A Sourcebook of Early Modern European History

A Sourcebook of Early Modern European History not only provides instructors with primary sources of a manageable length and translated into English, it also offers students a concise explanation of their context and meaning.

By covering different areas of early modern life through the lens of contemporaries' experiences, this book serves as an introduction to the early modern European world in a way that a narrative history of the period cannot. It is divided into six subject areas, each comprising between twelve and fourteen explicated sources: I. The fabric of communities: Social interaction and social control; II. Social spaces: Experiencing and negotiating encounters; III. Propriety, legitimacy, fidelity: Gender, marriage, and the family; IV. Expressions of faith: Official and popular religion; V. Realms intertwined: Religion and politics; and, VI. Defining the religious other: Identities and conflicts.

Spanning the period from *c.* 1450 to *c.* 1750 and including primary sources from across early modern Europe, from Spain to Transylvania, Italy to Iceland, and the European colonies, this book provides an excellent sense of the diversity and complexity of human experience during this time whilst drawing attention to key themes and events of the period. It is ideal for students of early modern history, and of early modern Europe in particular.

Ute Lotz-Heumann is Heiko A. Oberman Professor of Late Medieval and Reformation History and Director of the Division for Late Medieval and Reformation Studies at the University of Arizona. She specializes in European early modern history, especially the history of Germany and Ireland.

A Sourcebook of Early Modern European History
Life, Death, and Everything in Between

Edited by Ute Lotz-Heumann

LONDON AND NEW YORK

First published 2019
by Routledge
2 Park Square, Milton Park, Abingdon, Oxon OX14 4RN

and by Routledge
52 Vanderbilt Avenue, New York, NY 10017

Routledge is an imprint of the Taylor & Francis Group, an informa business

© 2019 selection and editorial matter, Ute Lotz-Heumann; individual chapters, the contributors

The right of Ute Lotz-Heumann to be identified as the author of the editorial material, and of the authors for their individual chapters, has been asserted in accordance with sections 77 and 78 of the Copyright, Designs and Patents Act 1988.

All rights reserved. No part of this book may be reprinted or reproduced or utilised in any form or by any electronic, mechanical, or other means, now known or hereafter invented, including photocopying and recording, or in any information storage or retrieval system, without permission in writing from the publishers.

Trademark notice: Product or corporate names may be trademarks or registered trademarks, and are used only for identification and explanation without intent to infringe.

British Library Cataloguing-in-Publication Data
A catalogue record for this book is available from the British Library

Library of Congress Cataloging-in-Publication Data
A catalog record has been requested for this book

ISBN: 978-0-8153-7352-0 (hbk)
ISBN: 978-0-8153-7353-7 (pbk)
ISBN: 978-1-351-24329-2 (ebk)

Typeset in Times New Roman
by Out of House Publishing

Printed and bound in Great Britain by
TJ International Ltd, Padstow, Cornwall

In Honor of Susan C. Karant-Nunn

Contents

List of figures	xvi
Preface	xvii
Acknowledgements	xxi
How to use this book	xxiii
BY UTE LOTZ-HEUMANN	

General introduction   1
BY UTE LOTZ-HEUMANN

I.
The fabric of communities: Social interaction and social control   21
Introduction   21
BY UTE LOTZ-HEUMANN

1. Show me your horse and I will tell you who you are: Marx Fugger on horses as markers of social status, 1584   25
   BY PIA F. CUNEO

2. From Bohemia to Spain and back again: Sports diplomacy in fifteenth-century Europe   29
   BY PAUL MILLIMAN

3. Resisting and defending noble privileges in the New World: García de Contreras Figueroa before the royal appellate court of New Spain, Mexico City, 1580   32
   BY MICHAEL CRAWFORD

4. "And so the old world has renewed": Magdalena
   Paumgartner of Nuremberg reveals the social significance
   of fashion, 1591   35
   BY ULINKA RUBLACK

5. In and out of the ivory tower: The scholar Conrad
   Pellikan starts a new life in Zurich in 1526   38
   BY BRUCE GORDON

6. A Protestant pastor should set an example for his
   community: Johannes Brandmüller of Basel gets into
   trouble in 1591   40
   BY AMY NELSON BURNETT

7. Spain, 1649: The Inquisition disciplines two Catholic
   priests who shot the baby Jesus   43
   BY ALLYSON M. POSKA

8. Canterbury, 1560: Slander and social order in an early
   modern town   46
   BY CATHERINE RICHARDSON

9. 'Popular duels': Honor, violence, and reconciliation in an
   Augsburg street fight in 1642   49
   BY B. ANN TLUSTY

10. Regulating day laborers' wages in sixteenth-century Zwickau   52
    BY SIEGFRIED HOYER

11. Ore Mountain miners stage a social protest in 1719   55
    BY HELMUT BRÄUER

12. Against corruption in all the estates: An early eighteenth-
    century Pietist vision for universal reform through education   57
    BY RICHARD L. GAWTHROP

II.
Social spaces: Experiencing and negotiating encounters   61
   Introduction   61
   BY UTE LOTZ-HEUMANN

13. Life at a German court: The importance of equestrian
    skill in the early seventeenth century   65
    BY PIA F. CUNEO

14. The constitutional treaty of a German city:
    Strasbourg, 1482   68
    BY THOMAS A. BRADY, JR.

15. Contested spaces: Bishop and city in late fifteenth-century
    Augsburg   71
    BY J. JEFFERY TYLER

16. Uproar in Antwerp, 1522   74
    BY VICTORIA CHRISTMAN

17. "We want the friar!" A civic uprising in Augsburg in 1524   77
    BY JOEL VAN AMBERG

18. Bourges: Public rituals of collective and personal identity
    in the middle of the sixteenth century   80
    BY JONATHAN A. REID

19. Castres, 1561: A town erupts into religious violence   83
    BY BARBARA B. DIEFENDORF

20. Swiss towns put on a play: Urban space as stage in the
    sixteenth century   86
    BY KASPAR VON GREYERZ

21. Smoke, sound, and murder in sixteenth-century Paris   89
    BY ALAN E. BERNSTEIN

22. Bologna's Feast of the Roast Pig: A carnivalesque festival
    in a sixteenth-century Italian city square   92
    BY NICHOLAS TERPSTRA

23. Taking control of village religion: Wendelstein in
    Franconia, 1524   95
    BY KATHERINE G. BRADY AND THOMAS A. BRADY, JR.

24. A Swiss village's religious settlement: Zizers in
    Graubünden, 1616 98
    BY RANDOLPH C. HEAD

25. Mapping the unseen: A Bohemian Jesuit meets the
    Palaos Islanders, 1697 101
    BY ULRIKE STRASSER

III.
Propriety, legitimacy, fidelity: Gender, marriage, and the family 105
   Introduction 105
   BY UTE LOTZ-HEUMANN

26. Housefather and housemother: Order and hierarchy in
    the early modern family 109
    BY UTE LOTZ-HEUMANN

27. Sexual crime and political conflict: An Alsatian nobleman
    is burned to death with his male lover in 1482 115
    BY CHRISTOPHER OCKER

28. "O abomination!" A sixteenth-century sermon against
    adultery 118
    BY CURT BOSTICK

29. Hans Gallmeyer: Seduction, bigamy, and forgery in an
    Augsburg workshop in 1565 121
    BY MARJORIE ELIZABETH PLUMMER

30. Professor Bryson's unfortunate engagement, Geneva, 1582 124
    BY KARIN MAAG

31. Gender relations in Germany during the Thirty Years'
    War: A groom refuses to marry his bride 127
    BY HEIDE WUNDER

32. Defining a new profession: Ordinance regulating
    midwives, Nuremberg, 1522 130
    BY MERRY E. WIESNER-HANKS

33. *A Chatty Comedy About the Birthing Room*: Johannes
    Praetorius observes women's lives in seventeenth-century
    Germany   133
    BY GERHILD SCHOLZ WILLIAMS

34. A letter sent from Augsburg in 1538: A Protestant
    minister writes to a friend about his illegitimate son   136
    BY MILTON KOOISTRA

35. Piedmont, 1712: Son forced into monastery by his father
    manages to get out   139
    BY ANNE JACOBSON SCHUTTE (†)

36. A mother tries to reform her son: Elisabeth of
    Braunschweig's "Motherly Admonition" to her son Erich,
    1545   142
    BY JILL BEPLER

37. Old age outside the bosom of the family: Elizabeth Freke
    of Norfolk (d. 1714)   145
    BY LYNN A. BOTELHO

IV.
Expressions of faith: Official and popular religion   149
   Introduction 149
   BY UTE LOTZ-HEUMANN

38. Reformation by accident? Martin Luther's Ninety-Five
    Theses of 1517   153
    BY SCOTT H. HENDRIX

39. Thomas Müntzer: A radical alternative   156
    BY GÜNTER VOGLER

40. Holy Scripture alone: Philip Melanchthon and academic
    theology   159
    BY NICOLE KUROPKA

41. Interpreting the Bible in the sixteenth century: John
    Calvin on the Gospels of Luke and Matthew   162
    BY BERNARD ROUSSEL

xii *Contents*

42. How to organize a church: John a Lasco on the election of ministers, 1555 — 165
    BY MICHAEL S. SPRINGER

43. What is a good death? Barbara Dürer, 1514 — 168
    BY HELMUT PUFF

44. A funeral sermon for Christian Röhrscheidt, law student in Leipzig, 1627 — 172
    BY CORNELIA NIEKUS MOORE

45. Pilsen, 1503: A wonderful apparition — 175
    BY KATHRYN A. EDWARDS

46. Hornhausen: A Protestant miracle well in seventeenth-century Germany — 178
    BY UTE LOTZ-HEUMANN

47. Gent, 1658: The miracle of the breast milk – or perhaps not — 181
    BY CRAIG HARLINE

48. A snapshot of Iberian religiosities: The inquisitorial case against the New Christian María de Sierra, 1651 — 184
    BY DAVID GRAIZBORD

49. Blazing stars: Interpreting comets as portents of the future in late seventeenth-century Germany — 187
    BY ANDREW FIX (†)

50. Picturing witchcraft in late seventeenth-century Germany — 190
    BY CHARLES ZIKA

51. Loftur the Sorcerer and clerical magic in eighteenth-century Iceland — 195
    BY THOMAS B. DE MAYO

V.
Realms intertwined: Religion and politics — 199
    Introduction 199
    BY UTE LOTZ-HEUMANN

52. Martin Luther defies Frederick the Wise: A letter from Borna, 1522 203
BY HEINZ SCHILLING

53. Philip Melanchthon justifies magisterial reform, 1539 206
BY JAMES M. ESTES

54. The courage to avow the truth: Philip Melanchthon on the Interim, 1548 209
BY IRENE DINGEL

55. 6 July 1535 – interpreting Thomas More's last words: God or king? 212
BY MARJORY E. LANGE

56. Mansfeld, 1554: Follow-up to an ecclesiastical visitation 215
BY ROBERT CHRISTMAN

57. Reformation mandates for the Pays de Vaud, 1536: How Bernese authorities tried to force their subjects to become Protestants 218
BY JAMES J. BLAKELEY

58. Ministers and magistrates: The excommunication debate in Lausanne in 1558 221
BY MICHAEL W. BRUENING

59. Who is in charge? Politics, religion, and astrology during the Thirty Years' War 224
BY SIGRUN HAUDE

60. Advocating religious tolerance: A Nuremberg voice of 1530 227
BY BERNDT HAMM

61. Assuring civil rights for religious minorities in sixteenth-century France 231
BY RAYMOND A. MENTZER

62. Turda, 1568: Tolerance Transylvanian style 234
BY GRAEME MURDOCK

63. Who suffered? A row in the Dublin Privy Council, 1605   237
    BY UTE LOTZ-HEUMANN

64. Is the throne empty? James II's supposed desertion of
    1688 discussed   240
    BY PETER FOLEY (†)

65. Dubrovnik: A Catholic state under the Ottoman sultan   243
    BY JAMES D. TRACY

VI.
Defining the religious other: Identities and conflicts   247
    Introduction   247
    BY UTE LOTZ-HEUMANN

66. The 'red Jews' and Protestant reformers   251
    BY ANDREW COLIN GOW

67. Debating the Reformation in Torgau, 1522   255
    BY CRAIG KOSLOFSKY

68. A Freiburg citizen's response to Luther in 1524   258
    BY TOM SCOTT

69. Augustin Bader of Augsburg (d. 1530): Weaver, prophet,
    messianic king   261
    BY ROBERT J. BAST

70. Should you consecrate bells? Johannes Eberlin von
    Günzburg argues against an established religious practice
    in 1525   264
    BY EUAN CAMERON

71. Catholic preaching on the eve of the French Wars of
    Religion: A eucharistic battleground   267
    BY LARISSA JULIET TAYLOR

72. How to convince Catholics that Protestants have sex in
    the open air: Gabriel du Préau's *Catalogue of All Heretics*,
    1569   270
    BY IRENA BACKUS

73. The Luther family's flight: A Counter-Reformation
    polemical broadsheet of the 1620s   273
    BY BARBARA STOLLBERG-RILINGER

74. God intervenes: A eucharistic miracle in the principality
    of Orange, 1678   277
    BY S. AMANDA EURICH

75. Different confessions, difficult choices: Theodore Beza
    converts after thirteen years of inner struggles   280
    BY SCOTT M. MANETSCH

76. "A priest you were on Sunday / Monday morning a
    minister": Clerical conformity in eighteenth-century
    Ireland   283
    BY MONICA BRENNAN

77. A great poet describes his own times: John Milton's
    Of Reformation, 1641   286
    BY DAVID CRESSY

78. Thomas Gage in Guatemala: A Puritan's memoir of
    preaching among the Maya, 1648   289
    BY KEVIN GOSNER

79. The morality of doubt: The religious skeptics of
    seventeenth-century Venice   292
    BY EDWARD MUIR

Map: Europe after 1648   295
List of contributors   296
Index   301

Figures

1.1	Jost Amman, emperor on horse performing a levade, woodcut illustration	27
1.2	Jost Amman, man on horse transporting cargo, woodcut illustration	27
21.1	Plan of Paris in the sixteenth century	90
25.1	Father Paul Klein's Map of the Palaos (1706 version by the Jesuit Procurator Andres Serrano, who added the title "Map of the New Philippines")	102
26.1	Woodcut "Vater – Mutter" ("Father – Mother"), second half of sixteenth century	110
26.2	Woodcut "Sohn – Tochter" ("Son – Daughter"), second half of sixteenth century	112
43.1	Albrecht Dürer, "Portrait of Barbara Dürer, née Holper, the Artist's Mother," charcoal drawing, 1514	169
50.1	Gottlieb Spitzel, *Die Gebrochne Macht der Finsternüß* …	191
50.2	Melchior Küsel, *Icones Biblicae Veteris et Novi Testamenti*	192
50.3	Johannes Praetorius, *Blockes-Berges Verrichtung* …	193
73.1	Broadsheet "Martin Luther, Nuhn Muess es Ia gewandert sein …," between 1620 and 1630	274
Map	Europe after 1648	295

Preface

This book is a tribute to Regents' Professor Emerita of History Susan C. Karant-Nunn, Director Emerita of the Division for Late Medieval and Reformation Studies at the University of Arizona, who for many years has been a friend, mentor, role model, and inspiration to me and to many others. Each of the contributors to this *Sourcebook* has his or her own story to share about receiving Susan's help or experiencing her kindness when interacting with her in various professional settings over the years. I had the pleasure of being told some of these stories when I first invited colleagues to write an essay for this volume. In fact, this volume was only made possible because so many of Susan's colleagues wanted to express their esteem for her by contributing.

Susan Karant-Nunn retired from the directorship of the Division for Late Medieval and Reformation Studies, which she held since 2001, at the end of June 2017. Before coming to the University of Arizona in 1999, she had been a professor of history at Portland State University. Her national and international reputation as a Reformation scholar has brought many graduate students to the University of Arizona, and her tireless fundraising has resulted in the Division boasting two endowed chairs – one named for her by an anonymous donor! – and several endowments to support graduate students.

Susan Karant-Nunn's work has been most influential in Reformation history. Her first two books, *Luther's Pastors: The Reformation in the Ernestine Countryside* (1979) and *Zwickau in Transition, 1500–1547: The Reformation as an Agent of Change* (1987) were concerned with the heartland of the Reformation, Saxony. These two books are exemplary works of social history. Since then, Susan Karant-Nunn has written three excellent works of cultural history that look at the German Reformation from innovative viewpoints: *The Reformation of Ritual: An Interpretation of Early Modern Germany*, which was published in 1997 and won the Roland H. Bainton Book Prize in History and Theology; *The Reformation of Feeling: Shaping the Religious Emotions in Early Modern Germany*, published by Oxford University Press in 2010; and her latest monograph, *The Personal Luther: Essays on the German Reformer from a Cultural Historical Perspective*, which appeared just in time for the 500th anniversary of the Protestant Reformation in 2017. Susan Karant-Nunn has edited and co-edited six volumes, and, as I write this, I have the pleasure of co-editing another volume with her which will document a conference on the cultural history of the Reformation that we organized together in 2016. She has published innumerable articles and book chapters, covering a fascinating range of topics in social and cultural history – from the reception of ghost stories in the late sixteenth century to the early modern evangelical parsonage as Christian exemplar.

From 1998 to 2010 Susan Karant-Nunn served as North American co-editor of the journal *Archiv für Reformationsgeschichte/Archive for Reformation History*. Among her many honors and awards, she received a John Simon Guggenheim Memorial Fellowship in 2003–2004, the Bodo Nischan Award for Scholarship, Civility, and Service from the Society for Reformation Research in 2016, and the Sixteenth Century Society and Conference Medal in 2017. Her invited guest lectureships and professorships have taken her to numerous universities in thirteen countries.

This volume is not only a tribute to Susan Karant-Nunn as a scholar, but also as a teacher. While she spent many hours of her career at the University of Arizona teaching and mentoring graduate students and giving community lectures, she also regularly taught undergraduate courses on the Renaissance and the Reformation. Susan's deep commitment to undergraduate education and her engaging teaching style were the inspiration for this volume.

Susan Karant-Nunn's books have deeply influenced the field of Reformation history – so much so that Professor Bernard Roussel, a leading French early modernist and contributor to this volume, in 1998 entitled a plenary lecture at the Sorbonne: "A la manière de Susan Karant-Nunn: réflexions sur la réforme du rituel dans l'espace francophone." It is therefore with deep gratitude and great admiration that I, along with all the contributors, dedicate this volume to her as a *Festschrift*.

This book has been in the making for a long time, and I owe many friends, colleagues, and graduate students a huge debt of gratitude. Above all, I would like to thank the contributors to this volume for their patience and understanding during a difficult period in my life when I was unable to move the project forward. Luise Betterton, Sandra Kimball, and Tom and Kathy Brady provided practical help and moral support at various points throughout the project, and I thank them with all my heart. I am also most grateful to my colleague Susan Crane for the subtitle for this volume. She originally suggested "Life, Death, and Everything in Between" as the title for my capstone seminar in early modern history, and it stuck, not only for the seminar. My new colleague, Beth Plummer, has long been very supportive of this project, and I thank her for a great first year together in the Division. Her willingness to move to Tucson within three months of being offered the Susan C. Karant-Nunn Chair in Reformation and Early Modern European History meant that I could finish editing this volume during my first year as director of the Division.

Unfortunately, we lost two treasured friends and colleagues, who wrote essays for this volume, in the last few years. In December 2016, Peter Foley, Associate Professor of Religious Studies at the University of Arizona, Associated Faculty of the Division for Late Medieval and Reformation Studies, and founding Director of the UA Institute for the Study of Religion and Culture (ISRC), passed away at the age of 55. He had battled brain cancer for a little over a year. Peter was a dear friend and a wonderful colleague, and we all miss him very much. I am most grateful to his wife Pia Cuneo, who is also a contributor to this volume, for signing Peter's contract and proofreading his contribution. In February 2018, Anne Jacobson Schutte, Professor Emerita of History at the University of Virginia, and for twelve years Susan Karant-Nunn's co-editor of the *Archive for Reformation History*, died of a cerebral hemorrhage. Anne supported me professionally in various ways over the years. I am very sorry that she will not see this volume in print.

Laura Pilsworth, editor for medieval and early modern history at Routledge, cheered me on from the moment she first heard about this project. Her editorial assistant Morwenna Scott has been most helpful and patient in sorting out various copyright questions and other matters. I am also very grateful to the five anonymous reviewers who agreed with me that this *Sourcebook* is a good idea.

Graduate students in the Division for Late Medieval and Reformation Studies translated contributions that were originally submitted in German. My thanks go to Paul Buehler, Sean Clark, Lizzy Ellis-Marino, Daniel Jones, Rebecca Mueller Jones, Mary Kovel, Benjamin Miller, and Amy Newhouse for taking on this task. Several of my research assistants over the years have helped with this volume in numerous ways. Many thanks to Adam Bonikowske, Tom Donlan, Patrick Meeks, and, above all, Hannah McClain and Benjamin Miller, who provided much-needed help during the final phase of the project.

My parents battled many illnesses over the last seven years, and my move to Tucson was not easy for them, but they have always supported me in everything I have done, and I cannot thank them enough for that. My father passed away in 2015, but his love, keen intellect, and his faith in my abilities as a scholar will always be with me. Last, but certainly not least, my husband Dirk has been at my side through the proverbial thick and thin, cheerfully tolerating my long work hours and my night-owl habits. I would like to thank him with the words of Katharina Schütz Zell who wrote about her husband, Matthias Zell, to Caspar Schwenkfeld in 1553: "My husband denied me nothing. ... He granted and allowed me space and will to read, pray, study, and be active in all good things, early and late, day and night: indeed he took great joy in that – even when it meant less attention to or neglect in looking after his physical needs and running his household."[1] Susan and her husband Fred Nunn have been instrumental in making Dirk and me feel at home in our adopted country. We thank them for all their help and friendship, from lessons in the rules of football to invitations to join their group of family and friends at their annual Labor-Day gatherings in Albuquerque.

Tucson, May 2018

Sadly, another contributor to this volume, Andrew Fix, passed away in June of 2018, as this volume was going to press. He co-edited with Susan Karant-Nunn *Germania Illustrata: Essays on Early Modern Germany Presented to Gerald Strauss*, published in 1992.

Note

1 Quoted in Michael Bruening (ed.), *A Reformation Sourcebook: Documents from an Age of Debate*, Toronto: University of Toronto Press, 2017, pp. 242–243.

Acknowledgements

We are grateful to copyright holders for permission to reproduce the following material:

Scripture quotations taken from *The Revised English Bible*, copyright © Cambridge University Press and Oxford University Press 1989. All rights reserved.

Figures 1.1 and 1.2: Marx Fugger, *Von der Gestüterey*, Frankfurt/M.: Sigmund Feyerabend, 1584, Niedersächsische Staats- und Universitätsbibliothek Göttingen, shelf mark 4 OEC I, 2742. By permission.

Ulinka Rublack, *Dressing Up: Cultural Identity in Renaissance Europe*, Oxford: Oxford University Press, 2012, extracts from pp. 232–241. By permission of Oxford University Press (www.oup.com).

Figure 21.1: Plan of Paris in the sixteenth century, detail (adaptation: Douglas Hollis). Sixième Plan de la Ville de Paris, Bibliothèque Nationale de France, département Cartes et plans, CPL GE DD-2987 (806), ark:/12148/btv1b7710749h; Vue de la Forteresse du Petit Châtelet, dessin de Victor-Jean Nicolle, Bibliothèque Nationale de France, département Estampes et photographie, RESERVE VE-53 (D), ark:/12148/btv1b10302741x; Le Grand Châtelet de Paris, Bibliothèque Nationale de France, département Estampes et photographie, RESERVE VE-53 (D), ark:/12148/btv1b10302745q. By permission.

Figure 25.1: Carta de Las Nuevas Philipinas [Palaos], Ministerio de Educación, Cultura y Deporte, Archivo General de Indias, MP-Filipinas, 15. By permission.

Figures 26.1 and 26.2: Woodcuts "Vater – Mutter" and "Sohn – Tochter," Germanisches Nationalmuseum Nürnberg, Graphische Sammlung, Inventar-Nr. HB 2013. By permission.

Gerhild Scholz Williams (ed.), *Mothering Baby: On Being a Woman in Early Modern Germany: Johannes Praetorius's Apocalypsis Cybeles. Das Ist Eine Schnakische Wochen-Comedie (1662)*, Tempe: Arizona Center for Medieval and Renaissance Studies, 2010, extracts. By permission.

Raymond A. Anselment (ed.), *The Remembrances of Elizabeth Freke, 1671–1714*, Camden Fifth Series, 53 vols, Cambridge: Cambridge University Press, 1993–2017, vol. 18, extracts. By permission.

xxii Acknowledgements

Copyright © Peter Matheson (ed. and tr.), *The Collected Works of Thomas Müntzer*, Edinburgh: T&T Clark, an imprint of Bloomsbury Publishing Plc., 1988, extracts from pp. 357–361. By permission.

Figure 43.1: Albrecht Dürer (1471–1528), "Portrait of Barbara Dürer, née Holper, the Artist's Mother," charcoal drawing, 1514, photo credit: bpk Bildagentur / Staatliche Museen zu Berlin, Kupferstichkabinett / Joerg P. Anders / Art Resource, NY.

Figure 50.1: Gottlieb Spitzel, *Die Gebrochne Macht der Finsternüß* …, Augsburg: Göbel and Koppmayer, 1687, Universitäts- und Landesbibliothek Sachsen-Anhalt in Halle (Saale), shelf mark AB 51 19/k, 35. By permission.

Figure 50.2: Melchior Küsel, *Icones Biblicae Veteris et Novi Testamenti*, Augsburg: Kysel, 1679, Herzog August Bibliothek Wolfenbüttel, shelf mark Tb 194. By permission.

Figure 50.3: Johannes Praetorius*, Blockes-Berges Verrichtung* …, Leipzig: Scheible, 1668, SLUB Dresden, Digitale Sammlungen, shelf mark Hist.Sax.inf.353,misc.1. By permission.

Jacqueline Simpson (ed. and tr.), *Legends of Icelandic Magicians*, Cambridge: D. S. Brewer for the Folklore Society, 1975, pp. 73–79. By permission of Jacqueline Simpson and The Folklore Society.

Heinz Schilling, *Martin Luther: Rebel in an Age of Upheaval*, Oxford: Oxford University Press, 2017, extracts from pp. 234–237. By permission of Oxford University Press (www.oup.com).

Gottfried G. Krodel and Helmut T. Lehmann (eds), *Luther's Works (American Edition)*, vol. 48: *Letters I,* Philadelphia: Fortress Press, 1963. Copyright © 1963 Fortress Press. Reproduced by permission.

Ralph Keen (ed.), *A Melanchthon Reader*, New York et al.: Peter Lang, 1988, pp. 155–156, 166–167. By permission of Peter Lang and Ralph Keen.

James M. Estes (ed.), *Whether Secular Government Has the Right to Wield the Sword in Matters of Faith. A Controversy in Nürnberg in 1530 over Freedom of Worship and the Authority of Secular Government in Spiritual Matters: Five Documents with an Introduction and Notes*, Toronto: Centre for Reformation and Renaissance Studies, 1994, pp. 41–52, here pp. 50–51. By permission.

Figure 73.1: Broadsheet "Marthin Luther, Nuhn Muess es Ia gewandert sein …," Herzog August Bibliothek Wolfenbüttel, shelf mark IH 23. By permission.

J. Eric S. Thompson (ed.), *Thomas Gage's Travels in the New World*, Norman: University of Oklahoma Press, 1958. Copyright © 1958 by the University of Oklahoma Press, Norman. By permission.

How to use this book

by Ute Lotz-Heumann

The title of this volume, *Sourcebook*, points to the most important feature of this collection, the presentation of a broad variety of primary sources that represent many different aspects of life in the early modern period. However, this book could also be called *A Reader* because the essays contextualize the primary sources and provide explanations for human behaviors as well as social and political phenomena that no longer spontaneously make sense in the twenty-first century. This volume hopes to be many things to many people, serving different purposes and assignments in both lower- and upper-division undergraduate history courses.

This book's primary purpose is as a companion volume to augment lectures and/or overview books of early modern European history. Therefore, the general introduction to the volume and the short introductions to the individual chapters are meant as supplementary material that may or may not be part of how the book is used in a class. In addition, the chapter introductions could potentially also serve as chapter conclusions, that is, they could be read after the essays, because they provide readers with further contextualization and group the essays into more defined subject matters. At the same time, these introductions represent only one – the editor's – view of how the essays relate to one another thematically.

While this collection has thematic chapters, the essays are consecutively numbered so that they can be combined in new ways. Each essay speaks to a variety of topics and certainly to much more than the subject of the chapter in which it has been placed. Therefore, instructors and students can put together groups of essays from different chapters to illustrate specific themes or geographical areas, such as essays showing the economic concerns of the common people, essays illustrating life in southern Germany or France, essays about the leading Protestant reformers, etc. The endnotes in the introductions to the individual chapters try to identify some of these thematic connections between essays without attempting to be exhaustive. Different groups of essays can thus be given as reading assignments to prepare students for lectures or classroom discussions on a particular subject.

While readers will certainly find many creative ways to work with this book, it is designed to serve above all as a starting point for further research.

This is why the essays in this book have only minimal endnotes and no accompanying bibliographies. These essays are meant to be the bases for micro-histories that students can research individually and collectively: Each primary source provides a glimpse of early modern people's lives and the accompanying explanation offers an interpretation of that source, but more research is needed to set the primary source into a larger context, to connect it with other sources, and to fully understand the themes explored in the essay. This volume can also be used for individual and group assignments in which students are asked to identify further themes and questions in early modern European history. In order to allow for such creative assignments, the volume provides an index of persons and places, but no subject index.

This collection can be used as a basis for individual reading responses, essay assignments, or research papers, and it can also be used as a foundation for classroom discussions and group work as well as role play and role-immersion games. Among many other uses, this book can serve: to introduce students to primary source analysis by asking them to analyze the relationship between the primary source and the historian's interpretation; for bibliographical exercises in which students find primary and secondary sources; to encourage students to think critically by asking them to develop discussion themes, research questions, and alternative interpretations about the different primary sources; for essay assignments in which students compare two or more primary sources; for research papers by using primary sources in the collection to develop broader historical questions; and for role play and role-immersion games in which students build on the information contained in the essays and develop them into more complex scenarios which can then be acted out.

But, above all, this volume wants to provide readers with an idea of the breadth and diversity of experiences in the early modern period, and the editor and contributors therefore hope that it will be read and enjoyed as a window into "life, death, and everything in between" in the early modern European world.

General introduction

by Ute Lotz-Heumann

The early modern era as a transitional period

The early modern period, the time between *c*. 1450 and *c*. 1750/1800, in many ways epitomizes our sense of the past as being both 'foreign' and 'familiar.' 'Early modern,' the term historians have been using since the 1950s to describe this period, references the fact that it was 'modern' because many of its structures are still familiar to us today, but also that it was 'early' because these structures were in their infancy. As a result of this 'dual nature' of the early modern period in Europe, historians have stressed different aspects of early modernity. Older historiography often focused more on early modern phenomena that they perceived as laying the groundwork for modernity like state formation, while recent historiography has emphasized the less familiar aspects of the period, like popular religious rituals and witchcraft trials. There is, however, no right or wrong way to describe early modernity; rather, we should acknowledge that the period had a unique quality all its own. This unique quality, the early modern experience of life, death, and everything in between, is the subject of this volume, which focuses on everyday social and political interactions and spaces, on social and religious conflicts and coexistence, and, above all, on how people lived their lives as individuals and in communities.

The transitional nature of the early modern period between the Middle Ages and the modern era, its combination of continuity and change, can be highlighted by various tensions. While an estimated 90 percent of the population in early modern Europe was illiterate, printing with movable type was responsible for a communication revolution. While early modern Europe remained a largely agricultural society, the early modern period also saw the rise of international trade and proto-industrialization. While so-called 'composite monarchies' or 'multiple kingdoms' were the norm in the early modern era, the groundwork for the nation states of the nineteenth century was being laid. While the Protestant Reformation resulted in the permanent split of Latin Christendom, popular religious culture changed much more slowly, often frustrating the reform efforts of Protestant and Catholic clergy alike.

The early modern period is also a transitional era in terms of the primary sources it has left for historians to examine. While the sources of the Middle

Ages often leave historians with considerable gaps to fill, and the modern era provides an overabundance of sources, the early modern period is the era when production of written material gradually expanded, giving historians a wide but manageable range of primary sources. Early modernists work with printed books and pamphlets, with images and material objects, and with many different kinds of handwritten sources, from the records of church and state to letters and diaries. While the number and variety of primary sources increased from the sixteenth to the eighteenth centuries, sources from the early modern period inevitably favor the perspective of political and ecclesiastical authorities and social elites; these institutions and groups produced the records. But historians have been diligently at work in recent decades to identify the voices of women, of the lower social orders, and of other non-privileged groups in these sources, even if they speak to us only indirectly.

The early modern period is a construct, of course, as are all historical periods. They are 'made up' by historians to give structure to historical narratives, as signposts, if you will, to organize the endless flow of history. While historical periodization is essentially a pragmatic tool, historians give this tool a lot of thought and discuss the reasons for and against a specific periodization. For the early modern period, these discussions concern not only the beginning and end of the period, but also the question of 'sub-periods' within early modernity. The beginning of the early modern era has sometimes been placed in the late thirteenth or mid-fourteenth centuries. This periodization focuses on the emergence of the artistic and intellectual movements of the Renaissance and humanism in Italy at that time. Humanist scholars and Renaissance artists looked to classical antiquity for their models in literature and artistic expression, and studied humans and their place in the world. However, most scholars now see the Italian Renaissance as part of the late Middle Ages. Current scholarly consensus defines the beginning of the early modern period by a series of events and processes which occurred between 1450 and the early sixteenth century.

Around 1450, Johannes Gutenberg ($c.1400$–1468) invented the printing press with movable type in the German city of Mainz. His invention changed not only the trajectory of the Protestant Reformation, but generally transformed communication through the mass production of books, pamphlets, and, later, newspapers. In 1453, the conquest of Constantinople, today's Istanbul, by the Ottoman Empire meant the end of the Byzantine or Eastern Roman Empire, thus leaving the Holy Roman Empire of the German Nation as the only successor of the ancient Roman Empire. More importantly, the expansion of the Ottoman Empire into the Balkans and eastern Europe resulted in multiple wars between the Ottoman Empire and central European countries during the early modern period; the 'Turks' laid siege to Vienna in 1529 and 1683.

Between 1492 and 1504, the voyages of Christopher Columbus ($c.1451$–1506) to the Americas – what he believed to be 'the West Indies' and Europeans came to see as 'the New World' – were the starting point of fundamental changes for the economic, political, and religious structures of Europe and the world. Ultimately, this led to the European colonization of territories in the Americas, Asia, and Africa, and the spread of Christianity around the world. It also ushered in the first age of economic globalization – from the creation of joint-stock companies for colonial trade and the establishment of overseas colonies to the shift in trade routes from the Mediterranean to the Atlantic seaboard.

1492 also marked the fall of Granada, the last Islamic foothold on the Spanish peninsula and therefore the end of the so-called 'Reconquista.' All remaining Muslims in the Spanish kingdoms of Aragon and Castile were forced to convert to Christianity or were expelled, and the same policy was extended to Jews. Nevertheless, 'New Christians,' i.e., either converted Muslims (*moriscos*) or converted Jews (*conversos*), were often suspected of crypto-Islam and crypto-Judaism and prosecuted by the Spanish Inquisition.

In 1517, the Augustinian friar and university professor Martin Luther (1483–1546) publicized his Ninety-Five Theses (he may or may not have nailed them to the door of the castle church in Wittenberg, Germany), criticizing the church's practice of selling indulgences. Luther thus started the Protestant Reformation, a religious movement which rapidly spread in central, northern, and western Europe, and which resulted in the permanent division of Latin Christendom. The effects of the Protestant Reformation and the response of the Catholic Church to it deeply affected early modern Europe, from the smallest village to the highest princely court.

The Renaissance and humanism also fall into this transitional period between 1450 and the early sixteenth century because by then, the impact of these movements was fully felt on the Italian peninsula and was also starting to be felt north of the Alps. The Renaissance papacy between 1420 and 1534, for all its political recklessness and worldly pursuits, was a great patron of the arts and transformed Rome into the Renaissance city we still see today. The popes patronized artists like Michelangelo (1475–1564) and Raphael (1483–1520), and built the Sistine Chapel and St. Peter's Basilica. (St. Peter's Basilica, of course, was funded in part by the indulgences against which Martin Luther protested.) Other famous Renaissance artists like Leonardo da Vinci (1452–1519) were active in the northern Italian city states.

The most famous humanist in central Europe, Desiderius Erasmus (1466–1536), the 'prince of the humanists,' who lived and worked in Rotterdam in the Low Countries, was an ardent supporter of educational and church reform and published the first printed Greek New Testament in 1516. Philip Melanchthon (1497–1560), the German humanist and colleague of Martin Luther at Wittenberg University, was called 'praeceptor Germanii' ('teacher of Germany') for his formative influence on educational reform in European Protestantism. Albrecht Dürer (1471–1528) in Nuremberg and Lucas Cranach the Elder (*c*.1472–1553) in Wittenberg created Renaissance art in Germany, especially paintings and engravings. Cranach, whose iconic images of the reformer Martin Luther were spread widely, became the artist of the

Lutheran Reformation. By the late sixteenth century, the Renaissance as a movement in literature made its impact fully felt in England with the works of William Shakespeare (1564–1616).

The internal periodization of the early modern period in Europe, its division into sub-periods, has also resulted in historiographical debate. Early modern Europe was made up of hundreds of territories, composite monarchies, and emerging states, and, starting in the nineteenth century, these have traditionally been claimed by one national historiography or another. This has resulted in very different sub-periods for the early modern period. For example, the strong influence monarchs had on political and religious developments in England has led to a periodization in English historiography that often favors monarchs over other considerations (for example, 'England under Henry VIII' or 'the Elizabethan age,' while the periodization of the seventeenth century indirectly refers to the presence or absence of the monarch: 'civil war,' 'the Interregnum,' and 'the Restoration').

In contrast, emperors did not influence the course of German history as much, so that the historiography of the Holy Roman Empire focuses periodization on political and religious processes and wars. Thus, central European history is often divided into the age of Reformation between 1517 and the Peace of Augsburg, the first religious peace in the Empire in 1555, followed by the 'confessional age' or 'age of confessionalization' between 1555 and the beginning of the Thirty Years' War in 1618. As an alternative periodization, many early modern historians have adopted the term 'age of Reformation*s*' to denote the overlapping processes of various Protestant Reformations and Catholic reform in the sixteenth and seventeenth centuries. The Thirty Years' War which ended with the Peace of Westphalia (also called Peace of Münster and Osnabrück) in 1648 is often constructed as its own sub-period.

Starting with the second half of the seventeenth century, periodization becomes less clear-cut. This is reflected in sometimes heated debates about the term 'age of absolutism' to describe the second half of the seventeenth and the eighteenth centuries, a sub-period which then overlaps with an 'age of Enlightenment' also starting in the later seventeenth or early eighteenth centuries. More recent historiography, however, has shown that religious identities and divisions set in motion in the sixteenth century had long-term effects lasting into the eighteenth century, which makes this traditional periodization less convincing.

The end of the early modern period can, on the one hand, be defined by two major political events, the American Declaration of Independence in 1776 and the French Revolution in 1789, both of which sought to establish the Enlightenment principles of equal rights and individual freedom. Events like the dissolution of the Holy Roman Empire of the German Nation, the political organization that had defined central Europe for a thousand years, by Emperor Francis II in 1806 and the political reordering of Europe after the Napoleonic Wars at the Congress of Vienna in 1815 also signify the major political shifts and upheavals that marked the end of the early modern period and the beginning of the modern era.

However, the end of the early modern period, even more so than its beginning, was also characterized by long-term processes. The Enlightenment as an intellectual movement which espoused the ideas of equality, liberty, religious tolerance, and progress and which culminated in the mid-to-late eighteenth century marks the end of the early modern era. It is, as mentioned above, often understood as a historical period of its own ('age of Enlightenment' or 'age of reason'). Other long-term processes that are associated with the transition from early modernity to the modern era are: a growing consumer society in which an increasing number of people had disposable income for consumption; population growth based, among other factors, on the gradual decrease of deaths from contagious diseases, notably the plague and smallpox; improvements in agriculture like crop rotation and fertilization which increased food production and thereby enabled Europe to feed its growing population; and the industrial revolution, which began in Britain in the second half of the eighteenth century.

Society and economy

Every society in human history has an ideal-type image of itself and of how people should relate to one another, from the most personal intimate relationships to the interactions between authority figures and those who are not in positions of authority, i.e., between rulers and ruled. Early modern European society was, in essence, hierarchical and patriarchal. Every aspect of life in early modern Europe tied into these two fundamental principles.

Early modern society was deeply patriarchal. While noble women became ruling queens or could act as queen-regents, women were regarded as the 'weaker vessels' and early modern society generally expected a woman to be under the authority of a man. Women could own property and, in certain circumstances, also control a business, but as a general rule, men held the reigns of princely power, exercised authority in the cities, and were the heads of households.

A Christian marriage between a man and a woman was seen as the basic unit of society in early modern Europe. As housefather and housemother they presided over a household which included not only their nuclear family, but also, from the middling classes upward, servants and apprentices. Marriage thus formed the backbone of early modern society. For example, an apprentice was not allowed to get married until he had made his masterpiece and been admitted by his guild as a master, at which point he was allowed to marry and set up his own household. As a result, many couples in early modern Europe married later, often in their late 20s, and thus also had a limited number of births and children. Ending a marriage was even more difficult than entering into it. In early modern Europe, an official divorce continued to be the exception, but couples who did not get along often separated.

These restrictions also meant that many men and women were excluded from having legitimate relationships and legitimate children. At the same time, entering into sexual relationships out of wedlock and having illegitimate children frequently resulted in hardships and potentially punishment by both ecclesiastical and temporal authorities. Generally, families, communities, the churches, and the secular authorities in early modern Europe often ignored sexual behavior they regarded as deviant as long as it did not result in 'scandal.' But at the same time, there was an increase in attempts to police and control sexual norms on all levels of society.

The idea that people would rarely leave the social sphere into which they were born formed the basis of the early modern social order in which everybody, from the highest nobleman to the lowliest beggar, had their place. This social hierarchy was often depicted as God-given, so that it appeared unchanging and unchangeable. The early modern social order is best envisioned as a pyramid, with very few people at the top and the majority of people at the bottom of the social scale.

Although historians often use the term 'social class' as a shorthand, early modern social 'orders' or 'estates' were, strictly speaking, different from 'classes' in the modern sense. In particular, 'class' implies a mostly economic descriptor, while 'order' or 'estate' denotes a social status that is determined by a complex matrix of birth and family connections, economic position, and the maintenance of one's honor and lifestyle. A person's educational, occupational, and financial status were related to these factors in complex ways, but they did not determine the definition of social status in the same way as they do today.

Social (and economic) hierarchies were ever-present in early modern life. Ideal-type depictions of medieval and early modern Catholic society show three estates: the nobility ('those who defend') with the emperor of the Holy Roman Empire of the German Nation at the top; the clergy ('those who pray') with the pope at the top; and a 'third estate' of people who work with their hands at the bottom. The first two estates vied for the position at the top, epitomized by the rivalry for precedence between the emperor and the pope which flared up repeatedly in the Middle Ages and continued into the early modern period. The vast majority of the population belonged to the 'third estate' in early modern Europe.

A monarch or prince presided over a court in which the high nobility of a country or territory were rivals for the rewards the prince could give – titles, offices, marriage opportunities, to name just a few. Members of the early modern nobility maintained their status in society through legal and tax privileges, land ownership, service to the crown, and maintaining and cultivating familial exclusivity and traditions which included restricting marriage partners to their own limited social group. While the nobility's elevated status had been derived from their service as warriors and knights, military service became less important over the course of the early modern period.

The clergy were the social group responsible for society's relationship with God, and as such they also enjoyed legal and tax privileges. Within the clergy, we encounter yet another pronounced hierarchy, from the pope, cardinals, and bishops at the top to the simple parish priests at the bottom. In Protestant areas, the Reformation brought about an important change in the status of the clergy. On the basis of Luther's theological concept of 'the priesthood of all believers,' clergy were no longer considered a separate social estate. Rather, clergymen became part of the 'third estate,' but they were still conceived of as a special group, a 'learned estate' of university-educated professionals.

At the top of the 'third estate' were the urban elites, usually rich merchants who dominated cities both economically and politically. Just like the nobility, they often formed tightly knit family networks and ruled cities as patriciates. The urban middle classes were mostly made up of master craftsmen who formed guilds which served to protect a particular craft by controlling prices, setting wages, and restricting the overall number of masters in a city. Merchants and craftsmen were burghers and they participated in the government of the city. Most cities in early modern Europe were governed by a council or councils in which these male burghers participated to varying degrees.

Everybody else was only an inhabitant of the city, not a burgher. Journeymen, apprentices, and male and female servants, who lived and worked in a master's household, all belonged to the lower urban social classes. Below these were day-laborers, who lived in small rented apartments and whose social and economic situation was precarious. They were always in danger of joining the ranks of the urban poor, who needed to beg or were dependent on social welfare.

In early modern Europe, 90 percent of the population worked the land. While the soils, climates, and types of agriculture varied considerably across the continent, the agricultural economy and rural life shared two basic characteristics: First, life in rural communities was fundamentally shaped by the agricultural year, the cycle of sowing and harvesting and tending to animals. Second, the agricultural economy – and by extension the early modern economy as a whole – as well as the livelihood of the individual peasant were dependent on the quality of the harvest which in turn was inextricably linked to the weather and changes in the climate. As a result, malnutrition and starvation were a constant threat in early modern Europe.

The social hierarchy in rural areas was dominated by the landholding nobility. Peasants were the largest social group in early modern Europe, but they were not a uniform group. Peasants were usually subject to a noble lord, but the patterns of landholding and self-government varied considerably across the continent, from serfdom in the northeastern Empire to autonomous peasant communes in Switzerland. Most peasants in central and western Europe were personally free, but few were freeholders; all others owed goods and labor services to their lords. All early modern villages had an internal social hierarchy, dominated by wealthy land-owning peasants at the top, cottagers with only a small piece of land in the middle, and poor and landless day-laborers at the bottom.

While the early modern European countryside continued to be dominated by agriculture, a major economic change took place in some regions of western and central Europe as rural manufacturing became more widespread. This involved urban-based merchants who gave raw materials, mostly textile fibers, and also equipment like spinning wheels to peasant families who were underemployed, often in the winter months. These rural households produced finished cloth or other products which the merchant collected and then sold on the regional or international market. This economic system has been called the 'putting-out system.'

The peasants received much smaller wages than urban workers, but they could augment their household income, and the merchants could be more flexible and avoid regulations that often applied to urban laborers. Historians call this form of rural manufacturing 'proto-industrialization' because this system was much less efficient than the later system of gathering workers in factories with steam engines which characterized the process of industrialization. This type of early modern rural manufacturing also led to social change when it allowed young people to marry and establish households earlier by participating in the putting-out system.

Early modern society characterized certain occupations, like executioners or gravediggers, as dishonorable trades whose practitioners were not accepted as full members of the community. Religious minorities, especially Jewish communities, but also radical Protestants like Anabaptists, were also disadvantaged and unable to attain full status as burghers or princely subjects. Except in England, where Jews had been expelled in 1290 and were only readmitted in 1656, Jews were present in continental Europe all through the early modern period. Jewish communities were often protected by the authorities because they provided the valuable service of money-lending to the Christian community (Christian churches regarded money-lending as usury). At the same time, Jews were severely restricted in their occupations and in their places of settlement. In cities and towns they were often forced to live in ghettos, and Jewish communities in early modern Europe were regularly targeted by pogroms.

As an ideal, early modern society thus constituted a large pyramid with several smaller pyramids within it, all well-ordered and strictly defining the place of each person and social group. However, this is not how humans operate. People are on the move, not only geographically, but also socially, and early modern Europe was no exception. Early modern cities could not sustain or grow their population through their birth rates, so migration was key to urban development. Cities provided opportunities, and even if early modern people rarely left the social estate into which they had been born, both the social and economic rise and fall of individuals and the gradual rise or decline of families over several generations did occur.

Most notably, those who belonged to the highest echelons of urban society, who were sometimes wealthier than the nobility, often tried to leave the ranks of the third estate and enter the nobility. This could be a multi-generational undertaking, involving the purchase of a landed estate and eventual ennoblement by the prince or monarch. However, being fully accepted into the nobility frequently proved to be an unattainable goal as the nobility did not want to marry such 'upstarts.' During the early modern period, the above-mentioned university-trained 'learned' professions, especially lawyers, physicians, and clergymen, began to form a defined group in society and developed into the educated bourgeoisie of the eighteenth century. Starting in the sixteenth century, university-trained lawyers were increasingly hired by princes to serve in their expanding territorial bureaucracies. This created a new class of professional civil servants and opened up the possibility of gaining noble status through princely service.

Early modern authorities saw it as their duty to stabilize society and therefore often played a cat-and-mouse game with people who aspired to a higher social status, or at least to the material culture and outward symbols of such a status. Since clothing was the most visible marker of social rank, the most obvious attempts to transcend social status involved fabrics, colors, and jewelry that were supposed to be exclusive to a higher social class. In an attempt to stabilize society and make the social hierarchy visible at all times, early modern authorities enacted sumptuary laws, clothing ordinances, and other measures of social disciplining. The fact that such rules and regulations were frequently ignored shows that early modern society was in flux and that people tried to show off beyond their social status, sometimes even more than they could afford.

Similar attempts at social control targeted the poor in early modern Europe. Early modern city authorities were faced with an increasing problem of poverty and destitution in their midst, and during the sixteenth century this led more and more cities to implement measures to control and combat poverty. Cities began to differentiate between 'the deserving poor,' inhabitants of the city who had fallen on hard times and were provided with relief by the city, and 'foreign beggars,' poor people from outside the city who were to be expelled. Over the course of the early modern period, orphanages, hospitals, and workhouses became the urban institutions in which the 'deserving poor' were taken care of, and, if possible, made into 'productive' members of society.

Religion and the churches

Although there can be no doubt that the Protestant Reformation,[1] involuntarily started by Martin Luther in 1517, fundamentally changed the course of early modern European history, historians have also stressed that this event was embedded in a long-term process of religious reform beginning in the Middle Ages. Important late medieval reformers were John Wycliffe (d. 1384), whose followers, the Lollards, probably laid some of the groundwork for the

Protestant Reformation in England, and Jan Hus (d. 1415), whose followers, the Hussites, managed to preserve their movement until the re-Catholicization of Bohemia in the 1620s. Other medieval religious sects like the Waldensians in France quickly merged into the Protestant tradition. In addition, reform efforts were underway in the medieval church. For example, the *Devotio Moderna*, a movement for religious reform, flourished in the Netherlands and spread to Germany in the late Middle Ages. Christian humanists like Desiderius Erasmus of Rotterdam and Francisco Ximénes de Cisneros (1436–1517), Archbishop of Toledo, sought a path of reform by combining Renaissance humanism and a program of revitalization of the church.

Nevertheless, Martin Luther's criticism of the selling of indulgences ultimately led to the Protestant Reformation and a split of Latin Christendom. Luther rejected many aspects of Catholic doctrine and religious practices. His principle of *sola gratia* ('by grace alone') emphasized that salvation could only be attained through God's grace. Thus, Protestants rejected good works, including indulgences, as a means to be saved and instead emphasized faith alone (*sola fide*). Luther also rejected the idea of priests and saints as mediators between the laity and God and advocated for the 'priesthood of all believers.' As a result, he regarded orders of monks, friars, and nuns as obsolete. And Protestants espoused the principle of *sola scriptura* ('Scripture alone'), relying only on the Bible as guidance for their theology. As a consequence, the reformers rejected the Catholic Church's tradition – its teachings and doctrines as they had been developed by the papacy and church councils – and also the papacy itself (Luther called the pope the Antichrist). Luther reduced the number of sacraments from seven to two, baptism and the Lord's Supper, and he advocated for the laity to receive communion in both kinds (bread and wine).

The Lutheran Reformation clearly touched a nerve in sixteenth-century Germany. Helped by the printing press, Luther's theology spread like wildfire and created a popular evangelical movement. Luther's ideas inspired many among the middling and lower orders, as is evidenced by the rapid spread of Protestantism in German towns and the role evangelical ideas played in the Peasants' War of 1524–1525.

However, the movement might very well have been doomed to failure if it had not been for two important developments in sixteenth-century Germany: City magistrates and territorial rulers within the Empire adopted the Lutheran Reformation in their territories and, starting with Luther's prince, Elector Frederick the Wise, provided protection to evangelical preachers and established reformed churches. While Emperor Charles V vehemently resisted this gradual spread of the Lutheran Reformation in Germany, he found himself unable to stop it. Charles was at war with the French king and the Ottoman Empire, and his power in Germany was limited, so he repeatedly made compromises with the Protestant princes and towns.

Eventually, these compromises led to a more comprehensive settlement, the Peace of Augsburg of 1555. Following upon similar bi-confessional arrangements in the First and Second Peaces of Kappel in Switzerland, the Peace of Augsburg established the *ius reformandi*, or 'right to reform,' also called the principle of *cuius regio, eius religio* ('whose territory, his religion'): Territorial princes in the empire (but not their subjects!) now had the right to choose between the Lutheran and the Catholic faith. Effectively, early modern European cities and territories were never confessionally pure, and recent research has uncovered many instances of toleration or at least bi- or multi-confessional coexistence. But the idea of the unity of state and church was nevertheless very powerful and led to many instances of intolerance and persecution in early modern Europe. Because religion was mostly experienced in community rituals like sermons and communal singing in Protestantism, and the Mass and processions in Catholicism, religious allegiance was closely intertwined with ideas of social belonging and political loyalty. As a result, people were often suspicious of neighbors who adhered to a different faith.

And the number of Christian faiths and churches proliferated rapidly. The three major continental reform movements were named after their founders: Martin Luther, Ulrich Zwingli (1484–1531), the reformer of Zurich, and John Calvin (1509–1564), the reformer of Geneva. Lutheranism spread not only in northern and central Germany, but also in the Scandinavian countries. Zwinglianism was most influential in Switzerland and southern Germany. Calvinism spread from Geneva into France, the Netherlands, Germany, and the British Isles, as well as into east central Europe.

Lutheranism, Zwinglianism, and Calvinism differed with regard to theology, church practices, and ecclesiastical institutions. The most important difference between Luther and Zwingli was their understanding of the Lord's Supper, with Calvin taking a compromise position in the middle. While Luther believed in the real presence of the body and blood of Christ in the Eucharist, Zwingli argued that the purpose of communion was to commemorate the sacrifice of Christ and that the bread and wine were therefore symbolic. One of the central aspects of Calvin's theology was 'double predestination,' the concept that God had preordained some to eternal salvation and others to eternal damnation. Lutheran, Zwinglian, and Calvinist churches also differed with regard to the ornamentation of churches, with Lutherans retaining images and other church decorations and the Reformed (Zwinglians and Calvinists) rejecting such ornamentations. Another important difference between these confessional churches arose in the area of church discipline, with members of the Calvinist churches seeing strict discipline and oversight by a consistory as a mark of the true church. Last, but certainly not least, Lutheran, Zwinglian, and Calvinist churches also differed with regard to institutional structures, which did, however, also vary through the influence of temporal rulers on their territorial churches.

While these major confessional churches came into being during the Reformation era, more radical groups also emerged. The radical preacher Thomas Müntzer was a leader of the German Peasants' War who was executed in 1525. 'Anabaptism' is a blanket term for a very diverse movement.

Its different branches held in common the belief in adult, or believer's, baptism as opposed to the baptism of infants that continued to be practised in all confessional churches in early modern Europe. The Anabaptist movement had multiple origins: It emerged from the more radical followers of Zwingli in Zurich; in southern Germany; and in the Netherlands through the influence of Melchior Hoffmann. Followers of Hoffmann gained influence in the Westphalian town of Münster, which they saw as the 'New Jerusalem' and transformed into a radical Anabaptist stronghold. The so-called Münster rebellion came to an end in 1535 when the city was successfully besieged by princely armies. Later, Anabaptists settled peacefully in various parts of Europe like the Netherlands and Moravia. They remained a minority faith and were often persecuted in early modern Europe.

During the early Reformation, the Catholic Church had difficulties in finding an adequate response to Luther and his followers. Protestants used the printing press much more effectively, and they successfully spread their message, first in Germany and then in many areas of western and northern Europe. Eventually, however, the Catholic Church responded to the challenge of Protestantism and also embarked on a reform process.

One of the most important institutions that changed and defined early modern Catholicism was the Society of Jesus. This religious order, whose members are called 'Jesuits,' was founded by Ignatius of Loyola in 1534 and approved by the pope in 1540. The Society of Jesus became a vanguard of Catholic reform and Counter-Reformation. The Jesuits were especially active as a teaching order in early modern Europe, and their missionary work took them to European colonies around the globe as well as to India, Japan, and China.

The most important event that defined early modern Catholicism was the Council of Trent, which was held between 1545 and 1563. Although attempts to convene a general council to overcome the religious schism created by the rise of Protestantism surfaced repeatedly in the Reformation era, the Council of Trent ultimately moved forward without Protestant participation. The council defined Catholic doctrine in opposition to the teachings of the Protestant reformers and also initiated institutional reforms of the church. For example, the Council of Trent rejected Luther's doctrine of 'justification by faith alone' and reaffirmed central doctrines and practices which had been rejected by Luther, among others indulgences, veneration of the saints, the seven sacraments, and clerical celibacy. Equally important were institutional changes which sought to address abuses and reform the church. For example, bishops and priests were to be resident in their dioceses and parishes, and bishops were to conduct visitations of their dioceses and ensure proper education of the clergy.

In France, the Reformation resulted in a situation in which Protestants and Catholics coexisted in a precarious relationship which eventually led to civil war. French Calvinists were called Huguenots, a term whose exact origin is unclear. The French Wars of Religion (1562–1598) culminated in the St. Bartholomew's Day Massacre of 1572, one of the bloodiest incidents of confessional violence during this era. Ultimately, King Henri IV (ruled 1589–1610) promulgated the Edict of Nantes in 1598, confirming France as a Catholic monarchy, but granting Huguenots certain rights and protections. In 1685, King Louis XIV (ruled 1643–1715) revoked the Edict of Nantes, resulting in the exodus of the vast majority of Huguenots from France and their settlement all over Europe and as far away as North America and South Africa. The refugee experience of the Huguenots was one among many in early modern Europe where the expulsion of religious minorities became a common occurrence.

In the British Isles, Calvinism was most influential in Scotland through the reformer John Knox (1513–1572), but Calvinist theology was also an important influence on the Protestant state churches of England and Ireland. After Henry VIII (ruled 1509–1547) had separated the English church from Rome, England only gradually became a Protestant country. During Elizabeth I's reign (1558–1603) the Church of England consolidated its status as the 'Established Church' which combined Calvinist doctrines on the one hand with much more traditional rituals and practices on the other. More committed Protestants, the so-called 'Puritans,' wished for further reform of the English church, but their hopes were not fulfilled, even when the Scottish King James I came to the English throne in 1603. Many of the Puritan critics of the Church of England found their way to the North American colonies.

Many countries in Europe experienced religious conflicts and wars during this era. In addition to the Religious Wars in France, the Netherlands fought the Eighty Years' War (1568–1648), or Dutch War of Independence, against Spain. This war had religious as well as political motives, and in 1618 it converged with the Thirty Years' War, the most destructive war in central Europe before the twentieth century. During the Thirty Years' War, which started in Bohemia and involved the German princes, the Habsburg emperors, Denmark, Sweden, and France as major players, religion and politics were also intertwined. The Peace of Westphalia in 1648 is often described as the end of the first half of the early modern period and of the confessional era in Europe.

Starting around the middle of the sixteenth century, the confessional churches in Europe consolidated, resulting in a process that has been called 'confession-building' or 'confessionalization.' This process, by which confessional churches, often in cooperation with the states, tried to exert more control over the beliefs and conduct of the clergy as well as the laity, has been among the most debated questions in recent historiography. Historians now agree on two things: first, that there were certainly strong, but mostly inconsistent efforts by church and state authorities to impose religious and social discipline; and second, that these efforts were often unsuccessful because they were frequently met with indifference, if not outright resistance.

However, there can be no doubt that church and state tried to establish confessional homogeneity in the towns and territories of early modern

Europe. These measures targeted the clergy, who were seen as 'multipliers' of confessional orthodoxy, and the laity. Churches aimed to define 'pure doctrine' in a declaration or confession of faith, for example the decrees of the Council of Trent and the Lutheran Book of Concord of 1580, and imposed these norms on the clergy through confessional oaths. Church and state established seminaries and universities to educate the clergy in their respective confessional orthodoxies, and they created schools on all levels so as to influence the younger generation. Through different measures of social control like visitations, consistories, and the Inquisition, church and state aimed at creating a confessionally homogeneous population. Religious practices and rituals were cultivated as markers of confessional belonging, and participation in the most important rituals like baptisms, weddings, and funerals was monitored through the keeping of registers. And finally, church and state used the printing press for propaganda purposes and tried to put in place a system of censorship.

On a more fundamental level, and beyond social class and confessional identity, early modern European Christianity shared a basic understanding of the world as deeply influenced by the supernatural. The world of the supernatural was understood to be constantly present in people's lives, and it could be read by paying attention to all manner of signs and portents. This shared early modern cosmology is borne out especially when looking at witchcraft beliefs. Belief in the power of witches to harm people by supernatural means and do evil in the world was universal in early modern Europe, both socially and geographically. 'Popular' and 'elite' culture put different 'twists' on these beliefs, but overall, witchcraft beliefs are a powerful reminder that shared beliefs in magic, the devil, and the supernatural permeated early modern European societies.

Even though recent historiography has emphasized these shared beliefs, there can also be no doubt that Protestantism resulted in a massive shift in social mores and cultural expectations in many regions of early modern Europe. Reformers emphasized preaching and writing in the vernacular languages as they wanted to bring the Word of God directly to the people. Protestant clergy were now married, making the pastor and his wife important role models in their parish. Because of the dissolution of monasteries and convents in many Protestant territories, an entire lifestyle largely disappeared. And Protestantism fundamentally changed the understanding of individual and communal experiences like miracles and death.

Politics and the state

Early modern Europe was not a continent of nation states as it is today. Rather, it was dominated by composite monarchies or multiple kingdoms. Multiple territories of various sizes, often (but not always) contiguous, were ruled by one monarch. This resulted in common characteristics and challenges for these composite monarchies. Under the conditions of early modern travel and communication, composite monarchies, especially geographically expansive multiple kingdoms, had to contend with the problem that directives from the central administration always reached their destination with considerable delay; nothing and nobody could travel faster than horses or a ship.

This tied in with the more general problem of how to build a governing structure in a composite monarchy. Frequently, territories would be acquired and lost through war or princely marriages, and the new monarch had to decide whether to leave old elites in place and rely on territorial self-government or whether to install political elites and a bureaucracy foreign to the territory. In both cases, conflicts might ensue, and rebellions in dependent territories were commonplace in early modern Europe. Another potential source of friction was religion. As the Reformation spread in Europe, central administrations generally aimed at unifying religion in all the territories ruled by a monarch, a goal that was often not attained and instead led to conflict and war.

A brief tour of early modern Europe can serve to illustrate these points. In central Europe, the Holy Roman Empire of the German Nation, usually called 'the Empire,' was a huge and complex political organization. It was a loose political union of mostly German and largely self-governing principalities and towns which were, however, under the authority of the emperor. The emperor was elected by a group of seven (later eight, and then nine) leading princes, the so-called 'electors.' The electors, the other territorial princes in the Empire, and the imperial towns met regularly at the political assembly of the Holy Roman Empire, the imperial diet.

During the first half of the sixteenth century, the Empire was actually part of an even larger composite monarchy under Charles V (born 1500, d. 1558), on whose empire the sun literally never set. Charles, the most powerful man in early modern Christendom, ruled over Spain (which itself consisted of the kingdoms of Castile and Aragon) and its southern Italian territories (from 1516), the hereditary Austrian Habsburg lands, the Holy Roman Empire (elected 1519), the Burgundian Netherlands (from 1506), and the Spanish overseas territories in the Americas. That his composite monarchy posed many of the problems described above can be gleaned from the fact that Charles was unable to suppress the Lutheran Reformation, and that his son Philip II (born 1527, d. 1598), who ruled over Spain, Portugal, Naples and Sicily, the seven provinces of the Netherlands, and briefly England, was confronted with the Dutch Revolt when he tried to tighten his political and religious control over the Low Countries.

In eastern Europe, the Polish–Lithuanian commonwealth constituted another geographically expansive composite monarchy. In Scandinavia, the kingdoms of Denmark and Norway, together with the northern German territory of Holstein, were ruled as a composite monarchy by the King of Denmark. And the King of Sweden held the multiple kingdom of Sweden–Finland. In western Europe, the British Isles also constituted a composite monarchy. The English crown had conquered Wales and Ireland in the late

Middle Ages, and beginning in 1603, the kingdoms of England and Scotland were united under one monarch. As a result, the crown in London frequently struggled with the religious and political administration of Catholic Ireland while at the same time ruling over a largely Calvinist Scottish kingdom. When King Charles I (ruled 1625–1649) proved unable to keep the peace in England, the situation in the dependent kingdoms of Ireland and Scotland made things worse and led to a quick descent into civil war.

While composite monarchies dominated early modern Europe, processes of state formation were underway in individual kingdoms and territories and eventually led to the nineteenth-century Europe of nation states. Even though processes of state-building were slow and uneven across the continent, there were certain trends which set early modern kingdoms and territories on a path to consolidating state power. Assemblies in which the higher and lower nobility, representatives of the church, and delegates of the towns (in rare cases also of the free peasantry) were represented had slowly developed into full-blown institutions in medieval Europe. These representative institutions – parliaments, estates, and diets – were able to counter-balance the ruler and provide a check on his or her activities, often by acquiring the right to consent to or refuse new taxes.

Over the course of the early modern period, rulers in most continental territories and kingdoms managed to diminish the role of these representative assemblies. This process took place in the territories of the Holy Roman Empire, where princes managed to expand their power especially during the rebuilding process after the Thirty Years' War. However, on the imperial level, no such state-building process occurred. The imperial diet was transformed into a permanent assembly in 1663, and during the eighteenth century the Empire was increasingly characterized by the rivalry of the two major territories within its borders, Brandenburg–Prussia and Austria.

Over the course of the seventeenth century, the French kings were increasingly able to move their kingdom toward a system of government historians have labeled 'absolutism.' By not calling France's representative assembly, the Estates General, after 1614 (it was only reconvened in 1789, at the beginning of the French Revolution), by managing to restrict the *parlements*, the provincial appellate courts, from resisting or delaying the king's edicts, and by defeating a noble revolt, the Fronde, in 1653, French kings managed to limit constraints on their rule and expand their authority.

As mentioned above, historians still argue about the term 'absolutism' or 'absolute ruler' because it has some misleading implications. Absolute rulers in early modern Europe, like the kings of France, Sweden, and Prussia, managed to tighten control of their territories and accumulate power in themselves and their central administrations, and this tendency has been embodied in the French King Louis XIV who famously said, "L'état, c'est moi" ("I am the state"). However, early modern 'absolute rulers' were never tyrants or dictators in our modern sense of the word – for several important reasons. First, under the conditions of early modern Europe, states lacked the means and technology to completely control their territories, especially the peripheries. Second, 'absolute rulers' did not destroy existing institutions, but tried to limit their influence. And third, early modern rulers recognized that they were subject to divine and natural law and that they would, ultimately, have to answer to God for their actions. Thus, absolute kings, while being hereditary rulers 'by divine right,' were not quite as 'absolute' in their authority as the term might suggest.

By the eighteenth century, under the influence of the Enlightenment, European rulers like Frederick the Great of Prussia (ruled 1740–1786) and Joseph II of Austria (ruled 1765–1790) saw their own role as – in the words of Frederick – "der erste Diener des Staates" ("the first servant of the state"). Basing their rule not on divine right, but on the idea of a social contract, these monarchs pursued educational, administrative, legal, and church reform and advocated for religious toleration. This 'enlightened absolutism' was thus in many ways an expression of the transitory nature of the early modern period: modern Enlightenment ideas about the state implemented by an 'absolute ruler.'

The political histories of the British Isles and the Dutch Republic were in many ways contrary to this general European trend. The Republic of the Seven United Provinces, after declaring its independence from Spain in the late sixteenth century and winning formal recognition in 1648, was a confederation of largely independent regions. Exhibiting both republican and monarchical elements, with the princes of the House of Orange-Nassau holding the office of *stadtholder* in most provinces, the Northern Netherlands represented a unique political structure in early modern Europe.

The early modern political history of England is notable for the fact that it took a very different route with regard to the relationship between monarch and representative assembly. It was certainly significant that parliament played an important role in legislating the religious changes of the sixteenth century. Overall, however, long-term prospects for parliament's role and the exact power balance between monarch and parliament were unclear in the sixteenth and early seventeenth centuries. During the reign of Charles I the absolutist policies of the king ultimately led to a power struggle and subsequently to a civil war between king and parliament. This mid-seventeenth-century crisis, which included the execution of King Charles I in 1649 and Cromwell's lord protectorship, was resolved in 1660 with the restoration of the monarchy.

Parliament's role as an integral part of the government of England was acknowledged by Charles II (ruled 1660–1685), but within a generation, England faced another crisis after the Catholic James II (ruled 1685–1688) had ascended to the throne. Parliament played an important role in the so-called 'Glorious Revolution' of 1688 which brought the Protestant Queen Mary and King William of Orange, daughter and son-in-law of James, to the English throne. In 1689, the new monarchs had to agree to the Bill of Rights, which affirmed a number of principles like parliament's power over taxation, free elections, and free speech in parliament. This set England on a path to becoming a constitutional monarchy.

In spite of these very different political routes taken by countries and regions in early modern Europe, a process of state formation was slowly underway everywhere. This state-building process was characterized by the gradual extension and professionalization of princely bureaucracies, accompanied by more elaborate and detailed administrative procedures and efforts at record-keeping. By the eighteenth century, the state tried to collect increasing amounts of demographic and economic data. This effort at more clearly understanding the people and territories under the authority of a ruler also included defining the borders of a territory and replacing the diffuse boundaries of the Middle Ages with the idea of a linear demarcation between neighboring states.

Another important aspect of state formation was trying to ensure the state's monopoly on the use of force. This included, among other things, ending the retention of mercenary armies by the nobility, preventing violent feuds between noblemen, and building a system of law courts that could serve to solve conflicts through the application of a code of law. Although there was by no means equality before the law in early modern Europe, early modern states made significant steps towards the rule of law. The state also increasingly asserted its monopoly on the use of force by moving from retaining mercenary armies as needed to building standing armies (or, in the case of England, a navy) during the second half of the early modern period. However, all of these were gradual developments which were still unfinished in many parts of Europe by the end of the early modern period.

Ultimately, the history of early modern Europe was one of simultaneous inertia and change. While ending one's life in the same social estate into which one was born was regarded as the norm, this patriarchal and hierarchical society was also constantly in flux. While beliefs in the supernatural were shared by the elites and the populace, religious divisions split apart families and communities and brought about massive social and political changes. While the state tried to reach into the furthest corners of the land, it continued to be faced with obstacles which were only overcome in the nineteenth and twentieth centuries. An age of transition, indeed.

Note

1 'Protestantism' describes a wide range of Reformation movements in early modern Europe. The term is now widely used, and serves a useful purpose as a short-hand. It is, however, vague. Its current usage in historiography is very far from its origin in the constitutional history of the Holy Roman Empire of the German Nation. It is derived from the Latin term *protestatio*. In the imperial diet, the minority could protest the majority's decision by handing in a 'protest,' or *protestatio*. The evangelical princes and towns did just that at the imperial diet of Speyer in 1529 to protest the decision of the Catholic majority. This is how the term 'Protestants' was born.

Further reading

Brady Jr., Thomas A., Heiko A. Oberman, and James D. Tracy (eds), *Handbook of European History, 1400–1600: Late Middle Ages, Renaissance, and Reformation*, vol. 1: *Structures and Assertions*, Leiden, New York: Brill, 1994.

Brady Jr., Thomas A., Heiko A. Oberman, and James D. Tracy (eds), *Handbook of European History, 1400–1600: Late Middle Ages, Renaissance, and Reformation*, vol. 2: *Visions, Programs, and Outcomes*, Leiden, New York: Brill, 1995.

Cameron, Euan (ed.), *Early Modern Europe: An Oxford History*, Oxford, New York: Oxford University Press, 1999.

Collins, James B. and Karen L. Taylor (eds), *Early Modern Europe: Issues and Interpretations*, Oxford: Blackwell, 2005.

Cook, Chris and Philip Broadhead, *The Routledge Companion to Early Modern Europe, 1453–1763*, London, New York: Routledge, 2006.

Dewald, Jonathan (ed.), *Europe 1450 to 1789: Encyclopedia of the Early Modern World*, Detroit: Scribner, 2006.

Koenigsberger, H. G., *Early Modern Europe, 1500–1789*, London, New York: Longman, 1987.

Kümin, Beat (ed.), *The European World 1500–1800: An Introduction to Early Modern History*, London, New York: Routledge, 2009.

Sangha, Laura and Jonathan Willis (eds), *Understanding Early Modern Primary Sources*, London, New York: Routledge, 2016.

Scott, Hamish (ed.), *The Oxford Handbook of Early Modern European History, 1350–1750*, vol. 1: *Peoples and Place*, vol. 2: *Cultures and Power*, Oxford, New York: Oxford University Press, 2015.

Whitford, David M. (ed.), *Reformation and Early Modern Europe: A Guide to Research*, Kirksville, MO: Truman State University Press, 2008.

Wiesner-Hanks, Merry, *Early Modern Europe, 1450–1789*, 2nd ed., Cambridge, New York: Cambridge University Press, 2013.

I
The fabric of communities: Social interaction and social control

Introduction

by Ute Lotz-Heumann

This chapter explores the dynamics of early modern social interactions in different types of communities and the forces that exerted social control in these various contexts. Pia F. Cuneo's essay draws attention to markers of social status, in this case the horse, in early modern society. Animals – just like skills,[1] clothing,[2] material objects, and legal privileges[3] – functioned as indicators of an individual's position on the social ladder, from the monarch at the top to the peasant at the bottom.

Paul Milliman's and Michael Crawford's essays focus on the highest ranks in early modern society. Jousting provided an opportunity for political and social interactions among the nobility through the means of sports, but this could also be a fraught undertaking. The case of García de Contreras Figueroa draws attention to the fact that noble privileges, especially the privileges of the lower nobility, were not always self-evident but needed to be asserted, and often came under pressure during the early modern period when they clashed with new developments like economic change, colonization, and state formation.

Ulinka Rublack's, Bruce Gordon's, Amy Nelson Burnett's, and Allyson M. Poska's essays focus on groups within the 'third estate,' the urban elites and the clergy in early modern Europe. In Magdalena Paumgartner's correspondence with her husband, clothes are revealed as markers of social identity among the urban merchant elite. Clothes displayed the tension between a desire for luxury and the need to fit in with the expectations of one's social and religious group (essay by Ulinka Rublack). Conrad Pellikan, a Hebrew scholar who moved from Basel to Zurich, belonged to the highest echelons of a new group of Protestant clergy and university professors. While pursuing their careers at newly reformed universities, these scholars also had to contend with novel expectations for their social group, namely organizing their home life and getting married (essay by Bruce Gordon). Johannes Brandmüller, a senior pastor and adjunct professor of theology in Basel, was also a member of this group, but his personal behavior as a husband, father, and community member did not fit the social expectations for the new Protestant clergy (essay by Amy Nelson Burnett).[4] While Basel's church leaders attempted to discipline Brandmüller in private, the two Catholic priests who accidentally shot an image of the baby Jesus in a shooting contest were publicly reprimanded and fined by the Spanish Inquisition (essay by Allyson M. Poska).[5] In both cases, church authorities tried to exert social control over the clergy as examples for the laity.

Catherine Richardson's and B. Ann Tlusty's essays draw our attention to the lower orders among the 'third estate,' and their definition of honor and social norms.[6] A case of slander brought in the ecclesiastical court of Canterbury by one woman of the lower urban classes against another for a claim of adultery shows these women's concern with preserving both their reputations and the social peace. The 'popular duel' fought between two members of the local guard in Augsburg[7] exemplifies the importance of defending one's honor in early modern society and shows that resort to arms was regarded as an acceptable form of social control.

Siegfried Hoyer's and Helmut Bräuer's essays address economic regulations and the economic concerns of the urban middling and lower classes. Day laborers found themselves bound by ordinances which set limits for their wages in a thriving economy in sixteenth-century Zwickau,[8] while miners in early eighteenth-century Saxony tried to stage a social protest to better their declining economic conditions.

Finally, Richard L. Gawthrop's essay introduces August Hermann Francke's vision of universal social reform through education. Francke, the leader of the Pietist movement in German Lutheranism, saw all social groups – "all the estates" – as corrupted and therefore aimed his campaign of reform at society as a whole.

Notes

1 See no. 13, Cuneo: Life at a German court: The importance of equestrian skill in the early seventeenth century.
2 See no. 4, Rublack: "And so the old world has renewed": Magdalena Paumgartner of Nuremberg reveals the social significance of fashion, 1591.
3 See no. 3, Crawford: Resisting and defending noble privileges in the New World: García de Contreras Figueroa before the royal appellate court of New Spain, Mexico City, 1580.
4 Gordon's and Burnett's essays also address the question of the new gender roles for Protestant clergy. See also no. 30, Maag: Professor Bryson's unfortunate engagement, Geneva, 1582; no. 34, Kooistra: A letter sent from Augsburg in 1538: A Protestant minister writes to a friend about his illegitimate son.
5 For another example of the activities of the Spanish Inquisition see no. 48, Graizbord: A snapshot of Iberian religiosities: The inquisitorial case against the

New Christian María de Sierra, 1651. For Protestant institutions and procedures of religious and social discipline see no. 56, Christman: Mansfeld, 1554: Follow-up to an ecclesiastical visitation; no. 57, Blakeley: Reformation mandates for the Pays de Vaud, 1536: How Bernese authorities tried to force their subjects to become Protestants; no. 58, Bruening: Ministers and magistrates: The excommunication debate in Lausanne in 1558.

6 For other essays that deal with the question of male and female honor see no. 26, Lotz-Heumann: Housefather and housemother: Order and hierarchy in the early modern family; no. 30, Maag: Professor Bryson's unfortunate engagement, Geneva, 1582; no. 31, Wunder: Gender relations in Germany during the Thirty Years' War: A groom refuses to marry his bride; no. 33, Williams: *A Chatty Comedy About the Birthing Room*: Johannes Praetorius observes women's lives in seventeenth-century Germany.

7 Other essays that are concerned with the German imperial town of Augsburg are no. 15, Tyler: Contested spaces: Bishop and city in late fifteenth-century Augsburg; no. 17, Van Amberg: "We want the friar!" A civic uprising in Augsburg in 1524; no. 29, Plummer: Hans Gallmeyer: Seduction, bigamy, and forgery in an Augsburg workshop in 1565. This is a reflection of the rich collection of early modern primary sources that has survived in Augsburg.

8 See no. 32, Wiesner-Hanks: Defining a new profession: Ordinance regulating midwives, Nuremberg, 1522, for another type of urban regulation.

1 Show me your horse and I will tell you who you are: Marx Fugger on horses as markers of social status, 1584

by Pia F. Cuneo

Now confined to the margins of Western culture and our present-day life, the horse in the early modern period played a central role in all cultural, social, political, and economic sectors. Different kinds of horses facilitated numerous activities essential to trade, transport, manufacture, agriculture, warfare, recreation, and entertainment. Consequently, the products of the early modern printing presses included books on the breeding, maintaining, training, and medical treatment of horses. These books were written by a range of authors that included humble craftsmen trained in farriery (blacksmithing) at one end of the social spectrum, and educated members of the nobility at the other.

Belonging to this socially diverse group of authors was the German humanist and patron Marx Fugger (1529–1597). The Fugger family had risen from modest beginnings in the fourteenth century as weavers in the southwestern German city of Augsburg to attain extraordinary wealth, prestige, and political influence during the course of the sixteenth century. In the ninth chapter of his book on the breeding and training of horses, printed in 1584, Marx Fugger muses at length about the many and profound ways horses are useful to humans. In his extended argument about the multifaceted and fundamental utility of this animal, Fugger also offers a cogent articulation of early modern social identity. In its ideal manifestation as he describes it, social status is portrayed as divinely ordained and therefore natural, hierarchical, clearly defined, and stable. Any attempted subversion of it would be immediately recognizable as laughably ridiculous.

"If one wants to observe accurately the utility derived by humans from horses, then one must consider first how many horses, and second how many people there are in this world. ... As there are many social groups and many kinds of horses, so must there be many kinds of utility. And if one observes such things carefully, and considers them from all angles, so one will discover in this ... a special and mysterious providence from God the Almighty. Because just as the lives and activities of people are different, so one also finds different kinds of horses that are appropriate for every individual person according to his social status, his activities and his way of life, and that these have been ordered and created by God for just that purpose. ...

For example, one would not tolerate it if a farmer wanted to be a prince, or a prince wanted to be a farmer; one would laugh at either one of them because they would both appear to have taken leave of their senses. So it would also be an enormous folly if a prince had his Spanish or Arabian horse costing many thousands of ducats hitched to a plow in order to work the land and instead sat himself upon a plow-nag to ride into battle or crusade to rescue and protect his subjects and territories. When, however, a farmer remains a farmer, and hitches a farmer's horse to the plow and works the land; and when a prince remains and is a prince and sits himself upon a Spanish, Arabian, or similarly precious horse and rides with that into battle to protect and defend his territories and subjects, then both are doing their part and both are to be praised because each behaves appropriately to his social status and his being. Because the farmer is ordained by God to till the soil and work the land, God has created for him an appropriate horse for this work. But the prince is ordained by God to govern territories and subjects, to lead them diligently ..., and to protect and defend them from enemies and similar dangers. For this, God has ordained for him different horses that are appropriate."[1]

In Fugger's text and in the images that accompany it (see Figure 1.1 and Figure 1.2), the farmer and the prince each have their own distinct social identity and a fixed place in the social hierarchy manifested in the specific activities they perform. They perform these activities because God has willed it so. It is also part of God's divine plan that the farmer and the prince should be aided in their characteristic activities by horses appropriate to the task. Thus, divinely sanctioned social status is visualized and performed not only in what one does but on what kind of horse one does it on.

In reality, early modern social status was not as unmistakable and immutable as texts like Fugger's make it seem. Individuals then as now dynamically inhabited and operated within a plurality of social relationships by which social identity and social status was structured and signaled in an ongoing, perpetually changing process. Social status was not merely a condition into which a person was born, and it was even less an indelible and eternal trait with which God marked someone. To some degree, social status did involve choices that individuals made according to social, economic, political, moral, and cultural possibilities and exigencies. This state of affairs explains the need, emphasized even by Fugger, for social identity to be performed; it had to be demonstrated so that it would be visibly and tangibly present for others to witness. Oftentimes, that demonstration of social status, such as plowing the field or riding into battle, involved the participation of animals, and early modern people regarded specific animals as effective indicators of the presence, absence, or degree of wealth and status. As Fugger tells us, what kind of horses a person had access to, and what that person actually did with those horses, sent a clear message about that individual's specific place in society.

Figure 1.1 Jost Amman, emperor on horse performing a levade, woodcut illustration to Marx Fugger, *Von der Gestüterey*, Frankfurt/M.: Sigmund Feyerabend, 1584, p. 16v

Figure 1.2 Jost Amman, man on horse transporting cargo, woodcut illustration to Marx Fugger, *Von der Gestüterey*, Frankfurt/M.: Sigmund Feyerabend, 1584, p. 9v

Note

1 Marx [Marcus] Fugger, *Von der Gestüterey*, Frankfurt/M.: Sigmund Feyerabend, 1584, pp. 18v–19r. Translated by Pia F. Cuneo.

2 From Bohemia to Spain and back again: Sports diplomacy in fifteenth-century Europe

by Paul Milliman

In their detailed analysis of the important role knightly tournaments played in medieval society, Richard Barber and Juliet Barker note that "throughout Europe from the late thirteenth century onwards ... diplomacy and jousting went hand in hand."[1] Perhaps the most spectacular early modern example of this was the Field of Cloth of Gold, the 1520 meeting between Kings Henry VIII of England and Francis I of France, the goal of which was to establish a lasting peace so a united Latin Christendom could fight the Ottoman Turks. But jousting and other aristocratic sports also played a very important role in everyday life in courts throughout late medieval and early modern Europe. Tournaments, which included banquets and dances in addition to jousts, provided nobles with an opportunity to display their courtliness and plead their cases in a common language that was recognized throughout Europe. Indeed, Geoffroi de Charny, a fourteenth-century French knight who wrote a manual on chivalry, describes how both traveling abroad and participating in tournaments were marks of chivalry.

In 1465, a dozen Bohemian nobles and a couple of Nuremberg patricians – all avid sportsmen – set out with Lev (Leo) of Rožmitál, the brother-in-law of Jiří (George) of Poděbrady, King of Bohemia, on a two-year journey that would take them from Prague to Santiago de Compostela in Spain and back again. Along the way, they stopped at the courts of rulers throughout western Europe. Two of these men – Václav Šašek and Gabriel Tetzel – chronicled the activities of the group. The goal of this Bohemian embassy was most likely to drum up support for King Jiří of Bohemia's 'European Union,' which had an objective very similar to the Field of Cloth of Gold – to make peace in Latin Christendom in order to make war on the Turks. Jiří hoped at least to keep the peace for the Hussites, a religious reform movement in Bohemia, who had been the target of a series of crusades a few decades earlier because the Catholic Church considered them heretics. However, neither writer talks about this diplomatic mission. Instead, Tetzel states: "The noble and well-born lord, Leo of Rozmital ... had proposed to undertake a knightly journey. ... He intended to visit all Christian kingdoms, also all principalities in Germany and foreign countries, ecclesiastical and lay, and above all to visit the Holy Sepulchre and [the tomb of] the beloved St. James [at Santiago de Compostela]."[2]

Šašek similarly explains in the preface to his account that there are two main reasons why noblemen leave their homelands: "... some are incited by a desire for glory, so that for this reason they increase the fame of their name and to gain a firmer knowledge of knighthood they undertake such labors; some having a pious manner of life, and led by a desire to visit the holy places, relics, and tombs of the saints, endure the dangers of pilgrimages; indeed some do it for both reasons."[3]

These two activities – pilgrimage and chivalry – dominate the narratives of both writers. Although they did not make it to Jerusalem, the Bohemians did see the important relics of each region they visited, and they also jousted at the courts of a number of secular and ecclesiastical magnates. Yet, not everyone allowed the Bohemians to realize their goals. When they visited René of Anjou, who literally wrote the book on late medieval tournaments, no jousting took place. This might have been because René favored the older form of the tournament, the mêlée, while the Bohemians (like most other late medieval knights) favored individual combat in the form of jousting. Or perhaps it was for the same reason that the Bohemians surrendered their jousting equipment to King Edward IV of England. Although neither writer explains why Edward, who was a patron of tournaments, prevented them from jousting in his kingdom, it might have been because sports can just as easily cause discord as concord. The Bohemians learned this at the beginning of their journey, when Count Palatine Frederick I refused to receive them. Šašek does not understand what happened: "In Heidelberg we found the Count Palatine of the Rhine. There my lord [Lev] with his companions displayed his heraldic emblem, desiring to engage in equestrian games at his [the Count Palatine's] court. But after arriving there, counselors of the Count Palatine met us at an inn and said their lord was away from home. Why they rejected him [Lev], I have not learned."[4]

But Tetzel thinks the Count Palatine was insulted by their challenge to joust with his men: "My lord and all his honourable company hung their jewels about their necks. This was done to honour the Palsgrave[5] and to show that we wished to run a course for them and tilt at his court. But my lord was informed that the Palsgrave had taken great offence at this and took it to mean my lord had done this because he thought that the Palsgrave had no people fit to joust and tilt with Bohemians. ... So we had to leave, since he declined to receive us. This all happened because my lord and his attendants had hung their jewels about their necks."[6]

While chivalry could complement diplomacy, it could also compete with it, particularly when knightly errantry was the primary motivation of the ambassadors, as appears to have been the case with Lev, Tetzel, and Šašek. These two interpretations of the same event also illustrate some of the problems in dealing with primary sources. Different writers had different interests, points of view, and access to information.

To further illustrate this point, it is worthwhile to compare the two accounts of the 1465–1467 journey with the diary of a Bohemian embassy to the King of France in the previous year. While this 1464 diary takes note of the attractions of the towns that Jaroslav (the author of the diary) and his fellow ambassadors passed through (relics, baths, fairs, etc.) and even mentions engaging in such tourist activities as climbing the towers of Notre Dame cathedral to get a good view of Paris, the ambassadors did not participate in tournaments. In fact, for the most part they did not mix with their hosts except when engaged in diplomatic discussions, although the two nobles leading the embassy went hunting with the Margrave of Brandenburg.

What accounts for these differences? Was it the different interests of the authors, the different motivations of their companions, or some combination of these factors? Can we read the Bohemian journey of 1465–1467 as an example of sports diplomacy, or should we believe Tetzel and Šašek, who say that it was simply an expression of knightly errantry, intended solely for the edification of the participants?

Notes

1 Richard Barber and Juliet Barker, *Tournaments: Jousts, Chivalry and Pageantry in the Middle Ages*, Woodbridge: The Boydell Press, 1989, p. 50.
2 *Des böhmischen Herrn Leo's von Rožmital Ritter-, Hof- und Pilger-Reise durch die Abendlande 1465–1467. Beschrieben von zweien seiner Begleiter*, Stuttgart: K. Fr. Hering, 1844, p. 145. This translation is from Malcolm Letts, *The Travels of Leo of Rozmital through Germany, Flanders, England, France, Spain, Portugal and Italy 1465–1467*, Cambridge: Cambridge University Press, 1957, p. 19. Letts translated excerpts from Tetzel's and Šašek's accounts. In what follows the translations from Tetzel's account are Letts's, while the translations from Šašek's account are by Paul Milliman.
3 *Des böhmischen Herrn*, p. 9. Šašek's account was originally written in Czech (as was the diary of the 1464 embassy), but only a later Latin translation survives.
4 Ibid., p. 15.
5 Count Palatine.
6 Letts, *The Travels of Leo of Rozmital*, p. 21; *Des böhmischen Herrn*, pp. 146–147.

just be seen in negative moral terms as an example of fanciful change. Rather, it could also be perceived as positive, skilled, decorous inventiveness which showed that the world can renew itself purposefully in aesthetic terms, and not just be foolish, sinful, and vain.

This was also a moment of triumph of the tasteful fashion of the urban elites in light colors and just a trim of gold against the small-spiritedness of the lower classes' clothing or any brash aristocratic expenditure. Silks and fine woolens were the materialized idiom of decorous civility, in which Italy met the northern Renaissance in the Nuremberg urban milieu. There was no Protestant austerity which denied the material among these ruling and merchant classes in early modern Nuremberg. Even medieval commentators had thought of beautiful, ingenious clothing as a source of joy, and Nuremberg Lutherans affirmed these assumptions.

Lutheran wedding sermons made it clear into the seventeenth century that female beauty was a sign of divine grace and was to be enjoyed, as long as the woman was pious. In a similar way, Magdalena and Balthasar socialized their child early on into thinking of clothing and other items of appearance as displaying piety and civility. When in 1589 little Balthasar wished for a small velvet bag as a gift from his father when he returned, Balthasar, the father, wrote to his wife: "… just tell little Balthasle [sic] that he should be pious for a while, for otherwise I will not bring him any presents, and if he is bad, I shall give the nice velvet bag, two pairs of shoes, and the red knitted stockings to another more pious boy."[5]

However, there were serious questions to consider: How much should they spend on shiny cloth? What would people say if they saw little Balthasar in clothes made of saffron-colored damask that his father wanted to obtain for him in Italy? Would the Paumgartners fit in with what other Nurembergers of their social status regarded as decent luxury? For all this could go horribly wrong: Others might think of them as vain-glorious, or worse, as breeding vanity in a small boy. They might then think that this showed that the Paumgartners were not pious at all. Material worlds lured, and the Paumgartners kept worrying. However, they were excited at the same time, since every piece of damask was a gamble about the social roles they could try and the smoothest textures they could inhabit and turn into a legitimate way of doing things in this world of Lutheran urban elites.

For example, in 1584, Magdalena got worried when Balthasar reported on the purchase of a piece of luxurious cloth to be made into a blanket: "You are writing me that the blanket will cost no more than the sum you mentioned. I was shocked in my heart. Another time we will think about this better beforehand."[6] On the other hand, in 1591, she wants to keep up with the neighbors: "Dear treasure, please, do not forget my Italian gown, like the one Wilhelm Imhoff has brought his wife from Venice, which one wears instead of fur. And please do not mind that I am asking you for something in every letter."[7]

Once again, in hopes and anxiously raised heartbeats, this was a world in which personal and social identities were not a matter of ideas, not a matter of following doctrine, but entwined with goods and the most luminous threads of silk. People related to themselves and others through their clothes. This is why dress was such an important part of the early modern psychic landscape. Is this a world we have lost, or a world that refracts our own?

Notes

1 Georg Steinhausen (ed.), *Briefwechsel Balthasar Paumgartners des Jüngeren mit seiner Gattin Magdalena, geb. Behaim*, Tübingen: Bibliothek des Litterarischen Vereins in Stuttgart, 1895. Translated by Ulinka Rublack.
2 '-in,' as in 'Paumgartner*in*,' is the female suffix denoting that she is Paumgartner's wife.
3 Sixteenth-century Nuremberg was a Lutheran city.
4 Magdalena Paumgartner to her husband, December 1591, in Steinhausen (ed.), *Briefwechsel Balthasar Paumgartners*, p. 150.
5 Balthasar Paumgartner to his wife, 21 September 1589, in ibid., p. 103.
6 Magdalena Paumgartner to her husband, 27 August 1584, in ibid., p. 64.
7 Magdalena Paumgartner to her husband, 9 December 1591, in ibid., p. 142.

5 In and out of the ivory tower: The scholar Conrad Pellikan starts a new life in Zurich in 1526

by Bruce Gordon

Basel and Zurich were two centers of the Swiss Reformation. Basel was the city of Erasmus, the printer Froben, and the university; it was a community of many humanist scholars devoted to the reform of the church. Zurich had introduced its version of the Protestant Reformation in 1525, led by Huldrych Zwingli, who had once studied in Basel. At the heart of the new Zurich church was the study of the Bible. Each morning in the *Grossmuenster*, the main church of Zurich, the Old Testament was interpreted in Latin, Hebrew, Greek, and finally German. This endeavor, often called 'prophesyings,' was possible because of an extraordinary collection of scholars in Zurich trained in the biblical languages.

In the following passage taken from the autobiography of Conrad Pellikan, Zwingli has attracted Pellikan to leave Basel and come to Zurich. In essence, this was a case of successful early modern academic 'head-hunting.' Pellikan, a former Franciscan monk and close colleague of Erasmus and Froben, was arguably one of the leading Hebraists of his day; Zwingli was most eager to have him come to Zurich to teach Hebrew:

"On the day thereafter (on the Festival of the Chair of St. Peter) I left Basel in the company of Fleck and Billing. Billing was, as the whole of Basel knows, a devout young man, a son of the wife of burgomaster Jakob Meyer, who at that time was still guild master. I had received about 20 gulden in cash from the city council and Froben. The first night we came to a village just before Schaffmatt.[1] The next day, the day of St. Matthew, a Saturday, we ate in Aarau and overnighted in Mellingen. On Sunday (Reminiscere[2]) we ate in Dietikon and about 4 o'clock arrived in Zurich to the great delight of the brothers, who showed great affection towards us. We both stayed as guests in Zwingli's house. Two days later good Huldreich Trinkler, empowered and instructed by the city council, presented me with the keys of my own home. It was empty but attractive and highly suitable for my studies, just as my patron Zwingli had promised. For the three next days I attended theological lectures (unfortunately I didn't have my books!). Leo Jud read and translated from the Old Testament. It was the first Hebrew lecture I had attended. – On March 1, however, the Thursday after Reminiscere, it fell to me (and not by chance) to take as the subject of my first lecture the 15th chapter of the second book of Moses.[3] I opened with this thought: 'Praise be to God, who has rescued me from Egypt and led me across the Red Sea to come out of Egyptian, i.e., papal imprisonment, so that I now join with the blessed in the song of the sister of Moses and full of joy can sing *Let us sing to the Lord, for he has done a great act.*'

"For about a week I ate in Huldrych Zwingli's house, until the time that my own home had been prepared for the needs of its poor occupant. Now my Peter sprang into action. He oversaw and organized everything that was needed at home, he planted and weeded the small garden and cooked, showing himself to be a servant who could do everything, even pruning the vines, sowing the beets, and purchasing and acquiring whatever was necessary. Zwingli oversaw conscientiously all expenses, and as a result it never crossed my mind at all to take a wife, not least because the gaudiness and less than moral behavior of the women and maidens of Zurich caused me concern. Also, I was already 48 years old, and therefore it would not have been right to bring a young woman into my household. I didn't want to try with one who was older, as they usually only bring trouble into the home. I therefore decided that at least I would not marry a woman from Zurich, for the morals of none, as far as I knew them, were pleasing to me."[4]

Pellikan describes his journey to Zurich, which he undertook with some hesitation, and the new life that awaited him there, although, as he says, he was not a young man. He speaks of the lectures held in Zurich and of the beginning of his own contribution, expounding the Old Testament in Hebrew. Pellikan would remain in the city until his death some thirty years later. During the 1530s, he wrote a commentary on the whole of the Bible, both Old and New Testaments, that was designed to enable ministers of the church to preach. However, this passage also reminds us that scholarship was not simply about dry texts, but that it involved practical arrangements and personal interactions within a community of scholars and beyond. As a teacher in Zurich, Pellikan received income from the secularized chapter house that brought with it a home and sufficient funds to support a small household. His scholarship took place within a circle of close-knit friends, evident here in Zwingli's hospitality and generous involvement in Pellikan's daily life. We note also, however, that there was an expectation for the new Protestant ministers to find a wife, a cause of considerable concern for Pellikan. Eventually, he did marry and have a son.

Notes

1 A mountain that marks the division of Basel land and Solothurn.
2 The second Sunday in Lent.
3 Exodus.
4 Konrad Pellikans, *Die Hauschronik Konrad Pellikans von Rufach: Ein Lebensbild aus der Reformationszeit*, ed. and tr. Theodor Vulpinus [from the original Latin], Strasbourg: Heitz und Mündel, 1892, pp. 104–105. Translated into English by Bruce Gordon.

6 A Protestant pastor should set an example for his community: Johannes Brandmüller of Basel gets into trouble in 1591

by Amy Nelson Burnett

The Protestant Reformation brought one major change to the ideal of the good pastor. Rejecting the clerical celibacy required by the Catholic Church, reformers insisted that their ministers should marry. A Protestant pastor was supposed to be a model housefather, setting a good example for his congregation in his interactions with wife, children, and servants. It therefore caused public scandal when a prominent pastor lived in open strife with family members, drank excessively, and drew shame or ridicule upon himself and others through his preaching.

These were the accusations made against Johannes Brandmüller, a senior pastor in Basel and adjunct professor of theology at the city's university in the later sixteenth century. In March 1591, Brandmüller's elderly father-in-law complained that Brandmüller was harassing him and his sick wife, and he asked that his son-in-law be ordered to stay away from their house. In response, the church convent – the board of pastors and senators who oversaw the city's church – held a private meeting with Brandmüller, himself a member of that board. At this meeting they confronted him with the following charges:

"1. That because he gladly attends all kinds of banquets in both city and countryside and also in his own house often drinks more than is good, he falls into a disorderly life, together with his sons, so that they belittle and insult honorable people who deserve better from them.

"2. That he struck his wife a few weeks ago, and again on the previous Thursday, and while liquored up he acted evilly with words and blows to her son and daughter, and didn't go to bed the entire night but went out in the street at 1 a.m., and in such a harsh frame of mind entered the pulpit the next morning ...

"3. That he is completely pleased with himself in all things and thinks he is right, and driven by his passions, he brings things into his sermons that are not fitting and that do not serve good, so that he sometimes begins his sermon in a mocking and laughable and even offensive way, like the monks used to do.

"4. That against the commandment to honor your father and your mother, he troubles his old father- and mother-in-law with surly words. ...

"This is indeed a pity, and this in spite of the mercy of the magistrate [shown] regarding his offensive and questionable affairs, for they spoke to him several weeks ago and admonished him to humble himself before God and amend his offenses and to get along with his fellow ministers. But we have perceived little humility and heard that in a public lecture in the cathedral he complained that love had grown cold among the ministers ... which unseemly words were heard by the syndic from Ensisheim and a mass priest ... to the disadvantage of our ministry and insult to our churches."[1]

Brandmüller's behavior was scandalous in several ways. Domestic violence, public drunkenness, and disturbing the peace were only the most obvious problems. In the sixteenth century, "insulting honorable people" was perceived as an attack upon character and social reputation that could not go unpunished. Instead of modeling appropriate conduct for his sons, Brandmüller involved them in his misbehavior. Protestant pastors were expected to teach God's Word from the pulpit with the seriousness it deserved, and without resorting to the anecdotes and extravagant gestures used by medieval preachers, who were often either Franciscan or Dominican friars.

Brandmüller's offenses also had broader ecclesiastical and political ramifications. Basel was a Protestant city-state surrounded by Catholic neighbors: the Habsburg lands to the north, with their administrative capital at Ensisheim in Alsace, the secular territory ruled by the Bishop of Basel to the west, and the canton of Solothurn to the south. As Tridentine reforms[2] took root in these areas, the religious situation polarized, and it became especially important that Basel's Protestant pastors live up to the high expectations concerning their personal and professional lives. But Brandmüller's domestic disturbances, his derisive preaching, and his disparagement of his fellow pastors had become public knowledge, and the leaders of church and state saw his behavior as harming the city's reputation among its Catholic neighbors.

When they confronted Brandmüller with these accusations, the church leaders reminded him that they acted "not as judge and jury, but as those who, on account of their [church] office, faithfully admonished him to cease his disorderly conduct."[3] Brandmüller refused to acknowledge any problems with his behavior, though, and he asked for the names of his accusers and a written copy of the accusations. Fearing that the pastor would take his complaints to friends in the Senate,[4] the president of the church convent wrote a full account of the meeting to submit to the entire Senate – the primary source from which the charges against Brandmüller are taken.

As so often happens in the study of the early modern period, there are no other records that tell us if the church convent's intervention eased the difficulties for Brandmüller's family or repaired his professional reputation. Nevertheless, the account of the meeting highlights several features of early modern society. The accusations made against Brandmüller demonstrate that early modern families did not live in isolation. His mistreatment of his wife and stepchildren caused others to complain to the church authorities; his in-laws too looked to the church to intervene. For their part, the church's leaders deliberately took a pastoral rather than a punitive approach to the situation. Their intervention made them the sixteenth-century equivalent of a social service agency today.

Brandmüller was not the only pastor they admonished for excessive drinking: Less than a month later the church convent rebuked one rural pastor for his drunken behavior on Palm Sunday and discussed the conduct of a schoolmaster who had a long history of drunken quarreling with his wife.[5] To some extent, however, Brandmüller's position as senior pastor protected him from the pressure applied by the church convent. The authorities did not want their disciplinary actions to become public knowledge, which would only reflect badly on the ministry as a whole, and so they met with him privately rather than summoning him to appear at one of their regular sessions. Ultimately, this desire to protect the reputation of one of their members probably undermined the church convent's ability to change his behavior. Given Brandmüller's unrepentant attitude, it seems unlikely that there was any significant improvement, and he retained his position as pastor and professor until his death five years later.

Notes

1 The document describing this meeting is found in the Staatsarchiv of the Kanton Basel-Stadt, Kirchen Archiv A6, no. 1, in the hand of the city's head pastor, Johann Jakob Grynaeus. Translated by Amy Nelson Burnett.
2 Reform measures undertaken by the Catholic Church as a result of the Council of Trent (1545–1563).
3 Staatsarchiv of the Kanton Basel-Stadt, Kirchen Archiv A6, no. 1.
4 The Senate was the council of elected guildsmen that governed the city-republic of Basel.
5 This second case is interesting in its own right. The schoolmaster, Heinrich Sundgauer, had jumped into a river in order to save someone from drowning, but rumors had reached the city that he had fallen in because he was drunk, and the other person had fished him out. Sundgauer was cleared of suspicion only after the church convent received letters from another pastor and a local official clearing his name – but the church convent still took the opportunity to admonish Sundgauer and his wife to sobriety. Basel Staatsarchiv D 1, 1, Acta Ecclesiastica (Kirchenratsprotokolle) vol. I, entries for 9 and 16 April 1591.

7 Spain, 1649: The Inquisition disciplines two Catholic priests who shot the baby Jesus

by Allyson M. Poska

The Spanish Inquisition has become infamous for its use of torture and its dramatic burning of heretics at the stake; however, after the first fifty years, such spectacular events were few and far between. The majority of the cases that came before inquisitors dealt with much more ordinary transgressions. In fact, inquisitors spent a considerable amount of their time and energy correcting the inappropriate, but not usually heretical, ideas and behaviors of Spanish clergy and their parishioners. As a result, Inquisition trials provide us with a glimpse into the daily lives of early modern Spaniards and their relationship with the Catholic Church, which in the wake of the Protestant Reformation articulated stricter expectations of its adherents and especially its priests. This summary of an Inquisition trial from 1649 is typical of the kind of cases that came before inquisitors and reveals how, well into the seventeenth century, many Spaniards failed to live up to those more rigid social norms.

"The accused: Antonio Fernández, the rector of the parish of Dumbría, and Gregorio Sobrino, rector of the parish of Santa Lucia in this archbishopric [of Santiago de Compostela] …

"The aforementioned were in the church of San Pedro dos Infantes at the funeral of a certain man who had died there in August of 1648. After having eaten at the home of the parish priest, the aforementioned fired some shots with a shotgun that hit a stone cross that was next to the house of the priest and with those shots they broke a leg of the image of the baby Jesus that the Virgin Mary Our Lady had in her arms. They made a scratch on its face that has resulted in a great scandal around there. … They both admit to having fired three shots with a shotgun at an iron ring on the said *crucero*,[1] having bet which of them shot better, and that after having figured out where the shots had gone, they saw that one was in the ring and the other was in the stone next to it and that the image of the baby Jesus that was in the arms of Our Lady was missing the little toe from its foot but did not know if that damage was from one of the shots.

"Sentence: They were gravely reprimanded and warned. They were told to repair the *crucero* to as it was before at their own expense. Each priest was also fined four thousand *maravedís*."[2]

The Council of Trent (1545–1563) emphasized the importance of a well-educated and well-behaved clergy. Yet bringing reform to Spain's vast countryside proved to be exceptionally difficult. Bishops were not only busy handling the daily affairs in the larger cities, but they had little incentive to make the difficult journey into rural areas over poor roads in bad weather to ensure the quality of parish clergy. Thus, inquisitors who made sporadic visits to the countryside often encountered priests with little understanding of Catholic doctrine and who were ignorant of the church's expectations about clerical behavior.

In this short summary, we see these two parish priests committing at least three acts that transgressed the Catholic Church's expectations of clergy after the Council of Trent. First, it is likely that these clergy were taking part in a long tradition of poor clergy going from funeral to funeral to partake in the free food and drink. These funeral feasts were often long and raucous. In order to prevent clergy from being associated with the social disorder that usually resulted, diocesan synods had forbidden clergy from excessive drinking and eating. Second, synods had also made it clear in their decrees that clergy were not to carry arms for any reason or engage in gambling. However, while it was considered bad form for the priests to be feasting, shooting, and gambling, it was the third transgression, the desecration of the image of the Virgin and Child, that caught the eye of the Inquisition.

After someone denounced the two priests to authorities, the inquisitor had to ensure that this seemingly harmless accident was not an act of blasphemy that indicated heretical ideas about either the Virgin Mary or the meaning of holy images. Protestant thinkers had denied Mary's authority and rejected the use of images as a part of worship. In response, the Council of Trent had reiterated the importance of the Virgin Mary as a spiritual intercessor and explicitly mentioned the importance of properly venerating images of Christ, the Virgin Mary, and the saints. Thus, shooting at the image of the Virgin and Child could be seen as an act of defiance against church doctrine.

However, the inquisitor clearly came to the conclusion that this case of clerical misconduct did not rise to the level of heresy. Poor and probably poorly educated, these priests were either unaware of the Catholic Church's expectations or they ignored them. So, the inquisitor admonished the priests and gave them a serious warning about their behavior, made them pay the equivalent of court costs, and sent them home. The fine was large enough to remind the priests that they had made a serious error in judgment, especially for parish priests who were expected to set an example for their parishioners.

On a daily basis, mundane cases like this one engaged the majority of the Inquisition's time and energy. As the Catholic Church was most interested in halting the spread of heresy, inquisitors rarely took serious action against poor and uneducated defendants. Rather, they used the denunciations as opportunities to correct misunderstandings and bad behavior and put their clergy and parishioners on the path to better Christian lives.

Notes

1 A large stone cross with the image of the Virgin and Child, common in the region.
2 Archivo Histórico Nacional, Madrid, Sección Inquisición 2042 #90 (1649), fol. 6b. Translated by Allyson M. Poska.

8 Canterbury, 1560: Slander and social order in an early modern town

by Catherine Richardson

One of the most important aims of urban government in the early modern period was social order – the quest for peace and harmony among citizens shaped the way towns were run. It also influenced the forms of urban life, determining the way men and women interacted with one another on a daily basis, as this primary source shows. The event described below took place in Canterbury, center of the Church of England[1] and the most significant market town in east Kent, with a population of approximately 3,700 inhabitants in the 1560s. In common with other provincial centers, Canterbury had a range of civic and ecclesiastical courts through which to maintain and disseminate ideas of social order.

Ecclesiastical courts tried moral crimes. They were extensively used in the period, and gave a high profile to the disputes they heard and the line they drew between acceptable and unacceptable behavior. Court machinery, from the serving of citations to public penance, was highly visible within society and this guaranteed informal discussion of local cases within the community. The courts prosecuted cases of tithe[2] dispute, matrimonial contention, sexual misconduct, contests over wills and slanderous utterances. Cases could be brought by the court itself, informed by churchwardens'[3] presentments from the parish, or by one party against another. A vast majority of disputes were settled outside the court by arbitration, and we must see those which were tried as the result of an explicit decision on the part of the plaintiff to elevate a private contention to a public level.

The court documents which we find in archives are answers to specific questions (which do not usually survive), and in recent years historians have become very sensitive to the way in which such evidence is shaped, paying attention to how stories told in court employ a range of strategies and elements which respond to legal requirements. They are thus particularly interesting primary sources for the study of ordinary people's responses and reactions, although it must be borne in mind at all times that the words spoken were mediated through the scribe who wrote them down, as is clear from the legal language used.

In 1560, in a case of slander brought by Margaret Raven against Margaret Richardson, Magdalen Lewys of the parish of St Paul's in Canterbury came to court to give her testimony. Apparently asked what she knew of the alleged slander, she recalls the events of the day in question. She begins by listing what she and her neighbors were doing at the time, thus stressing their gainful employment despite their poverty, and therefore her moral probity and trustworthiness as a witness:

"... in harvest last past and about mydd of the harvest tyme and that apon a workynday ... this deponent was sitting and spynyng at her doore situate in Ivy Lane, with other her poore neyghbours sitting by and spynyng as goodwif[4] Ward, goodwife Manley, Margaret Golding, goodwif Wieler[,] goo[d]wife Vallar and one Hanns wif whose husband is the sowgelder[5] with divers other."[6]

Having set the scene, she describes the slander itself:

"The foresaid Margaret Richardson cam[e] from the barton feld as she said, and told this deponent and other there present how that the mornyng of the foresaid workday betwene vi and vii she toke Margaret Raven in a hedge comyng out with a knave[7] ... and that she and the said man had plaid the whore and knave toigther."[8]

Magdalen then adds her own assessment of the words that Richardson spoke, and the evidence for her belief that they were untrue. She says she "said to the said Margaret Richardson that she had untruly reported of the said Margaret Raven, who as this deponent said to her went not furth of her doores that mornyng but kept her house with her husband who lay with her over night. And in the mornyng her husband about vi of the clock in the mornyng went furth abrode passing by this deponent sitting spynyng then at her doore, and shortely after within half an hower the said Margaret Raven went to the house of Mr Fookes over gainst this deponent with chekins to have them carved, and she this deponent saw her both going thither and comyng from thence agayn to her awne house wher[e] [she] remayned as this deponent thinckith."[9]

Magdalen's testimony is not unusual – there are many such slander cases in the ecclesiastical courts – but it does give us rich details of women's daily lives. If we are to interpret it appropriately, however, we must realize that it does so for several specific reasons. Firstly, the legal definition of slander requires an audience, so Magdalen is careful to list exactly who was there and therefore affected by the story that Richardson told. Helen Joyseman, who also deposed in this case, tells of a later occasion on which the slander was repeated, "being present this deponent and the said goodwif Gilbert, and the said Richardsons wif with other, countrey folkes about them in the market place aforesaid."[10] In other words, this slander took place in front of local people who might think ill of Margaret Raven as a result. It was for that reason that she brought the case against her neighbor. Second, detail substantiates Magdalen Lewys's testimony – for instance her statement that Raven crossed the road with chickens demonstrates the veracity of her memory and therefore 'proves' what she saw.

Every element of Magdalen's deposition is thus crucial to the making of moral meaning in the community. But it does not offer us evidence of exactly what happened, either what Margaret Richardson actually said or what Margaret Raven really did. Despite both deponents' use of telling detail, their testimonies differ at the crucial point of the description of Raven's alleged crime. As Joyseman recalls Richardson's words: "[I]n the hedge within the chauntrey stile in younges ground she played the whore, saying that she had gotten a whete sheef[11] from the stock in the said feeld and carryed into the hedge where she battrid the shefe abrode and saw her and a knave togithers."[12] This tale is as much a story of the stealing of corn as one of adultery.

What the evidence does show us is how women's reputations were negotiated in these small urban communities. Margaret Richardson is seen by both the deponents quoted here as a troublemaker, and both tell her so at the time. Joyseman says she "advised her to leave her talke and not to say any more so till she did knew more the truth."[13] This suggests the extent to which women themselves tried to keep the peace by making clear on a day-to-day basis their own sense of appropriate and inappropriate behavior, and it therefore demonstrates that the court was the last stage in a process of dealing with social tension. Whatever really took place in the small parish of St Paul's in 1560, these women understood the importance of showing that they valued social harmony. Although poor and presumably uneducated, they are skilled in such language and fluent in its ideologies, and they know how to construct a story in such a way as to demonstrate those proficiencies.

Notes

1 The Protestant state church in England.
2 A legally required payment of one tenth of one's yearly income to support the local parish church and clergy.
3 A lay parish official in the Church of England.
4 'Goodwife' used with a surname signified a married woman of good moral standing; notably, the epithet is not applied to Golding.
5 A sowgelder is a person who spays sows.
6 Canterbury Cathedral Archives and Library, X.10.7, fol. 110v, 1560. Contractions have been silently expanded, use of u and v regularized and modern capitalization adopted.
7 Knave denotes a dishonorable man.
8 Canterbury Cathedral Archives and Library, X.10.7, fol. 110v, 1560.
9 Ibid., fol. 111r.
10 Ibid., fol. 112r.
11 A bundle of wheat.
12 Canterbury Cathedral Archives and Library, X.10.7, fol. 111v.
13 Ibid.

9 'Popular duels': Honor, violence, and reconciliation in an Augsburg street fight in 1642

by B. Ann Tlusty

The word 'duel' usually brings to mind images of men of status meeting at dawn to face each other with pistols or swords in accordance with the rules of aristocratic honor. Recently, however, historians have begun to pay closer attention to the code of honor that governed violent encounters between ordinary townsmen, sometimes termed 'popular duels.' Prior to the eighteenth century, there was little to distinguish popular dueling among commoners from spontaneous swordplay between those of higher station.

Illustrative of such encounters is a sword fight that took place on the streets of Augsburg in 1642. Both of the participants were members of the local guard and seem to have been fighting mainly for the sake of a good fight. Of particular interest in the record of this sword fight is the general disregard demonstrated by both duelers and magistrates for the common-law expectation of 'retreat to the wall' as a prerequisite for claiming self-defense. Instead, behavior was both dictated and judged by the unwritten laws of male interaction, which included refusal to retreat when threatened and acceptance of resort to arms as an appropriate form of social control. These values are illustrated both by the responses of the killer, Caspar Morhardt, to the questions of the interrogators, and by the statements of witnesses to the fight.

From Morhardt's testimony:

"Q. Did [Morhardt] not last Sunday drink with Ernst Kratzer, and afterwards quarrel with him, then finally get into a sword fight and stab him so that he died of it the next day?

"A. [Morhardt] says that he was drinking not with Ernst Kratzer, but with others, and first met up with Kratzer on the way back. Ernst walked with him very peacefully from [the nearby village of] Oberhausen into the city. Afterwards, as they were passing by the artillery armory, Kratzer said to [Morhardt], 'Would you be ready to defend yourself at some point?' and he responded, 'Why not, if someone came after me?' Kratzer asked, 'You want a piece of me?' [Morhardt] answered, 'Of course not, God forbid, I don't want to start anything.' Then, in front of Neidthard the bell caster's house, Kratzer drew his sword, and Morhardt did so also, because a lot of people were on the street and he would have been embarrassed not to defend himself

… They crossed swords, and unfortunately during the fight he gave Kratzer this stab wound.

"Q. Did he carry a grudge or bear [Kratzer] ill-will, or why did he kill him?

"A. Certainly not, they had often guarded side by side and never said a bad word to one another."[1]

Witness 1 (a 30-year-old weaver): "Kratzer began to attack Morhardt with words as insulting as he has ever heard. [The witness] followed them and himself heard Kratzer say to Morhardt several times, 'I'm a soldier, but you're not, you're a bearskinner, dog's etc.[2] Defend yourself! Why are you wearing that sword at your side?' … [Morhardt] drew his sword mostly out of fear and shame, saying, 'You push me around like a hangman's knave and because it has to be, I'll defend myself,' upon which [Kratzer] attacked Morhardt with such force that, had his sword been a sharp-edged weapon, he would have split his head."[3]

Witness 2 (the wife of a gardener): "Caspar was very saddened. He went to the victim and offered him his hand, and said, 'Brother, brother, forgive me!' But Ernst didn't want to offer his hand, answering, 'No.' Then after a lot of urging, he finally offered Caspar his left hand after all. The people standing around told the defendant to flee, but he said, 'No, I won't flee, for it was a fair fight.'"[4]

Caspar Morhardt, then, drew his sword not in defense of his life, but in defense of his reputation. Because the incident occurred on the open street in front of many witnesses, the pressure to perform as expected was great. To ignore Kratzer's taunts in a public arena would both have compromised Morhardt's honor and masculine reputation and rewarded his adversary's inappropriate behavior. These pressures, to put it in the terms of the feminist philosopher Judith Butler, communicated acceptable ways of 'doing' gender, in this case emphasizing and legitimizing resort to arms as an appropriate means of restoring Morhardt's honor and devaluing Kratzer's drunken display of bravado.

At the same time, the sensibilities of the seventeenth century did not condone dispatching an opponent with callous indifference, even if he seemed to be asking for it. Morhardt knew that if Kratzer was dying, reconciliation with his victim was important to his own chances for social rehabilitation. Forgiving Morhardt was also important to Kratzer's own preparation for death. Both Catholics and Protestants understood making peace with God and with earthly adversaries to be essential to the process of dying well. By insisting that Kratzer offer the hand of peace, the killer both staged a good death for his victim, and demonstrated his own contrition and lack of malice.

This case is typical in that the witnesses to the fight and the surviving dueler were all careful to formulate their statements in support of the rules of fair fighting. The goal of their narrative was to convince the authorities that the killer acted honorably and the victim died well. In this case, the strategy was successful. Although Caspar Morhardt certainly could have avoided the fight without danger to his life, he was released without penalty. The city council required him only to pay for the food he consumed while incarcerated. Morhardt's irascible victim Ernst Kratzer, the council decreed, was himself to blame for his own death. Such a conclusion would hardly have been possible without the endorsement of witnesses for Morhardt's behavior. The fact that this fight took place in the public space of the open street in front of onlookers both increased the pressure on the duelers to properly perform their gendered roles, and also ensured that they would be judged according to popular norms of honorable conduct.

Notes

1 Stadtarchiv Augsburg, Urgicht Caspar Morhardt, 16 May–4 June 1642, Strafbuch 1633–1653, p. 254. Translated by B. Ann Tlusty.
2 Most likely the very common obscenity 'dog's cunt.'
3 Stadtarchiv Augsburg, Urgicht Caspar Morhardt, 16 May–4 June 1642, Strafbuch 1633–1653, p. 254.
4 Ibid.

10 Regulating day laborers' wages in sixteenth-century Zwickau[1]

by Siegfried Hoyer

From the early Middle Ages, employment opportunities in manufacturing and agriculture expanded for day laborers. With the upswing in economic transactions based on money and goods in the fourteenth and fifteenth centuries, these opportunities increased considerably. Wage labor supplemented the work of journeymen and tenant farmers. With the increase in literacy and record-keeping in the early modern period, authorities implemented written ordinances for their territories and towns, regulating the work conditions and payment of day laborers.

The example given here comes from the Saxon city of Zwickau in Germany. In the middle of the sixteenth century, Zwickau had a population of around 7,700 inhabitants and a thriving textile export industry, which made it one of the largest and most important cities in Saxony. As the city's records indicate, the city council of Zwickau first took up the regulation of payment for day laborers in 1506/07. Later ordinances were printed in 1542 and again, in expanded form, in 1565. While ordinances such as the one below regulated wages in the construction trade and in gardening and agriculture, parallel regulations were lacking for the textile industry – in which a workforce made up partly of women processed raw wool – as well as for the transport sector. In both of these areas, however, special agreements had most likely long been in place.

"Ordinance and Regulation of the honorable council of the city of Zwickau, concerning the day workers and day laborers, what and how one shall deal with their payment, so that no one shall in that regard be cheated or discriminated against. The order of the council shall in future be absolutely complied with by all inhabitants of the city and all those outside the city who wish to employ these citizens, under penalty of the formulated punishments.

"COMMON DAY LABORERS, from Easter to Michaelmas:[2] 1 groschen with board, 2 groschen without board; from Michaelmas to Easter: 10 pfennige with board, 20 pfennige without board.

"CARPENTERS and MASONS, when they take up day work, from the Feast of the Chair of St. Peter[3] to the Feast of St. Gallus:[4] for journeymen 18 groschen without board, for masters 1 florin without board; from the Feast of St. Gallus to the Feast of the Chair of St. Peter: for journeymen 15 groschen without board, for masters 18 groschen without board.

"WORKERS IN CLAY,[5] from Laetere[6] to St. Martin's Day:[7] 3 groschen per day without board. ...

"GARDEN WORK, DIGGING, for one day: 9 pfennige with board, 18 pfennige without board.

"HOPS STANCHIONING:[8] 15 pfennige per day with board, 2 ½ groschen without board.

"HOPS PICKING: 6 pfennige per day with board and not more. Concerning the other garden work, such as weeding, hops planting, and such work commonly performed by women: 8 pfennige per day with board and 16 pfennige without board.

"TREE CUTTING, GRAFTING: 2 ½ groschen per day without board.

"FIELD WORK and GRASS CUTTING: 2 groschen per day with board, 3 groschen without board.

"ROWEN[9] CUTTING: 15 pfennige per day with board, 30 pfennige without board.

"BARLEY and OAT CUTTING: 2 groschen per day with board, 3 ½ groschen without board.

"SOWING: 3 pfennige for a bushel of oats without board, 4 pfennige for other types of grain without board.

"GRAIN HARVESTING: 6 pfennige per day with board, 32 pfennige without board.

"GATHERING: 6 pfennige per day with board, 32 pfennige without board.

"BINDING [into sheaves]: 8 pfennige per day with board, 3 groschen without board.

"RAKING HAY, BARLEY, OATS: 8 pfennige per day with board, 16 pfennige without board.

"ROWEN RAKING: 6 pfennige per day with board, 14 pfennige without board.

"THRESHING, from St. Bartholomew's Day[10] to Michaelmas: 2 groschen without board, 1 groschen with board; from Michaelmas to Shrove Tuesday:[11] 20 pfennige without board, 10 pfennige with board.

"Punishment for violators: If anyone deliberately neglects and does not comply with the council's directives – whether they are a friend of the council or a bad burgher or inhabitant – for each broken regulation, as often as the breach occurs, without exception a penalty of 20 silver groschen shall be given to the council as a fine or punishment.

"But concerning the day laborer or worker who resists or refuses to work for the ordered and set wages, whether he is approached in the urban square where day laborers are hired or somewhere else: If he makes a separate agreement for wages and wants to compel people to honor it, he shall be reported to the council or the court. On account of his recalcitrance, he shall be arrested and punished or be commanded to forever give up work in the city. If a townsman does not want to seek out the council or the court in this matter, he shall report the worker to the bailiff. If such a worker, who enters into an unlawful employment contract, refuses to work or insists on special treatment, he shall be imprisoned so that the council can punish him. The townsman in this matter shall, however, show restraint and exercise no wilfulness toward the worker. Everybody has to adhere to this.

"Issued Thursday, the 1st of May 1565."[12]

At first sight, this *Ordinance and Regulation* appears to have been primarily passed as a protection for day laborers – to guarantee them a fair wage for their work. However, the punishments for workers who sought to work outside the system indicate that the Zwickau *Ordinance and Regulation* of 1565 also served another purpose; namely, that of preventing day laborers from negotiating for higher wages in a 'booming economy.' While masters who paid their workers less than the stipulated wage incurred a penalty which was only slightly higher than a carpenter's daily wage, laborers who tried to achieve higher wages through negotiations with their employers were threatened with punishment or exile from the city.

Notes

1 Translated by Sean E. Clark and Benjamin A. Miller.
2 Michaelmas, the feast of St. Michael the Archangel, is on 29 September.
3 The feast of the Chair of St. Peter is on 22 February.
4 The feast of St. Gallus is on 16 October.
5 Workers in clay spread clay on the walls of half-timbered houses.
6 The fourth Sunday of Lent.
7 St. Martin's Day, or the feast of St. Martin, is on 11 November.
8 Raising of hops-poles.
9 A second growth of grass or hay in one season.
10 St. Bartholomew's Day is 24 August.
11 Shrove Tuesday is the last day before the beginning of Lent on Ash Wednesday.
12 *Ordnung vnd Satzung eines Erbarn Radts der Stadt Zwickaw / die Tagwercker vnd Tagloener belangend / wes / vnd wie man sich jn belohnung gegen denselbigen zuhalten/ das niemands in deme vbersatzt / noch verkuertzt werde / Welche Ordnung gedachter Radt nun hinfort von allen Einwonern dieser Stadt / auch von den jenigen ausserhalb der Stadt / Welche sich der Burger arbeyt gebrauchen wollen / bey nach begriffener Straff / vnuorbruechlich wil gehalten haben ...* The ordinance was printed by Wolfgang Meyerpeck through the commission of the Zwickau city council and is kept in the Stadtarchiv Zwickau X, 34, p. 7. The whole text is framed by an arabesque border and in the upper left corner there is a woodcut image of three swans, again framed by an arabesque border. This is a symbol of the city that became part of the municipal coat of arms in 1566. See Helmut Claus, *Die Zwickauer Drucke des 16. Jahrhunderts*, part 2, Gotha: Forschungsbibliothek, 1986, p. 127. One part of the *Ordinance and Regulation* from 1565 was edited without the punishments by Otto Langer, "Zwickauer Lohntaxen aus dem 16. Jh.," *Mitteilungen des Altertumsvereins Zwickau* 8, 1905, 22–39.

11 Ore Mountain miners stage a social protest in 1719[1]

by Helmut Bräuer

The Ore Mountains in Saxony were among those regions of central Europe that, like Tyrol or the Harz Mountains, had played an important role as silver suppliers since the late Middle Ages. Saxon silver was profitable in Europe's markets and made the wealthy even wealthier. Silver mining peaked in the years between 1470 and 1550. The enormous profits which could be gained from mining were the result of complex processes, including oversight by territorial lords, technological developments, and the investment of capital from other cities, as well as the hard work and skill of the miners.

Since the end of the fifteenth century, a succession of urban communities had sprung up to house the miners, and these grew rapidly. While Freiberg dated from the twelfth century, Schneeberg, Annaberg, Marienberg, and some twenty other mining settlements now joined it. The Bohemian side of the mountains also saw similar developments. As may be observed in Europe generally, mining regions during that period had to import some of the most basic foodstuffs, grain and meat. These came principally from regions in Poland and Hungary, as well as from grain producing centers in Thuringia and northern Saxony. There were two primary reasons for this need to import: On the one hand, natural conditions in the mountains were harsh and barren, which diminished the crop yield; on the other hand, the mining industry gathered a relatively large number of men who, together with their families, had to be maintained. The territorial princes and urban magistrates had a high level of responsibility to secure adequate provisions.

Although silver production decreased significantly since the middle of the sixteenth century, the extraction of other metals enabled the mining industry to survive. Nevertheless, because of the dwindling findings of ore, miners earned less and less. They often moved from mine to mine in order to find employment, or they only worked half-shifts. As a result, female family members – wives and daughters – had to work harder as lace-makers. Some families subsisted on only the few pennies which the women earned from the production of lace.

In the seventeenth and early eighteenth centuries, production at the mines diminished even further. Often miners were only allowed to work short hours, and many were forced to rely solely on charity from the miners' guild fund to survive until they came 'to better times.' The miners' guild had become an important means of social support in such situations. It had been established in the fifteenth century as a religious and social organization for the purpose of prayer and mutual assistance. Over time, however, the significance of the guild's charitable fund increased more and more. Guild members deposited three pennies weekly and received, in the event of some misfortune, illness, or in old age, a small sum of money. Wives and unmarried daughters were also provided with charity. And the miners' guild had yet another function: It gathered, unified, and channeled the social protest of miners during highly charged situations such as those that occurred at the beginning of the eighteenth century.

Social divisions between miners and the authorities became notably confrontational in the early eighteenth century. Several times it resulted in demonstrations. When in 1719 noble landowners, several grain sellers, and also bakers in the mining towns hoarded grain and flour in order to inflate the price of bread, the hungry miners knew of no other recourse than to respond in protest. An undated paper, in which the protest organizers laid out their plans, was sent round the mines to rouse the miners to action:

"Good fortune to you fellow miners:

"We cannot refrain in this current, difficult, dangerous, and costly time, to write to the entire guild, because currently the difficult rise in prices weighs heavily on us and because everywhere our poor brethren may only work halftime at most mines. Consider well, therefore, how this matter is to be helped, for this is an increase in prices made by men and not by God. Should we therefore allow our wives and children to languish in hunger? We would much prefer this as our course: on the next payday we shall all gather in Freiberg and firstly send a dispatch to the city council of Freiberg, asking whether they would have some understanding and allow more bread to be baked or not ..., if they will not, then we will help ourselves ..., if they do not know what a rebellion is, we will teach them that we can help ourselves if we are not helped, so that we poor miners will not die."[2]

Members of the guild were then asked to circulate the letter and to assemble on the next payday on the castle square in Freiberg from 10 until 11 o'clock in the morning. When, however, news reached the authorities of the miners' plans, the mine overseers and the city council took steps to curtail the nascent rebellion and discipline the instigators. Unfortunately, this primary source does not tell us what happened next. Judging from other sources, it appears that the authorities punished the 'ringleaders' of such actions with dismissal.

Notes

1 Translated by Paul A. Buehler and Benjamin A. Miller.
2 Sächsisches Hauptstaatsarchiv Dresden, Loc. 9993/11, Acta das Getreyde Bedürfnis betr., vol. II, anno 1719, p. 137.

12 Against corruption in all the estates: An early eighteenth-century Pietist vision for universal reform through education

by Richard L. Gawthrop

In the early 1690s, the Pietist movement within the German Lutheran Church began to experience systematic hostility and persecution from the orthodox establishment. One of the targets of orthodox attack was August Hermann Francke (1663–1727), the leader of an 'awakening' in the city of Leipzig. Fortunately for Francke and the Pietist movement as a whole, the Reformed Elector[1] of the state of Brandenburg–Prussia, Frederick III, offered protection to the Pietists, who he hoped would assist his state-building efforts by supporting his plan to unite in one religious community the Reformed elite at the Berlin court and the overwhelmingly Lutheran population of his dynasty's lands in northeastern Germany.

Frederick appointed Francke to a professorship at the newly established University of Halle, as well as to a pastorate at a Lutheran Church in an impoverished Halle suburb. Francke's parishioners responded very positively to his ministry, and Francke quickly began to address Halle's socioeconomic problems by working to school the next generation in Christian values and vocationally useful skills. By the end of 1695, he had established a school for children of the poor, a Latin school for middle-class children, and a *Paedagogium* for sons of the nobility.

To shield the children of the 'poor school' from the harmful social environment outside the school, Francke and his associates mounted a successful campaign to raise money for a large orphanage. After the main building was completed in the late 1690s, the orphanage complex received a special 'privilege' of legal protection from the Prussian state, enabling it to continue expanding. Shortly thereafter, in the early 1700s, Francke wrote a series of tracts, publicizing the achievements of his Halle institutions and heralding them as a model for a 'reformation' of society as a whole. The following excerpt is from one of these, the "Great Essay":

"That everything is in a state of corruption and terrible decay – not just in the world at large, but also in so-called Christendom and even in the Protestant churches – can be quite easily recognized by those whose eyes God has opened only just a little bit ... As Christendom ... is divided into three main estates – namely, the governing estate, the household estate, and the teaching [clerical] estate, so is this corruption present to a roughly equal extent in all three estates ... In the governing estate, the Devil has his kingdom, reign, and government ... [but saying this] is not disrespectful to the governing estate itself, which was ordained by God ... [and] it cannot be denied that even in such an estate God has left a seed of redemption ... The Devil has his kingdom and reign in the household estate also, since robbery, lying, stealing, murder, fraud, whoring, adultery, and all kinds of horrible sins, vices, and shameful acts are exceedingly common [in it, ... but] God has also left seed for redemption in this estate – a greater abundance of it, moreover, among this lesser estate, than among the ... rich and powerful of this world ... The corruption of the teaching estate ... compared to that of the other estates is not any less grievous ... but God has also in this estate left behind a seed, through which He is awakening many every day to a true perception of their souls and their vocations – praise His name! ...

"One must, however, seek out further the foundations and sources of the corruption ... the veins and arteries through which the corruption in all the estates and the entire world spreads its harmful influence. Such a source is the bad upbringing of our youth. For it has come to pass that almost no one knows any more what comprises an upbringing that produces truly Christian adults who are useful, contributing members of society. Consequently, the youth grow up raw, dissolute, and wild, without any true knowledge and fear of God ... [Given the inability of parents to provide a good upbringing] what good can be hoped for, if people in their early childhood are neglected and the evil implanted in them by nature only becomes more hardened and entrenched ... It is the schools and no less the universities that are the places in which this situation can be improved, even if the children in their early upbringing at home were somewhat corrupted. But the schools as a whole are places where even children of pious parents are corrupted ... [and] the universities [have been permitted to develop] ... into an environment characterized by crudity, dissolution, and impudence ...

"In our time, however ... in a special act of divine Providence, a new university [i.e., Halle University] has been established and through it an open gate to the improvement of the universal corruption has been given ... For ... just as one might say regarding universities that through them evil can spread through all estates as from a poisoned spring, so on the other hand when the youth are taught there in ways pleasing to God these institutions are most emphatically capable of effortlessly remedying the general corruption ... Scarcely, however, was the new university inaugurated, than it pleased God in His goodness to open up still another special gate ... the many good and useful institutions [i.e., Francke's orphanage and school complex in Halle], which from the outset were aimed at nothing other than a fundamental improvement [in the education of youth, the training of future teachers, and the care of the poor]."[2]

What was the historical significance of Francke's reform vision? In many ways, it was simply an updated version of the sixteenth-century Lutheran Church's massive campaign of catechization and schooling designed to bring the light of Christ to a German population viewed by the reformers as deeply corrupted and spiritually blind. Francke's plan, however, was based on a different view of Christendom's prospects. Whereas the sixteenth-century reformers' efforts were intended primarily to save rank-and-file Protestants from spiritual perdition during a period perceived as very close to the Day of Judgment, Francke looked upon his pedagogical project as laying a foundation for a "fundamental improvement" not just of Halle, nor even of Germany, but of the entire world.

In other words, Francke was not, as Luther was, a pessimist regarding humanity's future; but an optimist – a millenarian, who believed that God's kingdom was in the process of being created on earth. Not surprisingly, Halle under his leadership was a founding partner, along with the London-based Society for the Promotion of Christian Knowledge, of the first wave of Protestant overseas missions. In addition, through the long-term impact of the thousands of graduates from Francke's schools, including the theology program at the University of Halle, Francke's confidence in the ability of education to transform society in a dramatic fashion would live on in Germany through the secular visions of reform put forward by Enlightenment thinkers like Kant and by early nineteenth-century German nationalists.

Notes

1 In early modern Germany, the electors were the princes who elected the emperor.
2 August Hermann Francke, "August Hermann Franckes Schrift über eine Reform des Erziehungs- und Bildungswesens als Ausgangspunkt einer geistlichen und sozialen Neuordnung der Evangelischen Kirche des 18. Jahrhunderts, 'Der Grosse Aufsatz,'" in Otto Podczeck (ed.), *Abhandlungen der sächsischen Akademie der Wissenschaften: Philosophisch-historische Reihe*, 53:3, 1962, pp. 70–72, 75–77, 86–90. Translated by Richard L. Gawthrop.

II

Social spaces: Experiencing and negotiating encounters

Introduction

by Ute Lotz-Heumann

This chapter is concerned with social spaces – courts, cities, villages, and the missionary frontier – in which encounters between different groups, cultures, and identities took place during the early modern period. People experienced and negotiated these encounters in various ways, running the gamut from peaceful interactions and carnivalesque events to hostilities and open conflicts within communities. Pia F. Cuneo's essay focuses on the socially most exclusive space in early modern Europe, the court, which was a very competitive environment for members of the nobility who sought to establish and defend their reputation and their place in the court's hierarchy.[1]

Most essays in this chapter, by Thomas A. Brady, Jr., J. Jeffery Tyler, Victoria Christman, Joel Van Amberg, Jonathan A. Reid, Barbara B. Diefendorf, Kaspar von Greyerz, Alan E. Bernstein, and Nicholas Terpstra, explore early modern towns and the encounters that happened in these spaces. As a result, cities and towns are without doubt over-represented in this chapter compared to the percentage of the population who lived in towns. Historians estimate that between 10 and 20 percent of the population in early modern Europe were town-dwellers, and that the overwhelming majority of the urban population lived in small and mid-sized towns of between 1,000 and 5,000 inhabitants. However, this over-representation has both historical and historiographical reasons: Cities and towns had a substantial impact on societies because they functioned as political, social, and economic centers for the rural spaces around them. And cities and towns produced a lot of written records in the early modern period. They have therefore been at the center of historiographical research for many decades.

The constitutional treaty, or 'oath letter,' of the city of Strasbourg exemplifies the careful political balance between patricians and guilds that late medieval and early modern cities tried to maintain. But keeping this civic political culture, which exhibited elements of oligarchy and communalism, intact, was often a challenge (essay by Thomas A. Brady, Jr.). Augsburg's relationship with its once-powerful episcopal overlord is another example of such a tenuous balance in the late Middle Ages. Allowing the bishop to ceremoniously enter the city and display his authority in the urban space required meticulous negotiations and careful execution (essay by J. Jeffery Tyler).[2]

In post-Reformation Europe, these power struggles in cities were complicated even further when religious interests and conflicts were added into the mix. The uproar in Antwerp in 1522 (essay by Victoria Christman) and the civic uprising in Augsburg in 1524 (essay by Joel Van Amberg),[3] both over early clerical supporters of the Reformation message, exemplify the different actors – central authorities, urban authorities, and the citizenry – involved. And they show why religious expression and identity were such powerful and potentially deeply disrupting factors in these compact urban spaces. Jean Glaumeau's account of urban celebrations and religious clashes in Bourges (essay by Jonathan A. Reid) and Jean Faurin's journal recording events which led up to the first War of Religion in Castres (essay by Barbara B. Diefendorf) show similar processes at work in sixteenth-century France.[4]

Cities were also spaces of communal festivals and acted as actual and virtual stages for plays, satirical depictions of social tensions, and carnivalesque interactions. The public staging of plays in sixteenth-century Swiss cities served to solidify political and religious bonds (essay by Kaspar von Greyerz). In contrast, the anecdote by François Rabelais satirizes the social tensions that characterized the city center of Paris (essay by Alan E. Bernstein). And Bologna's Feast of the Roast Pig exemplified the different functions of early modern carnivalesque rituals in the central urban square, from its marking of a saint's day to the display of urban authorities as benefactors (essay by Nicholas Terpstra).

Katherine G. Brady's and Thomas A. Brady, Jr.'s essay, and Randolph C. Head's essay take the reader to early modern villages, the spaces in which 90 percent of the population lived. Both Wendelstein in Franconia, Germany, and Zizers in Graubünden, Switzerland, exemplify the communal nature of life in these villages and show how – at least in some areas of Europe – villagers were able to have a strong say in their own affairs, including matters of religion.

Finally, Ulrike Strasser's essay takes us to the missionary frontier of early modern Europe, exploring how a map – the quintessential expression of European spatial perception through distances – could nevertheless reflect knowledge transfer between different cultural groups by displaying the Palaos Islanders' way of measuring travel time rather than distance.

Notes

1 See no. 2, Milliman: From Bohemia to Spain and back again: Sports diplomacy in fifteenth-century Europe, for courts as spaces for 'sports diplomacy.'
2 See below, note 3.
3 Other essays besides Tyler's and Van Amberg's that are concerned with the German imperial town of Augsburg are no. 9, Tlusty: 'Popular duels': Honor, violence,

Introduction: Social spaces 63

and reconciliation in an Augsburg street fight in 1642; no. 29, Plummer: Hans Gallmeyer: Seduction, bigamy, and forgery in an Augsburg Workshop in 1565. This is a reflection of the rich collection of early modern primary sources that has survived in Augsburg.

4 Several essays in this collection throw light on events leading up to and during the French Wars of Religion and the impact of these religious wars. Besides the essays by Reid and Diefendorf in this chapter, see also no. 61, Mentzer: Assuring civil rights for religious minorities in sixteenth-century France; no. 71, Taylor: Catholic preaching on the eve of the French Wars of Religion: A eucharistic battleground.

13 Life at a German court: The importance of equestrian skill in the early seventeenth century

by Pia F. Cuneo

Early modern courts were dynamic social and political institutions that were hierarchical in nature and structure. The social and political apex of each court featured a noble ruler and his family who were supported and aided by a host of advisors, bureaucrats, lesser peers, and servants. The court was the central institution of the early modern state. As such, it was essential to protect, preserve, and perpetuate the court's structure and thus to ensure a modicum of stability. Courts also became centers for the production and exercise of culture, from the literary and visual arts such as poetry and painting, to the physical and martial arts, such as fencing and riding. Because the social environment of the court was relatively fluid and dynamic, courtiers (members of the court excluding servants) used cultural production and exercise in order to compete with one another for the attention and favor of the noble ruler. A courtier's position within the court hierarchy usually coincided directly with the title and emoluments that were the ruler's to bestow upon whomever he deemed especially deserving. Conversely, falling out of favor with the ruler could result in the curtailment of privileges, reduction in rank, and in severe cases, even banishment from court. Thus attaining, preserving, and augmenting the ruler's good graces was a continuing concern and perpetual challenge for the individual courtier also because of the ever-threatening possibility that some other courtier would find more favor with the ruler and thus achieve social and economic superiority.

By the time he published his third book, *The Noble Art of Riding (Della Cavalleria)*, in 1609/10, Georg Engelhard Löhneysen (1552–1622) had been a courtier at various German courts. From 1575 to 1583, he served as the royal riding master at the court of Elector[1] August of Saxony at Dresden, and then as stable-master (among other positions) to the Princes of Braunschweig–Wolfenbüttel at their northern German courts in Gröningen and Wolfenbüttel. In the first main section of *The Noble Art of Riding* Löhneysen includes an extended discussion of life at court and the ideal characteristics of a courtier. Löhneysen describes the courtier's possibility for advancement as tightly circumscribed and narrowly limited by means that were deemed appropriate to his social status. Among other colorful topics, he addresses the issue "By what means a courtier may attain honor and wealth":

"Although the most noble means by which a courtier may attain the good graces and the respect of princes and knights are the art of riding and participation in knightly tournaments, especially because it is appropriate for every courtier to be well experienced and practiced in all matters relating to knightliness, these in themselves are still not sufficient. Instead, he must in addition know how to adapt himself to life at court in order that he may acquire and maintain the prince's grace and the officers' favor. Amongst all the other honest means available, a noble courtier can avail himself of only three in order to attain honor and wealth: princely service, warfare, and marriage. Regarding the first means, princely service, in this case the courtier must carefully attend to his own behavior towards the officers and towards all kinds of people at court so that he may obtain the prince's and others' grace and favor. To be deemed not only by acquaintances but also by strangers as praiseworthy and of good repute greatly helps and promotes a courtier in his quest. The primary means by which he may obtain and receive such a reputation, also as a bold courtier with beautiful, extraordinary, and swift horses, is through the art of riding …"[2]

Modern-day historians who have studied early modern European courts have noted the highly competitive nature that characterized the social relationships that bound members of court to each other and to their overlord. These historians have emphasized various behavioral strategies employed by courtiers in order to promote themselves within and thus to ascend the social hierarchy. One very prominent and influential historian of early modern courts, Norbert Elias, focused especially on the concepts of civility and etiquette as both the measure and the method by which courtiers could demonstrate and represent their social status and prestige within a competitive court hierarchy. In his book, *Court Society*, Elias maintains that etiquette enabled members of court "to enact their existence, to demonstrate their prestige, to distance themselves from lower-ranking people and have this distance recognized by the higher ranking. [The performance of etiquette] made visible the distancing relationship that both united them and distinguished them from each other and so publicly certified the order of rank they accorded each other. The practice of etiquette is, in other words, an exhibition of court society to itself."[3]

Within court society, a man's choice of words, his table manners, and his facility in making conversation were all serious matters. Even Löhneysen says in the above quote that a courtier must be mindful of his behavior towards others at court. Yet Löhneysen's text reminds us that it was not only social behavior but also physical skill that provided courtiers with the means to enhance their reputations and distinguish themselves from others. While it certainly served the personal interests of a riding- and stable-master like Löhneysen to stress the importance of equestrian skill as essential to life at court, his view is corroborated by abundant historical and cultural evidence.

Notes

1 In early modern Germany, the electors were the princes who elected the emperor.
2 Georg Engelhard Löhneysen, *Della Cavalleria. Gründtlicher Bericht von allem was zu der Reutterei gehörig und einem Cavallier davon zuwissen geburt*, Remlingen: 1609/10, p. 17. Translated by Pia F. Cuneo.
3 Norbert Elias, *The Court Society*, tr. Edmund Jephcott, in Stephen Mennel (ed.), *The Collected Works of Norbert Elias*, 2 vols, Dublin: University of Dublin Press, 2006, vol. 2, p. 110. The book was originally written in 1933 and first published in 1969 as *Die höfische Gesellschaft*, Darmstadt: Hermann Luchterhand Verlag, 1969.

14 The constitutional treaty of a German city: Strasbourg, 1482

by Thomas A. Brady, Jr.

From the fourteenth far into the sixteenth century, the cities of German-speaking Europe formed and consolidated their early modern political regimes. Most southern German (including Swiss) cities were racked by strife (called 'guild revolts') between established elites and corporately organized merchants, tradesmen, and craftsmen. The outcomes varied from Nuremberg, where the guilds were early on suppressed, through Ulm and Strasbourg, where noble/merchant elites shared civic governance with the guilds, to Basel, where, following the city's joining the Swiss Confederation in 1501, nobles and large merchants were excluded from the regime. In the evolution of these city governments, stages of revolt and riot were typically followed by negotiations and agreement on a new order, the terms of which were contained in a formal contract. Such documents deal with the issues that stirred the middling and lesser citizens: taxation, political inclusion of guilds, procedures for selecting magistrates, external ties of the patrician elites, the swearing of oaths by new magistrates and by the entire body of full citizens. Hence the name of the treaty, the "Oath-Letter."

This document, a kind of civic constitution, records the terms of Strasbourg's civic peace, which, negotiated in 1482, remained in force until the French Revolution. At around 20,000 inhabitants, Strasbourg was then a major southern city of the Empire,[1] subject to the emperor alone, and possessing extensive rights of autonomy. It was the seat of a (non-residing) bishop, a major center of manufacturing and commerce, and an important power in a politically highly fragmented region of the Empire.

The chief change agreed to in this document was the division of magistracies between the patrician elite (nobles and larger merchants) and the guilds, whose number was reduced from twenty-eight to twenty. The alliance of urban nobles and larger merchants, on which this contract rested, remained solid for the remainder of Strasbourg's history as a free city. A second element, also common in the southern free cities, was the formation within the regime of powerful, permanent bodies within the city council. At Strasbourg, the committees of the XV and the XIII were responsible respectively for internal and external security, and their members were co-opted for life. All of the prominent politicians sat in these councils, which formed the heart of the oligarchic tendencies in the city's political development.

The treaty was formally sealed on Christmas Eve 1482 by twenty patricians (some noble, some not) and fifty-two magistrates and other leading guildsmen. It declares the two parties' "judgment that the council shall consist of thirty-one persons: in the first place ten patricians, and a burgomaster from the guilds, and also twenty persons from the guilds. And ... each year half of the council shall stay in office. So that every magistrate shall stay in office for two years. And this is the manner of selection for half the council and the burgomasters. Each guild's own magistrates ... shall assemble in their guildhall early in the morning on Thursday after Epiphany, and there they shall elect another honorable, honest man from their guild to replace the departing one. ... Thereupon the whole old council, both patricians and guildsmen, who have been sitting that year, shall gather in the large council chamber in city hall, and there they shall elect in place of the departing patricians other pious, honest men into the council from among the knights, squires, and burghers, ... And they [all the magistrates, patricians and guildsmen] shall swear in person to God and the Saints to uphold all the measures, points, and articles which are written down, and to accept no gift or donation while they hold office. ... [Finally,] the aforementioned burgomaster, the four masters,[2] and the [other] magistrates shall swear to the knights, squires, burghers, guildsmen, and commune at Strasbourg – both rich and poor – that with life and goods they will as best they can loyally guard and protect the latter, rich and poor alike without exception. ... When they [the bells] are being rung, everyone shall come on foot to the square before the cathedral, gather before the burgomaster and other masters, and obey them. And when the burgomaster and the other masters dismiss them, they shall on their oaths go quietly to their homes."[3]

The communal act of swearing the oath, which bound magistrates and the entire citizenry into a single community of rights and obligations, took place in full publicity. All in all, the civic ritual was a kind of political sacrament. It is no wonder, then, that the treaty specifies that anyone who is known to have acted against the treaty's terms "shall be declared perjured and stripped of his citizenship, and he shall never again come within the jurisdiction, nor become a burgher, and his life and goods shall be forfeit to the master and council, who shall confiscate all of his property and holdings, in the city or in the countryside, as much as they can, on their oaths and without fail."[4]

The provisions of Strasbourg's treaty of 1482 and its language reflect both the political balance of forces at this time and the traditional language of civic political culture. Once the dominant force in the city, by this time the patricians, we know from other sources, were able to maintain their precedence only on the guildsmen's acceptance of their leadership. This is why there were no more guild revolts at Strasbourg. The language of the treaty expresses many of the central values in the political culture of German self-governing cities: the protection of God and his saint (the city's patroness was the Virgin Mary), the leadership of honest, pious (adult male) citizens, obedience to the magistrates, and the common duty of magistrates and burghers to fulfill their communal duties without fail and uphold the treaties to which they all had sworn. Behind the language are detectable both the formal symbiosis of political authority and civic communalism, of oligarchy and equality, which was the hallmark of the political culture of German cities at the dawn of the early modern era.

Notes

1 The Holy Roman Empire of the German Nation, usually called 'the Empire,' was a huge and complex political organization in central Europe in medieval and early modern times. It was a loose political union of mostly German and largely self-governing principalities and towns.
2 The principal patrician magistrates.
3 The original German text is printed in Jean Lebeau and Jean-Marie Valentin (eds), *L'Alsace au siècle de la Réforme 1482–1621*, Nancy: Presses Universitaires de Nancy, 1985, pp. 18–21, here pp. 18–20. Translated by Thomas A. Brady, Jr.
4 Ibid., p. 21.

15 Contested spaces: Bishop and city in late fifteenth-century Augsburg

by J. Jeffery Tyler

Gates and towers, markets and squares, church sanctuaries and civic halls – all places and spaces that were carefully defined and hotly contested in the late medieval and early modern city. The south-central German city of Augsburg provided the stage for a fierce struggle between churchly bishop and lay magistrates in the Middle Ages, a struggle won by magistrates when Augsburg became a free and imperial city under the Holy Roman Emperor. Even as citizens elected their magistrates and city hall embodied lay supremacy, the bishop – his clergy, churches, and ancient privileges – maintained a significant influence in Augsburg. One had only to look up to the cathedral's spires to recall a time when bishops and priests dominated political, economic, and religious life in the city. In the late fifteenth century, spaces and places in Augsburg still belonged to the bishop, pre-eminently the cathedral quarter – a city within a city – with its great church, elaborate cloister, residences of the bishop and cathedral chapter. Add to this neighborhood the many monasteries and churches under the bishop's spiritual authority, and the souls of all Augsburgers, for whom the bishop interceded with God.

Given their growing political impotence in Augsburg, bishops had come to reside in a small town to the west, Dillingen on the Danube, where they reigned with complete and unquestioned authority. Yet the cathedral – the bishop's true seat of authority and mother church of the diocese – remained in Augsburg; for certain holy days and ceremonies Augsburg alone sufficed as a stage for episcopal ceremony. Whenever the bishop did return, he seized the opportunity to dramatize his ancient claim to rule Augsburg and reveal his ties to great princes and lords, all of whom despised the free status of the city. No event displayed the contested places and spaces of Augsburg like a bishop's first entry. The chronicle of Hector Mühlich, a wealthy Augsburg merchant, tells us about one such event:

"In the year of our Lord 1470 John, Count of Werdenberg, the newly elected Bishop of Augsburg, reached an agreement with the city [of Augsburg] regarding exactly how he and his entourage would make his entry [into the city]. It was resolved that city magistrates on the one side and the bishop and his riders on the other should meet outside [the city walls] and before a city gate as agreed.

"So on the 17th of June of this year, on a Sunday eight days after Pentecost, Count John of Werdenberg, the newly elected Bishop of Augsburg, planned to ride into the city. The previous Saturday morning [prior to the entry], the city council of Augsburg had been in session. At their meeting, Hans of Stein, the bishop's overseer, appeared. He reported that his lord, the bishop, had 1,800 armed riders in his parade, who would all need lodging after entering the city on Sunday. This news shocked the city council, which had understood the bishop would only bring 800 armed riders ... The council took immediate action. The magistrates sent for all the carpenters of Augsburg and these craftsmen spent half a day constructing barricades along all the side streets [leading off the main parade route in Augsburg], so that the riders would have to stay on one street from the Red Gate all the way across town to the Cathedral of Our Lady.

"So on Sunday at midday Bavarian princes galloped over the Lech River toward Augsburg – Duke Louis and his train, the Duke of Munich and his entourage, the riders of Swabia and those from Zußmerhausen, and the bishop and the people of [the Count of] Württemberg. They gathered in the district outside the city – the Ziegelstädel. The entire train included 3 dukes, 1 bishop, and 28 counts. At the same time the mayor and magistrates of Augsburg along with 200 fully armed riders bearing military banners rode out of the city; the Red Gate was closed behind them. Then the mayor stood back and spoke as follows: 'Honorable prince and lord, the magistrates and whole community of Augsburg, rich and poor, welcome your princely grace with all devotion and all humility.' So both sides gave each other their respect and due. Then the mayor had the gate opened; he and our riders entered the city first and took up their positions on the side street before St. Margaret's. At that point the bishop's huge entourage rode [into the city] and made for St. Ulrich's. All the way they processed three abreast – exquisitely decked out, fully armed, and inflated with arrogance, especially the princely riders. All the way they rode with their pages on great war horses, bearing mighty banners before them. Meanwhile all along the street – on the salt barn, the dance hall, the guild houses, and beyond – armed residents of the city stood guard ...

"Then the relics were carried around. The bishop stood near Saint Leonharts in the Jewish lane and he donned the miter; the princes joined the bishop and proceeded into the cathedral ... Thereafter each one rode to his lodging. At that point the city magistrates presented Bishop John with a gift – a golden cup worth 100 gulden and with a further 200 gulden inside it ... The Bishop of Eichstätt received a similar cup and money while all the lords in their lodgings enjoyed wine and fish ...

"The next day at 8:00 a.m. the storm bell sounded. Then the bishop along with the princes rode to city hall, where the whole city council had gathered. There each side swore to the other to remain faithful to their ancient traditions. The bishop laid his hand on his breast and said, 'This I swear' – sic ego juro; thus was his oath. Then the bishop with the princes rode to the episcopal court, and the mayor and the magistrates ... and the princes and lords feasted with the bishop ...

"On the following Tuesday, the nobility departed while the bishop stayed behind; he sang the Mass for Corpus Christi day and carried the sacrament in the procession [through Augsburg]."[1]

The Red Gate and city streets, exquisite lodgings and feasting halls, the cathedral and city hall of Augsburg – all were contested spaces in which civic leaders and their soldiers maneuvered with the bishop and his massive, aristocratic, and armed escort. Such spaces and places provided the stage on which rivals flashed their power and prestige, the stage on which negotiations took place and oaths were sworn. Ritual and feast greased the wheels of peaceful resolution. Yet magistrates remained on guard against episcopal aggression and bishops continued to make public their ancient claims to lordship. In 1537 the magistrates in Augsburg embraced the Protestant Reformation and extinguished every last vestige of the bishop's power – his claims to political and spiritual rule, his rule over city, church, and soul.

Note

1 "Chronik des Hector Mülich, 1348–1547," in *Die Chroniken der deutschen Städte vom 14. bis ins 16. Jahrhundert*, vol. 22, Leipzig: Hirzel, 1892, pp. 228–230. Translated by J. Jeffery Tyler.

16 Uproar in Antwerp, 1522

by Victoria Christman

The city of Antwerp lies on the river Scheldt in the central part of the early modern Netherlands, in what is today part of northern Belgium. A bustling port city, it was one of the most important trade hubs in sixteenth-century Europe. In addition to the exotic spices, textiles, and printed works for which it was famous, new ideas flooded into and out of the city with ease. It was via these well-established trade routes that the religious ideas of the early Protestant Reformation found their way into the city. Already by 1519, Luther's works were being translated into Dutch, and circulating among the Antwerp population. There, they found an eager audience among a citizenry that was highly literate for its time, had rather ineffective clerical oversight, and was part of a region in which anti-clericalism and theological critique had a long history. Much of the reforming spirit in Antwerp can be specifically attributed to the work of a monastery of Reformed Augustinians there that was active, heterodox, and extremely popular. Its prior, Jacobus Praepositus, had studied with Luther in Wittenberg, and began preaching Lutheran ideas in Antwerp as early as 1519. His congregants received his sermons with such enthusiasm that the Augustinians often struggled to maintain order in the church during the services.

Charles V, Holy Roman Emperor and King of Spain, ruled the sixteenth-century Low Countries via his aunt and queen-regent, Margaret of Austria. These rulers sought with great passion to maintain the Catholicity of their Netherlandish holdings, and eventually removed Praepositus from his position as prior of the monastery, arresting him on charges of heresy. But the forced exit of Praepositus did not signal the end of Lutheran influence at the cloister. His replacement, Hendrick van Zutphen, was also a follower of the Wittenberg reformer and continued the heterodox preaching of his predecessor. Again the central authorities intervened, this time arresting all of the friars, imprisoning them in Vilvoorde, just outside Brussels, and placing van Zutphen under house arrest in Antwerp. The following excerpt from a contemporary chronicle describes the reaction van Zutphen's arrest elicited among the Antwerp citizenry:

"On St. Michael's day in the same year [1522] there was a great uproar in the city because of a preacher from the Augustinian monastery, and some of the things he had preached. Someone sent for him to visit a sick person in a certain part of town. But when he arrived there, the Margrave of Antwerp arrested him and imprisoned him in a room in St. Michael's cloister. News of these events spread like wildfire. As a result, a large group of locals, including some 300 women, came to St. Michael's, and ransacked van Zutphen's room, to the point that they managed to free him, and take him back to his own cloister. The next day he fled to Luther.

"Our lady Margaret [of Austria] was incensed by these events, and was determined to see justice done, insisting that the guilty parties be expelled from the city. Three or four women were imprisoned, but they were released shortly thereafter.

"On St. Franciscus' Day following, it was decreed that no one was to preach in any cloister in Antwerp, but only in the parish churches, although this changed quickly as well."[1]

The events here described reveal a great deal about the early Reformation in Antwerp and the reactions of those on all sides of it. We see here three groups of historical actors in the city: the Augustinians, the central authorities, and the Antwerp burghers. For their part, the Augustinians acted as devoted converts to Martin Luther's Reformation message. Despite several legal reprimands and the ongoing danger of arrest, they continued to preach the Reformation message in the heart of the city. Indeed, although the authorities convinced most of the imprisoned friars to recant their unorthodox beliefs, two of them, Hendrik Voes and Johann van den Esschen, refused to back down, even to the point of death. They were executed by fire in Brussels in July 1523, just one year after the events recounted above.

The second group of historical actors in this case is the central authorities. Here represented by Margaret of Austria, they moved swiftly and with determination against what they perceived to be heretics in their midst. After van Zutphen's flight, Margaret decided to teach the burghers of Antwerp a lesson to avoid such religious disobedience in the future. She traveled in person to the city, led a public procession to the monastery, and had it completely destroyed.

The final group of actors is the citizenry of Antwerp. Their reaction is fascinating. Clearly, the Augustinian friars were beloved by those who heard them preach, as these people were willing to risk punishment and even exile to stand up for them in this case. This indicates the religious fervor that existed even among those untrained in theology, who could vote only with their feet and their anger. It is also revealing of some level of organization among these people, who responded quickly to van Zutphen's arrest and came as a large group to help him.

This event broadens our view of the early Reformation in the city, clearly suggesting that it was not an arcane event in which only Latinate theologians were interested, but one in which the lowliest burghers were a dynamic force. It also raises a number of questions about the actions of the different groups involved. The story of the two Antwerp Augustinians raises the question of what motivated early Reformation converts to defend their new beliefs, even in the face of arrest and possibly death. In view of the harsh official reaction of the central authorities one wonders what Margaret was afraid of in this situation. What did she hope to accomplish by razing the monastery? By having the two friars executed? How might she justify such actions on legal and religious grounds? And why were her orders (to exile some citizens and to forbid preaching) not carried out in their entirety? Did the local magistracy intentionally ignore her mandates and, if so, to what end? One perplexing question that remains with regard to the Augustinians' supporters in the city of Antwerp is why so many of them were women. Several chroniclers of the time discuss this event, and all place the number of women involved at around 300, suggesting an enormous group of loyal female followers, though none of them address the reasons for the make-up of this group. Although answers to many of these questions remain elusive, the complex nature of this dramatic event reveals an urban society of mixed loyalties and competing jurisdictions in the earliest days of the Protestant Reformation.

Note

1 *Die excellente cronike van Vlaenderen*, supplement, fol. 13v, transcribed in Paul Fredericq, *Corpus Documentorum Inquisitionis Haereticae Pravitatis Neerlandicae*, Hoogeschool van Gent: Werken van den practischen leergang van vaderlandsche geschiedenis 9, 5 vols, The Hague: Martinus Nijhoff, 1889–1906, vol. 4, p. 137, doc. 97. Translated by Victoria Christman.

17 "We want the friar!" A civic uprising in Augsburg in 1524

by Joel Van Amberg

The Protestant Reformation came early to the prosperous free imperial city of Augsburg and quickly attracted the support of many in the city. By 1522, Reformation preachers were at work in Augsburg. Many people were particularly drawn to the Reformation sermons of the Franciscan friar Hans Schilling, who began preaching in spring 1524. The 1520s were a time of political and economic tension in Augsburg. Many citizens felt that an imperious merchant elite had come to dominate the political and economic life of the city. Schilling acknowledged, and some said exacerbated, these grievances in his sermons, weaving critiques of the elite together with his religious message. Eventually the city council came to believe that his sermons were too clearly directed against them, and that he was potentially encouraging rebellion. As a result, they arranged a secret meeting with Schilling that August where they pressured him to leave town quietly, offering him a horse and a large sum of money. Schilling accepted the offer and left, but not without first tipping off some of his followers. Shortly after his departure, the citizens of Augsburg responded:

"But just after the city council had taken their seats, all over the city a great cry was heard, and the report went out that people were going up to city hall to ask for the friar back. As a result, a great crowd of men, and only men, converged on city hall. They came unarmed and with the sole intention of lending their aid in petitioning for the friar's return. ... When the people entered city hall ... they established a commission of about 12–14 men and, as a condition obtained by the city council, ordered everyone else to wait on the large square outside. ...

"The commission's report apparently took the following form, namely, that they were appearing before this prudent body in all good will. But having been informed that the friar at the Franciscan church, Brother Hans Schilling, was removed from the city ..., they were unaware of the cause for this decision, other than that the priests ... decried ... the friar together with his listeners as heretics. They extended to the city council their submissive request ... that the friar be brought back and held accountable. If he were to be found in the wrong, he should receive his proper punishment. However, if his teaching and preaching were to be found correct, he and his listeners properly should continue to benefit from it. ... After this report, they withdrew from the city council and left the room. ...

"The city councilors' answer to the commission, which was waiting in the small room outside the council chamber, [was] that the honorable city council had heard their petition and although the honorable city council was always ... inclined to demonstrate fatherly intentions towards the honorable community ... this friar, who left for no other reason than to engage in further study, is no longer present. For this reason, as you can well understand, the honorable city council neither can nor will reinstall him. However, the honorable city council, with fatherly concern and good will, has favorably heard the honorable community in its request that the pulpit at the Franciscan church not remain vacant without an evangelical preacher. Thus, it has furnished this pulpit with Urbanus Rhegius, a learned, devout teacher, well grounded in the Holy Scriptures and holding his doctorate in the Bible. ...

"However, after the thronging crowd learned that the monk was no longer present and that the city council did not intend to restore him to them, they grew more heated and vehement, yelling ..., 'We want the friar and not Urbanus Rhegius!' ...

"Then the door of the council chamber opened and the city councilors went out ... to the small room where the people's commission and some other people who had pushed their way in waited. Then Mr. Ulrich Rehlinger, the former mayor ... began to speak in a soothing tone ..., 'Dear sirs and friends, the matter ... is under our authority as the government, as your properly constituted magistracy elected by you on your oath of obedience and your honor. ... And since the Holy Scripture ... commands ... that all magistrates ordained by God should be shown ... appropriate obedience by all their subjects at all times, it is the friendly desire of the city council that you show ... greater obedience this time and ... accept ... Dr. Urbanus Rhegius instead of the friar. ...'

"In the room a man stood up on the bench and cried out ..., 'If the friar is so unlearned, why did he preach God's word so biblically? There must be something else going on here.' ... the people outside on the square also ... cried out, 'We want the friar! We want the friar!' And they promised, 'We will not separate until they restore the friar to us!' and, 'Whoever approves of this put your hand up!' This, the majority did. ... And just as the city councilors had gone back in the council chamber, the great crowd on the lower square began to ... cry out tumultuously, so that their voices carried to the councilors ... Then, since they all felt like sitting ducks, so to speak, and fear ... was on every side, the city council shut up the council chamber so that no one could come in or out. ...

"Some in the crowd were calling the city councilors hypocritical and implacable enemies of the poor community, others called them whoremongers, ... Then the honorable city council answered the gathered people that the honorable city council ... promised to reinstall the requested friar ..."[1]

In the early modern German city, different views of the relationship between the government and the governed, and of the ultimate locus of sovereignty, competed with each other. Members of the urban commune, the body of citizens, were mostly willing to delegate the role of governing to the wealthy elite families. However, they assumed that sovereignty continued to inhere ultimately in the commune. If city councilors overstepped their role or ceased to rule for the common good, they believed that authority temporarily devolved back to the commune, which had the right to form *ad hoc* commissions to negotiate a return to good governance. Beginning in the second half of the fifteenth century, city councils, conversely, began to reconceptualize their relationship with the commune. Abandoning the language of fellow citizen, they turned to the language of magistrate and subject. Buttressed by appeals to paternalistic superiority and the divine will, they maintained that the commune had alienated its sovereignty and that it now inhered in the city council itself. The text above demonstrates how these different views of political authority and legitimacy clashed when a crisis arose.

People living in an early modern city would not have understood the modern notion of religion as a private matter. It was commonly assumed that the Christian religion offered normative rules for all major aspects of life. Furthermore, political authorities played an important role in regulating religious life in the city. This situation helps explain the explosive nature of religious disagreements. Since religion was considered to be a public matter affecting the whole community, urban communes during the Reformation reacted politically when they perceived that city governments were making decisions about the city religion without properly consulting the commune. This contributed to the vehemence of the commune's response to the city council's preemptory dismissal of Schilling.

Adding to these conflicts was the fact that the early modern city was a compact urban space. Rulers and ruled, rich and poor, met each other regularly at church, in the guild hall, and in the street. Physical proximity made it more difficult for elites to uphold the social and political boundaries they were working hard to construct. Additionally, city governments did not keep standing armed forces in their pay and were vulnerable to sudden surges of anger. With nowhere to escape from an angry group of citizens, quick action and temporary accommodation was often necessary to avoid a disaster. In the above account, a frightened, unprepared city council ultimately had to accede to the wishes of the commune.

Note

1 This handwritten account of the events, "Beschreibung der Aufruer so sich Allhie Im Augspurg wegen eines Mönchs als mann Nach Christi geburt zelete 1524 Jar den anderen tag Augusti Erhoben," was written during the 1530s, Stadtarchiv Augsburg, Evangelisches Wesensarchiv, 480, pp. 10r–19r. Translated by Joel Van Amberg.

18 Bourges: Public rituals of collective and personal identity in the middle of the sixteenth century

by Jonathan A. Reid

Located at the geographic center of France, Bourges was an important regional capital of some 12,000 inhabitants during the sixteenth century. Much like other French cities, it was socially and politically complex. Peopling its streets were swarms of priests, mendicants, monks, and nuns belonging to the town's dozens of independent churches; equal numbers of royal, ecclesiastical, feudal, and civic officials and justices drawn from the lower nobility and bourgeoisie; professors and students (many of them foreign) in its famous university; and, most numerous of all, the 'common people,' who worked in several industries, including textiles and agricultural commerce.

Jean Glaumeau, a beneficed priest in the collegial congregation of Notre-Dame de Moutiers–Moyen, recorded in his journal spanning the years 1541 to 1562 what he considered to be the major events occurring in Bourges and in his own family life leading up to the first War of Religion in France. It is a rare and precious primary source, for Glaumeau's observations reveal much about the social order as well as how contemporaries experienced and enacted their collective and individual identities within it, and even forged new ones as the rise of the Reformed Church undermined established structures.

In his journal, Glaumeau frequently described the staging of communal processions and demonstrations – in times of war, famine, drought, as well as peace and prosperity – along with other public rites of civic life. During times of peace, such rituals tended to promote unity. Participants reaffirmed the roles, authority, responsibilities, and relationships of the members of the constituent groups of the town. His detailed accounts of these rituals provide us, in effect, with a map of the socio-geography of Bourges.

Glaumeau devoted his longest journal entry to a week-long series of celebrations held at Bourges following the birth and baptism of François de Valois, the first son born to the *Dauphin* (heir apparent), Henri de Valois, son of the reigning king, Francis I. The year was 1544 and King Francis was in poor health. The boy's birth raised the hope that there would be a smooth transition of power from royal father to son for at least two more generations, thus promising future stability and prosperity. The people of Bourges' festivities reflected the social world they hoped the fortuitous event would preserve.

As Glaumeau reports, the people of Bourges fêted this boy's "nativity" (*nativité* in French, not a mere 'birth' or *naissance*) with fitting pomp:

"First, on Sunday, February 4, a general procession was held in which all the clergy, attired in vestments accustomed for the feast of Corpus Christi, carried several reliquaries from the cathedral of St. Étienne down the main road to the church of the Carmelites, where a High Mass of the Holy Spirit was celebrated. All the town officials, dressed in their ceremonial robes, attended, each one of them carrying a candle of virgin wax. Upon returning from the procession and entering St. Étienne, everyone commenced singing the *Te Deum laudamus* (We Praise You God) accompanied by bell ringing and the organ. It was very good to hear God honored for the new son born to my lord, the *Dauphin*.

"The same day, between three and four in the afternoon, the town officials, numbering 100 to 120, all on horseback or mule ... left from town hall and proceeded through the streets ... to see the triumphs and celebratory bonfires, which were as follows ..."[1]

Glaumeau goes on to describe in detail a lengthy block party attended by "a great multitude of common people, who danced and sang accompanied by several instrument players, all at the town's expense." The town councilors treated them to huge bonfires with fireworks, a simultaneous cannonade of thirty to forty pieces of artillery, free cakes tossed from balconies, "a vat of wine from which one could drink as much as one liked," and commemorative metals stamped with the *Dauphin*'s arms and the words of Isaiah, (which were typically used at Christmas), "To us a boy is born; to us a son is given."[2]

Never in living memory had there been such a joyous celebration. And the festivities, "too numerous to recount," did not stop. Over the next week, by turns in the different neighborhoods of Bourges, "all the estates [corporations] of the town put on some show or celebration. First the university and students, [then] the judges and lawyers, ..." and on and on across the occupational spectrum, including the guilds of manual laborers, such as vine-dressers, wool combers and carders, weavers, and cloth fullers. Glaumeau prayed, expressing the people's shared wish: "God grant that everything may come to a good end, and that he [the newborn] may someday, when a man, bring as much joy to the people as has his birth."[3]

The principal dimensions of the urban social order are on display in this collective moment of exuberance: the ties of affection binding people to the royal house; the religious dimensions of royal power and civic life; the divisions and order of precedence among clergy, lay authorities, educated elites, and the common folk; the responsibilities of the governing orders – king, clergy, and magistrates – to ensure the wellbeing of the town as well as those of the lower ones to give due thanks and respect to them.

However, such social structures and norms were severely tested by the rise of the Reformed Church in France. In Glaumeau's account of the tumultuous events at Bourges from 1557 to 1562, he describes new groups and uses new names to identify them when he tries to size up what was by then an unsettled social world, one in which he had trouble finding his place. In the deeds themselves and the categories Glaumeau uses to describe participants, we see that the old social identities and bonds were breaking under the strain of new competing religious ones. In 1559, hundreds of "men and women"[4] – apparently from across the social spectrum and hence otherwise defying categorization except by gender, with women appearing in this sense as a social group for the first time – gathered outside the city walls to sing Protestant versions of the psalms in direct contravention of the town officials' orders. By 1561, collective 'rites of violence' – repeated street battles involving as many as 2,000 armed people – pitted "those of the Gospel" against "those of the Roman church."[5] Iconoclasm, the burning of houses and clerical property, and murders ensued.

In January 1562, Glaumeau made his choice in this newly divided social and religious landscape: He publicly professed his long-secreted Protestant identity and joined "the church of the Christians," otherwise "named by evil ones as 'the church of the Huguenots.'"[6] He did so following the powerful symbolic moment when M. de Passy, the former Bishop of Nevers now turned Protestant pastor, celebrated the first public Reformed communion in Bourges.

In all this, we see that in times of social peace as well as of radical upheaval Jean Glaumeau and the people of Bourges mediated, contested, and expressed their corporate and individual identities through the idiom of collective rituals in public spaces.

Notes

1 Jehan Glaumeau, *Journal de Jehan Glaumeau: Bourges, 1541–1562*, ed. Alfred Hiver de Beauvoir, Bourges: Just–Bernard, 1867, pp. 9–10. Translated by Jonathan A. Reid.
2 Ibid., pp. 12–13.
3 Ibid., pp. 14–15.
4 Ibid., p. 103.
5 Ibid., p. 118.
6 Ibid., pp. 122–123.

19 Castres, 1561: A town erupts into religious violence

by Barbara B. Diefendorf

Although Luther's writings were outlawed in France as early as 1521, Protestant teachings continued to spread underground. In the mid-1550s, converts formed churches on the model of Calvin's Geneva so as to worship according to their beliefs. They also became increasingly militant, particularly in those parts of southern France where conversions were most numerous and local officials often sympathetic to the cause. Religious war broke out in March 1562 after Catholic-led troops attacked Protestants worshipping outside the town of Vassy, in Champagne, but the wars must also be understood in the context of the increasingly provocative behavior of militant Protestants. Taking advantage of the less repressive atmosphere introduced when Catherine de Medici became regent in December 1560, members of French Reformed churches became more open in their worship but also demonstrated their opposition to Catholicism by attacking Catholic churches and clerics. Protestants claimed to be cleansing the churches of error in removing side altars, saints' images, and other objects that they believed promoted false worship and superstition. To Catholics, however, these were deliberate and unforgivable acts of sacrilege and blasphemy.

Jean Faurin, a Protestant citizen of Castres, left a detailed record of events in this southern French town of approximately 5,000 people, as tensions built toward the first War of Religion. By his account, Castres' Protestants, tired of clandestine night-time meetings and the constant danger of attack, held their first public services in October 1560 in a local school. This resulted in several arrests and a prohibition against further services, but 500 people still gathered openly for a sermon in April 1561. Royal officials continued to interrupt public worship when they could, and yet the congregation continued to grow. 600 people publicly celebrated the Lord's Supper in July. By September, the membership was large enough and included enough local officials that Reformed church leaders demanded – and received – the keys to the Catholic church of Our Lady of La Platé, where they then established services. Thus, Protestants in Castres had taken over a central urban space. Jean Faurin's journal gives a good idea of what happened next:

"– On October 28, 29, and 30 [1561], on orders from the magistrates in Castres, all of the idols and all of the side altars were torn down in the temple[1] of La Platé, without opposition.

"– On December 14, in Saint Benedict Cathedral, a Franciscan sent by the Bishop of Castres, Claude d'Oraison, came to preach Advent sermons and said nothing but bad things about the Reformed faith. In short, everything was building toward an uprising. Then it happened that a Protestant school boy who was listening to [the Franciscan] preach, hearing him say bad things about the faith, publicly upbraided him and said that he lied. If the boy had not escaped at a run, several papists[2] would have killed him with the knives they carried, as they were certainly trying to do. That night, Protestants assembled in arms to seize this seditious preacher, who was lodged in Saint Benedict's cloister, in the sacristan's house. He was very hard to take but at last was made prisoner and brought by the Protestants to the town's criminal justice hall without opposition or resistance from papists. ... They [also] took prisoner Pierre Boissier, called 'Penchenery,' a local merchant; he was put in a house with several other papists who had provoked the uprising. Sometime later, the friar left the city alive and well with a rope around his neck.[3]

"– On December 16, members of the city's consistory[4] arrested everyone who was out in the streets, and the captain of the city's forces made them go to Protestant services, even if they were priests and others of that ilk. They even went to seek them out in churches while they were saying Mass.

"– On the afternoon of December 31, by order of the magistrates, all of the images and side altars were torn out of the following churches: first at Saint Benedict Cathedral, then at Saint James, Saint Clare, Saint Francis, Holy Trinity, Saint Vincent, and Saint John of Bourdelles, outside the city. The images and idols were also torn down in a number of other cities in France. The next day, January 1, the idols of Our Lady of Fagues, Saint John of Navés, and Saint Martin of Lodiés, outside the city, were torn down. ...

"– On January 4, the king's attorney for Castres, the *viguier*,[5] and the captain of the guard went to the convent of Saint Clare and removed all of the Franciscan nuns, about twenty in number, and sent them to hear Reformed services at Saint Benedict Cathedral, where Monsieur Fleury was preaching. They then took five to the notary Campardy's house, five to the house of Francis Buisson, and the others to the home of Antoine Marty, lord of Roquecourbe in Villegoudou. Their parents and relatives later came for them. ...

"– On Monday, February 2, the feast of Our Lady that the papists call *Chandeleur*, a Trinitarian friar named Brother Anthony was found secretly saying Mass in the refectory or sacristy of the Trinitarian church. Several local residents ... were in attendance. They took him and mounted him backwards on a donkey, making him hold onto its tail. The friar was still in his vestments from saying Mass, and they put a basket of figs garnished with feathers on his head and paraded him through the entire city on the donkey. They then brought him into the town square where they seated him on a stool, shaved his head, and, showing him the host[6] he had prepared for Mass, asked him if he was willing to die for the Mass. Then, in front of all who watched, he said no and that the Mass was worthless. Immediately afterwards, they took his cape and hood and all of his accouterments, his missal, and his host and burned them. The friar then said, in the presence of the entire crowd, that he would never say Mass again."[7]

Two weeks later, Castres' Protestants gave up their temple of La Platé in response to a royal edict promising freedom of worship if Protestants returned churches they had seized and only held services outside city walls. Many Catholics nevertheless vocally opposed the edict and war broke out at the beginning of March. Like other French Protestants, Jean Faurin blamed Catholics for starting the war and insisted it need never have happened, if only the edict promising freedom of conscience and a right to worship outside city walls had been observed. Perhaps so; French Protestants never made up more than 10 or 15 percent of the country's population and were well aware of their minority position. The behavior of Protestants in towns like Castres, where they enjoyed dominance over contested spaces, nevertheless raises interesting questions about just what it was the Protestants truly wanted and how far they were willing to go in pursuit of their own vision of religious truth.

Notes

1 French Protestants called the buildings where they worshiped 'temples' and reserved the word 'church' to refer to the congregation of believers.
2 A derogatory term for Catholics used commonly in Protestant writings.
3 Convicted felons were forced to beg pardon wearing a noose around their neck before their execution. Pious monks sometimes put on the hangman's noose as a mark of penitence, but in this case it is more likely that the Protestants forced the friar to wear it as a mark of shame.
4 Composed of lay elders and ministers, the consistory was responsible for administering the Reformed Church's affairs and disciplining its members.
5 A royally appointed judge and administrator.
6 The eucharistic wafer that, once consecrated, would, according to Catholic teaching, be transformed into the blood and body of Christ.
7 Jean Faurin, *Journal de Faurin sur les guerres de Castres*, ed. Charles Pradel, Marseilles: Laffitte Reprints, 1981, pp. 9–12. Translated by Barbara B. Diefendorf.

20 Swiss towns put on a play: Urban space as stage in the sixteenth century

by Kaspar von Greyerz

In sixteenth-century Swiss towns, the ritual function of urban plays, put on stage most frequently during Carnival and at Easter, was primarily that of a communal festival. In Catholic Lucerne the Easter plays were announced in advance from the pulpit. Members of the community eager to perform were asked to communicate their interest to the city council, who made the final decision about the distribution of the roles. Women (who, with few exceptions,[1] were not admitted to the theater stage before the second half of the seventeenth century) were excluded. Actors had to pay for their costumes – with the exception of that of Judas, which, at least in 1583, was paid for by the Lucerne council.[2] From the 1470s onward, when acting in Easter plays became the concern of laymen (hitherto it was in the hands of the clergy), two urban confraternities became the chief promoters of the annual performances. As in all other German and Swiss cities, the stage was erected in a public square; in Lucerne the wine market served as the location for performances.

In 1546, 10-year-old Felix Platter watched two plays in Reformed Basel: Valentin Bolz's *St. Paul's Conversion* (*Pauli Bekehrung*), which was presented on a stage erected for this special occasion at the Basel corn market,[3] and another play performed earlier that year, *Susanna*, which was presented on a stage at the fish market.[4] Platter's description, which he wrote in 1612, when he was 76 years old,[5] vividly illustrates the communal aspects of sixteenth-century urban theater:

"The play *St. Paul's Conversion* was staged at the cornmarket. Valentin Boltz had written it. I watched it from Felix Irmi's corner house at the Hutgasse. Burgomaster von Brun[6] was Saulus, Balthasar[7] played God the Father in a round heaven attached to the Peacock.[8] From there the lightning, a fiery rocket, took its course, which ignited Saulus's trousers when he fell from his horse. Rudolf Fry[9] was the captain. Under his standard he commanded about 100 burghers, all in his colours. The thunder up in heaven was made with barrels filled with stones, etc.

"A long time before that, Ulrich Coccius[10] put on stage *Susanna* at the fishmarket. I watched the play from the house of my tailor, Wolf Eblinger. The stage was erected on top of the fountain and there, directly at the fountain, was a case made of tin, where Susanna washed herself. There sat one in a red garment, a Merianin, engaged to Ulrich Coccius, but not yet married.[11] The role of Daniel was performed by Ringler,[12] [who] was still a little boy."[13]

Another Basel autobiographer, the minister and diarist Johannes Gast, throws additional light on the performance of *St. Paul's Conversion* and its highly communal nature:

"It was a very fine day, when the play about St. Paul's conversion, directed by Valentin Bolz, was performed publicly with great splendor by the burghers. The city council had decided on the venue, which, on its orders, was encircled by a wooden fence. Well-to-do burghers and city councilors took their seats within this enclosure. The common people watched from three ascending wooden scaffoldings. After the play, when the actors, as usual, took a walk in town, fairly strong rain surprised them. This is why, the next day, which was very sunny, they promenaded around almost during the whole day."[14]

In addition to serving as communal festivals, plays in sixteenth-century Swiss towns could also help to solidify urban religious identities or to strengthen political bonds between cities of the Swiss confederation which were strained by religious differences – two functions that could well contradict one another.

In the city of Bern, the painter, dramatist, and statesman Niklaus Manuel Deutsch wrote plays which gave eloquent expression to his early commitment to the cause of the Protestant Reformation. Most of these plays were put on stage in the center of town immediately following their composition and must have left a strong impression on the urban public. Take, for example, *The Eaters of the Dead* (*Die Totenfresser*), also called *About the Pope and his Priesthood* (*Vom Papst und seiner Priesterschaft*). Strongly anticlerical, this play explores countless criticisms of Catholic priests: the discrepancy between clerical and Christian life; indulgences; the incompetence of the priests; the so-called 'whore's levy,' which was the fee owed to the Bishop of Constance for every child fathered by one of the diocese's priests. The final scene shows the pope with all the worldly regalia of a prince at war, while Dr. Lüpold Schüchnitt (I'm-not-Afraid) seeks the nearness of Christ.[15]

However, Niklaus Manuel's plays were exceptional not only for the literary quality of his texts. In no other Swiss city was the public stage used as strategically in favor of the early Reformation movement as by Manuel in Bern. With his initiative, it became an instrument in the propagation and advancement of the new faith – elsewhere, this confessional instrumentalization of the theater did not become common until later in the sixteenth century.

In contrast to the propagation of urban religious identities, another play by Valentin Bolz, *Mirror of the World* (*Weltspiegel*), which was performed in Basel in May 1550, sought to strengthen political bonds between the Swiss urban communities. A moral play which lasted two days and involved 150 actors, it was above all concerned with the unity of the Swiss confederation, which was hampered by religious strife. In the final scene representatives of all thirteen cantons of the confederation got on stage and re-enacted the original oath which (supposedly) had created its nucleus in 1291.

These two examples from Bern and Basel are powerful reminders that the urban space as stage could unite as well as divide. A few generations later, however, the increasing confessionalism of the clergy brought about the demise of communal lay theater in the Swiss Reformed towns. Its reappearance in the later seventeenth century was in the hands of itinerant groups of professional actors.

Notes

1. The Basel performance of the play *Susanna* on 23 May 1546, discussed below, was one such exception.
2. Emil Ermatinger, *Dichtung und Geistesleben der Deutschen Schweiz*, Munich: C. H. Beck, 1933, p. 185.
3. This was printed twice by the Basel printer Jacob Kündig in 1551 and 1552 under the title *Tragicomoedia: Sant Pauls bekerung: Gespilt von einer Burgerschafft der wytberuempten frystatt Basel, im jor M.D.XLVI. Jetzund gebessert und gemert mit Figuren.*
4. In all likelihood *Susanna* was written by Sixtus Birk (Xystus Betulejus), c.1500–1554. Next to Pamphilus Gengenbach (d. c.1524), Valentin Bolz, and Johannes Kollros (c.1487–c.1558), he was one of the four prominent dramatists of sixteenth-century Basel.
5. Considering the time lag between the theater performances he enjoyed in his childhood and the actual composition of his autobiography, we should not be surprised that Platter misjudged the time that had passed between seeing *St. Paul's Conversion* and *Susanna*. The latter event did not take place "long before" *St. Paul's Conversion*, as he assumes. Rather, the two performances were held on 23 May and 6 June 1546, respectively. See Felix Platter, *Tagebuch (Lebensbeschreibung, 1536–1567)*, ed. Valentin Lötscher, Basel and Stuttgart: Schwabe & Co., 1976, p. 18 (editor's introduction).
6. Bonaventura von Brunn (1520–1591). He was actually burgomaster from 1570 to 1591; another instance where we have to be aware of the fact that Felix Platter wrote this long after the event. See ibid., n. 257.
7. Balthasar Han (1505–1578) was a city councilor and a noted glass painter. See ibid., n. 258.
8. The 'Peacock' (*Pfauenburg*) was the building at the corner of Sporengasse and the market square. See ibid., p. 82, n. 259.
9. Hans Rudolf Frey (1496–1551), city councilor and cloth merchant. See ibid., n. 261.
10. Ulrich Coccius (Koch) (1525–1585), a prominent Basel theologian. See ibid., n. 262.
11. Margareta Merian (1525–1570), later married to Ulrich Coccius. See ibid., p. 83, n. 266.
12. Ludwig Ringler (c.1535–1605), later a city councilor and well-known glass-painter. See ibid., n. 267.
13. Ibid., pp. 82–83. Translated by Kaspar von Greyerz.
14. Johannes Gast, *Das Tagebuch des Johannes Gast*, ed. Paul Burckhardt, Basel: Benno Schwabe & Co, 1945, p. 270. Translated by Kaspar von Greyerz.
15. For Manuel's plays see Niklaus Manuel, *Werke und Briefe*, ed. Paul Zinsli and Thomas Hengartner, Bern: Stämpfli Verlag, 1999.

21 Smoke, sound, and murder in sixteenth-century Paris[1]

by Alan E. Bernstein

François Rabelais (1483–1553), Franciscan priest, humanist, physician, advisor to cardinals, rebel, and novelist, wrote among other things *Gargantua* (1535), *Pantagruel* (1532), *The Third Book*, *The Fourth Book* (1552), and *The Fifth Book*, a posthumous and perhaps partly genuine compilation (1564). Within these works his writing ranges from coarse caricature to pedagogical pining. He exposed the foibles of humans and human society. His satire was so biting that the University of Paris, supported by the *parlement* of Paris, the country's highest court, placed *Gargantua* and *Pantagruel* on a list of prohibited books in 1545. The next year, he defiantly published *The Third Book*.

In that work, the misogynist Panurge (Overdrive) considers marriage but fears cuckoldry. Exercising due diligence, he consults a theologian, a physician, a philosopher, and a lawyer. His friend Pantagruel (Food-is-All) advises him to ask a fool and supports his suggestion with a Parisian anecdote:

"In Paris, where food stands are set up in front of the Petit Châtelet, by the grill of a cook who sold grilled meat, a porter flavored his bread in the smoke of a roast and considered it downright tasty. The cook stood by in silence, but after all the smoky bread had been devoured, the cook grabbed the porter by the throat and insisted that he pay for the smoke from his roast. The porter answered that he had done no damage to his meat, had taken nothing of his, and owed him nothing. The fumes in question were dispersing in the air anyway and going up in smoke. Never had anyone ever heard that in Paris the smoke from a roast had been sold in the street. The cook replied that the smoke from his meat was not intended to nourish porters and he threatened that if the porter didn't pay up, he'd take the hooks [used to carry heavy loads] as compensation."[2]

As the argument intensified, a crowd of gawkers, including Sire John, the town fool, gathered around. The cook proposed and the porter agreed to let the fool decide their case.

"Once he had heard their arguments, Sire John ordered the porter to take a piece of silver from his belt. The porter placed an old coin from the days of King Philip in the fool's hand. Sire John took it and put it on his left shoulder as if to check its weight, then he drummed it in the palm of his left hand as if to test its purity. Then he held it in front of the pupil of his right eye as if to check its minting. All this the gaping crowd watched in silence as the cook waited confidently and the porter in despair. At last the fool banged the coin several times on the grill. Then, with presidential majesty, holding his fool's wand in his fist as if it was a scepter, ... clearing his throat two or three times for effect, he said loudly: 'The court declares that the porter who flavored his bread with the smoke of the roast has adequately paid the cook with the sound of his coin. The court therefore orders that each party return to his particular domicile, without disbursement, and for cause.' The Parisian fool's decision seemed so equitable, indeed so admirable, to the aforementioned doctors that they doubted whether the case could have been heard as well by the parlement of the place, or even among the Areopagites [of ancient Athens] – so judiciously did it seem to have been rendered. Consider, therefore, taking the advice of a fool."[3]

The setting Rabelais assigned the story is crucial to its meaning. The Petit Châtelet is a gatehouse that defends the island in the Seine and the oldest bridge to the south, the Petit Pont, from the large square at the foot of the Rue Saint-Jacques. Its counterpart, across the Seine, is the Grand Châtelet, which defends the oldest northern bridges, collectively called the Grand Pont (see Figure 21.1). More important for the context of the story, the Grand

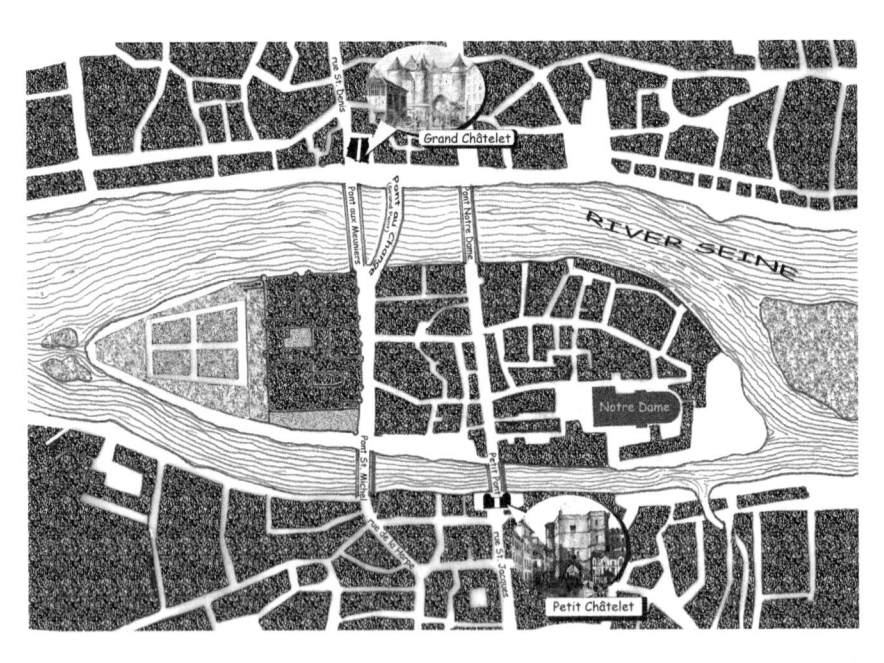

Figure 21.1 Plan of Paris in the sixteenth century, detail (adaptation from images in the Bibliothèque Nationale de France by Douglas Hollis)

Châtelet also houses the *parlement*. Therefore, Rabelais's contrast of the fool and the High Court is that between the Petit and the Grand Châtelet. In Rabelais's tale, the city center is a field that unites and separates polar opposites: the fool's wit and the High Court's law, literature and censorship, professional fools and foolish professionals. Thus, in the story of Sire John, it is "the aforesaid doctors," simple onlookers in the square, whom Rabelais sarcastically cast as doctors of law, who endorse the verdict.

Rabelais knew both sides of this contrast. As a youth he received a humanist education in Greek and Latin. He attended the University of Paris at the College of Montaigu, studied law, then became a physician at the medical school in Montpellier, and toured the universities of France. Throughout his life, though, established institutions limited his options. Despite censorship and the threat of the stake, he spoofed the nobility, chivalry, religious orders, prophecy, and visions. For example, in *The Third Book*, Pantagruel and Panurge go as pilgrims to consult the 'Holy Bottle.'

Strikingly, the social tensions Rabelais enfolded in his tale expressed themselves perversely – and tragically – some decades later. On 15 November 1591, while Paris endured military, political, and religious strife, assassins seized Barnabé Brisson, an accomplished jurist and president of the *parlement* based in the Grand Châtelet. Exploiting urban social dynamics similar to those in Rabelais's tale and hoping thereby to gain popular support for their murder, they hanged him at the Petit Châtelet. The next day, the assassins displayed Brisson's body at the Place de Grève, across the river. During the trial of Brisson's murderers, a witness testified how role reversal had excited one of the assassins, Adrien Fromentin, who, at the lynching, jeered, "He [Brisson] was judged as he had judged others!"[4]

Thus, what Rabelais made the dynamics of his joke, the murderers of 1591 took as a license to kill. This draws our attention to the danger, in history as well as today, that one person's spoof may be another person's plan of attack. Parody may properly inspire critical thinking, but it can become dangerous when it incites people to a literal re-enactment of itself.

Notes

1 I gratefully acknowledge help on this essay from JoAnne Gitlin Bernstein and Jonathan Beck.
2 François Rabelais, *Le Tiers Livre*, ed. M. A. Screech, Geneva: Librairie Droz, 1964, ch. 37, p. 259. Translated by Alan E. Bernstein.
3 Ibid., pp. 259–260.
4 Quoted in Élie Barnavi and Robert Descimon, *La Sainte Ligue, le juge, et la potence*, Paris: Hachette, 1985, p. 26. See Matt. 7:1–2.

22 Bologna's Feast of the Roast Pig: A carnivalesque festival in a sixteenth-century Italian city square

by Nicholas Terpstra

Early modern Italian cities had many public festivals that sent food and fists flying. Carnival time was the most popular, but others, like Bologna's annual Feast of the Roast Pig (*Festa della Porchetta*) on 24 August, the Day of St. Bartholomew, were no less chaotic. Bologna's premier balladeer and broadsheet writer, Giulio Cesare Croce, caught the public imagination with accounts like the one below that conveyed the *Porchetta*'s full carnivalesque energy, and hinted at the ever more elaborate spectacles that would mark the day until French armies put an end to many such early modern rituals in 1796:

"Four or six days before the feast day of St. Bartholomew, the illustrious members of the Council of the Elders ... find a great quantity of suckling pigs, and have them roasted and sent as gifts to many ladies and gentlemen and to pregnant women and their families, friends, and others. Then they order up a truly large one to be prepared carefully stuffed full of the best ingredients and the most perfect spices, and then roasted. The fragrance is so soft and appealing that it would bring a half dead person back to his senses. This roast suckling pig is thrown down from the balcony of the Communal Palace[1] an hour before sunset, when the piazza is full of people, carriages, and horses, with thousands more people at the windows, on the roofs, and in the towers. In short, there isn't a corner or hole that isn't crammed with people.

"Before the pig is thrown down, peacocks, geese, pheasants, turtledoves, quail, partridges, ducks, pigeons, and an infinite number of other living birds are thrown from the balcony and from the windows of the Palace. They have their wings clipped so that they can't fly very high but fall down and land on people all around the piazza. In order to catch one, everyone gets pretty crafty. All you can see is arms shooting up into the sky. This one grabs a duck, that one a peacock. It all goes on for two hours and more.

"Then, when the birds have all been launched, the cornets and flutes and trombones begin to play beautiful music as the roast suckling pig is carried in. It cuts quite a figure: all covered with flowers, and wrapped like a poetess with fronds of laurel. It lets off a fragrance so sweet that the entire piazza is filled with the most appetizing smells. This is when the gluttons expose themselves. Many are panting with the saliva pouring down their chins. People bring bags and sacks of all sizes and even sheets and other things like that. You'd even see fine gentlemen there if they weren't so concerned for their honor. Instead, the piazza is filled with manual labourers, low class types, and others who care less about their honor than about a half piece of pork.

"These all stay glued to their spots for a quarter of an hour, twisting their necks this way and that, now glancing down, now craning back – it all adds to the entertainment of the feast. They all push and shove forward a little, and then back a bit, all to keep in line with the table far above them where the roasted pig is sitting. At last, after endless foolishness and jesting, the servants throw the pig down. You barely see her falling before the arms all shoot up in the air to grab her. She hardly reaches the crowd before she's torn apart into a thousand pieces; one takes the snout, another a leg, another the head – one grabs this and another grabs that.

"Then to give even more entertainment to the people, they throw down a great caldron of hot soup. It rains down suddenly on the crowd, washing over their faces in such a way that they wouldn't want any other soap. The laughs double all round, and those destined to be drenched and splattered in this way suddenly break apart. They've really asked for it. With all these jokers giving each other jabs and blows, they would kill each other if something like this weren't done to break them up. Many go home with their eyes swollen like squids, and very well washed, and others are scalded and burned – in short, everyone has something. Nor are other amusements lacking on that day, because there is a race of a horse, a hound, and a hawk. ... they identify the horses with a cloth cap that has a feather stuck in it, because you often see riders thrown to the ground."[2]

Why celebrate the feast of Saint Bartholomew in this way? Certainly, the disciple of Christ was popular locally. Five churches within Bologna's city walls were dedicated to him, and another five outside, more than any other saint. While the day's festivities began with a Mass, it seems that there was more at work here than religious devotion. Some think that it marked a thirteenth-century military victory, and others now suggest that its roots extend deep into pre-Christian culture. Many popular proverbs point to St. Bartholomew's Day as the time when cooler weather and rain arrive, when harvest gets under way, and when shepherds begin moving their flocks down from the hills. Days with this kind of natural significance often made it into the Catholic calendar as saint's days, bringing with them ancient rituals like the sacrifice of pigs and the distribution of food to the poor.

Politics were also involved. The Bolognese raced horses on St. Bartholomew's Day from at least the thirteenth century, but there are no documents testifying to birds, roast suckling pig, and soup pouring out of city hall before the mid-sixteenth. This was a time of political upheaval, when authorities put a priority on distributing food to the poor. The day's rituals put these authorities on public display as civic benefactors in order to promote obedience, peace, and social cohesion. Yet for many, this was simply a day to gamble, fight, and feast.

Notes

1 City hall.
2 Giulio Cesare Croce, *L'eccellenza e il trionofo del porco*, Ferrara: Vittorio Baldini, 1594. Translated by Nicholas Terpstra.

23 Taking control of village religion: Wendelstein in Franconia, 1524

by Katherine G. Brady and Thomas A. Brady, Jr.

During the fifteenth and early sixteenth centuries, some villages in the southwestern German lands established new parishes. In these, and often in older parishes, they claimed the right to approve or depose their priests. They acted just as abbeys, nobles, and princes had in earlier times, endowing parishes and holding the right to nominate the local priests. This movement illustrates, therefore, how the power of communal village governments had grown in these lands since the fourteenth century.

This document is a statement (later issued in print) by the mayor and court of the Franconian village of Wendelstein, which lies south of Nuremberg and near the town of Schwabach. It concerns a new parish priest, Kaspar Krantz, who was installed on 19 October 1524. The village lay under the authority of Margrave Casimir of Brandenburg–Ansbach, a prince of the Hohenzollern dynasty, whose right to nominate to the parish pastorate the villagers did not challenge. They did, however, lay on their new pastor certain demands, which this text reports in detail.

This document comes from a time before the Peasants' War at the very beginning of the Protestant movement in this region. It combines individually familiar elements – the laity's religious needs, mutuality of pastor–flock relations, free administration of the sacraments – with a stern, even ominous, tone that makes the whole text a sign of a new time rather than a voice of tradition:

"Now, dear brother and good friend, since, though not called by us, you have come here at the command of our lord, the aforementioned Margrave,[1] to be our servant, you should take heed of our desires and wishes about how you should deport yourself in the future.

"1. We hold you to be no lord but a servant and employee of the community, and that you have not to command us, but we to command you. And we therefore command you to proclaim faithfully the Gospel and the Word of God loud and clear according to the truth and uncorrupted by human teachings.

"2. In the village community and in church, you should follow the Gospel as a true servant of Jesus Christ. You should distribute the sacrament of the covenant of Jesus Christ and in all things follow what the Lord has taught and commanded us to do.

"You should deal in similar fashion with the sacrament of baptism, so that the people shall understand it and be reminded of their own baptisms. Whatever, though, is useless or blasphemous, you should avoid entirely and at all costs, holding like a true pastor to the eternal and unique Word of God, and allowing yourself to be frightened from it by neither human law nor human command. ...

"If, however, you behave to contrary and play the lord and live as you please, you should know that we will not only regard you as a false servant, but we will drive you like a ravening wolf into the net and tolerate you no more among us.

"Also, in the past we often had trouble and enmity from the priests, who burdened us with collections, Mass stipends, fees for the sacraments, and other inventions, which cost us a lot of money. Now, however, since we have been taught by the Gospel that these things are given to us freely by the Lord [Matt. 10:8] and should not be sold for money, it is our opinion and decision that we are not legally obliged to pay you or anyone else such payments.

"Since, however, the servants of the Word may expect support and sustenance from those among whom they proclaim the Word, and since we are well aware that this office or pastorate was endowed by our ancestors and that from this endowment the community's servants and pastor can and should receive their pay, we do not intend to diminish what belongs to this office, whether tithe or rights to use the woods, the pastures, and or the plowland, but to leave them to you as agreed. You, as a true servant, may use them according to your needs, as we state above. Whatever else has been demanded and shorn from Christ's flock, on that you shall have no claim, but you shall be content with what you have. ...

"It happens from time to time that the sacrament must be carried to the sick in other villages that belong to this parish. When it has to be taken to Rayberßried,[2] we shall not be obliged to provide you with a horse. You shall nonetheless have care that no one is left untended.

"With this we consider the matter closed, and we affirm that this is the way it shall be, whether you occupy the office or not.

"And we admonish you in a brotherly manner to take the matter to heart, and to behave yourself as a humble servant of the Lord, who fashions his word according to the truth. May God help you and all of us! Amen.

"On such Christian terms the pastor of Wendelstein took up his office, agreeing to obey as a true servant of the parish, as God gives him grace. Wednesday after St. Gallus's Day, 1524."[3]

The community's demands mostly have to do with the villagers' insistence that the pastor was a servant of the village, not its lord, and he would be paid his dues only if he performed his sacramental duties faithfully, and demanded or asked for no more. The text shows that the village's officials – mayor and court – laid these conditions on the pastor's installation, an act for which the justification may have rested more on the parishioners' will than on ecclesiastical law. Their language is strongly communalist, especially in its characterization of the priest as subordinate to his flock. Not only do the village's officers address their new priest as "dear brother and good friend," much as they would have their neighbors, but the text contains no ambiguity about who must obey whom at Wendelstein, a subject on which the village officials will brook no opposition.

Not only does this document take a firm, even unyielding, position on the clergy as servants of the laity, but it also gives voice to common late medieval grievances which are, however, given edge and emphasis through an employment of a new language that, at this time, still possessed a radical ring: Phrases such as "the Gospel and the Word of God ... uncorrupted by human teachings" strongly suggest the biblicist influence of the early Protestant movement, which had already reached Wendelstein via preachers from Nuremberg. Every term, every phrase, every demand can be found in earlier documents, but their consistency and combination are not traditional. This is most strikingly true of the village officers' condemnation of charging fees for access to sacramental grace.

Notes

1 Margrave Casimir of Brandenburg–Ansbach (1481–1527).
2 Raubersried, 1.5 kilometers from Wendelstein.
3 The German text is printed in Günther Franz (ed.), *Quellen zur Geschichte des Bauernkrieges*, Darmstadt: Wissenschaftliche Buchgesellschaft, 1963, pp. 315–317, no. 97. Translated by Katherine G. Brady and Thomas A. Brady, Jr.

24 A Swiss village's religious settlement: Zizers in Graubünden, 1616

by Randolph C. Head

Nowhere in Europe, perhaps, was the freedom to take purely local decisions on the issues raised by the Protestant Reformation greater than in the Republic of the Three Leagues in Graubünden (now southeastern Switzerland). Some communities formally chose either Catholic or Reformed worship, while others, such as the district of the Four Villages (*Vier Dörfer*) near the region's capital in Chur, allowed individual villages to decide which of the two confessions to follow.[1] By the 1550s, three of the four main villages – Zizers, Trimmis, and Undervaz – had voted to retain Catholic worship in their churches, while the fourth, Igis, had opted for Reformed worship. Throughout the sixteenth century, this divergence caused few apparent difficulties for the villages' political unity, especially since religious dissidents in each village customarily could attend neighboring churches of their preferred confession.

This situation changed around 1600, when vocal Reformed Protestant minorities in Undervaz, Trimmis, and Zizers began demanding access to, or even control of, their villages' main churches. The Catholic majorities responded by pushing back, first with words and lawsuits, later with tumultuous assemblies and several near-riots. By 1614, the earlier confessional peace had given way to a series of tense standoffs, which were intensified by interventions on the part of powerful Catholic and Reformed actors from outside the Four Villages. Ultimately, high-level mediation led to negotiations in which the longing for communal unity confronted increasingly polarized separation in religion. The struggle to balance these realities led to documents such as the one translated here, which was signed at Zizers in 1616:

"An agreement of the people of Zizers concerning religion and the church there.

"We, the Evangelical and Catholic parties of the commune and parish of Zizers, make known and proclaim publicly and to everyone with this letter:

"After living for some years in our parish in a state of division and ill-will on account of religion, which has not only resulted in mistrust, envy, and hatred among us, but notably in considerable costs and damage, so that we must be concerned, unless God as the originator of peace should grant us by his grace the spirit of peace and love, that further and greater inconveniences must await us, and the spirit of disunity might cause us yet greater harm.

"Therefore, we from both parties collectively and in particular, for ourselves and for our descendants, have come to agreement and united on the following articles, and we promise one another faithfully and without deceit to hold and keep them to each other, and to live with and next to one another according to their provisions henceforth, as befits honorable communal citizens and neighbors.

"First, the two abovenamed religions shall be free in our entire parish, and neither party shall harass the other in the exercise of their religion, nor in offices, in the courts, or in communal benefits. And we shall be not as two parties or communes, but as one commune, and will hold our assembly henceforth also in the meeting room in the *Ballhütte*[2] after services, without any deceit, as in old times.

"And anyone who earnestly tries to convince another to stand with his party, and tries to persuade him to enter one or the other, shall be obliged to pay the other party a fine of 5 pounds for each instance, without reduction of the penalty.

"Next, the lower church shall serve the Evangelicals, to use it and to remodel it as they please, but at their own cost; only those parts that are used in common shall be maintained from the communal treasury, and the tablets[3] shall remain without damage in whichever church they are.

"The upper church shall serve the Catholics, and what they request, which the Evangelicals do not need for their services, shall be transferred to them willingly; they may provide the church with honorable priests, though without expense on the part of the commune, but not with foreign or wandering monks even at their own cost; and they shall not introduce any novelties, and shall conduct their burials with a priest in the lower customary graveyard.[4]

"Marriages shall be held according to whichever religion or church the groom, or the bride, request.

"The collection plate proceeds shall be divided in the lower church in a nonpartisan manner, and there shall be two supervisors of the collection.

"All public notices shall be made in the lower church by the village crier, as is customary. And the Evangelical churchwardens shall manage the entire church endowment now and in the future, according to their wishes, but without damage or deterioration to it. And in compensation, the Catholics shall be released from all damages, costs, contempt charges and fines resulting from religious matters. And if the entire commune should become Evangelical, then everything that had been donated to the endowment shall fall to the commune.

"Anything that the parishioners may have donated shall return to them or their heirs, in the line of the endower,[5] all according to our common law of endowment and inheritance; but on the contrary, if everyone should become Catholic,[6] then both churches and the entire endowment shall be given to them.

"Any remaining unpaid costs shall be paid from the communal treasury, provided the Evangelicals have approved them before today.

"The beadles shall be elected as formerly, and help each other, and shall divide the Mass offering equally.

"And everything shall belong to the entire commune undividedly, including both churches, the bells, the church decorations, to manage and control according to its wishes.

"And with this document, all earlier verdicts and recesses of the Three Leagues[7] and their courts shall henceforth be dead and cancelled, on both sides.

"Anything that shall come about outside these articles shall be resolved peacefully in all cases, according to our local custom and statutes. And if either party should disregard one or more of the articles, and no longer wished to follow it in full, or should protect anyone who acted against them, they shall be deprived of all the privileges described above.

"And as a true charter and for the greater security of exactly what stands above, now and for the future, we have drawn up two identical copies of this our contract; and both parties have requested Mr. Lorentz Göpfert, at this time *Landamman*[8] of Zizers, to confirm it with the communal seal, so that if one should be lost, the other would be given credit for all time. Given at Zizers on St. Martin's Day 1616."[9]

Tellingly, we possess the text of this document today only because when religious conflict flared up again in the 1640s, the settlement of 1616, copied in 1623 in the region's main city, Chur, was reproduced as evidence of how religious difference should be handled in a village now firmly divided into two religious communities.

Notes

1 The historical commune of the *Vier Dörfer* corresponds to the modern district of the *Fünf Dörfer*.
2 Literally 'ball-hut.' It cannot be determined where this structure stood, or why it carried this unusual name. Thanks to Dr. Silvio Margadant, Staatsarchiv Graubünden, for his inquiries on this matter.
3 These tablets (*Tafflen*) referred either to the priests' gravestones in the walls of the church, or more likely to the entire interior decoration.
4 The lower church, the larger one, had the communal graveyard.
5 The term used is *Stollen*, which in Swiss inheritance practices refers to one line within a larger kin group. See *Schweizerdeutsches Idiotikon*, vol. 11, col. 281. Online. Available at www.idiotikon.ch/Register/ (accessed 2 June 2017).
6 The expression used, literally "if everyone should fall to the Mass," reveals the Protestant sympathies of the scribe or drafters of this article.
7 The three federated leagues of Graubünden.
8 The chief magistrate.
9 "Convention deren zu Ziztzers wegen der Religion, und Kirchen daselbst," St. Martin's Day [11 November] 1616, in Staatsarchiv Graubünden, B 1538/15, pp. 94–97, a copy made in 1644 of an authenticated copy made in 1623. Translated by Randolph C. Head.

25 Mapping the unseen: A Bohemian Jesuit meets the Palaos Islanders, 1697

by Ulrike Strasser

Although early modern Jesuits went overseas in order to evangelize, their work also entailed the production of new knowledge about faraway lands for European audiences. Jesuits wrote detailed descriptions of diverse peoples and places, studied indigenous languages, classified the local fauna and flora, and made maps of previously unknown (from a European point of view) areas of the globe. This type of knowledge production on the 'missionary frontier' often took place in close collaboration with local inhabitants who were willing to explain their world to the Europeans. Such collaboration reflects that missionaries were in many ways dependent on the people whom they came to convert. It further illustrates that indigenous modes of knowing directly contributed to the burgeoning sciences in Europe, but that they were also regularly absorbed and made invisible by dominant European frames of reference.

The map reproduced below presents an intriguing case in point. It is the visual outcome of a cross-cultural collaboration between a Bohemian Jesuit named Paul Klein and islanders from the Palaos archipelago (today's Caroline Islands in Oceania). Klein chanced upon a group of Palaos on a beach in the Philippines where the islanders had been shipwrecked in December of 1696. Interpreting the shipwreck as a sign that God had ordained the discovery and conversion of their archipelago, Klein questioned the islanders about their world and how to reach it. Eventually, the most knowledgeable seafarers in the group used pebbles to outline the contours of the archipelagos in the sand. The pebble arrangement served Klein as the basis for a map that thereafter traveled to Europe (Figure 25.1). It appeared in missionary and scholarly publications in Spain, France, England, and Germany. Klein, who never set foot on the islands, became known as its creator.

Even if Klein translated the islanders' geographical knowledge into the language of European cartography, his map nonetheless reflects the important role of islanders in its making. Jesuit mapmakers often baptized new places with familiar Christian names, but Klein instead used only the islanders' names for all of the eighty-seven islands, a reflection of the fact that the depicted space was beyond European access and control at the time. More to the point still, the Jesuit retained elements of the islanders' distinct

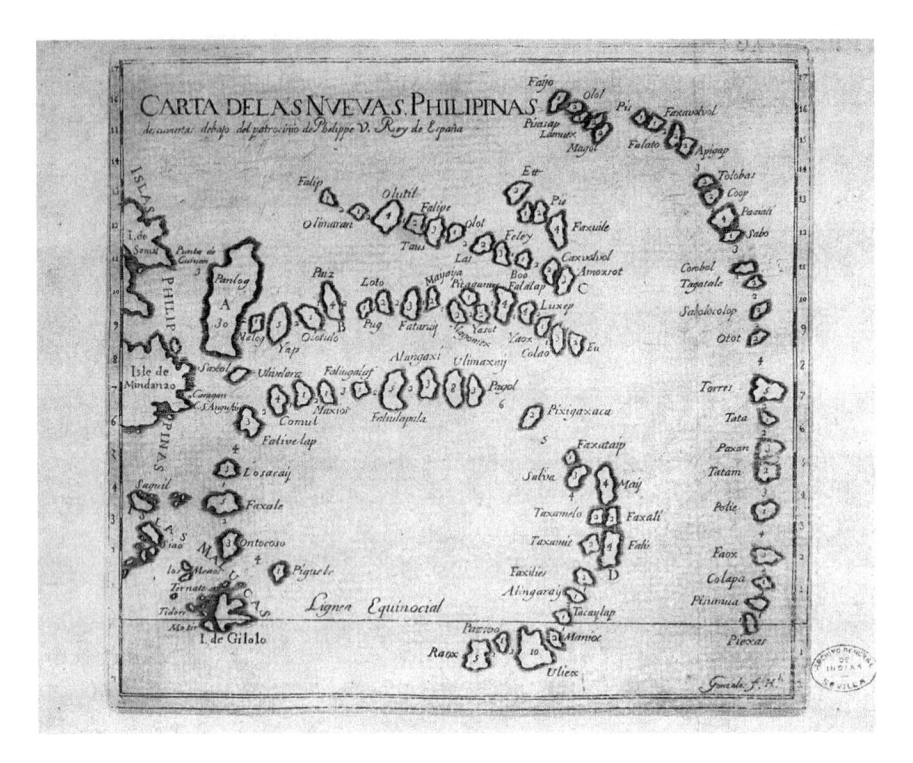

Figure 25.1 Father Paul Klein's Map of the Palaos (1706 version by the Jesuit Procurator Andres Serrano, who added the title "Map of the New Philippines"), preserved in Spain in the Archivo General de Indias, MP-Filipinas, 15, Carta de Las Nuevas Philipinas [Palaos]

mode of orienting themselves in space, some of them at odds with the increasingly standardized European cartographic conventions. Thus, on the Klein map, the size of the islands and the distance between them do not adhere to the rules of Euclidian geometry. Rather these dimensions are indicated with numbers derived from the spatial experiences of the islanders who alone successfully navigated the area. Island navigators measured distances in sailing days rather than sea miles. The numbers inscribed on the islands record the time it took for circumnavigation (e.g., thirty days to travel around Panlog). The numbers between islands mark the time required for transit from one to the next (e.g., two days from Panlog to the neighboring Malog).

The islanders' 'how long?' instead of the European 'how far?' emphasized the accessibility of islands and the connectedness of the archipelago. Voyages between islands throughout the huge archipelago were indeed frequent, and islanders experienced the biggest ocean of the planet as a relay and medium for exchanges rather than an obstacle as Europeans were prone to do. Especially for central Europeans like Klein who had developed their sense of environment in a place where the land dwarfed the water, the Pacific could seem like a monstrous disruption of natural territorial connections. It is therefore especially remarkable that Klein incorporated the islanders' 'how long?' into his map language instead of completely transforming their temporal experience of crossing a connecting sea into a geometric representation of separate bodies of land.

But European and islanders' experiences of navigating ocean space collided on a yet more fundamental level. Palaos seafarers worked exclusively with mental maps and by imagining their position from the vantage point of steering a canoe. They kept their eyes low on the horizon where they tracked the rising and falling of certain stars that pointed towards the island of their destination. This navigational system required memorization and recall of the relevant constellations for each island, what is also known as a 'star compass.' In addition, islanders picked islands to the side as reference points whose successive passage also aided them in charting the right course.

In several respects, the European system was diametrically opposed. European navigators charted their course with instruments and sea charts, and they did so in reference to fixed star positions that allowed them to determine their own location at a particular moment in time. Progress was measured by imagining oneself, from an aerial point of view, moving across a grid of longitude and latitude that enveloped the world. To create a European cartographic representation based on the islanders' cognitive maps therefore meant translating a practice-oriented horizontal view into a vertical perspective derived from Euclidian geometry. This was no small feat. Not surprisingly, Klein depicted parts of their archipelago as more divided than (we now know) it actually is, dividing islets linked within atolls into separate entities. On the other hand, the bend of some of the islands' arcs on Klein's bird's eye map, specialists have argued, is quite suggestive of the islanders' horizontal perspective in setting a course.

Over time, these traces of the islanders' authorship and spatial views disappeared as Klein's map was redacted for various reprints. This makes the version reproduced here the more valuable. Like a time capsule it contains a glimpse of a moment of knowledge transfer between cultural groups and of the competing visions of space that existed in the early modern world. Like the Europeans, the Palaos were highly skilled seafarers, yet their system of orientation existed only in the form of mental maps passed down orally from generation to generation. When Klein created the first European map of Palaos by relying on indigenous data, he thus also created the first permanent material representation of the islanders' mental maps. His distortions notwithstanding, this Jesuit still left us a historical record where otherwise none would have existed at all.

III

Propriety, legitimacy, fidelity: Gender, marriage, and the family

Introduction

by Ute Lotz-Heumann

This chapter explores the norms and realities surrounding gender, marriage, and family life in early modern Europe. Ute Lotz-Heumann's essay presents images and their accompanying captions which provided early modern Germans with an ideal-type depiction of the duties of fathers, mothers, sons, and daughters. These depictions reveal the norms and expectations that prevailed in the families and households of the urban middle classes.[1]

The essays by Christopher Ocker, Curt Bostick, Marjorie Elizabeth Plummer, Karin Maag, and Heide Wunder all address different aspects of the sexual norms and expectations with regard to relationships and marriage that prevailed in early modern Europe. At the same time, these essays draw attention to the fact that theory and practice were two very different things, and that circumstances often determined whether a person would be disciplined or prosecuted for their sexual and marital choices.

The case of the Alsatian nobleman Richard Puller of Hohenburg shows that homosexuality, although considered a capital offence in the late Middle Ages and early modern period, was only prosecuted if other, in this case political, factors led to the person concerned coming under scrutiny by the authorities (essay by Christopher Ocker). Early modern official norms, however, were very restrictive, and condemned any kind of sexual activity outside of heterosexual marriage. The "Sermon Against Whoredom and Uncleanness," which was regularly read in the Protestant Church of England, makes these norms and the alleged consequences that awaited those who broke them – both in this life and in the next – abundantly clear (essay by Curt Bostick).

The stories of Hans Gallmeyer, Alexander Bryson, and Henrich Holderbuel and his fiancée Orthie Kangiesser reveal how fraught early modern relationships could be. Because the breakdown of a marriage resulted in social stigma, the journeyman Hans Gallmeyer became a forger in order to enter into a second marriage (essay by Marjorie Elizabeth Plummer).[2] Alexander

Bryson, a Scotsman and professor at the University of Geneva, ran afoul of marriage rules which stipulated that one was not allowed to marry one's in-laws. After his fiancée's death he had promised marriage to her mother, but when Genevan church and city authorities prevented him from fulfilling his promise, Bryson chose to leave the city (essay by Karin Maag).[3] The case of Henrich Holderbuel and Orthie Kangiesser also shows how much ideas about marriage were connected to ideas about respectability and honor. Assuming that his fiancée had been raped by soldiers, Henrich refused to marry Orthie. But the ecclesiastical authorities demanded that Henrich keep his promise to his fiancée (essay by Heide Wunder).[4]

Once married, it was considered a woman's purpose in life to bear her husband's children. But childbirth also came with considerable health risks, and it was surrounded by a variety of social and religious customs. The essays by Merry E. Wiesner-Hanks and Gerhild Scholz Williams throw light on different aspects of childbirth. The Nuremberg ordinance regulating midwives of 1522 shows the gradual professionalization of this new profession as well as the authorities' expectations of midwives.[5] The seventeenth-century tract *A Chatty Comedy About the Birthing Room* reveals how fraught questions of childbirth, abortion, and illegitimacy, among others, could be in early modern middle-class society.[6]

The essays by Milton Kooistra, Anne Jacobson Schutte, Jill Bepler, and Lynn A. Botelho explore relationships between parents and children. The Protestant pastor Boniface Wolfhart of Augsburg had gotten married – as was expected of the new reformed clergy. He was, however, confronted with a woman from his past who claimed that they had an illegitimate son together. A letter by Wolfhart shows how he tried to provide for the boy without acknowledging him as his own (essay by Milton Kooistra).[7] The need to provide for children also played an important role when parents in Catholic areas of early modern Europe decided to force their children to enter monasteries or convents. Francesco Antonio Bottati had been pressured by his father to become a friar, but he later managed to win release from his vows (essay by Anne Jacobson Schutte).

The last two essays in this chapter exemplify fraught relationships between mothers and sons in the higher and lower nobility. Duchess and Regent Elisabeth of Braunschweig–Lüneburg, a Protestant, wrote a so-called 'political testament' for her son Erich in order to give him moral and political guidance upon ascending to the dukeship. Her advice ultimately fell on deaf ears (essay by Jill Bepler). And Elizabeth Freke of Norfolk did not only record in her diary her difficult relationship with her son and grandson, but also how she spent her final years sick and alone with servants who stole from her (essay by Lynn A. Botelho).

Notes

1 See below, note 6.

Introduction: Gender, marriage, and family 107

2 Other essays that are concerned with the German imperial town of Augsburg are no. 9, Tlusty: 'Popular duels': Honor, violence, and reconciliation in an Augsburg street fight in 1642; no. 15, Tyler: Contested spaces: Bishop and city in late fifteenth-century Augsburg; no. 17, Van Amberg: "We want the friar!" A civic uprising in Augsburg in 1524. This is a reflection of the rich collection of early modern primary sources that has survived in Augsburg.
3 See below, notes 6 and 7.
4 See below, note 6.
5 See no. 10, Hoyer: Regulating day laborers' wages in sixteenth-century Zwickau, for another type of urban regulation.
6 For other essays besides Lotz-Heumann's, Maag's, Wunder's, and Williams's that deal with the question of male and female honor see no. 8, Richardson: Canterbury, 1560: Slander and social order in an early modern town; no. 9, Tlusty: 'Popular duels': Honor, violence, and reconciliation in an Augsburg street fight in 1642.
7 Other essays besides Maag's and Kooistra's that address the question of the new gender roles for Protestant clergy are no. 5, Gordon: In and out of the ivory tower: The scholar Conrad Pellikan starts a new life in Zurich in 1526; no. 6, Burnett: A Protestant pastor should set an example for his community: Johannes Brandmüller of Basel gets into trouble in 1591.

26 Housefather and housemother: Order and hierarchy in the early modern family

by Ute Lotz-Heumann

Early modern society was hierarchical and patriarchal, and these notions about social order extended down to the smallest units, the household, the family, and marriage. Men and women could only be full members of society after they had married and established a household together. For the members of the urban middle and upper-middle classes, this usually meant that the man had to set up his own business as a master craftsman or as a merchant to be able to provide for his family. The resulting 'household' (*familia* in Latin) was much more than the nuclear family of today: An early modern household consisted of the 'housefather' (master of the house, husband, and father), the 'housemother' (mistress of the house, wife, and mother), their children, apprentices, servants, and, potentially, dependent blood relatives like widowed grandmothers. The housefather was at the top of the social hierarchy within the household, and he represented the household to the authorities.

Social expectations, legal norms, and religious values reinforced each other to establish an ideal-type image of the relationships between the members of a household. This image was inculcated through laws, guild regulations, sermons, and the so-called 'paterfamilias literature' (*Hausväterliteratur*),[1] among others. The primary source presented here, a late sixteenth-century woodcut (see Figure 26.1), is one such document. It presents a 'housefather' and a 'housemother' of the urban middle classes. Underneath the images, the text describes their relationship and their roles in the household in verse:

> "Father:
> Housewife, let us our life so live
> that an answer we may to our God give.
> Every housefather and husband
> With his house should take this stand:
> Love his child and wife in piety
> And carry out his trade with integrity.
> He should apply himself night and day

Figure 26.1 Woodcut "Vater – Mutter" ("Father – Mother"), second half of sixteenth century, Germanisches Nationalmuseum Nürnberg

that the household may profit in its way.
If he for his own faithfully cares,
the divine blessing his life daily bears.
And he is for God a true temple
because he gives his children a good example."

"Mother:
My dear master of the house I want to
honor God and you.
A wife who her God obeys
And with fear loves her husband in all her ways
urges her children to love
their parents by the word of God above.
It is also the duty of a pious wife
to watch over the servants and the house, their life.
In the kitchen with meat and drink she stocks her board,
which brings her usefulness, love, honor, and reward.
She also teaches her children throughout
manners, honest and devout."[2]

The 'housefather,' as head of the household, addresses his wife and reminds her that together they are responsible for leading a life that adheres to Christian norms. The 'housemother' responds to her husband, acknowledging his status as 'master' of the household and her responsibility to honor both him and God. The separate stanzas describing "father" and "mother" indicate that in the early modern household the husband and the wife had separate spheres in which their tasks were clearly defined. However, their shared responsibility for the household is also made clear, not least in their obligation to properly bring up their children.

The description of the housefather's duties is focused on the husband's role as master of the house and breadwinner for the family. He is reminded of his obligation to love his wife and children. But, above all, he has to conduct himself honorably – both as a member of the community and in order to be a role model for his children. The housemother's duties, as described, are more varied than her husband's; however, they are limited to the household and performed under the husband's authority. The wife and mother is admonished to "love her husband with fear," a reference to her inferior status. She has to keep an eye on all the other members of the household – children and servants – and has to ensure their good behavior. And she is responsible for getting food and drink on the table for all members of the household.

Another woodcut in the same series (see Figure 26.2) shows two younger people, son and daughter, dressed almost exactly like their parents, and the accompanying stanzas describe the expectations of children in early modern society:

Figure 26.2 Woodcut "Sohn – Tochter" ("Son – Daughter"), second half of sixteenth century, Germanisches Nationalmuseum Nürnberg

"Son:
I am obedient to my father
our Line relies on me, his heir.
A son who to seven years has come
shall leave his home.
He shall go to the gate
where he can diligently imitate
his father's honorable conduct
by learning a craft or trade.
If he fears God and his father's word,
God will bless him, be assured.
He avoids evil company
and accepts punishment willingly."

"Daughter:
I am the joy of my mother
I wish to be obedient to her.
A daughter who is no longer a child
takes care to be chaste, honorable, and not wild.
And she should learn especially
How with her needle to sew subtle and beautiful artistry.
She should help her mother in the household
and be friendly to young and old.
Her husband she should let her parents choose
and not decide herself, marry, and their trust abuse.
She avoids all fornication
because she is a precious fruit."[3]

Here the emphasis is on the children's duty to obey their parents. The expectations for their behavior are clearly laid out and heavily gendered. As was normal for early modern boys of the urban middle classes, the son is expected to be apprenticed to another master – usually at the age of seven – to learn a craft or trade. Often, but not always, the son followed in his father's footsteps. The reality of leaving his father's household at such an early age makes the admonition to be honorable, avoid bad company, and accept punishment from his new master all the more important.

The daughter's life is even more predictable. She needs to prepare to become a housewife herself by learning the skills and duties necessary from her mother. Above all, however, she is admonished to control her sexuality, her "precious fruit." A respectable marriage was the only legitimate space for sexuality in early modern Europe, and any hint of sexual misconduct in a young woman was highly damaging. Indeed, the daughter's choices were limited even further, because early modern society frowned upon 'secret' marriages, that is, engagements between two people without their parents' consent. The daughter is reminded that the 'proper' way to acquire a husband is by having her parents arrange a marriage for her.

While these woodcuts and their accompanying stanzas depict ideal gender roles in early modern society, the reality often looked very different. Reading these stanzas 'against the grain' draws attention to all the things that could go wrong: The husband and wife, trapped in an arranged marriage, might not love each other "piously;" the husband might abuse his wife or not conduct himself honorably in his business dealings; the wife might fail to run her household efficiently and squander money; the son might rebel against the master to whom he was apprenticed; the daughter might engage in sexual activities with a young man and then agree to marry him without ever consulting her parents. After all, early modern people were only human.

Notes

1 'Pater familias' literally means 'father of the household,' master of the house, in Latin. 'Hausväter' means 'house fathers' in German.
2 Caption, woodcut "Vater – Mutter" ("Father – Mother"), second half of sixteenth century, Germanisches Nationalmuseum Nürnberg, Graphische Sammlung, inventory no. HB 2013. Translated by Benjamin A. Miller.
3 Caption, woodcut "Sohn – Tochter" ("Son – Daughter"), second half of sixteenth century, Germanisches Nationalmuseum Nürnberg, Graphische Sammlung, inventory no. HB 2013. Translated by Benjamin A. Miller.

27 Sexual crime and political conflict: An Alsatian nobleman is burned to death with his male lover in 1482

by Christopher Ocker

In medieval and early modern Europe, 'sodomy' could refer to any sexual contact that intentionally resulted in non-procreative ejaculation, including but not limited to contact between men. Although sodomy had been progressively criminalized as a capital offense since the twelfth century, the prosecution of homosexuals as sodomites was rare. Homosexuality was sometimes quite public, in bath houses, for example, and there is little evidence that gay people formed a hidden social group. Gay sex could be routinely indulged, and when sexual persecution did occur, its context was broadly political, as illustrated by the execution of Richard Puller of Hohenburg, an Alsatian nobleman.

Richard was a member of the knightly order, whose father, in the service of the Prince Bishop of Strasbourg, greatly expanded the family's holdings across Lower Alsace. Shortly before the father died, he arranged for Richard to marry the daughter of one of Strasbourg's wealthiest and most powerful men. When Richard's elder brother passed away soon after, Richard consolidated his position as heir and reached property agreements with his brother's widow and his two sisters. Like many middling and lower nobles, Richard spent most of his adult life fighting to defend his properties or get more. He fought no fewer than sixty lawsuits over the course of his life, of which only one ended in a settlement.

Richard lost his most important fiefs in 1457. In 1463, he was first accused of homosexuality in a dispute that resulted in exile and the loss of many more of his fiefs, including some from the Prince Bishop of Strasbourg. On Richard's return to Alsace in 1474, Strasbourg's prince bishop threw him in prison for sodomy. He was released two years later after surrendering more properties, even though he had also confessed to the murder of an eyewitness to his sexual activity some years before.

Richard fled Strasbourg and spent the next five years plotting to regain control of his Alsatian lands. He eventually found refuge in Zurich and received citizenship there in early 1481. When his father-in-law died, he enlisted the Zurich council's support to win back his estate. The council took up Richard's cause, only to find themselves marching to war against Strasbourg while that city enjoyed the support of the entire Swiss Confederacy.

Tellingly, Zurich at first showed no interest in Richard Puller's well-known sexual preferences, however much the chronicler below emphasizes their moral stigma – until Zurich's political isolation became clear. Zurich's magistrates rescued their city by agreeing to turn on their new citizen. In the account below, Richard's sexual transgression is called "heresy" and Richard a heretic. He was arrested with his "unchristian bride," and they were executed as heretics in a carefully orchestrated public display. Richard Puller of Hohenburg died to avert a political and military disaster.

"On the knight-heretic who was burned at Zurich.

"As one counts from the birth of our Lord and safe-keeper Jesus Christ one thousand four hundred and eighty-one years, the city of Zurich received a knight named Richard of Hohenburg into citizenship. He was since his youth a great heretic and an unchristian man in the exact impudent manner that people in those days said openly of him, and [the accusation] was true and an open fact. … This knight-heretic … was extravagant with his things, and he also pretended, lying, that in the city of Strasbourg great violence and injustice was done against him, that there they withheld from him his legitimate wife and property, contrary to God, honor, and justice, and accused him of being a heretic, whereby he could not come to what belonged to him. … He also acquired, at great expense, citations from our holy father the pope and from the Roman king,[1] as was customarily done at courts back then – whoever has money unfortunately can use bribes to get whatever he wants – while the magistrates of Zurich thought everything he told was true. He acquired a large following of people in Zurich, who lent him money on the pledge of his father-in-law's property and his dishonest claims, since he was so exotic – splendid with horses, clothes, and other things – that those of Zurich accepted him as one of their own!

"At first, they [the Zurich council] wrote to the magistrates of Strasbourg, more than once, that Strasbourg should give him free and safe passage into their city, an assurance of safety, so he might get what is his. But the magistrates of Strasbourg did not think they were bound to do this, after the heretic's great offenses and knavery; … Afterward the magistrates of Zurich thought that, should the magistrates of Strasbourg … want to say something to their citizen, Zurich will want proceedings to occur before themselves. Still, the magistrates of Strasbourg did not think they were beholden to Hohenburg, because of his offenses. … And when both sides exchanged hostile words and gave no ground … to the other side, both parties, Strasbourg and Zurich, rode from place to place, … reciting their case … But it was the Zurich magistrates who first initiated the enmity and wrote confrontationally to the Strasbourg magistrates …

"The magistrates of Strasbourg explained their position regarding the heretic to the city councils of Bern and other members of the [Swiss] Confederacy … [asking the Confederacy to mediate between the cities, while Zurich prepared to attack Strasbourg]. The Zurich magistrates nonetheless armed … and went on the march to wreak havoc on the body and property of the people of Strasbourg ..., according to the threat of feud they had previously announced ...

"So, great trouble was taken ... and the matter was very cleverly and earnestly negotiated with the Strasbourg envoys, that Strasbourg should make a certain money payment to Zurich, and then the Zurich magistrates would try the knight-heretic, their citizen, and interrogate him and get a confession of his tremendous offenses. This was a bitter pill for the Strasbourg magistrates ... Yet the envoys of the Confederacy prevailed, and Strasbourg paid 8,000 gulden to the Zurich magistrates. When that happened, the Zurich magistrates were obligated to seize the heretic in their city and interrogate him as necessary concerning his offenses and bring him to justice according to the decision reached [by the Confederacy]. ...

"And so after these events and diets, even the Zurich magistrates reconsidered matters. ... And on a Thursday of the aforementioned eighty-second year, the ... knight-heretic, dressed in green silk, unsuspecting, was arrested together with his servant, his cutthroat and drumbeater, who was also a heretic, and led into the Wellenberg.[2]

"Immediately the servant admitted that the knight-heretic did rather unchristian things, and heresy, very many times with him, ... and it happened many times in Moser's bathhouse in Zurich and at other places ... At first, the knight-heretic did not really want to concede how indeed one had long reports and sure facts about his knavery, ... He was nonetheless condemned by the magistrates of Zurich, so that he and the servant should be burned ... to death as evil heretics. First his knightly estate, of which he was not worthy, was nullified by the Duke of Austria. And then the two were led together, the knight-heretic and his unchristian bride, to the usual place of execution. They were burned to ashes there, according to imperial law. ...

"That day many pious people were present, from Zurich, clergy and laity, nobles and others, and suitable envoys from Strasbourg and envoys from the Confederacy, ... The knight-heretic got his just deserts, and he deserved a still harsher death, after he tried to cause war and death and evil. Yet it pains and disturbs me to the core that the pious lords and honorable people of Strasbourg had to hand over 8,000 gulden on account of such a despicable heretic, who even the Zurich magistrates condemned to death and the pyre."[3]

Notes

1 "The Roman king" refers to the emperor of the Holy Roman Empire of the German Nation, the political entity that was the medieval and early modern precursor of modern Germany and Austria.
2 The "Wellenberg," or 'Wellenbergturm,' was the Zurich prison tower.
3 Diebold Schilling the Elder, *Die Berner Chronik ... 1468–1484*, ed. Gustav Tobler, 2 vols, Bern: K. J. Wyss, 1897–1901, vol. 2, pp. 255–268, no. 404–411. Translated by Christopher Ocker.

28 "O abomination!" A sixteenth-century sermon against adultery

by Curt Bostick

In the early modern era, one has a plethora of primary sources, not least church records, to draw evidence of attitudes towards illicit sexual behavior. The primary source presented here, "A Sermon Against Whoredom and Uncleanness," written by Thomas Becon, was the eleventh sermon in a set of twelve, first authorized in 1547 in the reign of King Edward VI and reissued under Queen Elizabeth I's direction in 1559. In 1563, a second set of sermons was published, and by 1582 the two volumes were printed uniformly and bound together to be used as a book of homilies in the Church of England.[1] The edition quoted here is the folio edition of 1623.

As the Edwardian and Elizabethan courts commissioned, authorized, and promulgated a sermon on the topic of adultery and ordered it to be read several times over the course of a year to all congregations, the "Sermon Against Whoredom and Uncleanness" encompassed what one might call the government's official position on adultery. As the guardians of morality, clergymen were required to communicate and inculcate in their flock the official norms in terms of proper moral and sexual behavior. Even though sermon literature is problematic for the reason that it does not provide us with statistical evidence, and one might therefore be tempted to dismiss these remarks as moralistic propaganda, there can be no doubt that a majority of English subjects were repeatedly exposed to this homily:

"A SERMON AGAINST Whoredom and Uncleanness.

"Although there want not, good Christian people, great swarms of vices worthy to be rebuked, ... yet above other vices, the outrageous seas of adultery, (or breaking of wedlock,) whoredom, fornication, and uncleanness, have not only burst in, but also overflowed almost the whole world, unto the great dishonour of God, the exceeding infamy of the name of Christ, the notable decay of true religion, and the utter destruction of the public wealth; and that so abundantly, that, through the customable use thereof, this vice is grown into such an height, that in a manner among many it is counted no sin at all, but rather a pastime, a dalliance, and but a touch of youth: not rebuked, but winked at; not punished, but laughed at.

"Wherefore it is necessary at this present, to intreat of the sin of whoredom and fornication, declaring unto you the greatness of this sin, and how odious, hateful, and abominable it is, and hath alway[s] been reputed before God and all good men, and how grievously it hath been punished both by the law of God, and the laws of divers princes. Again, to show you certain remedies, whereby ye may (through the grace of God) eschew this most detestable sin of whoredom and fornication, and lead your lives in all honesty and cleanness, and that ye may perceive that fornication and whoredom are ... most abominable sins, ye shall call to remembrance this commandment of God, *Thou shall not commit adultery:* by the which word *adultery*, although it be properly understood of the unlawful commixtion or joining together of a married man with any woman beside his wife, or of a wife with any man beside her husband; yet thereby is signified also all unlawful use of those parts, which he ordained for generation. And this one commandment (forbidding adultery) doth sufficiently paint and set out before our eyes the greatness of this sin of whoredom, and manifestly declareth how greatly it ought to be abhorred ... And that none of us all shall think himself excepted from this commandment, whether we be old or young, married or unmarried, man or woman, hear what God the father saith by his most excellent prophet Moses; *There shall be no whore among the daughters of Israel, nor no whoremonger among the sons of Israel.* ...

"*The Second Part of the Sermon Against Adultery.*

"YOU have beene taught in the first part of this sermon against adultery, how that vice at this day reigneth most above all other vices, and what is meant by this word *adultery*, and how holy scripture dissuadeth or discounselleth from doing that filthy sin; and finally what corruption cometh to man's soul through the sin of adultery. ...

"Great is the damnation that hangeth over the heads of fornicators and adulterers. What shall I speak of other incommodities, which issue and flow out of this stinking puddle of whoredom? Is not that treasure, which before all other is most regarded of honest persons, the good fame and name of man and woman, lost through whoredom? What patrimony or livelihood, what substance, what goods, what riches, doth whoredom shortly consume and bring to nought? What valiantness and strength is many times made weak, and destroyed with whoredom? ... What beauty (although it were never so excellent) is not disfigured through whoredom? Is not whoredom an enemy to the pleasant flower of youth, and bringeth it not gray hairs and old age before the time? What gift of nature (although it were never so precious) is not corrupted with whoredom? Come not many foul and most loathsome diseases of whoredom? From whence come so many bastards and misbegotten children, to the high displeasure of God, and dishonour of holy wedlock, but of whoredom? How many consume all their substance and goods, and at the last fall into such extreme poverty, that afterward they steal, and so are hanged through whoredom? What contention and manslaughter cometh of whoredom? How many maidens be defloured, how many wives corrupted, how many widows defiled through whoredom? How much is the public and common weal impoverished and troubled through whoredom? How much is God's word contemned and depraved through whoredom and whoremongers?

"Of this vice cometh a great part of the divorces, which now-adays be so commonly accustomed and used by men's private authority, to the great displeasure of God, and the breach of the most holy knot and bond of matrimony. For when this most detestable sin is once crept into the breast of the adulterer, so that he is entangled with unlawful and unchaste love, straightway his true and lawful wife is despised, ... Thus through whoredom is the honest and harmless wife put away, and an harlot received in her stead: and in like sort, it happeneth many times in the wife towards her husband. O abomination!"[2]

Separated into three parts of roughly equal length, this homily was meant to be read on three consecutive Sundays. In addition to providing a definition of adultery as any sexual contact out of wedlock and not for procreation, a number of rhetorical strategies are employed to convince listeners of the validity of the argument or frighten them into changing their (supposed immoral and ungodly) behavior. Apart from referring to the unlawfulness of adultery, both according to "the law of God and the laws of princes," the homily quotes extensively from the Bible to drive its point home to its audience. In addition, the social and personal effects of adultery are painted in graphic detail (and with the help of many rhetorical questions). The homily also addresses the question of divorce. In fact, divorce in the modern sense was usually not available in the early modern period, and most partners who wished to end a marriage simply separated, which is indicated in the text by the reference to divorce "by men's private authority" – a practice condemned by the authorities. Finally, the homily warns adulterers of the possible consequences for their eternal salvation: "Swift destruction shall fall on them, if they repent not, and amend not: for God will not suffer holy wedlock thus to be dishonoured, hated, and despised. He will once punish this fleshly and licentious maner of living, ..."[3]

Notes

1 The Protestant state church in England.
2 *Certain Sermons or Homilies, Appointed to be Read in Churches, in the Time of Queen Elizabeth, and Reprinted by Authority from King James I., A.D. 1623. ...*, Philadelphia: George and Wayne, 1844, pp. 108–109, 112, 115–116. See also *Certaine Sermons or Homilies, Appointed to be Read in Churches in the Time of Queen Elizabeth I (1547–1571)*, A Facsimile Reproduction of the Edition of 1623 with an introduction by Mary Ellen Rickey and Thomas B. Stroup, Gainesville, FL: Scholars' Facsimiles & Reprints, 1968, pp. 78–89.
3 *Certain Sermons or Homilies*, p. 117.

29 Hans Gallmeyer: Seduction, bigamy, and forgery in an Augsburg workshop in 1565

by Marjorie Elizabeth Plummer

On 3 March 1565, the Augsburg city council banished Hans Gallmeyer from their territories for bigamy and forgery. Gallmeyer, a cloth-shearer journeyman from Ulm, had worked in Hans Nadler's workshop since his arrival in Augsburg the previous July. After Gallmeyer seduced his daughter, Nadler forced the pair into a formal engagement. Nadler, and probably his guild, demanded that Gallmeyer complete his masterpiece in Ulm before the wedding. In order to do so, as Gallmeyer later testified, he needed to explain the absence of his first wife to the authorities in Ulm. Gallmeyer presented a letter from the Glotz city council that he hoped would persuade officials in Ulm to release his paternal inheritance so he could pay the guild fees for his masterpiece. The letter of character reference [*Kundschaftsbrief*], dated 12 November 1564, elaborately outlines the stellar career of a hardworking journeyman and the tragic circumstances of his fiancée's death:

"We, the mayor and city council of the city of Glotz, do officially certify ... with this letter that the honorable Hans Gallmeyer, a citizen and cloth-shearer journeyman from Ulm, came to Glotz two years ago to gain experience in his craft, as is required of an honorable journeyman, and worked for ... a year and five weeks ... for the honorable master Jochheim Geiger, a Glotz citizen and cloth-shearer. During this time, he achieved such professional standing that another Glotz citizen and cloth-shearer with the name of Anton Kunth promised him his legitimate and only daughter in marriage. It was agreed that Gallmeyer should return home to retrieve his birth certificate ... before the marriage. ... But God almighty ... wishing this promised maiden together with her father and mother ... to return to him, let them be visited by death. When ... Hans Gallmeyer returned ..., he found that she had departed in death. He left ... to follow his craft. He probably did not think, given the circumstances, to remember to ask for a letter of recommendation to show his character to his homeland in Ulm. But, now, Hans Gallmeyer has returned to Glotz and informed us that he wishes to marry once again in Augsburg and that he does not intend to return to his homeland in Ulm. ... he begged the honorable and wise Ulm city council to give him his parental inheritance ... that he may become a cloth-shearer and master. The city council refused to do that until he can ... bring a letter from Glotz to verify whether his affianced wife is living or dead ... He will not get any money from his inheritance and will not be allowed to lead the maiden to church and streets ... until he can bring this certificate from Glotz. He has ... humbly asked us to give him a true and public letter of recommendation and certification ... The honorable and eminent gentlemen, Hans Rosenberger and Jacob Schmaltz, citizens here in Glotz, have sworn ... under oath that the much-mentioned Hans Gallmeyer's promised bride died and that with this death he was released and ... that there is no ... other claim against him ... We also give our true certification of this truth together with the seal of the city of Glotz placed at the bottom of this letter."[1]

Shortly after his return to Augsburg, without a letter verifying his masterpiece, rumors began circulating that Gallmeyer's first wife was still alive. Investigating the charges, the Augsburg city council arrested Gallmeyer and ultimately determined that the above letter was a forgery which Gallmeyer had written himself, sealing it with a seal produced with the help of another journeyman. As his original story of his wife's death unraveled, Gallmeyer provided an alternative narrative in which Anna, his first wife, abandoned him, preferring life in a whorehouse to marriage, and later going to Vienna with another journeyman, freeing him formally from their union. The city council was unimpressed by Gallmeyer's attempts to explain that his marriage to Anna was "no proper marriage" and refused to believe his revised story. In the end he was banished from the city and its territories.

This case is as remarkable for the forgery and Gallmeyer's attempted cover-up of the private dissolution of his first marriage as it is for his unapologetic, repeated use of seduction and marriage to improve his economic position. Gallmeyer certainly understood that his marriages to Anna Kunth and Nadler's daughter, only children of workshop masters, would have brought him economic security, citizenship, and the chance to become a master craftsman, all of which were normally closed to him as an outsider. He also was aware that his first marriage's breakdown jeopardized his standing and potential guild membership not only in Glotz, but also in Ulm and Augsburg.

This case, however, is *not* remarkable in its transgressions of a secret marriage promise or bigamy. In 1565 alone, the Augsburg city council heard ten similar cases, three of which involved at least one of the couple already being married – a consistent statistic throughout the mid-to-late sixteenth centuries despite Augsburg's repeated marriage ordinances forbidding such actions. Gallmeyer was lucky to have escaped more serious punishment for his forgery, bigamy, or for the hints in his trial of his potential involvement in the disappearance of his wife.

The bi-confessional[2] Augsburg city council, like many early modern state authorities, sought to impose a single definition of marriage, using widely distributed Lutheran church ordinances regulating marriage as models for their own published marriage ordinances. However, they were less than successful in getting compliance. Yet they rarely implemented the imperial punishment of death by drowning for bigamy, choosing instead to treat most such cases as sexual misconduct. The case of Hans Gallmeyer shows just one of the numerous confrontations between state attempts to regulate marriage and the more informal practices of marriage and divorce.

Notes

1 Stadtarchiv Augsburg Urgichten Karton 37, Hans Gallmeyer, 3–26 February. Letter dated 12 November 1564. Translated by Marjorie Elizabeth Plummer.
2 Augsburg was a so-called 'bi-confessional' city; that is, its citizenry was split between Lutheranism and Catholicism and its city council was therefore staffed by members of both churches.

30 Professor Bryson's unfortunate engagement, Geneva, 1582

by Karin Maag

By 1582, Geneva was located at the heart of a Europe-wide network of Reformed churches that stretched from France to Hungary and from the Swiss cities to Scotland. The Genevan Academy had served as a well-known and highly respected center of Reformed higher education for over twenty years, attracting students from across Europe. The curriculum primarily included training in the humanities, in Greek and Hebrew, and in theology. Though the city's leading Protestant reformer and French exile John Calvin had died in 1564, the city continued to follow key Reformed practices, including a strong oversight of inhabitants' behavior. Genevans were expected to behave in ways that reflected their Christian commitments, since public sins in particular were held to damage the fabric of community and risked incurring God's wrath.

In this instance, the city council records of 1582 preserve the case of Alexander Bryson, a Scottish professor of philosophy, who had been appointed only two years earlier. Although it may seem far-fetched that a Scot would take up an academic post in sixteenth-century Geneva, Bryson's career was not unusual in Reformed centers of higher education at the time. The mobility of teaching faculty was greatly helped by the fact that all higher education took place in Latin, the international language of learning in the early modern era.

Over the course of his time in Geneva, Bryson had met and become engaged to a young woman, Marie Anastaize, who was the niece of the famous printer Henri Estienne. Sadly, in the spring of 1581, before the couple could marry, Marie Anastaize became ill and eventually died. It appears that during her illness, Alexander Bryson got to know her family quite well and, following Marie's death, Professor Bryson's friendship with Marie's widowed mother deepened into something more. By 1582, Professor Bryson and Catherine Estienne (Marie's mother) were planning to get married. The problem was that marrying the mother of one's deceased fiancée was considered a "cause of great scandal" by the consistory[1] and city council, because rules regarding affinity (relationship by marriage, or in this case, planned marriage) meant that people were not allowed to marry their in-laws. In March 1582, Professor Bryson was told that the marriage could not go ahead. In October 1582, the following item appears in the city council minutes:

"Mr Alexander Brisson, a Scot, professor of philosophy, presented a request noting that as he had obeyed *Messieurs*[2] in that they banned him from carrying out the marriage promises made between him and Catherine Estienne, and from any further contact with her, he knows that given that he will regularly have this sorrow and this object before his eyes, it will be impossible for him to have the calmness of spirit needed for his work, and thus he would be of no help either to the school or to himself. He informed the Company of Pastors and Professors[3] of this and was told that, although they do not support his departure, they do not however want to prevent him from doing so and are willing to accept whatever decision *Messieurs* come to. On this basis, he beseeches *Messieurs* to graciously grant him his release, stating however that he will never forget the support and favors he received from *Messieurs*, offering, if needed, to continue his work here for a little while. And because he is returning from here to his distant land, he will need to be able to show how the matter of the said promises occurred, as much to avoid the slander that may occur as to deal with any impediments he may face if he were to contract another marriage. He requested that *Messieurs* provide him with a certified and valid copy of their order, as it was declared to him orally. It was decided to grant him an honorable release and a copy of the said order which was principally based on the scandal."[4]

This primary source displays the power of the city and church authorities at the time and how important it was to maintain a good reputation. The fact that Professor Bryson asked for and received a formal attestation of what had occurred shows how vulnerable people were to slander and gossip, but also how powerfully written evidence could defuse such critiques. It is worth noting that, although Bryson was clearly distraught over being unable to marry Catherine Estienne, he still remained pragmatic enough to realize that a marriage to another woman in future years was not out of the question and thus asked for a certified copy of what had occurred. There is no further information on Alexander Bryson's later life or career. We do know that Catherine Estienne remarried in 1584 and died the following year.

Given the high rate of mortality in the sixteenth century, marrying more than once was the rule rather than the exception, whether it was a widower with small children looking for a new wife to help bring up his family or a woman whose husband had died and who needed to remarry to ensure ongoing financial security for herself. Yet as this primary source shows, we should not assume that early modern marriages were loveless or simply a matter of convenience. In this case, as in others, the evidence suggests that people selected their prospective spouses very much on the basis of compatibility and mutual attraction and were deeply affected when such marriages did not work out.

Notes

1 The governing body of the Reformed Church of Geneva.

2 The city council.
3 All the pastors of Geneva, together with the professors of theology, humanities, Greek, and Hebrew, made up the Company of Pastors.
4 Archives d'état de Genève, Registres du Conseil de Genève, vol. 77, fol. 47v–48v. See also Charles Borgeaud, *L'académie de Genève 1559–1798*, Geneva: Georg & Co., 1900, p. 187. Translated by Karin Maag.

31 Gender relations in Germany during the Thirty Years' War: A groom refuses to marry his bride[1]

by Heide Wunder

In 1638, the Reformed superintendent[2] Johannes Hütterodt, from the Hessian town of Eschwege (east of Kassel), recorded the following in his official journal:

"On the 5th of December, Henrich Holderbuel from Grossburschla and Orthie Kangiesser from Niederdünzebach, groom and bride, appeared in answer to a summons. The two church elders from Grossburschla, Hans Theias and Caspar Hospach, Jr., also came, and the pastor, Master Jacob Reischwein, sent me the minutes [of an earlier meeting] with them.

"To the question, if and when he had been engaged to be married to Orthie Kangiesser of Niederdünzebach, Henrich Holderbuel answered that it had happened about three years before. To the question, why he had not held a wedding, he answered that the wedding had been delayed due to the war.[3] After Count Götz's four regiments attacked the village and all the villagers had fled, his betrothed was taken captive by the horsemen and, everyone said, she had been with the horsemen. He said that because of this he could not marry her and also referred to the contract, a copy of which he brought with him.

"Dorothea [Orthie] answered the question, if, when and in whose presence she had been betrothed to Henrich Holderbuel as follows: This coming spring it will be three years ago, on the feast of the Annunciation, in the presence of Simon Hübethal and Lips Heerwig on her side, and Henrich's two brothers, Jacob and Conrad Holderbuhl [sic]. Not long after that, she had given him a ring as a token of faithfulness ... Regarding the wedding, she had always hoped that she would not have to remind him because he had received from her three *Malter*[4] of grain, three bushels of barley and a cartload of hay at Dünzebach.

"She had to admit that she had been captured by Count Götz's regiment, and had been led into the village, but, she argued, it was not her fault ... When the horsemen invaded the village, she ran into the forest like the others, but she – along with many others – was later driven back into the village. She had not been, however, touched by any of the soldiers. Even if she were to have been raped, which had befallen many honorable women, she would admit it; but since nothing had been inflicted upon her, she could not say so."[5]

This excerpt from the Holderbuel–Kangiesser matrimonial case records the effects of the Thirty Years' War on the life prospects of a young couple. True, the minutes of a church official offer only rough outlines of what actually happened, and can only hint at which moral judgments, interests, and emotions guided the actions of the parties involved. It is possible, however, to begin to discern in this document the different perspectives of the bride, the groom, and the village officials regarding the complex events as well as the significance of public opinion for one's reputation and honor in early modern rural society.

Henrich Holderbuel declined to marry his fiancée Orthie Kangiesser because, in his view, she had been made a prisoner, and presumably a 'whore,' by the horsemen of Count Götz's regiment. Although Holderbuel could furnish no evidence – such as Orthie's pregnancy – he obviously believed that his honor was being threatened. Orthie, on the other hand, answered the superintendent's questions elaborately: She named the witnesses at the betrothal, she referred to the ring which she had given to Henrich to vouchsafe the validity of the betrothal, and she mentioned the dowry she had already sent to Henrich at Dünzebach. She also described the episode with the horsemen differently than Henrich: She had indeed been taken prisoner like other villagers, but she had not been raped. Had that in fact happened, she would admit it, because it had been inflicted on many women who, nevertheless, were still held to be "honorable." With this argument, Orthie attempted to invalidate Henrich's position. Henrich saw the alleged rape as a hindrance to marriage, while Orthie did not see rape as a violation of female honor.

However, Holderbuel was not alone in his perspective on things, as he was able to persuade the local pastor and the two church elders that the rumor that his betrothed "had been with the horsemen" was a threat to his honor. He did, in fact, make a "contract" with Orthie in the presence of the pastor (Jacob Reischwein) and the elders, in which she agreed to release him from obligation to her if he returned her dowry of grain and hay. Apparently, all parties recognized this procedure as legitimate, and held that the marriage vow, sealed through the ring and the delivery of the dowry, could be dissolved through the assent of the two contracted parties.

Such an attitude is not surprising with regard to the laypeople, but it *is* surprising with regard to the pastor, since questions of the validity of betrothals fell under the jurisdiction of the church and were to be decided by the superintendent. When Henrich and Orthie answered the summons and appeared in front of the superintendent with the two church elders on 5 December 1638, Hütterodt found the conduct of all parties to have been unlawful. He gave the two elders a reprimand. A week later he also gave a reprimand to the pastor because the "contract" was, in fact, the equivalent of self-divorce by the betrothed pair and, as such, strictly forbidden by the church.

Our modern expectation – that the superintendent would attempt to resolve the question of whether Orthie remained, as she claimed, a virgin – is thoroughly disappointed. Although witnesses were without doubt available, he did not summon them because the question of the rape was not relevant to Hütterodt. For him, it all hung on the question of church law – whether the bond of betrothal between Henrich and Orthie still existed or not. In the end, Hütterodt decided that the two were 'promised,' and that therefore Henrich and Orthie must get married. (This corresponds to the fact that husbands whose wives had been raped were not able to divorce them in the early modern period.)

Henrich would not submit to this judgement, and was referred for further clarification to the chancery and marriage court in the capital city of Kassel. Henrich was not willing to do this, either, and he hoped that the Lutheran superintendent in the nearby Saxon city of Langensalza would perhaps give a more favorable ruling than the Reformed Hütterodt. This endeavor must not have been successful, however, because fourteen days later, Henrich declared that he was ready to marry Orthie. On 13 January 1639, Hütterodt noted contentedly that Henrich had "finally done some soul-searching" and that his wedding to Orthie had taken place in Grossburschla. To this he added "please God may it come to good." This 'pious wish' seems to have come true, despite this difficult beginning, since Henrich and Orthie do not appear again in Hütterodt's official journal, which covers the years 1638–1672.

The Holderbuel–Kangiesser case is unique in Hütterodt's journal, in which instances of alleged 'fornication' with soldiers predominate. The case nevertheless provides insight into the difficult situations which confronted young couples during the worst years of the Thirty Years' War in Germany, and the various strategies they employed to overcome them.

Notes

1 Translated by Elizabeth M. Ellis-Marino and Benjamin A. Miller.
2 A superintendent was a high-level official in certain Protestant territorial churches in Germany; he occupied the same level as a bishop.
3 The Thirty Years' War.
4 A *Malter* was a measure of capacity in early modern Germany which varied considerably between regions, even from village to village. Three *Malter* of grain were about 345 kilograms.
5 "Das Diensttagebuch des Eschweger Superintendenten Johannes Hütterodt (1599–1672)" [The official journal of the superintendent Johannes Hütterodt from Eschwege], a CD appendix to Martin Arnold and Karl Kollmann (eds), *Alltag reformierter Kirchenleitung: Das Diensttagebuch des Eschweger Superintendenten Johannes Hütterodt (1599–1672)*, Marburg: Historische Kommission für Hessen, 2009.

32 Defining a new profession: Ordinance regulating midwives, Nuremberg, 1522

by Merry E. Wiesner-Hanks

Women in early modern Europe, like those in most of the world's cultures in most periods, generally gave birth assisted by female relatives and friends. Women who had particular talents or inclination were often called to assist more regularly, and gradually such women began taking payment for their work, evolving into professional midwives. Midwives were trained by watching and helping more experienced midwives, but beginning in the sixteenth century in some parts of Europe, governments began to regulate midwifery and require midwives to swear an oath if they wished to obtain a license. The following is the first midwives' ordinance issued by the city council of the southern German city of Nuremberg in 1522. It served as a model for similar ordinances in many other cities:

"Every midwife should ... swear she will conscientiously care for and stand by every expectant mother in her time of need to whom she is called, whether she is rich or poor, to the best of her abilities and understanding. She should proceed to whomever she is called first, immediately and without opposition, and make absolutely no excuses or delays, as has often been the case, but faithfully stand by her. Also no woman is to be hurried or forced to deliver before the proper time; she should wait and hold out until the appropriate time.

"If the thing [the delivery] looks like it will be dangerous, she should call one or two of the women who oversee midwifery and proceed with the emergency according to their advice. In no case is she to wait or delay to call them until the need is so great they cannot handle it, or she will warrant serious punishment.

"If it happens that the birth takes so long and the first midwife has a pressing need to rest or sleep for a while, she should call another sworn midwife and not an apprentice, who will then be just as responsible to appear immediately without opposition. She should then steadfastly and helpfully care for the woman in labor just as if she had been called at first. ...

"If any midwives show themselves to be disobedient or disagreeable, the city council will not only remove them from office, but will also punish them severely, so that all will know to shape up and watch their behavior.

"The council has certainly experienced that the midwives deal very deceitfully and for their own profit with the city charity for poor new mothers, running back and forth to respectable women, who don't need the alms, promising them bedding and lard and other things if they will agree to call them as midwives. These lucrative operations are leading to a decline and breakdown of the charity fund. Because the council sees this with no little displeasure, from now on the midwives will be sworn by their oaths not to run after these women, ... If the council discovers any further incidents, she [the midwife] will be let out of her office, and will be punished in each case according to the severity of the deed, however the council decides. ...

"They [the experienced midwives] should not take on any flighty, young apprentices, as it so often happens that they marry during the course of their training and that all sorts of injuries result from their inexperience. They should rather take on apprentices well advanced in years and preferably living alone, from whom one expects more diligence than from younger ones.

"They should also not allow themselves to drink wine in excess, as all kinds of injury and harm have been inflicted on the pregnant women because of this. The council has decided to punish severely any who break this restriction.

"The honorable council has discovered that the midwives often send their maids (who have not completed their instruction or who have just completed it and have no experience yet) alone to women who are giving birth for the first time, through which these women are often neglected and deplorably injured. Therefore the honorable council orders that from now on no maid, whether she has half-completed her training or not, is to attend alone any woman bearing her first or second child, whether she goes with the knowledge of her instructor or not. After the passing of the normal years of training, the apprentice shall carry out her first birth in the presence of her instructor. In the case that the instructor is dead or not there, another sworn, experienced midwife should be present. Anyone who is convicted of this will be punished to the extent that the council's displeasure with the deed can be felt.

"The high honorable council has also had enough of midwives taking their proper salary for poor women not only from the established overseer of the charity for poor new mothers but also from the women themselves, and therefore receiving double payment. This gives the honorable council great displeasure. Because of this the midwives are to swear that when they receive their proper salary (that ... has been set at 20 *kreuzer* for each birth) from the overseer for caring for a poor woman, they are not to demand or want anything more, but let themselves be completely satisfied with their established salary. All of this is liable to punishment, which the high honorable council will set each time according to the crime and opportunities of the case.

"Recently evil cases have taken place, that those women who live in sin and adultry have illegitimate children, and during birth or before purposefully attempt to kill them by taking harmful, abortion-causing drugs or through other notorious means. Some of these cases never come to the attention of the authorities and proper punishment for them cannot be carried out. This the high honorable council, because of the God-given authority it carries, can no longer tolerate. Therefore they have made the recommendation that the midwives' oath be added to. They are to swear yearly that when one of them is called to deliver a baby for such a woman, one who is carrying an illegitimate child, she [the midwife] is obliged to ask with intent what the name of the child's mother is and who the child's father is. As soon as she has brought the child into the world, she is to report to the Lord Mayor whether the child is alive or dead, who its mother and father are, and where the mother is lying in bed. Also no dead illegitimate children are to be carried to the grave before she gives her report to the Lord Mayor. At least three or four unsuspected female persons are to go with the child to the grave. If one or more of the midwives act against this and will not comply with what has been sent forth above, the high honorable council will deal with them as perjurers with corporal punishment. Then they will finally know to conform to this."[1]

Along with various clauses about the character and training of apprentices and midwives' involvement in what we would now term 'welfare fraud' is a final clause ordering midwives to report all births out of wedlock and try to find out the names of the parents. The city council was worried that such children would need public financial support and wanted to know the identity of their fathers, so that they could be forced to pay for the upkeep of the children. It also thought that unmarried mothers might be driven to infanticide, and so prohibited midwives from attending the burial of an illegitimate child. Although there was no infallible way for midwives or physicians to tell if a child had been stillborn, died of natural causes, or been killed, authorities throughout Europe became convinced that there was a rising tide of infanticide. In some places, including Scotland and various German states, unmarried women who did not report a pregnancy risked the death penalty if the child died even if there was no evidence of actual infanticide. As a result, midwives could also be called as witnesses in trials for infanticide, which increased in frequency throughout the sixteenth century.

Note

1 Staatsarchiv Nürnberg, Amts- und Standbücher no. 100, fols 101–105. Translated by Merry E. Wiesner-Hanks.

33 *A Chatty Comedy About the Birthing Room*: Johannes Praetorius observes women's lives in seventeenth-century Germany

by Gerhild Scholz Williams

Although Johannes Praetorius (1630–1680) shared the misogyny of his age, his writings reveal, upon closer inspection, an astute observer of women's lives. In the tract presented here, he explores gender and social status as they play out in the roles of wives and their servants, while his sharp criticism of contemporary mores is often tempered by empathy for the women's lot and by his tongue-in-cheek humor. The tract humorously entitled *Celebrating the Mysteries of Motherhood, That is: A Chatty Comedy About the Birthing Room* (*Apocalypsis Mysteriorum Cybeles, Das ist eine Schnakische Wochen-Comedie*) represents the semiserious description of a new mother's six-week lying-in period after childbirth.[1]

During the six weeks of a new mother's confinement, the husband was banned from the conjugal bedroom; physical intimacy was frowned upon. However, the new mother could – in fact, was obliged – to formally invite and entertain with food and drink female family members, friends, and acquaintances. The confinement helped the mother to recover from the stresses and strains of pregnancy and birth. It kept her sheltered from the day-to-day challenges of domestic duties and conjugal obligations while her visitors saw to it that she did not lose touch with the goings-on in the community. At the end of the six weeks, the new mother left the no-man's-land of the lying-in chamber to be reintegrated into the life of the community and welcome her husband back into the conjugal bedroom.

This tract presents the reader with the visitors' conversations secretly recorded by various male listeners. These voyeuristic male *personae* note down the complaints, secrets, and confidences – in short, gossip – exchanged between the new mother and the women who come to keep her company, most importantly the baby's godmothers. Praetorius employs different masks as he sets about ridiculing male curiosity and female gossip with equal tartness. He also intersperses the women's conversations with several lengthy humorous poems on the topic of childbirth and confinement visits as well as a poem which regales the reader with an argument between a husband and wife about the pleasures and evils of tobacco which had, by the seventeenth century, become a staple of urban life and leisure.

The *Comedy* reviews the social pressures, superstitions, anxieties, and interactions that governed the lives of early modern middle-class women of childbearing age. We read about the prohibitions and rituals associated with pregnancy, birthing, and lying-in – a wealth of knowledge gathered over generations and passed from mother to daughter, from woman to woman. The confidences exchanged in the intimacy of the lying-in chamber also reveal just how much the women know about other women in their community and about their familial and social relationships.

The most obvious social chasm exists between the urban middle-class matrons and their maids and other servants in the household. For example, the young mother complains:

"… these days, unfortunately, we have to treat our maids well and not overwork them, lest they get to grumbling and become contrary. My foolish goose gets pretty annoyed that every four weeks she has to clean the house and scrub the parlor, kitchen, and bedroom; I'll leave aside what happens when I ask her to do a little more! Now these lazy horses' asses play the damsels, not wanting to serve their mistress any more."[2]

Little remains hidden as visitors and host share approbation and censure: The death of a child is public knowledge; the cause of death remains conjecture. The same is true for the paternity of a foundling recently discovered in the local cemetery:

"Frau[3] Christina: 'Let me tell you an amazing story, Frau Regina, that our maid told today just for fun when we were doing our wash. It appears that a newborn was found under the *Schwibbogen*[4] by the cemetery. The pastor from the *Spital*[5] came quickly to baptize it, naming it *Hans Schwiebboge* because it is a foundling and nobody knows who the father might be – although gossip has it that the whoremonger Jäckel produced it.'"[6]

The concealed circumstances of an illegitimate birth are part of gossip implicating parents, child, and community in a discourse of secrecy and conjecture about the truth that remains hidden:

"Frau Barbara: '… In our neighborhood there was a story going around about a young woman who had a baby, even though it was covered up; she spirited the baby out of town to be nursed and raised by a gardener woman.' The young mother: 'Where? Was it the *Rastrum*[7] seller?' Frau Barbara: 'I really don't want to say.'"[8]

And the women discuss with relish behaviors judged morally reprehensible, like public drunkenness, or the lasciviousness of a married, ostensibly respectable, burgher's wife, or the abortion of an untimely pregnancy:

"Frau Secretary: '… these foolish girls offer themselves to the whole town.' Frau Apothecary: 'Oh dear, and then the long pepper and unground saffron will be needed for that [to abort]; then the apothecaries will have something to sell; one little one after the other. It has been said that Frau Anna's[9] sweet young thing, the spoiled little bitch, aborted her "fruit" this way.' The young mother: 'Frau Anna's daughter? That's the first I've heard about it! They say the mother is not much better than the daughter. …'"[10]

The conversations among the women remind the reader of the smallness of the community that made privacy, in the modern sense, elusive, a social impossibility. As the visitors exchange confidences, criticisms, and gossip, the social differences and sexual tensions which divide the community surface time and again: whose daughter does what with whom; who would like to marry rich; who among the town's virgins got pregnant and had to leave town temporarily; who among the married women of the town keeps lovers; who has found out about her husband's infidelity, but must keep quiet; who wishes her husband dead.

Notes

1 Johannes Praetorius, *Apocalypsis Mysteriorum Cybeles. Das ist Eine Schnakischen Wochen-Comedie Oder verplauderte Stroh-Hochzeit*, Bojemo: 1662. This may be found at the Herzog August Bibliothek Wolfenbüttel, Germany, AB La 7169. The edition and translation used here is from Gerhild Scholz Williams (ed.), *Mothering Baby: On Being a Woman in Early Modern Germany: Johannes Praetorius's Apocalypsis Cybeles. Das Ist Eine Schnakische Wochen-Comedie (1662)*, Tempe: Arizona Center for Medieval and Renaissance Studies, 2010.
2 Ibid., p. 159.
3 German for 'Mrs.'
4 A *Schwibbogen* is a flying buttress.
5 In medieval and early modern times, a *Spital*, or hospital, was a place for the sick, the old, and the poor.
6 Praetorius, *Apocalypsis Mysteriorum*, in Williams (ed.), *Mothering Baby*, p. 97.
7 Beer.
8 Praetorius, *Apocalypsis Mysteriorum*, in Williams (ed.), *Mothering Baby*, p. 147.
9 Frau Anna was actually a visitor in the lying-in chamber before, but has left when this conversation takes place.
10 Praetorius, *Apocalypsis Mysteriorum*, in Williams (ed.), *Mothering Baby*, p. 151.

34 A letter sent from Augsburg in 1538: A Protestant minister writes to a friend about his illegitimate son

by Milton Kooistra

Beginning in the early 1520s, most Protestant reformers made the provocative step of entering into marriage, thus breaking their vows of clerical celibacy and making manifest their breach with the Catholic Church. Many reformers, such as Martin Bucer and Martin Luther, married ex-nuns, and the majority married women of their own social status. Protestant reformers believed that compulsory clerical celibacy and monasticism were not only unbiblical but also unnatural, and upheld clerical marriage as a means to prevent 'fornication.' Many wrote treatises on marriage and defended their actions before ecclesiastical and secular authorities. They hoped that by marrying and raising legitimate children they might become models of connubial bliss and domestic propriety for other Christians. These clerical marriages and their resulting families supplanted the priestly household presided over by a celibate but not always chaste clergyman, his cook or housekeeper (euphemisms for concubines), and their illegitimate offspring.

The transition from celibate priest to married pastor, however, was not always smooth. The following letter, written by Boniface Wolfhart (d. 1543), a Protestant minister in Augsburg, to Wolfgang Capito (d. 1541), a Protestant reformer in Strasbourg, on 25 April 1538 demonstrates how one reformer reacted when confronted by a woman from his past and the offspring of their alleged act of fornication:

"Greetings in the Lord. I had already responded to your letter with the same courier that brought yours, but I understand from your more recent letter that you had not yet received mine, for you threaten me with some dreadful fate if I don't respond. Therefore, my esteemed Capito, I am writing to the same effect as I did before. First, that the mother of the boy is acting unfairly with me since she is now at last attempting to force the boy upon me. I could not even persuade her to give him to me, when I asked her long ago, perhaps because she had a bad conscience, knowing that he was not my son, something which I can easily deduce from various signs. Yet, such is my good nature, I would have brought him up for duty's sake and would still [offer to] do so, if I had not already adopted another orphan, whom I have no right to renounce. He seems to be of an excellent nature and worthy to be raised for the good of the church.

"Second, my wife, who is otherwise nagging enough to me, would provoke new quarrels if I were to acknowledge him as my own, a boy long since in someone else's custody. Perhaps Satan used this occasion to sow strife between us and scandalize the church. Finally, my means are too limited for me to be able to support the schooling of the boy – even if I was willing to do so and he was the fruit of my loins (if only his mother were not lying about that) – unless Maecenases[1] come forward.

"Therefore I ask you, through Christ, to consider if you judge him cut out for literature and to see if he can be publicly supported. But, if it were better that in time he should learn some trade, I would advise that he become a tailor, since you write that he is physically weak. I myself am going to support him. Believe me, dearest Capito, I shall be compelled now and in the future to borrow money, for I have not saved anything out of my stipend and do not wish to amass a treasure, rather I am liberal to strangers and to the poor. But by incurring such expenses – supporting two boys at home and one abroad – the source of my liberality would soon run dry. I write this to show you that I am not given to avarice, a vice from which I have always been far removed. If there is anything I can do to pay you and your family back, I shall attempt it, even if it surpasses my strength. Farewell along with your wife and children. I hope that they, along with you, are healthy."[2]

This letter is interesting for a number of reasons, but it nonetheless raises more questions than it answers. It begins with the acknowledgement of the exchange of a few letters between Wolfhart and Capito that no longer exist, but were pressing in nature. Wolfhart, who lived in Strasbourg from 1525 to 1531, explains that a woman (her identity is unknown) had approached him, claiming that he was the father of her son, and was now demanding that he provide financial support for his education or training. Next, he describes that his wife – nothing is known about his wife, except that Wolfhart was married by the early 1530s – wants nothing to do with that boy, and that Wolfhart cannot afford to provide a stipend for him, since he is already supporting two other boys.

Despite his claims to the contrary, reading between the lines, it is quite evident that Wolfhart was indeed the father of the boy, which helps explain his wife's refusal to allow him to acknowledge the illegitimate son as his own and his request that Capito secure a stipend for the boy or else find a placement for him as an apprentice to a tailor, which belies a paternal concern for the wellbeing of his son, legitimate or not. This interpretation is further bolstered by a comment that Capito wrote on the reverse of the letter, below the address, in which he provides the name of the boy: "Regarding his son David, that he be hired out to a tailor." Furthermore, a year later, Wolfhart again wrote to Capito, congratulating him and his wife Wibrandis Rosenblatt on the birth of their baby, contrasting that happy occasion with his grief over David, who had ended up in the home of an untrustworthy man – possibly a tailor – and was suffering from a hernia.[3] This letter thus shows how reformers, despite their best efforts to enter into sanctioned marriages and raise legitimate children, could still be subject to the ghosts of their past and how they strove hard to cover up any scandal that might "sow strife" and "scandalize the church."

Notes

1 Wealthy patrons.
2 The autograph original of this letter is in Universitätsbibliothek Basel, ms. Ki. Ar. 25a, no. 28. Translated by Milton Kooistra.
3 The autograph original of this letter is in Universitätsbibliothek Basel, ms. Ki.Ar. 25a, no. 11.

35 Piedmont, 1712: Son forced into monastery by his father manages to get out

by Anne Jacobson Schutte (†)

Early modern parents often determined that one or more of their offspring would enter monastic life, whether or not they had any desire to do so. Usually, the main purpose was to eliminate individuals from the inheritance stream, thus fattening the patrimony that would pass to a single heir. By employing force and fear, elders achieved this objective. Eventually, however, spiritual advisers persuaded some of them to repent and allow sons and daughters in religious houses to petition the pope for release from their vows. When interrogated under oath on an unspecified date not long before his death in April 1710, Francesco Bottati – a notary in Trinità, near Mondovì in the northwestern Italian region of Piedmont – admitted that eight years earlier he had compelled his son Francesco Antonio to become a friar. He now affirmed support for his son's attempt to return legally to secular life.

The elder Bottati began by "recognizing myself, unfortunately, to be an irascible, ill-tempered, rather passionate man, both in words and in laying hands on my children, servants, and anyone else who contradicts me in the slightest way."[1] On one occasion, he recalled, when he was suffering from quartan fever, his son (about sixteen at the time) came to the door of his bedroom to apologize for having offended him:

"I got out of bed, enraged, and said to him, 'Rash and impertinent as you are, you have the nerve to come before me! Go away! Get out of here! Go to the devil, go to hell, and never show up again or dare to call me father!,' and many other injurious and inappropriate things. And as he left, he said, 'Oh, poor me, what in the world will I do and where will I go?' Hearing this, I told him, 'Go make yourself a Discalced Augustinian friar,' and with that he left. I told him that if he didn't become a religious in that order, which he now is, I never wanted to see him again or put up with his carefree, lazy behavior, paying no attention to his studies or undertaking any other worthwhile occupation."

At a servant's suggestion, Francesco Antonio apologized again the following day. "Having persuaded myself that he would change his life and behavior," his father suspended the order. Francesco Antonio, however, continued to neglect his studies and refused to amend his life. About a year later, another confrontation occurred in the presence of Francesco's brother-in-law and nephew: "Overcome by rage," the father testified, "I began to yell at and reprove him," insisting that he must enter the Discalced Augustinian friary near Mondovì. Beating Francesco Antonio with his cane, he shouted, "You little idiot, you still dare to disregard my wishes and refuse my orders!" Not long thereafter, thoroughly intimidated by his father's verbal and physical violence, Francesco Antonio unwillingly took the habit in a Discalced Augustinian house near Turin. On 9 April 1702, under the religious name Angelo Francesco di San Benedetto, he professed the solemn, irrevocable vows that made him a full-fledged friar.

His son, Francesco Bottati went on to say, became a friar not of his own free will but solely "on account of the insults I used." He made clear to Francesco Antonio that he must forget about returning home, "for I absolutely did not want to recognize an unfrocked friar as my son." When he learned from some Discalced Augustinians that the young man intended to apply for annulment of his monastic profession, Francesco sent a message reminding him that unless he remained a friar, their father–son relationship would be over. However, five or six months before testifying, Francesco had a change of heart. He stated in the conclusion of his interrogation that, "counseled by a religious of complete integrity who is my confidant, I repented of the error I had made." Therefore, he decided to withdraw his objection to Francesco Antonio's seeking release. His only motive, he insisted, was "relieving my conscience."

Another witness whose testimony was included in the printed submission presented by Francesco Antonio's attorneys to the Congregation of the Council, whom the pope regularly charged with adjudicating such cases, told a rather different story. According to the petitioner's elder brother, Carlo Lorenzo, Francesco Antonio had originally been studying to become a secular priest. When the bishop deferred his ordination, father Francesco flew into a rage, "telling him that he no longer wanted to incur so much expense in sending him back and forth, and he didn't want any more priests in the house."[2] First he tried unsuccessfully to force his son into the Discalced Carmelite order. When those friars refused to accept him, Francesco sent him to the Discalced Augustinians, one of whom was the young man's uncle. Around Christmas of 1709, after learning of his brother's intention to petition for release, Carlo Lorenzo tried to persuade his father to put up the money for legal expenses; after Francesco's death, he himself assumed that responsibility.

The newly available money to finance an appeal was crucial. On 12 April 1710, the cardinal-members of the Congregation of the Council had rejected Bottati's petition, most likely because it was inadequately supported. On 5 April 1712, having received his lawyers' summary of evidence demonstrating that force and fear exerted by his father had driven him into the friary, they approved his release from monastic vows. Assuming that he had been ordained during his years as a friar, he probably took up a career as a secular priest, as did most male religious who won their cases.

Francesco Antonio Bottati's ordeal illustrates several common features of forced monachization. Elders employed harsh words, threats of financial and emotional alienation, physical assaults, and much else to thrust sons as well as daughters into monastic life. Few adolescents disinclined to become religious could resist such pressure. In most cases, ingrained 'reverential fear,' which persisted as long as their forcers remained on the scene, dissuaded them from appealing. That Bottati's legal effort swung into high gear only after his father's demise is no coincidence.

Notes

1 This and the following quotations are from Archivio Segreto Vaticano, Congr. Concilio, Petitiones, 354, Turin, Bottati, *Summarium*, Rome: De Comitibus, 1712, fols A1r–A3v. Translated by Anne Jacobson Schutte.
2 Ibid., fols A6v–A8r.

36 A mother tries to reform her son: Elisabeth of Braunschweig's "Motherly Admonition" to her son Erich, 1545

by Jill Bepler

With one notable exception, Maria of Jever (1500–1575), there were no women in early modern Germany who ruled a territory in their own right. This stands in stark contrast to the number of widowed dynastic women who ruled territories as regents and co-regents for their sons until they came of age. These regencies could last for very extended periods and the transition of power from mother to son was not always without complications. The female regent had to come to terms with a marked change in her own status within the court system in which she was relegated to the position of dowager. One contemporary source stressed that this meant that from one day to the next her capacity to command and be obeyed was replaced by the mere right to request and an expectation that she would be treated with respect.

Many women regents had steered their territories through difficult periods of political or confessional strife and were proud of their achievements – women like Amalie Elisabeth of Hessen–Kassel (1602–1651), who was recognized as a skilful military strategist and political negotiator in the Thirty Years' War. Elisabeth of Braunschweig–Lüneburg (1510–1558), also known as Elisabeth of Calenberg, was 15 years old when she married Erich of Braunschweig–Lüneburg (1470–1540). In 1538 the young duchess openly converted to the Lutheran faith. Two years later her husband died, and Elisabeth became regent of the territories of Calenberg–Göttingen which she ruled in the name of her son Erich, who was 12 years old at the time. Elisabeth introduced the Protestant Reformation into her territories and carried out a number of social and economic reforms aimed at improving the ruinous financial conditions left by her husband. The political and confessional situation in Germany in which Elisabeth handed over the reins of power to her son Erich in 1545 was highly unstable. Erich himself was a difficult and recalcitrant son, and Elisabeth was right in fearing that he might revert to the Catholic faith and undo her work of Reformation.

In Germany there was a tradition of 'political testaments' written by male rulers laying down their principles of government for their successors. It is in this tradition that the "Motherly Admonition," a text written in the form of a manuscript letter from Elisabeth to her son Erich, should be seen. In 1545 she set out on 392 small pages the moral, political and administrative advice which would make him a good ruler:

"Our, Elisabeth, by God's grace born Margravine of Brandenburg etc., Duchess of Braunschweig and Lüneburg, widow, instruction and order, which from motherly affection and a true heart we have set out for the high born Prince Erich, Duke of Braunschweig and Lüneburg, our friendly beloved son, as a friendly and useful instruction for the beginning of his future rule, showing how he may direct and comport himself in the same in blessed manner towards God and in his worldly government towards all people. In the Year 1545."[1]

In her preface Elisabeth stressed the value she attached to her manual of advice, which was why she had written it in her own hand. She stated that she expected it to be kept as a family heirloom and used not only by Erich but by successive generations of male rulers from their dynasty. Elisabeth clearly anticipated the problems which soon ensued by imploring her son to remember that she had sacrificed her youth and health to the good of his realm and his education and reminding him not to treat her disrespectfully or badly after his accession to power:

"Please note diligently that I would like to see you, my beloved child, warned about and protected from ruin and misfortune, both in eternity and in this life, and that I ... wish you well. Therefore, I hope that as a pious son you will follow your beloved mother in this [i.e., her advice] and be mindful of the fact that ... I have, both through my own person and through this written exhortation, conveyed to you what leads to godliness and princely welfare, ..."[2]

The ideal which Elisabeth projects in her text is the *princeps christianus*, the Christian prince guided by biblical example, which remained a mark of Lutheran political theory well into the seventeenth century. Elisabeth divides her text into 49 sections in which she touches on all aspects of government, all of which she underpins with biblical examples and citations. She begins with the most important articles of the Lutheran faith, exhorting Erich to personal piety and the upholding and enforcement of the Ten Commandments as the only good works leading to salvation. She attempts to bind him to the precepts of the Lutheran catechism and her own published church ordinance of 1542. She instructs him on baptism, communion, and prayer, and warns of the dangers which stem from religious radicalism and the Anabaptists, a movement he must suppress at all costs.

In a section entitled "What pious princely works pleasing to God consist in," Elisabeth sets out ten precepts for Erich, the first of which is: "Consider God as great and majestic and yourself as a nothing." She commands him "to bring comfort to, protect, nurture, and defend widows and orphans," be a patron of the clergy, build up the school system, and ensure that the Ten Commandments and the catechism "are taught diligently to the young."[3] The sick and the poor should be his particular concern and he should punish vice severely and administer justice equitably.

Elisabeth's instructions on his marriage express the contemporary view of the requirements of a good consort, above all her exemplary piety. Erich is warned that he must take a wife in order to avoid sinful relationships, and also that adultery will be punished with eternal damnation. On the other hand, Elisabeth warns of the dangers of excessive love in marriage, which can lead a ruler to neglect God's will or set his wife up as an idol. In all matters, the wise Christian prince should seek the middle path: "And when God gives you a pious wife, do not despise her, but honor her as is her due; for an honest and virtuous wife brings honor to her husband's household. Rule over her with love and reason and don't be bitter towards her, but cherish her as your own body; ..."[4]

Elisabeth's instructions on the running of the territory go into the greatest detail. She addresses the administration of monasteries, hospitals, courts, and the minting of coins. She advises her son on ways of finding good counsel, the necessity for care in forming alliances, and exerting moderation in taxation. She goes through the entire office structure of the court, giving advice on appointing good staff and implementing control mechanisms, from the councilors' meetings to the stables and kitchens.

Elisabeth's instructions to Erich did not fall on fruitful ground. He converted to Catholicism, tried to rid himself of his wife Sidonie of Saxony, and became a mercenary leader who spent most of his life abroad, neglecting his territories in northern Germany. Elisabeth herself died after years of impoverishment and resistance to Erich's efforts to return the territory to Catholicism.

Notes

1 The original manuscript was kept in the library at Königsberg, but was lost during the Second World War. The Herzog August Bibliothek in Wolfenbüttel has a certified transcription dating from 1823. The text was edited by Paul Tschackert, *Herzogin Elisabeth von Münden: Die erste Schriftstellerin aus dem Hause Brandenburg und aus dem braunschweigischen Hause, ihr Lebensgang und ihre Werke*, Berlin: Giesecke und Devrient, 1899, pp. 22–44, here p. 22. Translated by Jill Bepler.
2 Ibid., p. 23.
3 Ibid., p. 27.
4 Ibid., p. 28.

37 Old age outside the bosom of the family: Elizabeth Freke of Norfolk (d. 1714)

by Lynn A. Botelho

One of the most enduring stories about the past is that families were always close-knit and loving, and that it was typical for three generations – grandparents, parents, and children – to happily and harmoniously co-exist around a single family fire. Then, like now, this was not always the case. *The Remembrances of Elizabeth Freke, 1671–1714*,[1] is an account of one old gentlewoman, a mother and grandmother, who was usually neglected by her husband, son, and grandson. As a result, she grew increasingly frustrated and bitter. After having nursed her husband through a long illness before his death in 1706, she lived out her final years in ill health and at the hands of thieving servants. Elizabeth's family relations were a far cry from that warm and loving fireplace scene of our imaginations. Instead, her old age was mostly spent physically separated from her immediate family. Elizabeth's account records what life could be like for the elderly who struggled with difficult familial relationships and who therefore had to live outside of the bosom of the family.

Elizabeth's marriage to her husband, Percy Freke, had broken down, so they lived apart for years on end. In addition, she started to be in poor health by her 60s, and both her husband and her son ignored Elizabeth during the best of times and even when she was ill. When Elizabeth was sixty-one, she suffered an illness that confined her to her bedroom for more than two months: "In all which time neither my husband or son have binn soe kind to lett me heer a word from either of them, which has much aded to my greatt misery and sickness."[2]

Elizabeth's son would go years without visiting his mother. After a nearly seven-year absence, he snubbed his mother at church, so that Elizabeth concluded that he wanted her dead and his inheritance secured:

"And twas with the greatest of diffyculty and the help of fowre servants I compassed to my church and misery I sate ther (and nott lessened to see my son sett frowning on me ther for an howr for I know nott whatt) (except itt were his feare of my coming alive home againe). This his cruell usuage of me gave me a greatt trouble, ... And afftter diner ..., I asked him iff hee had nott latly received mercyes enough from God: first from his deliverance by the severall tempest by sea ..., and since thatt, his youngest son, John Redman, lay sick heer with me (and att my charge) allmost a month given over of the small pox; besids severall other mercyes received. His answer to me was I talked to him as iff he were butt eighteen years of age, ..."³

To her dismay, Elizabeth found that both her son and her grandson continued to ignore her, even when she was bedridden after her outing to the church:

"And since Sunday, which is now fowre days, my son hass gone by my chamber doore and never called on me to see how I did butt twice (and I soe very ill). My greatt and good God forgive hime and supportt unhappy mee, his wretched mother, ... The like was his eldest son Percy Freke dereicted to doe, who for above a week pased my chamber neer twenty times a day [and] never once call'd in to see mee, his grandmother."⁴

Away from the nuclear family, the elderly were forced to rely upon their own resources or to call upon the charity of others. Being physically alone when in frail health was dangerous. Elizabeth knew she was vulnerable, writing: "I am confined to a chaire and helpless."⁵ In 1710, she narrowly escaped being killed by a house fire:

"Fryday nightt, November 3d, I were sitting in my chamber all alone reading, when on a suden my head caught on fire and in three minits time burntt all my head close close [sic] to my haire. And I being all alone could nott gett them off or any body to me thatt it was Gods greatt mercy I was nott burntt to death, ..."⁶

As a gentlewoman, Elizabeth was wealthy enough to be able to hire servants to do what her family would not, but she knew, too, that she was at her servants' mercy. When she feared she would die, she took what she regarded as the necessary precautions:

"I being very ill sentt for my cosin John Frek downe to me to settle my affaires and my will, ... and to remove five hundred pounds of mine which lay in the house by me of which I expected every day being robed by my servants and other rogues iff I should dye – which I dayly expected, I were soe ill."⁷

On another occasion, she found out "thatt my servantt John Preston was a rogue ... and thatt he had gott into my service under a falce cirtificate contrived with by my own maid Sarah Flowrs, who had lived with me above three years [and] was privy to itt and all this his theiffreys and rogeryes whilst with mee. ... I nott knowing the many severall things they had stole from me, haveing hardly gon cross my chamber for allmost two years and then with a hard shifft⁸ to see my house allmost gutted by this rogue and whore [her servant Sarah]."⁹

Another maid, whom she had cared for during a bout of smallpox, with "as much care ... as of a neere relation," proved equally unsteady; when she recovered, "after neer all my care and charge, ... she run away."¹⁰ Sadly for Elizabeth, neither kin or hired help provided her with steady care and comfort during her later years.

Because this handwritten book was written about Elizabeth by Elizabeth, we never learn how her tale ended. Did Elizabeth continue to worry about theft and runaways? Or did her son return to her during her dying days? We do not know. This remembrance draws our attention to the complexity of family life in the early modern past: Husbands might not have loved their wives, children their parents, and grandchildren their grandparents. Families could be every bit as fractured as some are today, and the elderly did not always receive the respect ordered by the Ten Commandments: 'honor thy father and thy mother.' What also emerges from Elizabeth's account of her old age is the vulnerability and emotional strain that can accompany living alone and feeling helpless. In many ways, the life of Elizabeth Freke illustrates the many continuities between our world and the past.

Notes

1 Raymond A. Anselment (ed.), *The Remembrances of Elizabeth Freke, 1671–1714*, Camden Fifth Series, 53 vols, Cambridge: Cambridge University Press, 1993–2017, vol. 18.
2 Ibid., p. 76.
3 Ibid., pp. 197–198.
4 Ibid., p. 198.
5 Ibid., p. 99.
6 Ibid., p. 156.
7 Ibid., p. 157.
8 Great effort.
9 Anselment (ed.), *Remembrances of Elizabeth Freke*, p. 159.
10 Ibid., p. 194.

IV

Expressions of faith: Official and popular religion

Introduction

by Ute Lotz-Heumann

This chapter explores the wide variety of religious expressions and rituals – from official to popular – in early modern Europe and the various ways in which they often overlapped and sometimes clashed. The essays in this chapter make it very clear that 'religion' could mean many things to different people and groups in early modern society, ranging from theological teachings to ideas about death, magic, the universe, and witchcraft.

The essays by Scott H. Hendrix, Günter Vogler, Nicole Kuropka, Bernard Roussel, and Michael S. Springer explore different aspects of the thinking and teachings of major reformers. The history of the Ninety-Five Theses makes it clear that Martin Luther did not want to start a new church. But his vocal criticism of indulgences, indulgence preachers, and the curia – combined with the spread of his theses in print – led to events beyond his control (essay by Scott H. Hendrix).[1] The reformer Thomas Müntzer initiated a more radical movement. He advocated for a complete renewal of the church and the world, including detachment from material possessions and worldly power (essay by Günter Vogler). The reformers, among them Philip Melanchthon, Luther's colleague in Wittenberg, and John Calvin, the reformer of Geneva, shared a strong belief in the principle of 'Scripture alone,' of the Bible as the sole basis of Protestant theology. The humanist Melanchthon used the rules of ancient rhetoric and historical knowledge to interpret the Bible (essay by Nicole Kuropka).[2] John Calvin studied the biblical text equally carefully in his commentaries, emphasizing his role as servant of the truth contained in the Scriptures (essay by Bernard Roussel). John a Lasco closely followed the New Testament and practices of the early church when advocating for the election of ministers by the laity (essay by Michael S. Springer).

The essays by Helmut Puff, Cornelia Niekus Moore, and Kathryn A. Edwards address early modern people's understanding of the meaning and rituals associated with death and the deceased. The famous German Renaissance artist Albrecht Dürer carefully documented his mother's sickness and death in 1513–1514, including drawing her portrait. While Dürer described the medieval Catholic rituals surrounding his mother's death, his own death as a Protestant in 1528 was probably very different (essay by Helmut Puff). The law student Christian Röhrscheidt's death was accompanied by one of the new rituals of the Lutheran Reformation, the funeral sermon, which was often also published as a 'funeral book' (essay by Cornelia Niekus Moore). The ghost of Wenceslaus Haimblichen that appeared to a group of priests and laypeople in Bohemia in 1503, although rooted in both time and place through his references to purgatory and fifteenth-century Bohemian sects, is also an example of late medieval and early modern popular religiosity (essay by Kathryn A. Edwards).

The essays by Ute Lotz-Heumann, Craig Harline, and David Graizbord explore further aspects of lay cultural and religious practices as well as the way these practices sometimes aligned and sometimes clashed with official church doctrine, be it Protestant or Catholic. Lutheran miracle wells, like the one in Hornhausen in northern Germany in 1646, were sixteenth- and seventeenth-century phenomena which fulfilled a popular need for cures in a world full of disease. But these wells were also enthusiastically embraced by Lutheran clergy (essay by Ute Lotz-Heumann). The experience of Maria Caroens reflects how early modern Catholic worshippers sought help and miracles from praying to saints, and how the ecclesiastical authorities sought to control these popular miracles (essay by Craig Harline). The case of María de Sierra, a New Christian accused of performing Jewish rituals, shows the overlaps and interactions between popular and official religious cultures in early modern Spain. Prosecuted by the Inquisition as a result of accusations by her neighbors, María personifies the dilemma *conversos* often found themselves in (essay by David Graizbord).[3]

The essays by Andrew Fix, Charles Zika, and Thomas B. de Mayo explore different aspects of early modern beliefs in portents, witchcraft, and magic. The three cases examined here – comets as portents of God's punishment in the form of future disasters (essay by Andrew Fix),[4] witchcraft images that were created by seventeenth-century defenders of the belief in witchcraft (essay by Charles Zika), and the legend of an eighteenth-century clerical magician (essay by Thomas B. de Mayo) – focus on early modern elites and their understanding of, or relationship to, the supernatural. But these beliefs penetrated deeply into early modern societies.

Notes

1 See below, note 2.
2 Other essays besides Hendrix's and Kuropka's addressing the actions and teachings of Luther and Melanchthon are no. 52, Schilling: Martin Luther defies Frederick the Wise: A letter from Borna, 1522; no. 53, Estes: Philip Melanchthon justifies magisterial reform, 1539; no. 54, Dingel: The courage to avow the truth: Philip Melanchthon on the Interim, 1548.

3 For another example of the activities of the Spanish Inquisition see no. 7, Poska: Spain, 1649: The Inquisition disciplines two Catholic priests who shot the baby Jesus. For Protestant institutions and procedures of religious and social discipline see no. 56, Christman: Mansfeld, 1554: Follow-up to an ecclesiastical visitation; no. 57, Blakeley: Reformation mandates for the Pays de Vaud, 1536: How Bernese authorities tried to force their subjects to become Protestants; no. 58, Bruening: Ministers and magistrates: The excommunication debate in Lausanne in 1558.

4 For another essay about early modern understandings of astronomical phenomena see no. 59, Haude: Who is in charge? Politics, religion, and astrology during the Thirty Years' War.

38 Reformation by accident? Martin Luther's Ninety-Five Theses of 1517

by Scott H. Hendrix

Recalling in 1545 his twenty-eight-year career as a reformer, Martin Luther (1483–1546) wrote: "I got into these turmoils by accident and not by will or intention; I call upon God himself as witness."[1] Those "turmoils" were controversies with the pope and his theologians over the Ninety-Five Theses that he had composed for debate at the German university of Wittenberg in 1517.[2] According to tradition, on 31 October of that year Luther posted the theses on the front door of the castle church to catch the attention of a crowd that was expected the next day, the festival of All Saints. They were hoping to shorten their stay in purgatory by winning indulgences for viewing the large collection of relics amassed by Luther's ruler, Elector[3] Frederick of Saxony. Since the Ninety-Five Theses questioned both the power of indulgences and the authority of popes to grant them, it was easy to conclude that Luther knew full well he was arousing a controversy which could be taken as an attack on the Roman church. Countless images have pictured Luther as a rebellious monk nailing the Ninety-Five Theses to the church door in a public act of defiance that ignited a 'Protestant' Reformation.

That assumption was still popular in 1961 when the Catholic church historian, Erwin Iserloh, called attention to the fact that Luther never mentioned a posting of the theses. Nor do we have evidence that a debate ever took place. Luther did mail a copy of the theses to his ecclesiastical superior, Archbishop Albert of Mainz, who forwarded them to Rome. But the posting was reported after Luther's death by Philip Melanchthon, his younger colleague, who arrived in Wittenberg one year after the alleged event. In 2006 another indirect piece of evidence for a posting was discovered. A jotting made by Luther's close coworker, Georg Rörer (1492–1557), shortly before the reformer died reported that the theses had been affixed to the doors "of the churches" in Wittenberg on the eve of All Saints' Day 1517. Does it matter, however, whether the theses were nailed or mailed? What does either mode of transmission say about the accidental character of the Reformation?

On the one hand, the answer is: very little. First, it was Luther's duty as a university professor to prepare theses for his students to debate. A different set with ninety-eight theses, also by Luther, had just been debated at the university the previous month. Second, written in Latin, the theses could have been understood by very few people who came through the church doors. Normally, a posting of theses was the announcement of a debate intended only for scholars and students who could read and understand them. Third, much of their content was theologically above the head of ordinary folk. Luther could scarcely have intended to stir up resentment against the church among the populace at large. Finally, Luther's main target was not the Roman church or the pope's office but the claims being made by indulgence preachers who were authorized by Albert. Then, as later, Luther never thought he was starting a new church.

On the other hand, Luther minced no words. Indulgence letters were advertised as guarantees that the guilt of sin would be forgiven once and for all before death and that after death they could 'spring the soul' from purgatory. According to church law, however, they could only indulge, that is, set aside the penalties (penance) imposed after sins were confessed to a priest. The guilt of sin was forgiven only by God; not even the pope could forgive that guilt – for souls on earth or in purgatory. "It is vain," wrote Luther, "to trust in salvation by indulgence letters even though the indulgence commissary, or even the pope, were to offer his soul as security" [thesis 52].[4] Luther also knew that income from the sale of this indulgence was allocated for the new St. Peter's basilica in Rome. Therefore he asked:

"Why does not the pope, whose wealth is today greater than the wealth of the richest Crassus,[5] build this one basilica of St. Peter with his own money rather than with the money of poor believers?" [thesis 86].[6] – "Christians are to be taught," he declared, "that he who gives to the poor or lends to the needy does a better deed than he who buys indulgences" [thesis 43]. – "Christians are to be taught that he who sees a needy man and passes him by, yet gives his money for indulgences, does not buy papal indulgences but God's wrath" [thesis 45].[7]

Nor did he spare the indulgence preachers. Blessed are those, he said, who guarded against the lust and license of the preachers, especially when they claimed that papal indulgences would forgive the raping of the mother of God, or that St. Peter could not grant greater graces if he were alive, or that the processional cross erected beside an indulgence preacher was equal to the cross of Christ:

"Let him who speaks against the truth concerning papal indulgences be anathema and cursed. [thesis 71] – But let him who guards against the lust and license of the indulgence preachers be blessed. [thesis 72] – To consider papal indulgences so great that they could absolve a man even if he had done the impossible and had violated the mother of God is madness. [thesis 75] – To say that even St. Peter, if he were now pope, could not grant greater graces is blasphemy against St. Peter and the pope. [thesis 77] – To say that the cross emblazoned with the papal coat of arms, and set up by the indulgence preachers, is equal in worth to the cross of Christ is blasphemy. [thesis 79]."[8]

In effect, indulgences were superfluous: "Any truly repentant Christian," he wrote, "has a right to full remission of penalty and guilt, even without indulgence letters" [thesis 36]. – "Any true Christian, whether living or dead, participates in all the blessings of Christ and the church; and this is granted him by God, even without indulgence letters" [thesis 37].[9]

Luther's biting comments about financial chicanery in the curia and excessive claims for the potency of papal indulgences provoked the "turmoils" he did not expect. The issue of papal authority soon pushed indulgences into the background, and a case opened against Luther in 1518 concluded with his excommunication on 3 January 1521. Seen in that light, the Ninety-Five Theses did ignite the Protestant Reformation, and it was not entirely accidental on Luther's part. By mailing them to Archbishop Albert, Luther made the theses more politically provocative than if they had circulated only around Wittenberg. Moreover, the Latin theses were soon translated into German, and printed copies reached the hands of savvy people who immediately saw their political import. Luther probably spoke honestly when he maintained in 1532: "God knows, I never thought of going as far as I did. I intended only to attack indulgences. If anybody had said to me when I was at the Diet of Worms,[10] 'In a few years you'll have a wife and your own household,' I wouldn't have believed it."[11] Once, however, the theses reached Rome and a literate German public, their impact was out of Luther's hands.

Notes

1. "Preface to the Complete Edition of Luther's Latin Writings, 1545," in Lewis W. Spitz and Helmut T. Lehman (ed.), *Luther's Works (American Edition)*, vol. 34: *Career of the Reformer IV*, Philadelphia: Muhlenberg Press, 1960, p. 328.
2. Martin Luther, "Ninety-Five Theses or Disputation on the Power and Efficacy of Indulgences, 1517," in Harold J. Grimm and Helmut T. Lehmann (eds), *Luther's Works (American Edition)*, vol. 31: *Career of the Reformer I*, Philadelphia: Muhlenberg Press, 1957, pp. 17–33.
3. In early modern Germany, the electors were the princes who elected the emperor.
4. Ibid., p. 30.
5. Marcus Licinius Crassus (115–53 BC), Roman general and politician, whose wealth was legendary, both in his own and later times.
6. Luther, "Ninety-Five Theses," p. 33.
7. Ibid., p. 29.
8. Ibid., pp. 31–32.
9. Ibid., pp. 28–29.
10. At the imperial Diet of Worms in 1521, Luther had refused to recant his teachings.
11. Martin Luther, "Table Talk, Between June 12 and July 12, 1532," in Theodore G. Tappert and Helmut T. Lehman (eds), *Luther's Works (American Edition)*, vol. 54: *Table Talk* (Philadelphia: Fortress Press, 1967), p. 160, no. 1654.

39 Thomas Müntzer: A radical alternative[1]

by Günter Vogler

At first glance, the Protestant Reformation was a movement initiated and fostered by Martin Luther and his supporters with the aim of renewing church and society. So powerful was this view that for a long time alternatives to Luther's understanding of the Reformation, and the people who formulated and defended them, were not adequately explored by historians. Recently, however, scholars have become more aware of the fluidity of the early Reformation period, and so potential alternatives to Luther's Reformation have received more attention. Thomas Müntzer (1489–1525) is among those historical figures who are of particular interest in this context. Müntzer was born in Stolberg, Saxony. He studied in Leipzig and Frankfurt on the Oder and was actively involved in school and church ministries. In May 1520, Müntzer assumed his first position as a preacher in the city of Zwickau, Saxony. However, after fierce quarrels with clergy who adhered to the old faith, he was forced to leave the city. Müntzer went to Prague in Bohemia, convinced that in the territory of Jan Hus the 'new apostolic church' would come into being and spread. In Prague, Müntzer finished his first work, which explicated his developing theological ideas. Soon, however, new conflicts arose, and once again he was forced to leave.

Müntzer conceptualized this first work as an "open letter" (the widespread belief that it was to be a 'public notice' or a 'manifest' cannot be traced to the author himself). The first draft of 1 November 1525 does not have a title, but Müntzer gave the title "A protestation concerning the case of the Bohemians" to an expanded version (dated 25 November). In addition to the German text, translations into Latin and Czech are extant. Even though Müntzer did not succeed in publishing the document, it attests to the author's intention to make public his own understanding of the Reformation; in this first work Müntzer speaks of God and the world in a manner previously unheard of. In his first draft, Müntzer argued:

"I, Thomas Müntzer of Stolberg, do declare before the whole church and the whole world – wherever this letter may be shown – that I can testify with Christ and all the elect who have known me from my youth up, to having shown all possible diligence, more than any other man known to me, in pursuing better instruction about the holy and invincible Christian faith. For at no time in my life (God knows I am not lying) did I learn anything about the true exercise of the faith from any monk or priest, or about the edifying time of trial which clarifies faith in the spirit of the fear of God, showing the need for an elect man to have the seven-fold gift of the holy spirit. I have not heard from a single scholar about the order of God implanted in all creatures, not the tiniest word about it; while as to understanding the whole as a unity of all the parts those who claim to be Christians have not caught the least whiff of it – least of all the accursed priests. I have heard from them about mere Scripture, which they have stolen from the Bible like murderers and thieves; in chapter 23 Jeremiah describes this theft as stealing the word of God from the mouth of your neighbour; for they themselves have never heard it from God, from his very mouth. In my opinion these really are fine preachers, consecrated for just this purpose by the devil. But St Paul writes to the Corinthians, in the third chapter of the second epistle, that the hearts of men are the paper or parchment on which God's finger inscribes his unchangeable will and his eternal wisdom, but not with ink; a writing which any man can read, providing his mind has been opened to it; as Jeremiah and Ezekiel say, this is where God writes his laws, on the third day, that of the sprinkling: when man's mind is opened up. God has done this for his elect from the very beginning, so that the testimony they are given is not uncertain, but an invincible one from the holy spirit, which then gives our spirit ample testimony that we are the children of God. For anyone who does not feel the spirit of Christ within him, or is not quite sure of having it, is not a member of Christ, but of the devil, Romans 8."[2]

When Müntzer was thinking about the way in which true Christian faith was to be attained, he did so with the whole church and the whole world in mind – and for Müntzer both church and world were in need of a radical renewal. His criticism of monks and priests was rooted in the conviction that they denied faithful Christians access to the Gospel; God, however, revealed his will not only in the past through the biblical texts, but also in the present by writing on "the hearts of men." In order to live and act according to God's will, steadfast faith is necessary, and this, according to Müntzer, could only be attained by those who were willing to follow the 'bitter Christ' and to suffer temptations. This is the main theme of Müntzer's later writings.

Müntzer's programmatic call to restore "the order of God implanted in all creatures" resulted from the conviction that God revealed his plans for mankind and the world to the faithful. In this first "open letter," Müntzer did not yet explain what "the order of God" comprised, but he soon after reached the conclusion that its restoration demanded above all that people detach themselves from all material possessions and worldly powers. For Müntzer, this detachment was the prerequisite for bringing about a radical and universal Reformation. It was necessary to overcome social differences so that justice would prevail through Christian charity. This would only be possible, however, once the political balance of power had also been changed.

For Müntzer, God's "elect" were the enforcers of the divine will. He did not restrict himself to a specific social class, but rather made his call to all people, including the nobles and the Saxon princes – if they were ready to follow God's Word. It was not until after the latter disappointed him that Müntzer desired to gather the "elect" into a covenant in order to remove from power the godless and tyrannical lords and princes. It was for this reason that he turned to the prophecy of Daniel and argued that God was able to confer all power on the 'common folk.' Müntzer perceived that the 'time for the harvest' had come, and he was convinced that God had appointed him as the reaper.

This was the first document in which Müntzer outlined the manner in which he intended to radically renew church and society. Even though Müntzer's hopes were not fulfilled in Bohemia and his "open letter" did not reach the public, this first work already contained his key ideas which prove his theological independence and which he developed into a full doctrine in his later writings.

Notes

1 Translated by Benjamin A. Miller and Rebecca Mueller Jones.
2 Peter Matheson (ed. and tr.), *The Collected Works of Thomas Müntzer*, Edinburgh: T&T Clark, 1988, pp. 357–361, here pp. 357–358.

40 Holy Scripture alone: Philip Melanchthon and academic theology[1]

by Nicole Kuropka

Martin Luther not only repudiated the pope and the councils, but also suggested a return to the Holy Scriptures alone. Luther argued that the Bible, and not the words or statutes of men, should be the foundation of theology and church life (*sola scriptura*). In line with this effort, Luther encouraged and supported a younger colleague, Philip Melanchthon (1497–1560), who was appointed to the newly created professorship of Greek at the University of Wittenberg in 1518. Unlike Luther, Melanchthon had received a humanistic education, and one of the defining characteristics of humanism was a new understanding of language. Humanism above all emphasized the correct use of terms and logical argumentation (dialectic), as well as the development of a line of reasoning through elegant language, form, and structure (rhetoric). During the Middle Ages, the discipline of dialectic had developed into a labyrinth of pedantic rules of linguistic logic. In new primers of dialectic and rhetoric, humanists such as Rudolph Agricola and Desiderius Erasmus argued for an understanding of language which focused on its practical application in the social life of the community.

Melanchthon was committed to this understanding of language and brought competence and drive to bear on the reading and analysis of the Bible in the Wittenberg movement. Thus, Melanchthon contributed not only his knowledge of original biblical languages (Hebrew and Greek) to the Reformation, but he also applied his humanistic understanding of language to the Lutheran theology of *sola scriptura*. Through the reading and analysis of the Bible in its original languages, Melanchthon deployed the new understanding of dialectic and rhetoric as the key to understanding the biblical texts. He emphasized the linguistic transmission of the Word of God to man and argued that man must internalize the rules of language so as to correctly understand the Bible. For Melanchthon, it was neither sufficient to, as was common in the Middle Ages, search after the four levels of meaning nor to pick apart the Bible in single sentences. As he wrote in his *Elements of Rhetoric* (1531):

"Many theologians have foolishly asserted that the Bible has four meanings: a literal, a tropological, an allegorical, and an anagogical.

Without exception they have construed every verse in all of the Scriptures in this four-fold manner. It is now easy to understand how wrong this is, for when language is plucked apart into so many levels of meaning it becomes insecure. These men have contrived and invented this nonsense. They have no scholarly education and, although they see that the Holy Scriptures are full of rhetorical figures, because they have no understanding of language they cannot assess these rhetorical figures appropriately. ...

"We, however, should remember, that one must always search the rules of grammar, dialectic, and rhetoric for a single, firm, and simple meaning. For a sentence that does not have a single and simple meaning teaches us nothing with certainty. If any figures of speech occur, these should not produce multiple levels of meaning, but rather a single understanding according to linguistic usage, and this meaning should be compatible with the rest of the passage. It is for this purpose that elementary training in rhetorical figures of speech and in the entire method of language has been developed. With this training, one learns to evaluate an expression and to extract a single and firm meaning from any sentence. Thus one must likewise ensure that the interpretation of the Holy Scriptures conforms to language use. As a result, we will be informed with certainty about the facts which are described therein."[2]

For Melanchthon, the Bible was clear and its sense could be unlocked. He stressed that the biblical texts should be understood as a single unit and that they should always be interpreted according to linguistic rules. In this way, Melanchthon wanted to ensure a scholarly interpretation that rested on the literal sense of the text and so to support theoretically a theology founded on Scripture alone. This is impressively displayed in his dialectical–rhetorical exegesis of the Apostle Paul's Letter to the Romans. Melachthon interpreted this text for the Lutheran Reformation using the rules of ancient rhetoric and thus provided the scholarly evidence that the doctrine of justification by faith represented the central notion of the Letter to the Romans. However, Melanchthon was not only interested in a methodologically sound interpretation from the perspective of linguistic theory. He also aspired to historical precision and was thus eager to accurately pinpoint the geographic places in the Scriptures as well as to verify the historical narratives of the Bible by making use of the historical knowledge of his day.

Although Melanchthon never held a professorship in Bible studies within the university, for forty years he interpreted the central biblical texts for his students. Martin Luther reported that as early as the first years of Melanchthon's tenure 500 listeners attended his lectures. Beyond the borders of the auditorium, his commentaries were printed and read throughout Europe. Many reformers – John Calvin and Heinrich Bullinger among others – are known to have studied Melachthon's commentaries intensively. Melanchthon's broad impact in word and print can therefore not easily be overestimated.

Notes

1 Translated by Sean E. Clark and Benjamin A. Miller.
2 Philipp Melanchthon, *Elementa rhetorices: Grundbegriffe der Rhetorik*, ed. Volkhard Wels, Berlin: Weidler, 2001, pp. 193–195, 197–199.

41 Interpreting the Bible in the sixteenth century: John Calvin on the Gospels of Luke and Matthew

by Bernard Roussel

John Calvin (1509–1564) wrote commentaries on all biblical books but one, Revelation. Before being published in 1555, his *Commentary on a Harmony of the Evangelists* (i.e., on the Books Matthew, Mark, and Luke) matured as lectures to the weekly congregations of the Genevan ministers. They were published in Latin and French almost simultaneously in order to avoid discriminating between an educated audience and the common people.

The commentaries are annotations inserted in the course of an 'interrupted reading' of the biblical text. Calvin wanted them to be brief, simple, and edifying. He aims for brevity when he criticizes or quotes swiftly other authors without naming them (e.g., Erasmus of Rotterdam and Martin Bucer of Strasburg). Calvin strives to keep the topics simple by not focusing on the historical and literary discrepancies between Matthew and Luke – under the guidance of the Holy Spirit, they are said to bear witness, each in his own way, to Jesus's doctrine that Calvin, as an exegete, brings to light. Finally, Calvin seeks to be edifying: He abandons a didactic style and instead often expresses an opinion by using the pronoun "I," which both affirms personal authority and appeals to the judgment of the listeners. Furthermore, through occasional use of "we" he suggests that, through the mediation of the text, both he and the faithful of Geneva benefit from Jesus's words as did the disciples of old.

This brief fragment shows why Calvin's commentaries, written in a clear and persuasive style, were well-received in Reformation Europe and why Calvin's intellectual competence and religious authority were respected among the Genevan people and among many contemporary readers in other countries.

"MATTHEW.

"V.1. And when Jesus had seen the multitudes, he went up into a mountain, and when he had sat down, his disciples approached to him. 2. And opening his mouth, he taught them, saying, 3. Happy are the poor in spirit: for theirs is the kingdom of heaven. ...

"LUKE.

"VI. 20. And he, lifting up his eyes on the disciples, said, Happy (are ye) poor: for yours is the kingdom of God. ...

"Matthew V.1. *He went up into a mountain.* Those who think that Christ's sermon, which is here related, is different from the sermon contained in the sixth chapter of Luke's Gospel, rest their opinion on a very light and frivolous argument. Matthew states, that Christ spoke to his disciples on a mountain, while Luke seems to say, that the discourse was delivered on a plain. ... For the design of both Evangelists was, to collect into one place the leading points of the doctrine of Christ, which related to a devout and holy life. ... Pious and modest readers ought to be satisfied with having a brief summary of the doctrine of Christ placed before their eyes, collected out of his many and various discourses, the first of which was that in which he spoke to his disciples about true happiness.

"2. *Opening his mouth.* This redundancy of expression (pleonasm) partakes of the Hebrew idiom: for what would be faulty in other languages is frequent among the Hebrews, to say, *He opened his mouth,* instead of, *He began to speak.* Many look upon it as an emphatic mode of expression, employed to draw attention to any thing important and remarkable, either in a good or bad sense, which has been uttered: ... I shall ... dismiss the ingenious speculation of those, who give an allegorical turn to the fact of our Lord teaching his disciples on a mountain, as if it had been intended to teach them to elevate their minds far above worldly cares and employments. ...

"Now let us see, in the first place, why Christ spoke to his disciples about *true happiness.* We know that not only the great body of the people, but even the learned themselves, hold this error, that he is the happy man who is free from annoyance, attains all his wishes, and leads a joyful and easy life. ... Christ, therefore, in order to accustom his own people to bear the cross, exposes this mistaken opinion, that those are happy who lead an easy and prosperous life according to the flesh. For it is impossible that men should mildly bend the neck to bear calamities and reproaches, so long as they think that patience is at variance with a happy life. The only consolation which mitigates and even sweetens the bitterness of the cross and of all afflictions, is the conviction, that we are happy in the midst of miseries: for our patience is *blessed* by the Lord, and will soon be followed by a happy result.

"This doctrine, I do acknowledge, is widely removed from the common opinion: but the disciples of Christ must learn the philosophy of placing their happiness beyond the world, and above the affections of the flesh. ...

"3. *Happy are the poor in spirit.* ... [on Matthew:] Christ pronounces those to be happy who, chastened and subdued by afflictions, submit themselves wholly to God, and, with inward humility, betake themselves to him for protection. ...

"*For theirs is the kingdom of heaven.* We see that Christ ... leads [the minds of his own people] to entertain the hope of eternal life, and animates them to patience by assuring them, that in this way they will pass into the heavenly kingdom of God."[1]

Calvin, like other commentators of the sixteenth century, represents himself less as a creative author than as a servant of the truth embedded in the biblical text he studies so carefully. He identifies the figures of speech (here a 'pleonasm') and rejects any allegorization – such as that which could be reached by playing on the words "on the mountain" (i.e., a solemn discourse for a few people) vs. "in the plain" (i.e., a discourse for the common people). Because of the introductory word "happy" (Mt 5:3), Calvin focuses on a Christian paradox: Happy are those who carry their own cross for Jesus's sake (i.e., who 'follow' Jesus's path under the conditions of their own lives) and who meditate about the eternal life to come.

Overall, this excerpt from Calvin's *Commentary on a Harmony of the Evangelists* shows his purpose when interpreting a biblical text: he avoids illuminism[2] by referring to the pages of the Bible and fundamentalism through a methodical exegesis; guarding against Catholic criticism, he places in the forefront the textual source of Christian traditions and theology; he distinguishes himself from the humanists while borrowing elements of their way of studying the ancient literature.

Notes

1 *Commentary on a Harmony of the Evangelists, Matthew, Mark and Luke, by John Calvin*, ed. and tr. William Pringle, Edinburgh: Calvin Translation Society, 1845, pp. 257–261.
2 A belief that one has attained direct enlightenment by God.

42 How to organize a church: John a Lasco on the election of ministers, 1555

by Michael S. Springer

The sixteenth-century Reformation transformed the clerical estate, replacing Catholic priests and their sacramental function with evangelical ministers who focused on preaching God's Word. Protestants introduced new methods for choosing their clerics, too. The Polish-born reformer John (Johannes) a Lasco (1499–1560) addressed the different historical approaches to elections in the *Form and Manner of the Ecclesiastical Ministry*, a church ordinance he published in 1555. The text described the rites and practices for the London Strangers' Church, a community of Dutch and French exiles living in England's capital:

"We see that the manner for electing ministers in congregations was observed differently, not only in antiquity but also in the present church, according to each congregation's needs and what the circumstances appeared to require.[1] In the past, in the ancient church that followed the apostles, ministers were chosen by the votes of all the people according to the example the disciples had established when electing deacons. Later Cyprian[2] taught that this custom was observed in his own time but that piety began to diminish everywhere and people in the church fell into disagreement, quarreling with each other. The whole matter of elections appeared to be thrown into great discord and enmity, and everything seemed to be motivated by private emotions. Finally, the entire authority to choose ministers in the church was handed over to the magistracy (the guardian of public tranquility charged with maintaining political order in the church), who followed, without doubt, the example of the ancient church under Moses, in which the magistracy had ordained all of the highest ministers in the temple. More recently it came to pass, through the foreign tyranny of the pope in Rome, who is clearly the Antichrist, that he (I don't know which one) claimed that power for himself over all churches in the entire world, by right or by wrong … The authority over elections, having been restricted therefore, had passed from the people to the magistracy and, finally, to the pope himself and his accomplices. We see that the pure and legitimate ministry of all churches was nearly destroyed, which now, presently, by the singular grace of God, we witness it being turned back and restored in many locations day by day."[3]

A Lasco went on to describe the procedure for electing clergy used by his London congregation, which he modeled on the apostolic practice. He wrote that one week before choosing a new superintendent,[4] preacher, elder, or deacon, church leaders should give a sermon about the vacant post and its duties. They then instructed lay members to vote by submitting the names of suitable candidates. A Lasco warned current ministers to consider who had received the most nominations from the people. Once completed, the clergy announced the newly elected person's name and the congregation had seven days to register any objections. If the laity made no complaints, the ministers ordained the new man in his position. The Polish-born reformer thought this procedure most closely followed the original practice.

Although Protestants stressed the Bible as an authoritative source and the important model the apostolic church provided, they instituted different policies for appointing ministers. In Martin Luther's town of Wittenberg, for example, representatives from the university, city council, and congregation chose new ministers. Jean Calvin introduced a different approach in Geneva, where clerics, acting on behalf of the community, nominated and elected preachers, elders, and deacons. The congregation and magistrates then gave their approval to the newly chosen person. A Lasco, in contrast, argued for a policy that returned to the early church and emphasized a greater role for the laity in selecting clerics.

The excerpt from the *Form and Manner of Ecclesiastical Ministry* demonstrates how the Polish-born reformer read and understood Scripture, as well as his thoughts on historical practices in the church. The London superintendent argued that his plan closely followed the New Testament where, in Acts 6, the disciples had chosen seven men to assist them. He added that in the years following the apostles, the people voted for new ministers. Other reformers emphasized later historical practices for choosing ministers in the church. Calvin, for example, conceded that the laity had selected new ministers in the early church, but that disagreements during the third century led ecclesiastical leaders to restrict the people's role. The reformer from Geneva agreed with this limited participation, explaining that people make poor choices, and he established clerical elections in which ministers and magistrates chose new clerics. The two theologians differed on which historical model to follow: A Lasco advocated for a return to the apostolic procedure for elections, while Calvin pushed for the practice developed in the third century.

A Lasco's comments in the ordinance shows the difficult task Protestants faced in reforming ecclesiastical practice. Although they agreed on the need for change and the Bible's authority on doctrinal matters, they struggled to find consensus concerning rites and ceremonies. Different interpretations of the Scriptures and church history made it increasingly difficult to reach consensus and led to a variety of practices among Protestant communities.

Notes

1 "Acts 6:14" is printed in the margin, referring to a verse from this book in the Bible explaining the growth and development of the church. This particular passage speaks of the changing laws introduced by Christ: "For we have heard him say this Jesus of Nazareth will destroy this place and alter the customs handed down to us by Moses" (*The Revised English Bible with the Apocrypha*, Oxford, Cambridge: Oxford University Press, Cambridge University Press, 1989, Acts, p. 108).
2 Cyprian of Carthage (d. 258).
3 Johannes a Lasco, *Forma ac ratio tota ecclessiastici Ministerii, in peregrinorum, potissimum vero Germanorum Ecclesia: institute Londini in Anglia, per Pientissimum principem Angliae &c. Regem Eduardum, eius nominis Sextu[m]: Anno post Christum natum 1550. Addito ad calcem libelli Privilegio suae majestatis*, Frankfurt, 1555, fols D8v–E1v. Translated by Michael Springer.
4 A superintendent was a high-level official in certain Protestant churches in early modern Europe; he occupied the same level as a bishop.

43 What is a good death? Barbara Dürer, 1514

by Helmut Puff

Death and dying were of vital concern in the late Middle Ages and the early modern period. How one died, it was said, reflected one's life and foreshadowed one's afterlife. Since every human was believed to be irredeemably sinful, dying was the source of great spiritual anxiety and the dying were thought to be in need of support. A good death, therefore, was a death in the company of others, of family members, neighbors, servants, and friends. They were called upon to tend to the dying at the same time as their presence at another person's deathbed prepared them for their own hour of death. By contrast to the much-feared sudden departure from life, a well-ordered death involved a cleric who would administer the sacraments to the dying. In other words, death and dying were governed by familiar rituals. The theologian Jean Gerson called the art of dying "the art of all arts," a lifelong preparation for the defining hour of one's life.

Barbara Dürer was the mother of the German Renaissance artist Albrecht (1471–1528). Whereas her husband and Dürer's father, Albrecht the Elder (d. 1502), had been a goldsmith, her son, Albrecht the Younger, became one of the most recognized artists of sixteenth-century Europe, thanks, above all, to his brilliant use of prints. His talents allowed him to rise socially in Nuremberg, his native city – a place that prided itself in mercantile daring and technological innovation; but the city was also a hotbed of civic humanism and a religious center. Albrecht Dürer wrote a detailed account of his mother's sickness and death in 1513–1514:

"... in the year 1513, on a Tuesday before Rogation week,[1] my poor and pitiable mother – I had taken her in two years after my father's death – ... all of a sudden fell deadly sick. ... My pious mother gave birth to and raised eighteen children. She often had the plague as well as many other grave illnesses. She also suffered great poverty, mockery, contempt, insults, frights, and great adversities; yet she was never vindictive. Over a year after the day she fell sick, on May 17, 1514, a Tuesday, two hours before midnight, my pious mother, Barbara Dürer, passed away in a Christian manner, with all the sacraments and absolved of her sins by the plenary power of the pope.[2] She blessed me and wished me the peace of God with good instruction that

Figure 43.1 Albrecht Dürer, "Portrait of Barbara Dürer, née Holper, the Artist's Mother," charcoal drawing, 1514, Kupferstichkabinett, Staatliche Museen zu Berlin, inventory no. KdZ 22

I should avoid sins. She also asked for and received St. John's blessing.[3] She feared death greatly but she did not fear to come before God. She had a tough death. I noticed that she saw something fearful because she requested holy water after not having talked for a while. Then her eyes closed over. I saw how death dealt her two blows to the heart, how she closed mouth and eyes, and she departed from life in pain. I led her in prayers. I experienced such pain from this that I cannot express it. God have mercy with her. Her greatest joy was always to speak of God, and she liked to behold the honor of God. She was in her sixty-third year when she died. I buried her honorably and according to my means. May God grant me that I also have a blessed end and that God with his heavenly host, my father, mother, relatives, and friends will be there at my side. May God Almighty give us eternal life. Amen. And in her death she looked much more peaceful than when she was still alive."[4]

What is exceptional about this account is the fact that Dürer felt compelled to leave an extensive record about his mother's parting on a double-page leaf that contains notes on various subject matters and was part of a larger collection of memorabilia no longer extant. From the writings, scribbles, and additions, one can tell that Dürer went back several times to add to his description. Meticulously, he notes the care he afforded his mother, and he presents her as a figure whose life and death resembled that of Christ. The scattered religious formulae and many emotional registers capture well the considerable anxieties that clustered around death, the death of others as well as one's own death. What animates Dürer's account, among other things, is the question whether his mother's was a good death. The gift of careful observation evident in the account is manifest also in the charcoal drawing Dürer produced of his sick mother, a moving portrait of a woman on the verge of death and one of the first portraits of an old woman whose identity we know. (See Figure 43.1)

When Albrecht Dürer died in Nuremberg in 1528 without leaving progeny, he probably died a death different from his mother's. In 1525, Nuremberg had turned Lutheran. Early on, Dürer had expressed great enthusiasm for Martin Luther's cause. As a result of the Protestant reforms, however, spiritual life in Nuremberg changed radically. The community of the living and the dead disintegrated: According to Luther, once a dying person's rigor mortis had set in, there was nothing the living could do on behalf of the deceased in order to alleviate their suffering in the afterlife; no human intervention, only God's grace, could bring about salvation. An indulgence like the one Dürer acquired for his mother would no longer have been available, nor the last ointment, a sacrament not considered biblical by the reformers. The history of death is therefore an excellent example for the momentous changes in collective beliefs, behaviors, and practices brought about by the Protestant Reformation.

Notes

1 The week that starts five Sundays after Easter, that is, 26 April 1513.

2 An indulgence.
3 A liturgical farewell drink.
4 Excerpt from Dürer's "Gedenkbuch," in Hans Rupprich (ed.), *Albrecht Dürer, Schriftlicher Nachlass*, 3 vols, Berlin: Deutscher Verlag für Kunstwissenschaft, 1956–1969, vol. 1, pp. 36–37. Translated by Helmut Puff.

44 A funeral sermon for Christian Röhrscheidt, law student in Leipzig, 1627

by Cornelia Niekus Moore

What is a funeral book? The Lutheran funeral tradition began with the funeral of Martin Luther (22 February 1646) in the Wittenberg castle church. First, Johann Bugenhagen preached a sermon, a practice which had been recommended by Luther as a replacement of the traditional Requiem Mass. Then Luther's colleague Philip Melanchthon presented a Latin oration, a classical tradition that had been reinstituted in the Renaissance with which learned men honored their departed colleagues and rulers. This oration was largely biographical. For a person as famous as Martin Luther, the funeral sermon and the oration appeared in print. With the funeral of Martin Luther we see, therefore, the combination of religious and secular practice which would become standard for the Lutheran funeral service. The sermon explained a Bible text and the biography served to exemplify the points that had been made in the sermon.

Lutheran funeral books began to appear fairly soon after the death of Martin Luther, proving once more that practices initiated in Wittenberg were adapted elsewhere in Lutheran Germany. They contained the funeral sermon, the biography, the acknowledgment speech, in which the funeral attendees were thanked for coming, and poems written especially for the sad occasion by family and friends. In the 1550s, we see this practice at the funerals of the ruling houses of Germany; the nobility followed suit, and around the beginning of the seventeenth century the higher and educated bourgeoisie also began to honor their dead with funeral books. The booklets, mostly in quarto format, were sent to family and friends as a memorial to the departed. Although most Lutheran funeral services must have included a sermon, people of lower rank could not afford the printing costs of funeral books.

More than 220,000 of these funeral books are still extant in German libraries and archives. Since they were printed for men as well as women, even for young children, they contain detailed biographical accounts about persons who otherwise would not have made it into the history books. But they are tendentious literature. When reading them, one should keep in mind why they were written, printed, and distributed.

The following is an excerpt from a funeral book that was composed for a law student, the scion of a prominent Leipzig family, Christian Röhrscheidt

(1602–1626). Not only does it contain a funeral sermon and a biography, both written by Polykarp Leyser, Jr., at that time pastor and superintendent[1] in Leipzig, but, as was customary for anyone associated with the university community, also a 'program' by the rector of the university with a biography in Latin and several poems and words of condolence in Latin by members of the university community, including fellow students.

The fifteen-page sermon is an exegesis of the biblical text of the Book of Wisdom, 4:7–14: "But the just person, even one who dies an untimely death, will be at rest. It is not length of life and number of years which bring the honour due to age; ... His soul was pleasing to the Lord, who removed him early from a wicked world."[2] To prepare for this sermon, the preacher would write an outline called a concept and use it as the basis for his sermon. Here the outline went as follows:

"It is really a sad thing in this life for all of us, but especially for parents, that even children are called from this earth, but the Book of Wisdom consoles all pious parents that it is indeed the Lord who calls children away at an early age. First we will hear, to whom this text applies, namely the righteous. Secondly, how the righteous fare in this world. Although they die at an early age, they do gain eternal rest. Thirdly, their death is timely, because they die according to God's will."[3] Throughout the sermon, these points are made to give consolation to the bereaved.

In the succeeding funeral biography (nine pages), the young man's life is told in the traditional order of birth, baptism, education and career (in this case omitting marriage and children), evidence of a pious life, tribulations including illnesses, and death:

"And so we have brought to his last resting place, the honorable and learned Christian Röhrscheidt, student here in Leipzig. He was young in years but he was old enough in the eyes of the Lord, who tore him away from this evil world and made him whole. ... He was born in this city[4] of Christian, honorable and distinguished parents on 31 May 1602. His father ... was the honorable, esteemed, and highly learned Marcus Röhrscheidt, doctor of law and attorney at the Elector[5] of Saxony's palace court. ...

"His mother who is still alive and who has accompanied her son's body with tears and sadness is the honorable and virtuous Barbara, daughter of the right honorable, highly respected, and very wise Mr. Caspar Graf, erstwhile mayor of this city and judge at the highest court of the Electorate of Saxony. From a very young age, these parents brought him up to be God-fearing and to employ all Christian virtues. When he was a few years old, his maternal grandfather took him into his household and saw to it that he learned diligently. He lived there until his grandfather died. His grandmother would have loved to have kept her grandson with her ..., but ... his father thought it better that he would be educated by a private tutor in the house of his parents together with his brother Johann Caspar who has now chosen a military career. This arrangement was continued not without considerable expense when the father died and the boys came under the tutelage of their mother and a guardian, Andreas Schneider, doctor of law and judge at the highest court of the Electorate of Saxony. When, through the grace of God and his own diligence, he had proceeded to the point that he could attend the public lectures of the University of Leipzig, Christian Röhrscheidt ... made such great progress that after a while he was ready to choose a major. With the advice of his guardian, he chose law ... He proved himself so well prepared that there was great hope that if he would have continued on this path he would have become a very valuable jurist. As far as his Christianity is concerned, his family attests that he was a pious, God-fearing, and Christian youth, that he was not enamored with the worldly life which is so popular with young people today, but much rather stayed at home and helped his mother, and did not knowingly cause her any worry. At home he read the Scriptures and attended church services regularly, took the Lord's Supper several times a year, was charitable to the poor and friendly to all.

"It has pleased the Lord to take him from this world at such a young age. A year ago he attracted a high fever, from which he never quite recuperated. Although the doctors used everything that was within their power, nothing seemed to help. About ten weeks ago he suddenly showed a large tumor, which sapped his strength even more, so that in the end he passed away.

"During his illness he showed great patience, put his will into the hands of the Lord, received the Lord's Supper a few days before his death, said goodbye to all, and thanked all who had taken care of him. He passed away last Friday at 12 o'clock amidst the prayers of all who were there. He was 24 years, 20 weeks, and 1 day. May the Lord who took him into eternal rest console the bereaved mother and remind her that He means well and takes away those He loves early, so that they will not experience the evil of this world. ... Amen."[6]

Notes

1 A superintendent was a high-level official in certain Protestant churches in early modern Europe; he occupied the same level as a bishop.
2 *The Revised English Bible with the Apocrypha*, Oxford, Cambridge: Oxford University Press, Cambridge University Press, 1989, The Wisdom of Solomon, pp. 77–78.
3 Polykarp Leyser, *Christliche Leichpredigt / Aus dem Buch der Weißheit am 4 Capitel. Der Gerechte / ob er gleich zu zeitlich stirbet / ist er doch in der Ruhe / etc.: Beym Begräbnis des Erbarn und Wolgelarten Jungengesellen Christiani Rörscheidts Lipsiensis, Iuris Studiosi, Welcher den 20. Octob. Anno 1626 ... entschlaffen / und den 22. Octob. Christlich zur Erden bestattet worden / Gehalten durch Polycarpum Leisern ...*, Leipzig: Mintzel, 1627, p. Aiii v. Translated by Cornelia Niekus Moore.
4 Leipzig.
5 In early modern Germany, the electors were the princes who elected the emperor.
6 Leyser, *Christliche Leichpredigt*, pp. Cv–Civ r.

45 Pilsen, 1503: A wonderful apparition

by Kathryn A. Edwards

On St. Stephen's Day (26 December) 1503 a ghost appeared before three painters in Pilsen, Bohemia. Later that same day the ghost interrupted a priest right after his sermon and, without hesitation, declared, "I'm the soul of an old man with the name of Wenceslaus Haimblichen."[1] After being asked if he needed any Masses said or alms given to ease his way out of purgatory, Wenceslaus proceeded to tell the assembled that on Christmas Day God gave purgatorial souls permission to return to earth to ask for help. He promised to return on the eve of the feast of the Three Kings (6 January), implying that he would then provide his audience with more specifics. He broke that vow, suggesting one reason he was in purgatory in the first place. Instead, he appeared on the feast day in the rooms of a young man from Schmichow who had somehow known to gather a group of fifteen people around him, including three priests. Although initially reluctant to speak before such a crowd, Wenceslaus bent to the priests' will and described why Christ had permitted him to appear.

The story of Wenceslaus's manifestation and eventual return to purgatory is told in a short pamphlet, *A Wonderful History of a Spirit Who Spoke Before Many People in Pilsen in the Land of Bohemia.*[2] Aware that skeptics assumed apparitions to be the product of a fevered imagination rather than God's benevolence, the printer invoked influential local authorities. He claimed that the pamphlet was based on a letter sent by the captain of nearby Märheim and was confirmed by the lords of Schmichow and reputable priests who had seen and heard the ghost themselves. Such legitimation was essential because his message was so important. Wenceslaus provided a local and personal example of the sufferings of sinful souls, and the bulk of the pamphlet recounted dialogues about those sins and the trials of purgation:

"We [the priests and authorities] asked the spirit what pain or torment in hell was like. It answered, 'It's a fire in hell and purgatory and it looks like blood; the difference is that the souls in purgatory wait for the final hope, but there's no such hope in hell.' It was further asked who are those who descend to be eternally damned. He answered, 'The *Pickhartenketzer*[3] and Jews were robbed for eternity of the sight of our God.'

"Item it was also asked what most offended our Lord, for what reason was the soul so tormented in purgatory, and how could he receive help. He answered, 'For the particular sins of poor, lesser, unbaptized people. And while I was in the world near my corpse, I muttered and growsed about the weather. Also I leered at and mocked women, and [more] women, and other people.' After that it [Wenceslaus] had not wanted to talk for awhile … [A priest demanded,] 'Tell us why we finally should believe that you're a real spirit. Was it lawful for our Lord to throw the devils out of heaven?' He [Wenceslaus] answered, 'He [God] was lawful.'"[4]

While communities found such visitations shocking and frequently suspicious, spirits appeared often enough in late medieval and early modern Europe to form 'normal exceptions': extraordinary events that were nonetheless perceived as being possible or even likely, atypical yet plausible elements of an early modern life. Pamphlets, chronicles, and legal briefs throughout Europe provided examples of the dead returning to instruct, cajole, and even terrorize the living. In particular, the warnings that God permitted such spirits attested to the doctrines surrounding purgatory, especially the consequences of sin, the community of the living and the dead, and the beneficence of God. Many scholars have stressed purgatory's centrality to late medieval Christianity, and ghosts played a central role in making it personal, immediate, and vivid.

In Bohemia, however, such pamphlets did more than express God's continued care for humanity and humanity's need for purification; they were a testament in a region known for its religious divisions. While the area around Pilsen in western Bohemia had been a site of battles during the Hussite Wars, an uneasy truce existed at the time of Wenceslaus's appearance between the two main confessions in the area: Catholic and Utraquist.[5] Although Pilsen was officially Catholic, religious dissenters could find a sympathetic audience among some who were dissatisfied with the religious status quo. The spirit showed his local knowledge and, thus, legitimacy from his earliest testimony when he stressed that he was an "old man" and when he condemned the "Pickhart heretics" to the lowest level of the damned.

Yet the very individualism that made him a plausible messenger also points to the tensions within late medieval Christianity and the problems scholars face when attempting to integrate such cases with more doctrinal pronouncements. Wenceslaus showed little respect for the clergy. He preferred to appear to the laity and only grudgingly answered the priests' questions. Even then he often delivered incomplete or vague information. He testified repeatedly to God's and Christ's power but seemed openly contemptuous of clerical prerogatives and ritual trappings; he broke off an account of his sins to ask, "Why are you sprinkling that holy water on me?"[6] When asked to testify to the legality of God's treatment of the devil, Wenceslaus reemphasized that God's actions were thoroughly legitimate, but when a priest asked him to kiss the cross, his reply was a nonchalant, "Why not?"[7]

His audience was both skeptical and hopeful, and the pamphlet's resolution reflected this ambiguity. After testifying that his current body was not the one he once had, Wenceslaus disappeared. His audience waited, then turned the lights on and looked throughout the room for ways they could have been tricked into believing that a spirit had been there. Finding none, they could only assume that he was an angry, suffering spirit in need of their prayers.

Notes

1 Anonymous, *Ein wunderbarlich geschicht von einer Sel die geredt hat vor vil leüten zu Pilsen in dem land zu Behem*, n.p.: s.n., [1503], p. 1r. Translated by Kathryn A. Edwards.
2 Ibid.
3 Literally 'Pickhart heretics.' The Pickharts were an early fifteenth-century Bohemian sect who argued against transubstantiation and are often associated with Adamites and Free Spirits. See Gordon Leff, *Heresy in the Middle Ages: The Relation of Heterodoxy to Dissent*, Manchester: Manchester University Press, 1999, esp. pp. 395–400, 701–703.
4 Anonymous, *Ein wunderbarlich geschicht*, p. 2r.
5 'Utraquism' refers to the Latin phrase *sub utraque specie*, which in turn denotes the sacrament 'in both kinds,' one of the principal beliefs of the Hussites.
6 Anonymous, *Ein wunderbarlich geschicht*, p. 2r.
7 Ibid.

46 Hornhausen: A Protestant miracle well in seventeenth-century Germany

by Ute Lotz-Heumann

In 1646, two years before the end of the Thirty Years' War, a healing well sprang up in the village of Hornhausen, near Magdeburg in northern Germany. Healing wells were common phenomena in early modern Germany, but the Hornhausen well was somewhat special: Soon after it appeared, the well was touted all over Germany as a Protestant pilgrimage site. So popular did the Hornhausen well become, in fact, that more than fifty pamphlets written at the time have survived. While 'a Protestant pilgrimage site' seems to be a contradiction in itself, this was not the case in early modern German Lutheranism. Even though contemporary Lutheran theologians did not use the term 'pilgrimage' to describe what happened in Hornhausen (that term was clearly Catholic), Hornhausen had all the markings of a Lutheran pilgrimage site. Chief among these was that the Hornhausen well was regarded as a 'miracle well,' directly given by God. This interpretation was enthusiastically embraced by Lutheran laymen and pastors alike, and thousands of people went there in the hope of finding a cure for their illnesses.

An anonymous pamphlet entitled *Impartial and Well-Meaning Opinion about the Newly Sprung-Up Healing Well at Hornhausen in Lower Saxony. Whether its Potency is Solely Due to its Mineral Content or Whether it Comes From an Additional God-Given Miraculous Power. Given by the True Medicine's Servant*, argues:

"In Hornhausen a well has sprung up and it has been reported that through the powerful effects of this healing well's virtues many and diverse illnesses have been swiftly cured. Among these illnesses were several which could not be cured by natural means and which wise physicians, however high they had risen in their profession, could not dispel. ... There are different opinions about the potency of this healing water. Some ascribe its potency to nature alone, while others want to attribute it all to miracles. Therefore, as a Christian physician, I want to express my honest German opinion. I do not want to deny God our Lord's honor, but I also do not want to deny nature's honor (as far as this is possible), and I say frankly: It is impossible that all illnesses are cured and turned away at this well in a natural way and by natural means. Rather, a special and miraculous power given by God is here present and has the most eminent effect: And that these illnesses are not cured and taken away by the natural potency of the water, but by God's miraculous grace, given to us freely, by his merciful effect and miraculous hand. And in order to prove this, one should consider this: While God the Almighty has occasionally before our times and today caused powerful bathing springs and healing wells spring from the earth, nevertheless none of them healed such incurable diseases as is happening at this [Hornhausen] well."[1]

In the early modern period, illness was a constant companion. To name but a few maladies, apart from the plague and other epidemics, women were vulnerable during pregnancy and childbirth, people suffered from cancer, had strokes, and developed ulcers. And life prospects could change from one minute to the next through work or travel accidents. People did not, however, take their illnesses as inescapable fate. Instead, they looked actively for cures, and in the early modern period, there were just as many cures available as there were diseases: From bloodletting to cancer surgery, from herbs to healing waters, there were many options. There were many healers as well: Folk could turn to the physicians who had studied medicine in the universities, but these did not enjoy the monopoly that they do today. The sick could also go to barber surgeons, midwives, priests, and itinerant healers.

Some of this diversity can be explained by the fact that in the early modern period, many phenomena in life – from illnesses to thunderstorms – could not be explained scientifically. Instead early modern contemporaries often explained their world in religious terms. While people knew from experience that certain mineral waters had healing qualities, they did not know how the water actually affected the human body. As a result, healing wells were interpreted both as natural phenomena and as God-given miracles. Religious interpretations of healing wells were enthusiastically embraced by both Catholic and Lutheran laymen and clergymen in the early modern period. In Catholicism, healing wells were often integral parts of pilgrimage sites dedicated to saints, whereas in Lutheranism, newly discovered wells were frequently interpreted as God-given 'miracle wells.'

The anonymous author of this pamphlet, presenting himself as a "Christian physician," takes a middle ground in the contemporary discussion about how the Hornhausen wells should be interpreted. He says that, while the minerals contained in the water are able to heal *some* illnesses, many cures that have occurred in Hornhausen cannot be attributed to nature alone because all kinds of medicines administered by the best doctors were ineffective. The anonymous author accepts the Lutheran interpretation of Hornhausen as a miraculous well given by God's grace. In accordance with all Lutheran pamphlets about miracle wells, he focuses the reader's attention on God as the provider of the miraculous power of the well. In order to clearly differentiate Lutheran wells from Catholic ones, the idea of a saintly intercessor or the attribution of 'holiness' to the water itself were carefully avoided. Unfortunately, this source tells us little about what the sick people thought and did when they visited a Lutheran miracle well or a Catholic pilgrimage site. It is, however, clear that they were desperately looking for cures in a world full of disease.

Note

1 Anonymous, *Unvergreiffliches und wohlmeynendes Guttachten / von dem newentsprungenen Heil-Brunn zu Hornhausen in NiederSachsen / Ob desselben Kräffte allein von den inwohnenden Mineralien oder aber von einer mit-würckenden Göttlichen Wunder-krafft herkommen. Gestellet durch Der Wahren Medicin Dienern*, n.p.: s.n., 1646, pp. Ai v–Aii r. Translated by Ute Lotz-Heumann.

47 Gent, 1658: The miracle of the breast milk – or perhaps not

by Craig Harline

Since the later Roman Empire, Christians visited holy places distant and near in search of divine intervention, often in the form of miraculous healing. During the early modern period, the practice continued, especially among Catholics, but the process of declaring a miracle grew more rigorous, filled with formal hearings organized by the nearest bishop and including expert medical advice as to whether a cure was 'beyond nature' or merely 'natural.' This rigor was meant partly to ensure that laypeople would believe only in 'true' miracles, and partly to avoid the embarrassing claims of miracles that Catholics sometimes made and that Protestants eagerly exploited in their criticisms of the Catholic Church. In August 1658, 42-year-old Maria Caroens appeared before the vicariate of the diocese of Gent[1] to testify under oath regarding an alleged miracle that had recently happened to her.[2] Maria's case reveals great detail about the world of miracle-seeking and the careful process used to control it.

As was common in such proceedings, Maria told her background first. She had been married twice, had born fourteen children (at least five of whom had died), and had known poverty her entire life. Her current husband, the blacksmith Anthony de Witte, regularly had to travel without her in order to find work, while she stayed with the children and earned what she could by baking waffles. She had also traveled in search of more income, once setting up shop in the Dutch Republic, to the north, where her Protestant brother lived, but she now lived in the Savaanstreet in Gent.

Then she came to the miracle. In April 1657, she bore her fourteenth child. She had never had much milk for any of her children, but for this last she had none. "And because she found that she had no milk in her bosoms, she went and had them pulled" by a widow named Margariet Doosens, a midwife or healing woman expert in such things. "The same widow said to the witness that it was wasted effort, that she had no milk," thus Maria left her baby with Margariet to be nursed, as Margariet had a baby of her own. Maria "brought the baby home at night to lie at her breast" in the hope that this might stimulate the flow of milk, "but she believed that the baby got out none or very little, first because she neither saw nor heard it swallow, and second because it cried the whole night through." She tried all the known remedies of the day, "rubbing on wheat germ and boiled wheat, and drinking milk mixed with boiled wheat, all without effect."

Because she could not afford to keep her baby out to a nurse any longer, Maria "went more out of desperation than devotion" to see her friend Cristine, "to borrow five stivers, with which she bought two wax breasts, in order to offer them before the image of Our Dear Lady at the church of the Recollect Fathers,[3] on All Saints' Day 1657," following the common practice of offering at an altar the part of the body in need of a cure. But the offering also had no effect. Maria grew "very despondent," until she heard a new idea. It happened that Margariet the wet-nurse was in great sorrow now too, for her own child had fallen into the household fire and suffered serious facial burns. Yet another woman, named Maeyken Bernaerts, had told Margariet, in Maria's hearing, to take the burned child "to the image of Our Dear Lady in the church of the Jesuit Fathers," which, she had heard in a sermon, "was a miraculous image, for it had once been cast into a fire by a heretic and had lain there for long without being burned." Maria thought to herself that "if that same image could heal a burned child or give it health, then surely it could grant her milk in her bosoms."

Thus it happened that she went a few days later to hear Mass "in the Jesuit church." In the small chapel containing the image, Maria "stood and began to make her request and pray in this manner: 'Holy Mother Maria, I can't leave money or a particular gift, but I offer you my soul and body and my poor household if it would be possible for a miracle to happen to this poor sinful person: take my child from the world, grant me milk, or move someone to pay for my child to be nursed.'" She then "heard a Mass or two," and returned home without effect. She did the same thing a second day.

"And as she continued her devotion on a third day, and was hearing Mass in the chapel of Our Dear Lady, celebrated by a certain very tall father, she thought to herself, 'Lord, the Mass will soon be finished and I still haven't been consoled,' adding to this, 'Holy Maria, if I am comforted, I promise you, as long as I live in this city, that I will come visit you here every day, with a short or long prayer, or at the very least a Mass.' And at that she fell into something like a dream or sleep, though she remained kneeling the whole time," without being exactly sure of her state. "Coming out of it, she felt that she was sweating, and that milk was running out of her left breast, through her collar, and that she also had milk in her right bosom, which none of her children had been able to suck because there was no nipple," but now it was running out of her right breast too.

Yet another of Maria's friends, a certain benefactress of hers named Juffrouw Beeclaere, encouraged Maria to tell the story to a confessor, and she did so, on the second or third feast day of Christmas 1657, again in the church of the Jesuits. And Maria thought that with this the matter had ended. But then one day at the shop of Little Adriana, "who sold butter and cheese at the Walgate," Adriana said that the Jesuits had put out word that they wanted to find the woman with fourteen children and no milk, and "had charged

Adriana with inquiring among all who came into or out of her store if they didn't know such a woman." When Adriana realized that she had found the woman, she told Maria to return to the Jesuit church immediately and tell them where she lived, for they wanted to investigate her story. And Maria did so, finding the same confessor, and saying that "she lived in the Waffle Shop in the Savaanstreet." Soon afterward, a Pater van Delft visited and wrote down Maria's testimony. At the end of the testimony, she declared that she still continued her devotion at the church, and that she had had more milk for this child than for any of her others. Then she signed her name with a mark, a simple cross.

As usual, the vicariate soon called upon medical experts, four of them in this case, none of whom actually examined Maria but who were simply presented with the facts and asked whether this event "transcended nature." All four agreed that it did. But then a complication: It emerged that the image before which Maria had found her cure was most likely a fraud, given to the Jesuits of Gent as a joke by a "heretic," who pretended that the image had survived a fire. Not wishing to give more ammunition to Protestant propagandists waiting pen in hand just over the border, the vicariate quietly asked two physicians to reconsider the facts. These two suddenly decided that in fact it could be perfectly "natural" for a 42-year-old woman, who had born fourteen children and had never had much milk and for her last child had had no milk at all, suddenly to start producing milk in abundance. The investigating panel agreed. Maria's miracle was not an official miracle at all, but simply natural. Of course, Maria and her friends were free to believe what they wanted, but the church would not proclaim it – as they would not for the vast majority of cures claimed by such thankful people as Maria Caroens.

Notes

1 The previous bishop had just died and a new one had not yet been named, so the vicariate had temporary jurisdiction over the diocese and such cases as claims of miracles.
2 Rijksarchief Gent, Bisdom B3035, document dated 19 August 1658. All quotations are from this document which was translated by Craig Harline.
3 Franciscans.

48 A snapshot of Iberian religiosities: The inquisitorial case against the New Christian María de Sierra, 1651

by David Graizbord

Among the primary targets of the Spanish Inquisition (1478–1832) was a small population of 'New Christians' or *conversos*, the Christianized descendants of Iberian Jews. For centuries, *conversos* fell victim to the charge of 'Judaizing,' a heresy that consisted of thinking and/or behaving in (mostly quotidian) ways that the inquisitors deemed, codified, and publicized in various 'Edicts of Faith' as standard 'evidence' of 'Judaism.' Scholars disagree as to what extent the records of inquisitorial trials shed light on the religiosity of the deponents. Few disagree, however, that much of the preserved testimony, especially the suspects' confessions, tends toward the formulaic, and was conditioned by the threat of physical coercion, continued incarceration, destitution, and public disgrace. In that sense, inquisitorial dossiers serve as evidence of harsh attempts to inculcate an officially-sanctioned Catholic religiosity. Paradoxically, these trial records may also reveal interesting gaps between what the agents and the subjects of confessional discipline knew, thought, felt, and did about their shared religious culture. The document excerpted and translated below is a case in point.

From 1651–1653, inquisitors in Toledo investigated María de Sierra, a 28-year-old New Christian of Portuguese origin who earned her living from a tobacco stand that she and her husband owned and operated in Pastrana, a village in La Mancha. Echoing the Edicts of Faith, María's neighbors, former employees, and relatives, some of whom were her fellow prisoners, had accused her of performing 'Jewish' actions, such as avoiding pork. In María's first hearing on 9 March 1651, inquisitors demanded that she cross herself and recite a few prayers. She did this "all wrong,"[1] and admitted that she knew neither the decalogue nor the Catholic credo. Still, María said that "she considered herself a Christian who guards, believes, and confesses what the ... church commands."[2]

Two days later, she responded to standard allegations that she had engaged in 'Jewish' fasting:

"About eight to ten years ago, [a visiting aunt] told her to fast one day in order to be a good Christian and serve God. And [the suspect] does not remember when and for what reason the fast was to take place ... She is also doubtful as to whether the woman told [her] to fast all day or ... eat at midday, and therefore [the suspect] does not know if it was good or bad, she merely had a bad presumption that [the old woman] should tell her to fast, because she was of such a young age."[3] "[Upon further prodding, the defendant] said that the reason it seemed bad to her [to fast as the aunt had instructed], and that she did not do it, was that the ... woman had beaten her, and thus she did not wish to fast, neither to obey her."[4]

At another hearing a few of María's denunciators made unusual and sensational claims. The prosecutor summarized (and supported) these allegations as follows:

"With great contempt for the holy images, this detainee [María de Sierra] and a person closely related to her were [secretly] mistreating and whipping an image and likeness of our Lord [on the] crucifix, [and] just to hear of this criminal sacrilege makes the heart of the least decent and Catholic Christian tremble ... Two persons witnessed this sacrilegious atrocity, and fearing that it would not be publicly revealed and that people would say that [María de Sierra's accomplice] would give them a violent death, [the two witnesses fled from the village], which caused a notable scandal and whispering [in Pastrana]."[5]

María confessed under torture to minor crypto-'Judaic' infractions, yet denied abusing the icon. She hazarded that her accusers (whose identity remained secret to her) were two resentful maids she had recently fired. In turn, María accused them of having the "soul of Judas." Oddly, María's final sentence omits any mention of the ritual abuse. In discarding the most incendiary allegations, were the judges merely following their own rules of evidence, or were they also looking askance at plebeian forms of incitement against *conversos*?

We can only speculate, yet we may still argue that María de Sierra's dossier provides a snapshot of at least three expressions of early modern Iberian religiosity. These expressions were articulated at a crossroads of popular and learned cultures, within a social framework of local rumor-mongering and inquisitorial probing. First, the dossier allows glimpses of a socially authoritative piety that demanded adherence to quasi-ethnographic definitions of deviance, and to the 'proper' institutional remedies that the Inquisition represented.

Second, the dossier reveals the relatively spontaneous religiosity of commoners steeped in anti-Jewish folklore. The accusers drew from a trove of medieval anti-Jewish canards that ordinary Iberians shared with their better-educated countrymen, and which had generated major persecutions of *conversos* since the fifteenth century. Notably, in 1632, and then again in 1654, inquisitorial investigations had yielded claims almost identical to those lodged against María de Sierra that Portuguese *conversos* in Castile had reenacted their Jewish ancestors' supposedly deicidal hostility by ritually whipping statues of the crucified Christ. The first cluster of these allegations had become a *cause célèbre* that led to several executions.

Third, the dossier reveals a similarly spontaneous popular religiosity, one expressed by poorly catechized believers like María. Granted, one could approach her as a clever crypto-Jew who, under extreme physical and psychological pressure, tried to deceive her interrogators with pious locutions such as "soul of Judas" and (while tortured) "O, most sacred Virgin!".[6] An alternative interpretation, however, might allow us to consider these phrases, and the rest of María's testimony, as tokens of an ordinary believer's 'good faith' – in the double sense of 'earnestness,' and of a reflexive – and very Christian – 'piety.'

Notes

1 Archivo Histórico Nacional, Inquisición de Toledo, legajo 184, expediente 12, fol. 71v. Translated by David Graizbord.
2 Ibid., fol. 71r.
3 Ibid., fol. 72v.
4 Ibid., fol. 73v.
5 Ibid., fols 77r–v.
6 Ibid., fol. 130r.

49 Blazing stars: Interpreting comets as portents of the future in late seventeenth-century Germany

by Andrew Fix (†)

Comets, since time out of mind, have been of interest and concern to Europeans. Unusual events in an otherwise seemingly unchanging celestial realm, they required equally special explanations. In antiquity, Aristotle's view was influential and it became the standard theory of comets until at least 1577. Aristotle, who believed the heavens were perfect and unchanging, saw comets as atmospheric events: exhalations from deep in the earth, drawn into the upper atmosphere, and set alight by the realm of fire. He also saw comets as portents or predictors of future disasters that would strike the earth. Since comets brought hot, dry air, they predicted events that would also flow from such atmospheric conditions: drought, famine, pestilence, earthquakes, and other such things.

In the Middle Ages, Aristotle's view was substantially modified by early church fathers and theologians. Comets came to be seen not as natural exhalations but as supernatural phenomena, miracles of God created to warn mankind of God's anger with humans' sins and of forthcoming supernatural punishment from God, such as wars, revolts, murders, the deaths of princes, and the fall of states and empires as well as disasters such as floods, high winds, storms at sea, and the usual droughts, diseases, earthquakes, and severe heat.

During the religious uncertainty, confusion, and anxiety of the early modern period, when the lives of people became intertwined with confessional hatred, intolerance, and violence, comet portents were taken even more seriously as predictors of the outcome of the religious struggles and of the end of the world. Thus, comet portents and religious prophecy, astral as well as terrestrial signs, were combined into a powerful mixture of popular religion and confessional propaganda. Comet portents were perfectly designed for a worldview steeped in conflict, uncertainty, desperation, and an intense desire to know the future and thus the approaching outcome of all human suffering.

Johann Philip Hahn's *Short and Urgent Report of the Most Recently Appearing Comet in December Anno 1664*, published in Dresden in 1665, is a traditional treatment of comets as was current during the early modern period. Hahn, a lawyer, poet, and author of almanacs, was spurred to write when he witnessed this important comet which appeared in December 1664 and was visible until early February 1665. What appears below are excerpts translated into English of a twenty-two-page pamphlet:

"God the Lord of heaven and earth created the world and put stars in the firmament, wonderful signs to see. This Holy Scripture teaches us, and this is also confirmed by our daily viewing of the heavens and our human reason. But when God puts in the sky another and new light he wants to indicate something unusual. And it is certain that God is especially angry about the evil of man when he causes new stars and comets to appear.

"New stars and comets are put in the sky for our admonishment and conversion, quite apart from the fact that they have their natural causes. God is a righteous judge and wants only that men master their sins. Thus he sends these signs as warnings that he will come with hard punishments.

"It is totally certain when comets appear that God is very angry and they are sure signs of his nearing wrath. Because now every corner of the world is full of sins; idolatry, whoring, breaking honor, despising God's Word and sacraments, cursing, slandering, and other abominable sins are swelling up. ...

"This newly appearing comet is a proud Peacock-tailed star that sets dragging its tail after it. Like other comets, it has its origin in the greasy exhalations of the sun. Comets are formed from collisions of exhalations coming out of the body of the earth and especially out of the sun. They are slung together heavenly clouds that from a distance appear to be a star, but not a thick one, rather a body transparent to the sun's penetrating rays. ...

"Our comet appeared on the second of December according to the testimony of several pastors from Laussniss.[1] They all saw it at the same time, early in the morning around 3:00. It was seen for four consecutive days and then was hidden by bad weather. It was seen again on 15 December at night. We do not know at this time how long it will last. ...

"Comets are neither stars nor planets, and therefore they have no certain color. Most are pale. Some are clear – like the one of 1572. Some are dark like those of 1652 and 1660. Our new star was at first pale, but afterwards it was different and the body appeared smaller and brighter, the tail dark. ...

"The position of comets is twofold: physical and optical. A comet has its natural place that it fills up with its body and tail. The optic place is determined by instruments. I have not seen enough of our comet to determine its physical place. But by considering its setting we can get an approximate position. On December 16th it set in the early morning at 20 minutes until 6:00. According to all appearance and judgment it is in the Tropic of Capricorn in the Milky Way next to the Big Dog, with its tail streaming upward and to the right side of the Little Dog, to the left of Orion. ...

"Princes and Lords who take astrologically experienced people as their mathematicians and consult them are fairly praised. This is a noble art and highly necessary science. ...

"That comets are something special, as the *arcanum*[2] of their nature testifies, no intelligent person denies. Experience teaches us this and histories give examples and proof. ...

"God is in the habit of not giving men betterment of life, but on the contrary of punishing their sins, because He is an eternal God and wants to pay men with fair and well-deserved wages for their evil. But he always shows his charity to repentance that is before the fact of punishment, and that is why he sends before us wondrous warning signs and comets, which bring nothing good with them. ...

"Physically comets mean high winds, dryness, bad weather, earthquakes, barrenness, and unhealthy air. Astrologically they mean war, bloodshed, murder, robbery, burning, destruction of cities, changes of wealth, deaths of princes and kings, the coming of new kings, and other public miseries. ...

"What does our comet mean? The meaning and effect are known to God alone. Man cannot know it immediately, but only after several years of experience. Some take the meaning from the figure and color of the comet. Its tail resembles a Peacock, which causes pride, so it may mean the pride of the Israelites will be punished. The color is Saturnical and Mercurical. Saturn wants to be the gravedigger and Mercury the poisoner, so perhaps it brings pestilential air and poisonous mist from its burning. The comet may bring a cold, dry winter and an arid summer with high winds. By its nature it attacks the bile of men and causes great heat, pestilential sicknesses, sudden deaths, and floods.

"Astrologically it causes in kingdoms if not transferences, at least changes because of the death of a head or some unrest. Bad defeats will occur, and beautiful, long-standing cities will become hostile and fall. The foreigner and strangers will win the advantage. ...

"God be gracious and charitable to us, and turn away the misfortunes, if not completely, at least so as not to damage our souls. In the meantime let us be repentant."[3]

The early modern view of comets gradually changed from the seventeenth century onward, resulting in the current view of comets as natural parts of the physical universe, having no meaning beyond their physical characteristics and no role in terrestrial drama as portents. They became a cornerstone of classical physics when Book Two of Newton's *Principia* (1687) was devoted almost entirely to comets and their orbital characteristics.

Notes

1 Lausnitz, a town near Dresden.
2 Mystery.
3 Johann Philipp Hahn, *Kurtz eilfärtiger Bericht Von Dem im Decembr. Anno 1664. Neulichst erschienen Cometen / Benantlich Was dessen Betrachtung / Natur / Gestalt / Zeit / Farbe / Größe / Lauff / und muthmaßliche Bedeutung betrifft*, Dresden: Berge, [1665], pp. 1–22. Translated by Andrew Fix.

50 Picturing witchcraft in late seventeenth-century Germany

by Charles Zika

By the later seventeenth century the number of witch trials throughout Europe had seriously declined, and the reality of witchcraft was increasingly questioned. The defense of witchcraft beliefs often became florid, as did the pictorial images created in support. An image that appeared in three demonological treatises exemplifies this development. It first appeared in 1687 as an engraving prefacing part two of *The Broken Power of Darkness* (*Die Gebrochne Macht der Finsternüß*), written by the Pietist pastor of St. Jakob's church in Augsburg, Gottlieb Spitzel, and published by Gottlieb Göbel and Jakob Koppmayer, also in Augsburg.[1] (See Figure 50.1.) Spitzel had been involved with a number of witchcraft and demonic possession cases involving children in the 1670s and 1680s, not least that of the young demoniac Regina Schiller, whom he had long tried to exorcise.

Six years later, the engraving appeared in reverse, and was therefore clearly a copy, in part two of the 1693 edition of Nicholas Rémy's *Demonolatry: Or Description of Witches and Sorcerers* (*Daemonolatria, Oder: Beschreibung von Zauberern und Zauberinnen*) published by Thomas von Wiering in Hamburg.[2] This German translation was a vastly expanded version of the work of the well-known chief prosecutor of Lorraine, first published in Lyon in 1595.

The engraving served printers' interests well, for it appeared for the third time, and now as a frontispiece engraving, in Peter Goldschmidt's *Witness to the Depravity of Witches and Sorcerers* (*Verworffener Hexen und Zauberer Advocat*), published in Hamburg in 1705 by Gottfried Liebernickel.[3] Goldschmidt was a Lutheran pastor from Schleswig and a stern defender of witchcraft trials. In 1698 he published a stinging attack on the Dutch Reformed minister and critic of witch-hunting, Balthasar Bekker, the *Hellish Morpheus* (*Höllischer Morpheus*). He now directed his *Witness to the Depravity of Witches and Sorcerors* against another critic of witchcraft trials and beliefs, the professor of law at the University of Halle, Christian Thomasius. Goldschmidt himself created the frontispiece engraving, a poor copy of that in the *The Broken Power of Darkness*.

We still know too little about the different ways prints circulated through early modern Europe, and in this case how they made their way from Augsburg to Hamburg. Was it via a network of printers or publishers, of engravers,

Figure 50.1 Gottlieb Spitzel, *Die Gebrochne Macht der Finsternüß ...*, Augsburg: Göbel and Koppmayer, 1687, p. 207

192 Charles Zika

booksellers, or authors? Was the link direct or through key publishing and intellectual centers such as Frankfurt, Leipzig, or Halle? What this chain of image-making does show is how images were recycled by artists and printers across space and time; how they were combined and adapted for authors, artists, and readers; how they picked up messages and motifs from different visual and literary genres.

The composition and iconography of these three engravings is virtually the same. (See Figure 50.1.) In the foreground a young female witch in a magic circle pours powder from a horn into a cauldron. Nearby sits a devilish beast with beady eyes, dragging on a pipe; and in the opposite corner are the woman's tools of trade. The background displays a different scene. A satyr-like devil with flaming hands leads a procession of dancers, some half naked and gyrating to the sounds of two musicians, towards a group lining up before a goat on a table. The goat is carefully positioned, tail raised to receive the so-called obscene kiss from the line of women and children. Two witches ride through the air above – one on a goat, grasping its horn; the other on a forked cooking stick, her garment falling free to reveal her upper body and her hair flying out wildly behind her. A bright crescent moon sets the scene at night.

An unknown artist created this image from two different sources. The foreground, depicting the witch and her paraphernalia, was taken from a woodcut by the Augsburg artist, Melchior Küsel, which he had used to illustrate the biblical story of the witch of Endor (1 Samuel: 28) in a 1679 Augsburg picture

Figure 50.2 Melchior Küsel, *Icones Biblicae Veteris et Novi Testamenti*, Augsburg: Kysel, 1679, I. Sam. Cap. XXVIII.3 seq. PYTHONISSA, table 40

Figure 50.3 Johannes Praetorius, *Blockes-Berges Verrichtung* ..., Leipzig: Scheible, 1668, frontispiece

Bible, the *Icones Biblicae Veteris et Novi Testamenti*. (See Figure 50.2.) Küsel in turn had taken his witch of Endor from a 1626 engraving by the Dutch artist Jan van der Velde II, which illustrated the seductions of various vices. The background was modeled on a woodcut first published in Leipzig in 1668, as a frontispiece to *Performance at the Blocksberg* (*Blockes-Berges Verrichtung*), by the prolific Baroque poet, Johannes Praetorius. (See Figure 50.3.) This bawdy and scatological representation of a Witches' Sabbath was very much in the spirit of Praetorius's work, a mixture of demonological themes and fantastic tales of exotic lands and strange spirits. The model for Praetorius's print in turn was a widely circulating engraving by Matthaeus Merian the Elder after a drawing by Michael Herr, first published in 1626.

The 1687 Spitzel engraving (Figure 50.1) modified the Praetorius woodcut (Figure 50.3) in ways that accorded with the content of Spitzel's treatise and with his zealotry in prosecuting witchcraft in Augsburg. The obscene kiss now became the central collective ritual; and it was a ritual exclusively involving women and children. These significant changes support the view that this was a carefully constructed combination print modeled on images that would have been well known to Spitzel, his Augsburg publishers, and the artist.

One intriguing aspect of these engravings is how a female ritual magician modelled on the biblical Witch of Endor found her way into general images of witchcraft in the later seventeenth century – for the development is not limited to these images. Does the attack by Goldschmidt and Spitzel on the so-called 'atheism' of witchcraft skeptics like Balthasar Bekker and Christian Thomasius suggest why this biblical witch might have become attractive to those defending belief in witchcraft?

Notes

1 Gottlieb Spitzel, *Die Gebrochne Macht der Finsternüß / oder Zerstörte Teuflische Bunds- und Buhl-Freundschafft mit den Menschen: Das ist: Gründlicher Bericht / wie und welcher Gestalt die abscheuliche und verfluchte Zauber-Gemeinschafft mit den Bösen Geistern angehe ... und denen Teufflischen Bunds-Verwandten ... wider geholffen werden könne / Allen Heyl- und Gnaden-begierigen ... verstrickten Seelen / zum nothwendigen Unterricht ... beschrieben ... wie auch einigen Kupffer-Bildern ausgezieret von Gottlieb Spitzeln ...*, Augsburg: Göbel and Koppmayer, 1687, p. 207.
2 Nicolas Remi [= Nicholas Rémy], *[Nicolai Remigii Daemonolatria, Oder: Beschreibung von Zauberern und Zauberinnen]*, Part Two: *Der Bösen Geister und Gespensten Wunder-seltzahme Historien und Nächtliche Erscheinungen: Wie auch der Zäuberer und Zauberinnen Gottslästerliches Unwesen und Gewalt ...; Aus vielen so wol alten als neuen glaubwürdigen Scribenten ... zusammen getragen*, Hamburg: Wiering, 1693, p. 325.
3 Peter Goldschmidt, *Verworffener Hexen- und Zauberer-Advocat: Das ist: Wolgegründete Vernichtung Des thörichten Vorhabens Hn. Christiani Thomasii I.U.D. & Professoris Hallensis, und aller derer, welche durch ihre Superkluge Phantasie-Grillen dem teufflischen Hexen-Geschmeiß das Wort reden wollen ...*, Hamburg and Lauenburg: Liebernickel and Pfeiffer, 1705, page opposite title page.

51 Loftur the Sorcerer and clerical magic in eighteenth-century Iceland

by Thomas B. de Mayo

The practice of magic of various sorts was widespread in pre-industrial Europe, as is evidenced by the large number of surviving manuscripts of spells and incantations. The form known as 'necromancy' or 'nigromancy' was a learned art and a by-product of the high medieval translation movement: It drew upon Arabic and Hebrew works to summon and command named demons. Magical ritual required knowledge of Latin and of Christian liturgical formulae, particularly exorcisms. Thus, as Richard Kieckhefer points out, practitioners of learned magic were predominantly clerics with at least some schooling in Latin.

Iceland, which converted to Christianity only around the turn of the millennium, lay far from the center of Latin Christian culture. Nevertheless, folklore from Iceland connects various church figures with necromancy, Latin magic, and the devil. The following account comes from a story collected by Jón Árnason about the post-Reformation figure of *Galdra* Loftur (born *c.*1700).[1] *Galdur* means 'sorcery' in Icelandic. The sinister character of Loftur combines the figure of the clerical magician with a typically Icelandic concern for the revenant dead, and the story shows clearly the fear and suspicion directed towards Latin learning and the Catholic past in Lutheran Iceland:

"1. *Bishop Gottskálk's Book.* Bishop Gottskálk the Cruel[2] was the greatest wizard of his day; he gathered together all the black spells, which had never been used since the heathen times, and wrote them all down in a magical book called Red Skin. ... The Bishop grudged that this book should pass to anyone else after his time, and therefore he has it buried with him, ...

"2. *Loftur the Magician.* Two hundred years after Bishop Gottskálk's time, there was a scholar in the Cathedral School at Hólar named Loftur, who spent all his time studying magic ... Loftur got a maidservant with child, and then killed the mother of his child with sorcery. ...

"The Rev. Thorleifur Skaftason, who was the [Lutheran] Rural Dean and the Cathedral Vicar at the time, rebuked Loftur for his ungodliness, but Loftur did not mend his ways – indeed, Loftur now began to attempt to harm the Dean, though, because of the Rev. Thorleifur's piety and wisdom, he was unable to hurt him ...

"Loftur did not let up till he had learned everything there was in the magicians' manual called Grey Skin, and knew it thoroughly; he then made enquiries from other magicians, but no one knew more than he did. ...

"One day in early winter Loftur spoke to a boy whom he knew to be courageous and asked him to help him raise all the ancient bishops of the see from the dead. ... Loftur [said] that he need only stand motionless in the bell-tower with his hand on the bell-rope, and stare steadily at him until he gave him a signal with his hand, and then ring the bell straight away.

"'I,' said Loftur, 'will now explain my plan to you. Those who have learned as much magic as I have can only use it for evil, and must all be lost whenever they die. But if a man knows enough, then the Devil will have no power over him ... It is not possible to attain this degree of knowledge nowadays, since the Black School closed down, and Gottskálk the Cruel had his book Red Skin buried with him. That is why I want to raise him up and force him by spells to let me have Red Skin. ... I cannot touch the later bishops, because they were all buried with the Bible on their breasts. ...'

"They agreed on this, and rose up soon after bed-time and stole out into the cathedral. The moon was shining, and the church was bright inside; the other boy stepped in the bell-tower, while Loftur went into the pulpit and began to conjure. Shortly afterwards, a man rose though the floor; his expression was mild, but serious, and he wore a crown, and the boy felt sure that this must have been the first Bishop of Hólar.

"He said to Loftur: 'Cease, miserable man, while there is time, for my brother Gvendur's prayers will weigh heavily against you if you disturb him.'

"Loftur took no notice, but went on conjuring. ...

"Still Gottskálk resisted, and Loftur now began to conjure in earnest, ... He turned the penitential psalms of David to the Devil's name, and made a confession of all the good he had ever done as if it were a sin. ... Then a tremendous rumbling was heard, and a man rose up through the floor with his crozier in his left hand and a red book under his right arm; ... [he] turned and grinned at Loftur, who was now conjuring with all his might.

"Gottskálk moved a little closer, and said sarcastically; 'Well sung, son, and better than I expected, but you won't get my Red Skin.'

"At this Loftur fell into a berserk fury, and conjured as if all he had done till then was nothing. He recited the Lord's prayer to the Devil, and gave the blessing in the Devil's name, till the whole church shook and rocked as if in an earthquake. The other boy felt that Gottskálk edged nearer to Loftur, and unwillingly reached a corner of the book out to him. Up to then he had been frightened, but now he shook with fear and everything went black in front of his eyes, but it seemed to him that the bishop held up the book and ... Loftur put out his hand to take it. At this point he thought Loftur gave him the signal, and he pulled the bell-rope – and at once all the dead sank down though the floor, with a great rushing sound."[3]

Because of the failure of his assistant and his own mistakes, Loftur admits that he is now damned. Not too long afterwards, he vanishes when a hairy hand pulls a boat in which he is sitting with another man under the water.

The story combines Latin, Icelandic, and Lutheran features into a composite picture of the nature and dangers of clerical magicians. Loftur's magic strongly resembles Latin necromancy. In the magical duel he inverts and perverts Christian ritual. The magical use of the dead is a particularly Icelandic motif. In Old Norse literature the dead (especially the heathen dead) often guarded treasure in their tombs. As with Gottskálk, they are prone to physical manifestations, sometimes engaging heroes in violent combat. Gottskálk's book burial demonstrates how thoroughly magic was seen as a medieval pagan survival, made dangerous by its eruption into early modern Lutheran society. Indeed, there is a triple-layering of the past, for Gottskálk was a Catholic bishop in a now-Lutheran country, and Loftur therefore has greater power over him than over the later Lutheran bishops who "were all buried with the Bible on their breasts."

Notes

1 Jón Árnason, *Íslenzkar þjóðsögur og Aevintr*, new edn., ed. Árni Böðvarsson and Bjarni Vilhjálmsson, 6 vols, Rejkavik: Þjóðsaga, 1954–1961, vol. 1, pp. 572–575.
2 Bishop Gottskálk Nikulásson of Hólar (1497–1520) was a historical figure, but his activities as a wizard are probably fictitious. The book *Red Skin* may be a remembrance of a red-bound tax register particularly hated by his subjects. See Simpson, below.
3 The translation is in Jacqueline Simpson (ed. and tr.), *Legends of Icelandic Magicians*, Cambridge: D. S. Brewer for the Folklore Society, 1975, pp. 73–79.

V

Realms intertwined: Religion and politics

Introduction

by Ute Lotz-Heumann

This chapter is concerned with the ways in which religion and politics were often intertwined in early modern Europe. Unity of state and church was a strong ideal in the eyes of contemporaries. As a result, rulers in early modern Europe showed a strong will to unify religion and politics and to use religion as an instrument of state formation, while church leaders were willing to cooperate with the state to provide their church with a privileged status and to discipline the population. However, these relationships were not without friction, and often conflicts erupted between various actors.

The essays by Heinz Schilling, James M. Estes, Irene Dingel, and Marjory E. Lange are concerned with the attitudes and actions of churchmen in their relationships with political authorities. In his letter of 1522, Martin Luther defied his ruler, Frederick the Wise, by casting himself in the role of an Old Testament prophet. Declaring his obedience in worldly things, but his independence with regard to the evangelical truth, Luther effectively defended the indefensible: being disobedient to his prince (essay by Heinz Schilling). That the reformers' stance toward temporal authorities was complicated is clear from the writings of Philip Melanchthon. In 1539, when he wrote his treatise *Concerning the Office of Princes*, he articulated Lutheran teachings that God had put secular authorities in place to ensure that "true doctrine" (i.e., Lutheran theology) would be taught (essay by James M. Estes). In 1548, when Emperor Charles V imposed the so-called Interim on German Protestants, Melanchthon wrote another treatise in which he argued that Protestants should resist any changes to the "true doctrine" of their churches as stipulated by the Interim. While he reminded his immediate temporal lord, the Elector of Saxony, of his responsibility – as Melanchthon saw it – to defend Lutheranism as 'the true church,' Melanchthon also argued that the Emperor, the Elector's overlord, had no authority to change religious doctrine (essay by Irene Dingel).[1] Thomas More, Lord Chancellor of England, experienced a similar dilemma when he was tried for refusing to take the oath of supremacy after Henry VIII had severed the English state church from

Rome. Shortly before his execution, More asserted that he served both the king and God. Thus, More did not choose between Henry and God, although he clearly exposed the problem of the choice considering the fact that King Henry had acted against the papal church which – in More's mind – was the true church (essay by Marjory E. Lange).

The following three essays by Robert Christman, James J. Blakeley, and Michael W. Bruening focus on the theory and practice of ecclesiastical discipline and the ways in which secular and ecclesiastical authorities handled visitations and other disciplining measures in a variety of Protestant contexts. These essays also throw light on how the populace targeted by these efforts at religious, social, and moral control responded.[2] In the visitation directives issued in the small German territory of Mansfeld in 1554, the procedures and responsibilities of temporal and ecclesiastical authorities are discussed in detail (essay by Robert Christman). In the Pays de Vaud, a territory under the rule of the Swiss city-republic of Bern, the Reformed faith was imposed on the Catholic population by fiat. Mandates prescribed the 'proper' form of worship and moral behavior, but people found ways to evade the authorities (essay by James J. Blakeley). The 'excommunication debate' in the Swiss town of Lausanne, located in the canton Bern, in 1558 focused on how ecclesiastical discipline was to be administered. Pierre Viret, following Calvin, argued that excommunication fell within the jurisdiction of the church, while the magistrates of Bern, following Zwingli, saw it as belonging to the secular authorities (essay by Michael W. Bruening).

Sigrun Haude's essay draws attention to another kind of tension between politics and religion. She analyses recording calendars, or almanacs, during the Thirty Years' War and shows how religion, politics, and astronomical-astrological explanations for the war were intertwined.[3]

The essays by Berndt Hamm, Raymond A. Mentzer, and Graeme Murdock tackle the difficult question of toleration, or at least the peaceful coexistence of different religious communities in early modern Europe. The memorandum and letter which Georg Fröhlich, a Nuremberg chancellery clerk, penned in 1530 were highly provocative. He advocated for religious freedom and tolerance for all faiths. His position was firmly rejected by the city's Lutheran authorities (essay by Berndt Hamm). After the French Wars of Religion, the Edict of Nantes, issued by King Henri IV in 1598, attempted to impose a workable structure of coexistence on Catholics and Protestants. One of the ways in which religious pacification was attempted was by establishing biconfessional law courts (essay by Raymond A. Mentzer).[4] In early modern Transylvania, where the influx of Reformation ideas resulted in religious diversity, the necessity to keep the peace led to limited religious freedom and a measure of protection for religious minorities (essay by Graeme Murdock).

The essays by Ute Lotz-Heumann and Peter Foley reveal the challenges of defining identity and legitimacy when politics and religion were not aligned in early modern Europe. In Ireland, English authorities expected that government pressure and imprisonment would coerce Catholic urban elites into conformity with the Protestant state church. Instead, they were met by resistance and found that religious and political grievances could make people see the same events in very different lights. The same was true in England in 1688, when William of Orange, a Protestant, invaded the country to take the throne from King James II, a Catholic. While many in England regarded this so-called 'Glorious Revolution' as legitimate, others viewed deposing a ruling monarch as an illegitimate act.

Finally, James D. Tracy's essay takes us to Dubrovnik, a Catholic republic and a tributary of the Ottoman Empire in the early modern period. In Dubrovnik the urban magistrates charted a careful course of fostering the Catholic faith while at the same time avoiding alienating the powerful Ottomans.

Notes

1 Other essays besides Schilling's, Estes's, and Dingel's addressing the actions and teachings of Luther and Melanchthon are no. 38, Hendrix: Reformation by accident? Martin Luther's Ninety-Five Theses of 1517; no. 40, Kuropka: Holy Scripture alone: Philip Melanchthon and academic theology.
2 For parallel examples of religious and social disciplining in a Catholic context see the essays on the Spanish Inquisition: no. 7, Poska: Spain, 1649: The Inquisition disciplines two Catholic priests who shot the baby Jesus; no. 48, Graizbord: A snapshot of Iberian religiosities: The inquisitorial case against the New Christian María de Sierra, 1651.
3 For another essay about early modern understandings of astronomical phenomena see no. 49, Fix: Blazing stars: Interpreting comets as portents of the future in late seventeenth-century Germany.
4 Several other essays in this collection throw light on events leading up to and during the French Wars of Religion and the impact of these religious wars. See no. 18, Reid: Bourges: Public rituals of collective and personal identity in the middle of the sixteenth century; no. 19, Diefendorf: Castres, 1561: A town erupts into religious violence; no. 71, Taylor: Catholic preaching on the eve of the French Wars of Religion: A eucharistic battleground.

52 Martin Luther defies Frederick the Wise: A letter from Borna, 1522

by Heinz Schilling

Martin Luther's letter to the Elector[1] of Saxony, dispatched from Borna, the final stop on his return to Wittenberg from Wartburg castle, on 5 March 1522, is in many respects noteworthy – as a testament to Luther's tactical thinking, as a work of artful speech, but above all as a world-historical document on individual freedom.

In his letter, Luther tried to achieve multiple objectives. On the one hand, he wanted to create a *fait accompli*, while on the other hand he did not want to irritate Elector Frederick the Wise further, who alone could grant him protection from the 1521 Edict of Worms and who had sheltered him in Wartburg castle for almost a year. Therefore, he emphatically expressed in his letter that he was indebted to the elector. However, he saw his work of reform, which was worth more to him than his life, in mortal danger: In Wittenberg in the first days of January 1522, radicals led by his colleague at the University of Wittenberg, Andreas Bodenstein of Karlstadt, who, Luther insisted, were in league with the devil, had resorted to iconoclasm and won the upper hand in the town. In this situation Luther decided to return to Wittenberg immediately.

He did not allow himself to be dissuaded, even when the bailiff of Eisenach, Johann Oswald, delivered a message from the elector strictly forbidding Luther to return home. Frederick the Wise had reason to be worried and to want the reformer to remain in Wartburg castle. The Nuremberg imperial council, prompted by the unrest in Wittenberg, had recently sent a sharp rebuke to the elector, and the Catholic Bishop of Meissen had announced plans for a visitation in Saxony. Should Luther, who was still under imperial ban, return to Wittenberg, political reprisals from the Empire[2] seemed unavoidable.

Luther realized that his public appearance could subvert the Saxon government. Nevertheless, he didn't hesitate for a moment. He left without further negotiations with the Saxon court and announced his return as a virtual *fait accompli*. Thus, when the elector received the letter from Borna, the rebellious monk had already returned to Wittenberg:

"To the Most Serene, Noble Sovereign and Lord, Sir Frederick, duke of Saxony, elector of the Holy Roman Empire, landgrave of Thuringia, margrave in Meissen, my Most Gracious Lord and Patron. …

"I need not say that I know your Electoral Grace has the very best of intentions, for I am certain of it as a man can be. On the other hand I am convinced by more than human means of reckoning that I too have good intentions. But this does not get us anywhere. ... I hope that it will always be that I have a thoroughly unaffected love and affection for Your Electoral Grace above all other sovereigns and rulers. ...

"Your Electoral Grace knows (or, if you do not, I now inform you of the fact) that I have received the gospel not from men but from heaven only, through our Lord Jesus Christ, so that I might well be able to boast and call myself a minister and evangelist, as I shall do in the future. ... I have served Your Electoral Grace well enough by staying in hiding for this year to please Your Electoral Grace. The devil knows very well that I did not hide from cowardice ...

"I have written this so Your Electoral Grace might know that I am going to Wittenberg under a far higher protection than the Elector's. I have no intention of asking Your Electoral Grace for protection. Indeed I think I shall protect Your Electoral Grace more than you are able to protect me. And if I thought that Your Electoral Grace could and would protect me, I should not go. The sword ought not and cannot help a matter of this kind. God alone must do it – and without the solicitude and co-operation of men. Consequently he who believes the most can protect the most. And since I have the impression that Your Electoral Grace is still quite weak in faith, I can by no means regard Your Electoral Grace as the man to protect and save me. ...

"Inasmuch as I do not intend to obey Your Electoral Grace, Your Electoral Grace is excused before God if I am captured or put to death. Before men Your Electoral Grace should act as an elector, obedient to the authorities and allowing His Imperial Majesty[3] to rule in your cities and lands over both life and property, as is his right according to the Imperial constitution; Your Electoral Grace should by no means offer any resistance or request such resistance or any obstruction on the part of others in case [His Imperial Majesty] wants to capture me or put me to death. For no one should overthrow or resist authority save him who ordained it; otherwise it is rebellion and an action against God. But I hope they will have the good sense to recognize that Your Electoral Grace occupies too lofty a position [to be expected] to become my executioner. ...

"I have written this letter in haste so that Your Electoral Grace may not be disturbed at hearing of my arrival [in Wittenberg]. ... If Your Electoral Grace believed, you would see the glory of God. But because you do not believe, you have not yet seen. Love and praise to God forever. Amen."[4]

The letter is a masterpiece: Luther treated his prince, who was one of the most prominent territorial rulers of the Empire, with all necessary respect, and he expressed his thanks and obedience – but only regarding wordly things. More important than political considerations, even more important than Luther's own life, was the evangelical truth. While prepared to die for his faith, the reformer believed that he returned to Wittenberg under God's protection, "a far higher protection than the Elector's." At the same time, Luther underscored his independence of, even superiority to, any secular ruler with a candor that could hardly have been surpassed.

Casting himself in the role of an Old Testament prophet, Luther relativized the significance of secular authority in light of sacred history. In an unabashed expression of his charge as pastoral admonisher he writes: "And since I have the impression that Your Electoral Grace is still weak in faith, I can by no means regard Your Electoral Grace as the man to protect and save me." These are not the words of a prince's servant, but they are also not the words of a revolutionary. After all, Luther urges Elector Frederick not to act counter to imperial law in order to defend him against violence to his person. For many of his contemporaries the complexities of the reformer's stance and his personality were too difficult to comprehend. Elector Frederick, however, understood the language of his Wittenberg professor and the attitude expressed in the letter. He accepted the prophetic claim with which 'Doctor Martinus,' as he always respectfully called him, legitimized his unyielding behavior, and he adjusted Saxon politics accordingly.

Notes

1 In early modern Germany, the electors were the princes who elected the emperor.
2 The Holy Roman Empire of the German Nation, usually called 'the Empire,' was a huge and complex political organization in central Europe in medieval and early modern times. It was a loose political union of mostly German and largely self-governing principalities and towns.
3 Charles V, Holy Roman Emperor.
4 Luther's letter to Frederick of Saxony, Borna, 5 March 1522, in Gottfried G. Krodel and Helmut T. Lehmann (eds), *Luther's Works (American Edition)*, vol. 48: *Letters I*, Philadelphia: Fortress Press, 1963, no. 117, pp. 389–393.

53 Philip Melanchthon justifies magisterial reform, 1539

by James M. Estes

As a general rule, the Protestant Reformation survived only where it won the support of friendly rulers who were able to defend it and to foster the organization of new churches independent of the church of Rome. Although the Bible and church history were full of examples of pious emperors, kings, princes, and other sovereign rulers who established and maintained true religion, magisterial support for the Protestant Reformation had to be defended against: first, those who regarded such support as a flagrant violation of the authority of the Catholic hierarchy; and, second, those who maintained that Protestant rulers had no authority (or no need) to impose uniformity of doctrine and practice on religious non-conformists who did not threaten the public peace. It was Philip Melanchthon (1497–1560), Luther's colleague in Wittenberg, who, in answer to these critics, provided the definitive version of the Lutheran teaching that God had established secular government 'for the sake of the church.' Although Melanchthon's mature teaching on the subject had been fully worked out by 1534, he argued it most brilliantly and cogently in the 1539 treatise *Concerning the Office of Princes, That God's Command Instructs Them to Remove Ecclesiastical Abuses*:

"[P]rinces and magistrates must abolish ungodly worship and see to it that true doctrine is taught and that godly ceremonies are established in the churches. I shall establish this proposition with many clear arguments. ...

"[1.] God expressly admonishes rulers to submit to the Gospel and to allow it to be propagated. Psalm 2[:10–12]: 'Be wise now therefore, O kings: be instructed, you judges of the earth. Serve the Lord with fear, and rejoice with trembling. Kiss the Son, lest the Lord be angry [with you].' ... Isaiah 49[:23]: 'And kings shall be your foster fathers, and queens your nursing mothers,' that is, princes and the rulers have the duty to support and defend the ministry of the Gospel and provide the material support of pastors and preachers. For this is the reason that God has established political authority, that the Gospel might be spread. All rulers must obey these commandments, even if superior lords and popes object. ...

"[2.] The magistrate is the custodian of the first and second tables of the law,[1] as regards external discipline; that is, he must prohibit external impieties, punish those guilty of them, and set a good example. Now it is clear in the first and second commandments that idolatry and blasphemy are prohibited; therefore it is necessary that the magistrate should abolish blasphemy and external idolatry[2] and assure that true doctrine and godly ceremonies are established. For although the magistrate does not change hearts or have a spiritual office, he does nonetheless have the office of preserving external order in those things that pertain to the first table. It was certainly for these reasons that the [Christian] emperors Constantine[3] ... and Theodosius[4] issued laws prohibiting the worship of idols and imposed capital punishment on those who sacrificed in public. ...

"[3.] If the bishops [who should reform the church] do nothing, or if the bishops themselves teach falsehoods, the rest of the church must remove bad pastors from office. And in any [ecclesiastical] assembly whatsoever the foremost members ought to have precedence over all the others and help them, so that the church might be reformed. Princes and other magistrates are necessarily the foremost members of the church: They are therefore duty bound to initiate and support that reformation. [This] is obvious, for the following commandments pertain to the whole church and to individual members: 'Beware of false prophets' [Matt 7:15] ... 'If anyone preach any other Gospel, let him be accursed' [Gal 1:8]. These texts command every individual to abhor the defenders of ungodly doctrine and worship as persons cursed and banned. ... Thus whenever it is certain that doctrine is ungodly, there is no doubt that the sounder part of the church ought to remove bad pastors and abolish ungodly worship. And the magistrates in particular, as the foremost members of the church, ought to support this reformation. ...

"[4.] The preeminent and particular goal of human society is that God become known. The magistrate is the guardian of human society: Therefore he ought above all else to be the guardian of this chief goal, because in every action the principal goal is to be sought and defended, just as health is chiefly to be sought and defended by a doctor in healing. Thus in the government of society, too, the proper goal of society is principally to be sought by the governor. Hence those magistrates err who separate government from its goal and judge themselves to be the guardians only of peace and a full belly. For they have, to a much higher degree, another office, namely the defense, as pertains to external discipline, of the whole law of the first and second tables. For the sake of this divine office, God shares with them his name, saying: 'I have said, you are gods' [Ps 82:6], that is, those divinely chosen to maintain true religion, to prohibit and abolish idolatry, to preserve justice, marriage, peace, to forbid depravity, etc. In Deuteronomy 17 [:18–19] God makes the king custodian of the law and of the teaching of religion. And in the Book of Wisdom [1:1], this precept is taught at the outset: 'Love righteousness, you that be judges of the earth: seek the Lord,' etc. ...

"[5.] But I say [that the magistrate] is custodian of the law, as far as external discipline is concerned, in order to preserve the distinction between the ministry of the Gospel and the office of magistrate. The ministry of the Gospel proclaims the Gospel by which the Holy Spirit is effective in believers ... Meanwhile, however, the magistrate has his external office: He prohibits public idolatry, just as he prohibits adultery or murder, in order that there be no cause of offence. Paul clearly teaches this, saying [1 Tim 1:9] that the law is made for the unrighteous, the profane, and the disobedient toward God. And this use of the law Paul calls legitimate, that is, when by external discipline the magistrate restrains crimes that are contrary to the first and second tables."[5]

Notes

1. I.e., the two tables or tablets containing the Ten Commandments (Exod. 20:1–17). The commandments in the first table (the first three or four, depending on one's theological tradition) describe one's duty to God; those in the second table (the remaining six or seven) describe one's duty to one's fellow human beings. Melanchthon here follows tradition in treating the Ten Commandments as God's own capsule summary of natural law, with which (along with divine law) all human law must be in harmony.
2. For the reformers, this meant abolishing Catholic practices, e.g., the Catholic Mass.
3. Ruled 312–337.
4. Theodosius I, ruled 379–395.
5. Philip Melanchthon, *De officio principum, quod mandatum Dei praecipiat eis tollere abusus ecclesiasticos*, in Robert Stupperich (ed.) in cooperation with Hans Engelland et al., *Melanchthons Werke in Auswahl*, 7 vols, Gütersloh: Bertelsmann, 1951–1975, vol. 1, pp. 387–410. The passages translated here are found on pp. 388, 389–391, 392–393, 394–395, 400. Translated by James M. Estes.

54 The courage to avow the truth: Philip Melanchthon on the Interim, 1548[1]

by Irene Dingel

To restore unity, peace, and justice to the Empire[2] – this was the goal of Emperor Charles V (1500–1558) when he waged war on the Schmalkaldic League in 1546/47. The League was an organization formed in defense of the Protestant territories of the Holy Roman Empire in 1531. From a legal standpoint, Charles V's military action was within the bounds of the imperial constitution because he portrayed it as an 'imperial execution,' an intervention by the central authority against specific princes to enforce observance of imperial law – in this case against the Elector[3] of Saxony and the Landgrave of Hesse, both rebellious leaders of the Schmalkaldic League. However, the Schmalkaldic War was a *de facto* religious conflict because Charles V wanted to end the religious divide in the Empire. All previous attempts at reuniting the church, including the imperial colloquies, had collapsed. Upon his victory at the battle of Mühlberg on the Elbe, on 24 April 1547, Charles V called for a new religious law to be enacted by an imperial diet[4] at Augsburg in 1548.

Since it was only to serve as a temporary solution until a decision could be reached by a general council, the law was called the 'Interim.' Its goal was the re-unification of the church through an extensive 're-Catholicization' of the territories and cities which had adopted Lutheranism. Only lay communion and clerical marriage were conceded; in teaching and ceremony, a return to the pre-Reformation status quo was compulsory. Any opposition to the law was prohibited, and numerous pastors who would not acquiesce were forced into exile. The presence of imperial troops, mostly in the south of the Empire, gave teeth to the law and enforced obedience. Nevertheless, there were centers of resistance, primarily the city of Magdeburg, which was besieged by the imperial ally, Maurice of Saxony. Here, the printing presses never stopped, and every variety of Protestant propaganda was produced.

One of the first publications to come out expressly against the Augsburg Interim was a pamphlet entitled *Thoughts on the Interim by the Venerable and Learned Philip Melanchthon*.[5] These *Thoughts* had at first only been circulated in manuscript form, and, besides Philip Melanchthon, were signed by the Wittenberg theologians Johannes Bugenhagen, Johannes Pfeffinger, Caspar Cruciger, Georg Major, and Sebastian Fröschel. Matthias Flacius Illyricus – a former student and friend of Melanchthon's, but now his theological opponent – was responsible for the unauthorized printing of Melanchthon's work in Magdeburg. Shortly before, Flacius had published his own fiercely negative judgment on the Interim. Melanchthon's text was published without his knowledge – though it bore his name – and should be seen as an attempt by Flacius to discredit Melanchthon's more moderate stance.

Despite this, the impact of Melanchthon's *Thoughts* and his influence on further oppositional statements was considerable. Unlike Flacius, Melanchthon chose his words carefully. With historical hindsight it is clear that this was due to the larger political context in which Melanchthon was writing, as the new Saxon prince, Elector Maurice, had requested the work. Melanchthon wrote this paper at an early point in the process: Although he assumed the official status of the Interim, he had yet to receive a printed version of the edict. Melanchthon, therefore, did not know of the law's exclusive applicability to the Protestant cities and territories as later revealed in the preamble ("prologue") to the Interim (since it had originally been intended to also include those of the old faith). It was for this reason also that Melanchthon's thoughts are expressed rather diplomatically:[6]

"The prologue recently written to the book of the Interim was not brought to us, and therefore we cannot discuss it at this time: but we see that it is a very serious, grave and perilous text, if it is its intention to condemn our churches, and that the acceptance of this book would be an acknowledgement, as it were, that our churches have hitherto taught wrongly and created devious dissension and division. Therefore it is necessary that all the men of understanding in our churches answer to it, for if we should now ourselves deny the known and acknowledged truth, ... that would be a blasphemy toward God, which should never be forgiven; from which may God graciously defend us. And although war and destruction are threatened us, still we must set more by God's word, and not deny the known truth.

"... let men also consider, if false learning and idolatry should be again brought in and begun in our churches, how great an offense and slander should be occasioned in it: for many godly men and women would fall into great burdens and grief, and true prayer and calling upon God would be hindered. ...

"We strive not of our own frowardness, arrogance or pride, as some men have accused. God who knows all men's hearts knows how gladly we want to see and have peace with all our hearts.

"But this earnest and strong commandment, that we shall not forsake or persecute the knowledge of the truth, drives us to the defense of the true learning which is preached in our churches: and as for the danger, we will have to have trust in God.

"And since we now see and feel that the bishops and the participants will reach no agreement: and that the discord of doctrine and certain ceremonies will still remain, and that they will make or ordain no priests for us: it would be better if we indeed stayed calm, quiet, and peaceful in our churches, and did not raise disquiet, discord, debate and offense among ourselves.

"For this book[7] will surely not be received in many countries and cities.

"But as different as the articles in the book may be, some are right and some are wrong, some speak of the chief articles of belief which all men must know and understand, and some of other matters which are not so necessary to be known: we will in order declare our obedient meaning, and, since it is the right thing to do, we will not strive against it with calumny and sophistry, but plainly and simply acknowledge it, and again, what is not right, we will not allow. ...

"And since it was recently written to us, that it is highly forbidden in the prologue[8] to preach, teach, or write against this Interim, necessity forces us humbly to say this, that we will not change the true doctrine which we have hitherto preached in our churches. For no creature has power or authority to change God's truth. And no man may also deny or forsake the known truth. Since then this Interim is against the true doctrine in many articles, ... we must show a true declaration and answer to it, ..."[9]

In Melanchthon's view, whoever accepted the Interim would consent to the persecution of the truth of the Gospel. The truth he spoke of was the core of Protestant teaching: justification by God's grace alone. This truth, Melanchthon asserts, was not upheld in the Interim. He explains to the elector that it would therefore be blasphemy to consent to the law's implementation. In fact, the elector had a responsibility to ensure access to the Word of God and thus a denial of the recognized truth for political reasons was not permissible. Melanchthon's call to resistance focused on the courage to avow the truth – against political pressures and superior secular authorities. In this conviction, despite denigration from some of his contemporaries, he stood firm.

Notes

1 Translated by Daniel Jones and Benjamin A. Miller.
2 The Holy Roman Empire of the German Nation, usually called 'the Empire,' was a huge and complex political organization in central Europe in medieval and early modern times. It was a loose political union of mostly German and largely self-governing principalities and towns.
3 In early modern Germany, the electors were the princes who elected the emperor.
4 The imperial diet was the political assembly of the electors, princes, and imperial cities in the Holy Roman Empire.
5 *Bedencken auffs Interim Des Ehrwirdigen vnd Hochgelarten Herrn Philippi Melanthonis*, Magdeburg: Michael Lotter, 1548; it is edited in Irene Dingel (ed.), *Reaktionen auf das Augsburger Interim: Der Interimistische Streit (1548–1549)*, Göttingen: Vandenhoeck & Ruprecht, 2010, pp. 40–75.
6 Later in 1548, in his advisory note for the meeting of the Saxon territorial diet at Meissen, he was openly critical.
7 The Interim.
8 The preamble of the Interim.
9 Philip Melanchthon, "Thoughts on the Interim (1548)," in Ralph Keen (ed.), *A Melanchthon Reader*, New York et al.: Peter Lang, 1988, pp. 155–156, 166–167.

55   6 July 1535 – interpreting Thomas More's last words: God or king?

by Marjory E. Lange

When the executioner's axe ended Sir Thomas More's life on 6 July 1535, it was an internationally significant event. More (1478–1535) was famous within England. He had been the first layman to be chancellor and had assisted Henry VIII (1491–1547) with the writings that won the king the title "defender of the faith." On the continent, too, More was a man of renown. A long-time friend and associate of figures such as Desiderius Erasmus, the famous humanist, he was recognized as a strong proponent of the humanist movement, and known in the courts of Europe. More was also author of *Utopia* and *The History of Richard III*, the basis for Shakespeare's play and subsequent negative interpretations of that king. He had been very popular with Henry VIII until Henry's lack of a male heir led him to repudiate Catherine of Aragon in favor of Anne Boleyn.

When the pope refused to grant the king a divorce, Henry elected to break with the Roman church and caused parliament to enact two laws, one making the English ruler head of the English church (the Act of Supremacy) and the other changing the order of succession by placing his children with Anne Boleyn before his daughter with Catherine (the Act of Succession). Thomas More carefully maintained silence about both acts, on the grounds that his silent conscience could not be considered treasonous. Although he never abandoned his belief in papal supremacy, he never spoke against Henry. However, his refusal to take the oath supporting the Act of Supremacy was eventually enough to bring him to trial. The trial was a carefully contrived affair (More was, after all, an able lawyer and very learned in the laws of his day), but he was eventually convicted and condemned.

News of More's execution traveled with almost modern speed to the continent via a document now called *The Paris Newsletter*. The French document appeared as soon after his death as travel would have permitted, perhaps as early as 4 August. Very shortly after that, virtually the same text, translated into German and Spanish, was published in those countries. Finally, within a matter of months a very widely circulated erudite version in Latin, the *Expositio fideles*, appeared. In every case the text is a tightly written, convincing, and very detailed narrative of More's trial, conviction, and last personal experiences, including a report of his final words before he died. The tone of *The Paris Newsletter* is quite neutral in comparison with later polemical documents written in support of More. Notably, it contains no commentary; there is no evaluation of More's words or actions. It is as objective a piece of news reporting as the sixteenth century produced. Subsequent biographers have relied on this account, even though it is anonymous, has no provenance, and seems to have appeared from nowhere.

The bulk of the *Newsletter* recounts More's words at his trial, replying to the charges leveled against him, where, only after his conviction, did More unburden his conscience about the Act of Succession, and the Act of Supremacy under which he had been condemned.

According to the *Newsletter*, "More then spoke as follows: 'Since I am condemned, and God knows how, I wish to speak freely of your Statute, for the discharge of my conscience. For the seven years that I have studied the matter, I have not read in any approved doctor of the Church[1] that a temporal lord could or ought to be head of the spirituality.' The Chancellor[2] interrupting him, said, 'What More, you wish to be considered wiser and of better conscience than all the bishops and nobles of the realm?' To this More replied, 'My lord, for one bishop of your opinion I have a hundred saints of mine; for one parliament of yours, and God knows of what kind, I have all the General Councils [of the Roman church] for 1,000 years, and for one kingdom[3] I have France and all the kingdoms of Christendom.' Norfolk[4] told him that now his malice was clear. More replied, 'What I say is necessary for discharge of my conscience and satisfaction of my soul, and to this I call God to witness, the sole Searcher of human hearts. I say further, that your Statute is ill made, because you have sworn never to do anything against the Church,[5] which through all Christendom is one and undivided, and you have no authority, without the common consent of all Christians, to make a law or Act of Parliament or Council against the union of Christendom. I know well that the reason why you have condemned me is because I have never been willing to consent to the King's second marriage ...'"[6]

Throughout his defense, More spoke consistently in favor of papal supremacy, against the establishment of a national church, and used this stand as his reason for opposing Henry's marriage to Anne Boleyn.

The *Newsletter* ends with a moving account of More's last meeting with his daughter, Margaret, wife of his principal biographer, William Roper, concluding, "A little before his death he asked those present to pray to God for him and he would do the same for them ... He then besought them earnestly to pray to God to give the King good counsel, protesting that he died the King's good servant, and God's servant first."[7] For More, there was no inherent conflict in serving God and king, provided the king also served God.

This last phrase, "that he died the King's good servant, and God's servant first," has been the source of misunderstandings. The first published English translation has it "... *but* God's servant first." Not only is this clearly not the sense of the French original, but it creates a very judgmental and critical persona for More. If, as the original has it, he is the king's servant *and* God's first, then Henry and God are (at least potentially) on the 'same side,' and More could conceivably serve both. However, if More is only 'the king's servant, *but* God's first,' he appears to assert that Henry is irrevocably in the wrong and cannot be supported. Given More's great care to avoid anything resembling such a stand, it seems a clear misreading.

Thus, *The Paris Newsletter* is a significant document for several reasons: It presents a lucid account of the trial and execution of one of the most prominent of Henry's courtiers, one who was, moreover, a major player on the stage of international politics, and it demonstrates the speed with which news could be disseminated when the cause was important enough. In addition, it provides an early instance of the power of journalism to maintain anonymity in a difficult political situation: In over 450 years, no one has discovered the identity of the author, nor how the document was dispatched to France.

Notes

1. "Approved doctor of the Church" is an official title bestowed by the pope to a saint who is regarded as having made important contributions to theology and doctrine.
2. The Lord Chancellor, Thomas Audley.
3. England.
4. The Duke of Norfolk.
5. The Roman Catholic Church.
6. The translation is in James Gairdner, *Letters and Papers, Foreign and Domestic, of the Reign of Henry VIII*, vol. VIII, London: Longman, 1885, pp. 394–396, here p. 395. Gairdner used a copy of the text found in the memoirs of Bishop Anthony Castelnau, where it carries the date 4 August 1535. The original French text is found in Nicholas Harpsfield's *Life and Death of Sir Thomas Moore, Knight*, ed. Elsie V. Hitchcock, London: Published for the Early English Text Society by the Oxford University Press, 1932.
7. Gerard B. Wegemer and Stephen W. Smith (eds), *A Thomas More Sourcebook*, Washington, DC: The Catholic University of America Press, 2005, p. 355. They, among others, remark upon the error in the last sentence.

56 Mansfeld, 1554: Follow-up to an ecclesiastical visitation

by Robert Christman

In the 1530s and 1540s, and even more so during the second half of the sixteenth century, the Lutheran Reformation in the Holy Roman Empire[1] went through a process of institutionalization. As a general rule, each territory developed its own autonomous church polity (ecclesiastical authorities), usually under the ultimate control of the territorial lord or city council (temporal authorities). Common oversight over the church and state institutions reflected the significant overlap in each body's objectives. Territorial churches sought believing, obedient, and principled parishioners, taking seriously the control of morality as an important part of the pastoral function; the state wanted disciplined and obedient subjects. Although it occasionally led to tensions, maintaining proper behavior among the people became the joint responsibility of both bodies.

This tendency is perhaps most apparent in ecclesiastical visitations, events in which groups of visitors comprised of clerics and representatives of the temporal government traveled from parish to parish throughout the territory, reporting on the situation in each congregation. Already early in the Reformation, ecclesiastical visitations performed an important role. The first, conducted in Saxony between 1528 and 1531 by Martin Luther and his immediate circle, addressed primarily the teachings of the pastors, church practice, and the material condition of the churches. But during the second half of the sixteenth century, the laity increasingly became a focus of attention, as visitors began to investigate public sins and record their observations.

Normally, a visitation began with a short sermon to the entire congregation describing the process, its biblical precedents, and its goals. Next, the local pastors were asked about the performance of their duties, then about their parishioners' behavior. Thereafter, the visitors examined the beliefs of the laity, testing them on their knowledge of the catechism. Finally, the visitors asked the laity about the behavior of their fellow parish members, particularly about cases of adultery, use of magic, pilgrimages, blasphemy, failure to attend church services and the sacrament, usury, slander, unlawful divorce, and children who despised parents.

Methods and means for punishing offenders varied. In some territories, reports were passed to the consistory, a church court made up of both ecclesiastical and temporal authorities, but in others the first line of defense was the local temporal authorities who were told to admonish public sinners. Major offenses were handed over to the temporal courts or reported to the pastoral synod, an annual gathering of the territory's pastors. In the following excerpt from the directives for visitors in the small German territory of Mansfeld in 1554, the means of deciding and enforcing punishments for problems uncovered during the visitation are addressed. These issues brought the ecclesiastical and temporal authorities into intimate contact:

"The visitor, for his part, must record every confessed sin he rebukes in a visitation book, along with the individual's name and the circumstances, so that the superintendent[2] can be well informed and aware of the state of ecclesiastical and spiritual matters. Moreover, the sentence or punishment by our blessed lords,[3] as explained in the *Execution*,[4] will follow after the visitation is completed. Under no circumstances should this be left undone, because a visitation without an *Execution* is more destructive than constructive, as experience teaches us.

"The form and method of the *Execution* is as follows: Our blessed lords sit down with their councilors after the visitations and hear the misdeeds, transgressions, and sins recounted in their entirety. They then determine the sentences and penalties, and means of improvement. Spiritual visitors[5] can be asked about those problems that clearly concern ecclesiastical and entirely spiritual matters, and their advice can be added to the other determinations on civil judgments.

"After this has been completed, all temporal authorities and local sheriffs should be informed, each in his own district, that the sentences must be carried out within a set time. It would especially please me if the punishments consisted of a prison sentence rather than fines, so that the poor women and children, who are not guilty of their husbands' and fathers' transgressions, won't suffer under the burden of financial penalties. In cases where individuals have been punished by the temporal authority for serious and scandalous deeds, reconciliation with the church should be made through public penance and absolution. In this way the scandal is removed and the others are deterred from that sin. This should be done according to the liturgy of absolution as prescribed in the booklet of spiritual discipline used in this territory.

"Moreover, so that no one wonders why we insist that the temporal authorities handle all punishments of the abovementioned sins, we do this for good reason: So that the princely councilors do not accuse the clergy of grasping for the temporal sword and intruding in the government and rule. For it matters less to us who punishes the transgression and sins as long as they are punished. At the same time, we do not intend with this recommendation to take away from the consistory the right to punish sins and to exercise ecclesiastical punishment. Indeed the temporal and spiritual authorities must act harmoniously and in concord, so that all scandals and sins be punished."[6]

Two significant late-Reformation trends present themselves in this text. The first is the way in which the temporal and ecclesiastical authorities worked together. Representatives from each body took part in the visitations. Both the superintendent and the counts, heads of their respective polities, were informed of the results. And while the counts decided upon the punishments, they also received input from the clerics. It is difficult to imagine a situation in which the two groups of authorities were more intertwined.

The second issue that arises is the possibility of tension between the two groups, as acknowledged by the author himself. He seems to expect criticism for the state's expanded role in disciplining the people; he argues that his plan does not impinge upon jurisdictional boundaries; and he reminds the reader that the two groups of authorities have the same goals and interests in mind. Although their goals often overlapped significantly, it seems that sometimes the ecclesiastical and temporal authorities came into conflict with one another.

Notes

1 The Holy Roman Empire of the German Nation, usually called 'the Empire,' was a huge and complex political organization in central Europe in medieval and early modern times. It was a loose political union of mostly German and largely self-governing principalities and towns.
2 A superintendent was a high-level official in certain Protestant churches in early modern Europe; he occupied the same level as a bishop.
3 "Our blessed lord" was the way in which subjects referred to their princes. Here the reference is to the local counts, who stood at the apex of the temporal authority.
4 The term *Execution* refers to the directives regarding the imposition of penalties; it also refers to the implementation of the punishments themselves.
5 The term "spiritual visitors" refers to members of the visitation team who are clergy.
6 Erasmus Sarcerius, *Form und Weise einer Visitation / Fur die Graff un[d] Herschafft Mansfelt. Durch Erasmum Sarcerium Superintendente[n] zu Eisleben / gestellet Des Jahrs 1554*, Eisleben: Bärwald, Jakob, 1554, pp. B2v–B3v. Translated by Robert Christman.

57 Reformation mandates for the Pays de Vaud, 1536: How Bernese authorities tried to force their subjects to become Protestants

by James J. Blakeley

In 1536, the city-republic of Bern conquered and seized the nearby francophone territory of the Pays de Vaud. The politically fragmented and militarily weak Vaud was no match for the formidable Bernese army. Conquest meant that Bern would impose its Reformed faith on the Roman Catholic population. Converting the people would not be as quick as military conquest. There was little native attraction to the Protestant Reformation in Vaud; many were reluctant to give up the old faith. Thus, one of Bern's first steps was to issue religious mandates that clarified its religious creed and forbade the Catholic Mass and practices. Such mandates were an aspect of the process of confessionalization in which states dictated to their inhabitants and subjects the religion that was allowed in a particular territory. Although the secular and religious officials, ensconced in urban centers, could order religious change, they relied on local officials to communicate directives. The following selection is taken from the October 1536 mandate that Bern issued to end Catholic worship:

"We order and command each and every one of our bailiffs, chief magistrates, lords of manors, lieutenants, and other officers, after having seen this document, to travel forthwith from one church to the other and also to every cloister and monastery ... and to tell them that we have ordered an end to [papal] ceremonies, sacrifices, offices, papal institutions, and traditions and that they must completely end all of these immediately if they wish to avoid our bad graces and heavy punishment. We also expressly advise that all images, idols, and altars in these said churches and monasteries be taken down without delay."[1]

In December 1536, a second mandate was issued that clarified and expanded on the first. It was longer, more detailed, and focused on specific behavioral changes that residents were expected to make in order to conform to Bern's religious vision:

"*On The Blessings of Voyages, and Pilgrimages:* We have also ordered that all blessings of voyages and pilgrimages are forbidden and that those who are bold enough to disobey will be fined ten *florins* for men, seven for women."[2]

"*On Rosary Beads:* To avoid scandal and conflict we have ordered that no one should carry rosary beads under the threat of being fined 30 *sols* for men and 15 *sols* for women."[3]

"*On The Ave Maria:* We are certain that all are of the opinion that no one should worship anything other than one God, our Lord Jesus Christ. Therefore, on account of this, no one shall say the Ave Maria in a place of prayer and no one should ring the bells to publicize it as was done previously."[4]

"*On the Ringing of Bells Against Ill Weather and After Death:* The ringing of bells during periods of foul weather and for those who have passed away is in vain, therefore we abolish it and forbid it."[5]

Religious officials in Bern believed that such ritualistic practices had no biblical basis and were only superstitious forms of idolatry. Likewise, if a true Reformation were to take place, the sacred space of the church itself was to be cleansed of all statues of the saints and the Virgin, side altars, and other vestiges of Catholicism. For the population, such traditions were important spiritual expressions that had been carried out for generations. They bound communities together in common practice and, in the case of bell ringing, were a means of keeping at bay danger, injury, and threats to crops that could, in a largely agricultural society, devastate a village. Similarly, the church interiors contained significant religious statues and objects, many of which had been dedicated by village residents or their ancestors and thus were important for individual and communal worship. It is not surprising, then, that officials faced resistance in eliminating them.

Mandates that ordered religious change, acceptable behavior, and new ways of worship were common during the Protestant Reformation throughout Europe. Often, they set the punishments to be imposed if the mandates were broken. Some historians have questioned the effectiveness of such religious ordinances: Authorities could dictate what religious and moral behavior was acceptable, but did that mean that subjects obeyed? Interestingly, in the case of the Pays de Vaud, most parishes were very close to Catholic villages in the territory of Fribourg, a separate member of the Swiss Confederation. Thus, it was relatively easy to cross the border for worship, festivities, and dancing. Records of violations of the mandates exist which demonstrate that some preserved their Catholicism long after Bern ordered that it be given up. Moreover, this demonstrates a willingness on the part of the inhabitants to plot their own religious course even if that meant defying orders. Thus, while religious mandates show what was officially expected of inhabitants, they only reveal one side of the story. Nevertheless, they do demonstrate the confessionalizing spirit of the age, in which secular and religious authorities sought to control and modify both religious belief and behavior.

Notes

1 Regula Matzinger-Pfister (ed.), *Les sources du droit Suisse, 19ᵉ partie: Les sources du droit du canton de Vaud, C: Époque bernoise, 1: Les mandats généraux bernois pour le Pays de Vaud 1536–1798*, Basel: Schwabe, 2003, no. 2d, p. 14. Translated by James J. Blakeley.

2 Ibid., no. 2e, p. 18.
3 Ibid., p. 18.
4 Ibid., p. 18.
5 Ibid., p. 18.

58 Ministers and magistrates: The excommunication debate in Lausanne in 1558

by Michael W. Bruening

In early 1559, Pierre Viret, the chief pastor of Lausanne, Switzerland (and one of John Calvin's closest friends), was banished from the city and the other territories governed by canton Bern. The city's other ministers, as well as nearly all of the professors and hundreds of students at the Lausanne Academy, followed Viret into exile. Viret's banishment – ultimately for disobeying Bern's order to administer the Christmas Eucharist of 1558 as scheduled – was the culmination of twenty years of debate between the ministers of Lausanne and the magistrates of Bern over the proper jurisdictions of church and state in enforcing moral behavior.

For the magistrates, particularly in a city such as Bern that adhered more closely to Zwinglian thought, the regulation of moral behavior, just like all other behavior, properly belonged to the state. For Viret and his colleagues, who followed Calvin's teaching on this matter, the enforcement of morals was properly called 'ecclesiastical discipline.' As such, it fell within the jurisdiction of the church, particularly to the consistory, which was understood by Calvinists as the body of church elders. The crux of the debate was whether or not the consistory should possess the right of excommunication. Viret and his colleagues insisted that it should. In June 1558, they prepared a manuscript entitled "Advice of the Ministers of the Class of Lausanne on the Matter of Ecclesiastical Governance," in which they explained their position in detail to the Bernese:

"As for the government of daily affairs for the maintaining of order and control in the church, this duty pertains to those who are for this reason called 'governors,' and are also named 'elders,' the assembly of whom we call today the 'consistory' ... We believe this correction[1] is highly necessary to the church, since it was established by Jesus Christ (Matt. 18) and practiced continually since then, not only by the apostles and from the time when the rulers were infidels, but even more in the time of Christian princes, by the entire early church without any contradiction. For, in fact, since it is forbidden to give what is holy to dogs and pigs, how could this be enforced if there is no discipline for knowing who they are and for separating them from the children of God? ... In sum, experience shows us more clearly that it would not be possible to maintain a pure church without this order established by the

Lord against heretics, evil-doers, and trouble-makers, just as the secular state cannot be preserved for long if the magistrate does not administer reasonable punishment to delinquents.

"We call excommunication a sentence of punishment legitimately made and pronounced by those who have this duty in the church, that is to say, the assembly of the elders legitimately established. By this sentence an individual is declared shut out of the church in the name and by the power of Jesus Christ, and consequently shut off from Jesus Christ and his goods and treasures. The sign of this is that he is also shut out from the use of the sacraments, which are the marks and seal of the communion of Jesus Christ and his members, for as long as he remains obstinate in the sin for which he has been separated from the church."[2]

This section on excommunication constituted a small portion of a much larger plan for reforming church discipline – so comprehensive, in fact, that the Bernese accused the Lausanne ministers of trying to create a "new Reformation" to replace "our Reformation," as the Bernese consistently referred to their church order and religious decrees. They refused to enact any of the proposals, despite Viret's continued objections. Viret's postponement of the 1558 Christmas Eucharist was the last straw; he and his supporters had to go.

Key differences between Calvinist and Zwinglian eucharistic theology and ecclesiology underlay the excommunication debate in Lausanne. Zwinglian sacramental theology removed Christ's presence from the Eucharist; instead, the bread and wine were symbolic, memorial representations of Christ's body and blood. The focus of the sacrament was not personal but communal; the administration of the sacrament bound the entire ecclesio-civic community together as Christian citizens in remembrance of the Last Supper. In Calvinist eucharistic theology, by contrast, the elements continued to have real power, and *worthy* individual communicants fed spiritually on the true body and blood of Christ. Hence, the bread and wine were not mere symbols but retained their holiness; they were not, therefore, to be given to "pigs and dogs." Only excommunication could ensure that *unworthy* communicants did not pollute the sacrament by their presence.

With regard to ecclesiology, the Lausanne ministers insisted on the consistory's right of excommunication in order to maintain a "pure church." For them, the earthly church, properly understood, was the collection of the living members of the community of the elect. As such, the visible church was a subset of the larger political community. Since it constituted the body of Christ on earth, it needed to be as pure as humanly possible, uncontaminated by the most wanton sinners and clear 'enemies of the Gospel.' In Zwinglian thought, by contrast, the visible church and the political community were coterminous; in Zwingli's words: "A Christian is nothing other than a good and faithful citizen, and the Christian city nothing but the Christian church."[3] Excommunication would therefore sever the bonds of both church and state and, hence, as Bern's 1532 church order stated, "no one should be easily excommunicated."[4]

Notes

1 Excommunication.
2 "Advis des ministres de la classe de Lausanne sur le faict du gouvernement ecclesiastique," here as printed in Michael W. Bruening, "*La nouvelle réformation de Lausanne*: The Proposal by the Ministers of Lausanne on Ecclesiastical Discipline," *Bibliothèque d'Humanisme et Renaissance* 68, 2006, 21–50. Translated by Michael W. Bruening.
3 Preface to the *Commentary on Jeremiah* (1531), in Emil Egli et al. (eds), *Huldreich Zwinglis Sämtliche Werke*, vol. 14, Braunschweig: C. A. Schwetschke, 1905–, p. 424. Translated by Michael W. Bruening.
4 Gottfried W. Locher (ed.), *Der Berner Synodus von 1532: Edition und Abhandlungen zum Jubiläumsjahr 1982*, vol. 1, Neukirchen-Vluyn: Neukirchener Verlag, 1988, p. 209. Translated by Michael W. Bruening.

59 Who is in charge? Politics, religion, and astrology during the Thirty Years' War

by Sigrun Haude

Politics, religion, and astrology were often closely interwoven in the early modern period, which is evident in many recording calendars (*Schreibkalender*) or almanacs. These constituted a popular contemporary genre providing meteorological and astronomical information for each day, month, and season of the year, as well as space for one's own notes. Typically, such calendars also furnished an astronomical–astrological section including predictions about the future ranging from weather to politics, as well as sections on war and other events. The production of consecutive yearly calendars was a thriving business because not only were people eager for data regarding the weather, but during this war-torn era they also thirsted for forecasts on the course and possible outcome of military conflicts.

The following excerpts are translated from recording calendars written during the Thirty Years' War (1618–1648), a political and religious conflict between Protestants and Catholics that started as a regional confrontation in Bohemia and soon engulfed much of Europe. The recording calendars' various explanations reveal a wrestling with fundamental questions: Who was responsible for this long, miserable, seemingly endless war? The greedy, selfish politicians; the people with their sinful, blasphemous lives; the planets and stars; God himself; or all of the above?

Martin Horky (born *c.*1590, died before 1648), mathematician and physician in Lochowitz, Saxony–Anhalt, and well-known author of astronomical–astrological literature and calendars, published his 1636 *Schreibkalender* when the emperor and the imperial estates had just signed the Peace Treaty of Prague (1635). His writing reflects the uncertain hope for peace at the time. Horky underlines "that it would be desirable if we Christians cherished unity among ourselves and lived and believed in the way we did in times past. If we can suffer the Jews, who surely are public blasphemers of God and the Son of the Virgin Mary, in the [Holy] Roman Empire,[1] why can we not tolerate the Augsburgers [i.e., the Lutherans] and the Reformed? Why do [the Catholics] force the poor Lutherans with severe imprisonment, fire, and sword to accept the anti-Christian faith [i.e., Catholicism]?"[2]

Rather than supporting military conflict, Horky advocated a political and legal solution similar to the one established in the Peace of Augsburg in 1555 which would allow Lutherans and Catholics, and now also the Reformed, to live side by side without fighting one another. From the constellations of the planets and stars, he concluded that the war was not yet over:

"Therefore there is great cause to hasten toward penance and to tame God's anger with diligent prayer and a God-pleasing life. Since this Bohemian war began 19 years ago, we have experienced misfortune and unbelievable damage in many kingdoms and beautiful regions. ... in countless places people acted tyrannically and barbarically. Even the Turks would never have used such tyranny as the Christians did amongst themselves (God have mercy) ..."[3]

Like many others, Horky believed that war was a punishment from God and that penance would bring peace, but he was also horrified about the conduct of many "Christians."

In his chapter "On war, illnesses, and the fruits of the earth," Horky introduces God's providence into his argument when gauging what might happen in the future:

"... even though this year there are good constellations of the heavenly planets that suggest a worthy peace, I do not believe that war will end completely among Christians in Europe until, through special godly providence, the high potentates, princes, and powerful lords have united and turned their might against the Turks, the archenemy of the Christian name. But I fear, although many conventions and peace negotiations are underway, that these two small words 'mine,' 'yours,' that is: this is mine, not yours, will cause much evil among high and low persons. May God the Almighty preserve what is pious; ..."[4]

Horky's caution was well founded. War continued, since neither France nor Sweden signed on to the Treaty of Prague. In his 1640 *Schreibkalender*, Hermann de Werve (1584–1656), a Lutheran minister and astrologer in East Frisia and another successful author of calendars, gave voice to the general disappointment with politicians:

"Someone who walks underneath the windows of city hall is often smarter than those holding counsel within. It would have been and still is beneficial to pay attention to the counsel and suggestions of common people. This way many thousands of people and money would have been saved and spared. The world is blind because of greed, pride, envy, or stupidity."[5]

At the same time, de Werve criticized people for thirsting for news about the war:

"Now, the eager and smart-alec hearts and minds (which in the exploration of new things so rarely can be satiated) are not yet satisfied and content when one writes that, according to astrological opinion and political judgment, there is no hope for lasting peace ... (God can bestow peace and may he desire to do so). Instead, they crave and want to know who will finally retain the upper hand and be victorious ..."[6]

After twenty-two years of war, de Werve's forecasts were mostly pessimistic but, like many others, he expressed hope that a renewed orientation toward Christian virtues might end the political stalemate and the war's dire effects:

"... it will be such an exceedingly sad summer due to fire, robbery, murder, and bloodshed on water and land that I shudder when I think about the miserable situation ... But I hope that the Christians of this [Holy] Roman Empire will grow tired of the war, will come to an agreement, and will resist the bloodhound."[7]

In other words, only if both political leaders and their subjects embraced a Christian mindset and pious lifestyle would the war end. Still, since humans were weak, de Werve kept imploring God to have mercy on them.

Notes

1 The Holy Roman Empire of the German Nation, usually called 'the Empire,' was a huge and complex political organization in central Europe in medieval and early modern times. It was a loose political union of mostly German and largely self-governing principalities and towns.
2 Staatsarchiv Nürnberg, (Rep. 129) Staats- und Schreibkalender, no. 255 Jahreskalendersammlung 1544–1820, vol. 8, 1630–1639, *1636 Schreibkalender* by M. Martin Horky von Lochowitz, Nürnberg: Wolff Endters, 1636, fol. Bj v. Translated by Sigrun Haude.
3 Ibid., fols Bj v–Bij r.
4 Ibid., fol. Dij v.
5 Bayerisches Hauptstaatsarchiv Munich, Manuskriptensammlung no. 345, *Alter und Newer Schreibkalender, 1640*, with underlinings and short notes by Hermann de Werve, Nürnberg: Wolffgang Endters, 1640, fol. Bj r. Translated by Sigrun Haude.
6 Ibid., fol. Ciiij r.
7 Ibid., fol. Biij r.

60 Advocating religious tolerance: A Nuremberg voice of 1530[1]

by Berndt Hamm

In the spring of 1530, a debate broke out in the imperial city of Nuremberg concerning the toleration of religious beliefs which deviated from the official Lutheran position adopted by the city. Emotions ran especially high at that time regarding the punishment of Anabaptists.[2] In this situation, the chancellery clerk, Georg Fröhlich, who was a subordinate and close colleague of the city's council clerk,[3] Lazarus Spengler, composed a memorandum entitled "Whether secular government has the right to wield the sword in matters of faith."[4] Fröhlich did not make his memorandum public, but passed it to Spengler confidentially. Spengler was so alarmed, however, that he made Fröhlich's document available to Nuremberg theologians and outside experts like Martin Luther and Johannes Brenz and requested their opinions. They all confirmed Spengler in his firm rejection of Fröhlich's position.

Fröhlich's assertion of religious freedom was extremely unusual and provocative in the religious and political context of the early sixteenth century – especially considering that it did not come from the quill of a persecuted Anabaptist or Spiritualist; on the contrary, it came from a representative of the urban authorities and a supporter of the council's oversight over the Lutheran Church in the city. Personally, George Fröhlich was strongly influenced by humanism and probably harbored secret sympathies for Zwinglianism and Zwingli's understanding of communion.

In his memorandum, Fröhlich looked beyond the situation in Nuremberg and raised the question of religious tolerance in a more general way. He argued that secular authorities should allow all faiths – Catholics, Lutherans, Zwinglians, Anabaptists, "re-baptizers," Jews, and Turks – in their cities and territories. Invoking Luther's doctrine of the two kingdoms, Fröhlich rejected the use of force by the secular government in fundamental questions of religion and faith. He predicted that religious intolerance would lead to an escalation of hostilities, to violence and the shedding of blood. As he states in his report:

"Furthermore, if a Christian government forbids false faith, it thereby gives governments that adhere to false doctrine a pretext for combatting the true faith. For as soon as one admits that a government may impose penalties upon unbelievers, then every government will assume this right for itself – for none of them will admit to having a false faith – each one executing and banishing one after the other all those who are not of its faith."[5]

"For otherwise [i.e., without tolerance] the daily torture and execution of both true and false believers will not cease. And it is much to be feared, that one day, precisely for the reason that one seeks to exterminate false belief by the sword, governments will come into conflict and whoever is the strongest will teach the doctrine to the others. Then there will be a real blood-letting, which the devil, as the signs already indicate, diligently seeks and promotes."[6]

Following the intense reaction of Spengler to his memorandum, Fröhlich defended and clarified his position in a letter to Spengler in March 1530. In this letter, Fröhlich discusses how authorities were to be noncommittal toward different religious groups and what measures of autonomy should be conceded to them:

"For it is not my opinion that a government should not have the power, in the faith to which it adheres, to conduct visitations, to appoint and dismiss preachers, and to establish ceremonies. Indeed, I say more: not only should a government have the power to do this with respect to its own faith, but so also should every group or sect in its own faith, so that Christians, Jews, Anabaptists, etc., all would be free to establish and observe without hindrance those doctrines and ceremonies which they regard as right and by which they hope to come to God, but in separate places, namely the Christians in their churches, the Anabaptists and Jews in their designated houses or synagogues.

"I also say further that not only the government in its faith but also every sect – the Jews, Anabaptists, or others – should have the power to dismiss preachers or ministers whom they had appointed and subsequently found unfit for office, and to appoint others in their place, just as a government or community appoints and dismisses schoolteachers or shepherds.

"But just as the Jews or Anabaptists may not tell a Christian secular government how it shall order its worship or whom it should have for teachers, so also the government should not forcibly impose preachers, ceremonies, or doctrines upon the Jews or Anabaptists.

"This alone should be the government's office: if in its principality or territory anyone among the Jews, Christians, or Anabaptists resorts to force or crime, as for example if one party forcibly invades the synagogue or church of the other in order to establish its worship there, to attack the doctrines or disturb the ceremonies of the other, the government should not suffer this but administer penalties and restore peace."[7]

"... the government should ... restore peace in such a way that every faith or sect, in such cases or in others that might arise, may have peace and quiet in its worship, doctrine, and ceremonies, as otherwise in secular affairs, just as hitherto peace was everywhere maintained for the Jews in their synagogues."[8]

Fröhlich argued that full freedom of religious worship should be granted to all, even to those whose beliefs he held to be wrong and associated with the works of the devil (for example, the Anabaptists). The Nuremberg chancellery clerk believed that the true faith would ultimately prove itself through God's Word in this officially protected space of religious freedom. For Lazarus Spengler, such a tolerant stance was completely unacceptable. On 26 March he wrote to the reformer Johannes Brenz in Schwäbisch Hall:

"But if a government were absolutely required to tolerate in its territory those incontrovertibly recognized as public idolaters, deceivers, and heretics, whether they be pagans, Jews, or Christians, and to allow discordant preaching, idolatry, rebaptizing, and polluted sacraments and ceremonies, above all the public abomination of the mass, in the churches, houses, cloisters, or assemblies under its jurisdiction, just imagine what improprieties would result and what would, in time, become of all authority."[9]

In contrast to Fröhlich, Spengler argued for religious homogeneity in one dominion under one secular authority. That authority was to subordinate itself to the higher authority of the Bible as the Word of God. For Spengler, Fröhlich's standpoint raised the question: "And when would one ever again be able to maintain a uniform Christian order and a unanimous godly religion in any territory if one had to tolerate all these scoundrels and deceivers and could not expel them?"[10]

Spengler's concept of confessional unity would determine Protestant confessional politics during the Reformation era and the confessional age. Fröhlich's plea, together with many other voices of the sixteenth century asking for freedom of religious worship, anticipated the modern age. This freedom of worship would begin to gain gradual acceptance starting in the seventeenth century.

Notes

1 Translated by Amy Newhouse and Benjamin A. Miller.
2 The term 'Anabaptism' refers to radical groups during the Reformation period who practiced believers' (adult) baptism rather than infant baptism.
3 The council clerk was the head of the Nuremberg council chancellery.
4 "Ob ein weltliche oberkeit recht habe, in des glaubens sachen mit dem schwerdt zu handeln," in Lazarus Spengler, *Schriften*, ed. Berndt Hamm, Felix Breitling, Gudrun Litz, and Andreas Zecherle, vol. 3: *Schriften der Jahre Mai 1529 bis März 1530*, Gütersloh: Gütersloher Verlagshaus, 2010, no. 143, pp. 377–390.
5 James M. Estes (ed.), *Whether Secular Government Has the Right to Wield the Sword in Matters of Faith. A Controversy in Nürnberg in 1530 over Freedom of Worship and the Authority of Secular Government in Spiritual Matters: Five Documents Translated with an Introduction and Notes*, Toronto: Centre for Reformation and Renaissance Studies, 1994, pp. 41–52, here pp. 50–51. When Estes translated this primary source, he did not yet know that Georg Fröhlich was the author of this memorandum. He therefore assumed an anonymous author.
6 Ibid., p. 52.

7 German original in Spengler, *Schriften*, no. 148, pp. 401–403. Here quoted from Estes, *Whether Secular Government Has the Right to Wield the Sword in Matters of Faith*, pp. 52–53.
8 Ibid., p. 53.
9 German original in Spengler, *Schriften*, no. 150, pp. 405–411. Here quoted from Estes, *Whether Secular Government Has the Right to Wield the Sword in Matters of Faith*, p. 38.
10 Ibid.

61 Assuring civil rights for religious minorities in sixteenth-century France

by Raymond A. Mentzer

The fierce antagonism between Catholic and Protestant, the horrific collective violence associated with the religious warfare, and individual acts of brutality remain the popular image of the Protestant Reformation and the confessional turbulence that accompanied it. Less well-known are the various efforts to promote reconciliation among opposing religious groups and to safeguard the basic rights of various religious minorities. In France, the Wars of Religion erupted in 1562 and continued, despite repeated yet ineffective attempts at pacification, until the end of the sixteenth century. Over time, all sides came to agree, however reluctantly, on certain measures that ultimately enshrined Catholicism as the official religion of the realm while offering security guarantees to the Protestant minority who, when the fighting finally ended, constituted no more than 6 to 7 percent of the French population, roughly 1.4 million people.

The signal achievement in the pacification of the kingdom was the Edict of Nantes, issued by King Henri IV in 1598. While the legislation did not grant French Reformed Protestants, often known as Huguenots, full equality with Catholics, it created an intelligible and logical structure in which followers of the two faiths might live together without violence and bloodshed. The Edict allowed the exercise of the Reformed religion under restricted circumstances. The Huguenots also received guarantees of their civil and political rights. The crown allowed them to have so-called surety towns, which they could fortify and garrison with their own soldiers in order to protect the Reformed form of worship. Huguenots were also assured access to public and royal offices as well as admission to educational institutions. Finally, to allay Reformed fears of religiously prejudiced Catholic judges, the Edict recognized special bipartisan law courts known as chambers of the Edict (*chambres de l'Édit*). Equal numbers of Protestant and Catholic judges staffed the tribunals, which were competent to adjudicate any civil or criminal case in which at least one of the litigants was Protestant.

The Huguenots had called for independent justice from the time that violence first erupted in the early 1560s. Simply put, the prospect of trial by Catholic judges frightened them. Already in 1576, well before the end of the

Wars of Religion, the Edict of Beaulieu established the principle of bipartisan justice. The text of article 18 made clear the crown's intent:

"And in as much as the administration of justice is one of the principal means for maintaining our subjects in peace and concord, acceding to the request which has been made to us by our Catholic allies and members of the 'so-called Reformed religion,' we have ordained and ordain that a chamber composed of two chief justices [*présidents*] and sixteen associate judges [*conseillers*], half Catholics and half from the said religion,[1] will be established in our court of the *parlement*[2] of Paris."[3] Subsequent articles in the edict envisioned similar bipartisan courts for the other *parlements* throughout the realm.

Although this particular royal legislation was never fully realized and the religious strife continued for more than twenty years, the underlying concept – bipartisan courts composed of equal numbers of Catholic and Protestant judges who would adjudicate all civil as well as criminal cases involving Protestants – remained a fundamental element in attempts to bring lasting peace to the French kingdom. Full endorsement and implementation came only with the famous Edict of Nantes of 1598.

The Edict of Nantes organized chambers of the Edict for the *parlements* of Bordeaux, Grenoble, Toulouse and, in more limited fashion, for the high court at Paris. The royal legislation reiterated in much the same language as the earlier Edict of Beaulieu the judicial guarantees accorded the Protestants. Article 30 stated:

"To the end that justice be given and administered to our subjects, without any suspicion, hatred or favor, as being one of the principal means for maintaining peace and concord, we have ordained and do ordain, that in our court of the *parlement* of Paris shall be established a chamber ... which shall be called and entitled the chamber of the Edict, ..."[4]

Article 31 confirmed the status of the bipartisan tribunal which was already functioning at the Protestant town of Castres for the jurisdiction of the *parlement* of Toulouse and created new chambers within the *parlements* of Bordeaux and Grenoble:

"In addition to the chamber already established at Castres for the jurisdiction of our court of the *parlement* of Toulouse and which will continue as is, we have ... ordained and ordain that in each of our courts of the *parlement* of Grenoble and Bordeaux a similar chamber will be created, ..."[5]

The chambers within the *parlements* of Bordeaux, Grenoble, and Toulouse were bipartisan, that is to say, composed of equal numbers of Protestant and Catholic judges. The chamber for the *parlement* of Toulouse had two presidents and sixteen associate judges drawn equally from each faith; those for Bordeaux and Grenoble two presidents and twelve associate magistrates, again with a balance of Protestants and Catholics. The chambers for Paris, on the other hand, had but a single Reformed judge; the remainder of the bench was Catholic.

The Protestant and Catholic judges who staffed these tribunals had the power to hear all civil or criminal cases in which at least one of the litigants was Protestant. According to article 34 of the Edict of Nantes:

"All the said chambers ... shall have competence and shall judge in sovereignty and last appeal ... the proceedings and differences ... in which those of the Reformed religion are or shall be parties ... in all matters civil as well as criminal, ..."[6]

Collectively, these bipartisan tribunals adjudicated tens of thousands of cases before their dissolution in 1679 on the eve of Louis XIV's revocation of the Edict of Nantes. The courts assured Protestants access to unbiased justice or, at least, as dispassionate and impartial as possible in the religiously divided world of early modern France.

Notes

1 Protestantism.
2 High court.
3 André Stegman (ed.), *Édits des Guerres de Religion*, Paris: Vrin, 1979, p. 102. The original French texts of the various edicts of pacification, including the Edict of Nantes, promulgated during the French Wars of Religion can be found in this edition.
4 English translation of the Edict of Nantes adapted and modernized from E. Everard, *The Great Pressures and Grievances of the Protestants in France*, London 1681, reprinted in Roland Mousnier, *The Assassination of Henry IV*, London: Faber and Faber, 1973, pp. 316–363, here p. 326.
5 Ibid.
6 Ibid., p. 327.

62 Turda, 1568: Tolerance Transylvanian style

by Graeme Murdock

In January 1568 the diet[1] of Transylvania met in the town of Turda (Torda to its Hungarian-speaking residents). The diet discussed – and not for the first or the last time – how to resolve problems posed by religious divisions. By the 1560s Transylvania was a social and geographic patchwork of religious loyalties. These divisions were mirrored in the diet, which was made up of three privileged groups; German-speaking urban magistrates, Hungarian-speaking nobles, and Szekler lords from eastern Transylvania. The diet was called together by the territory's elected ruler, János Zsigmond Szapolyai. Szapolyai styled himself 'Elected King of Hungary,' but his rule was confined to the province of Transylvania and to some counties of the eastern Hungarian plain.

Transylvania had long been divided between a Latin Catholic community and an Eastern Orthodox community. During the middle decades of the sixteenth century, support for the Roman Catholic Church collapsed. Lutheranism came to dominate the German-speaking towns of Transylvania. Hungarian-speaking towns and nobles were first influenced by Lutheran preaching, but then mostly embraced a second wave of reform in favor of the views of Swiss Reformed theologians. A Hungarian-speaking Reformed Church emerged during the 1560s, but then divided as ministers argued over the doctrine of the Trinity. Some clergy defended Trinitarianism and adopted the Second Helvetic Confession. Others supported the insights of some Italian exiles and established contact with anti-Trinitarians in the Polish–Lithuanian Commonwealth.

How did the elite of the Transylvanian state respond to these dramatic religious changes? In January 1568, the diet decided that "ministers should everywhere preach and proclaim the Gospel according to their understanding of it, and if their community is willing to accept this, good, if not however, no one should be compelled by force if their spirit is not at peace, but a minister retained whose teaching is pleasing to the community. Therefore, no one should harm any superintendent[2] or minister, nor abuse anyone on account of their religion, in accordance with previous laws, and no one is permitted to threaten to imprison or deprive anyone of their position because of their teaching, because faith is a gift from God which comes from listening to the Word of God."[3]

At first sight, this resolution suggests that Transylvania became an extraordinary haven of religious tolerance in early modern Europe. The diet strictly prohibited violence against anyone "on account of their religion," while ministers were permitted to preach and proclaim the Gospel according to their understanding of it.

However, it is crucial to consider the context and practical impact of this resolution. For example, the diet apparently offered communities the right to decide on who should be appointed as their minister. However, we should not imagine that they intended for local plebiscites to be organized. Rather, the views of landowners and church patrons often remained decisive in determining which church had access to which buildings. We also need to read with care the language used by the diet. This resolution explicitly linked true faith with "listening to the Word of God." This reflected the ideology of religious reformers. While Lutheran, Reformed and anti-Trinitarian (or Unitarian) ministers came to different conclusions from reading the Scriptures, all maintained a shared interest in asserting the superiority of biblical authority over the authority of the Roman Catholic Church. The 1568 resolution reflected this anti-Roman agenda in "accordance with previous laws" about religious life in Transylvania.

In 1566, the diet had expelled all priests who did not want to learn from the Bible or who practiced 'idolatry.' Neither the Catholic Church nor the Orthodox Church therefore benefited from the provisions of the 1568 resolution. Only in 1595, thanks to the intervention of a Catholic prince, was the diet finally persuaded to accept that Transylvania had four "received religions," and that the "Catholic or Roman, Lutheran, Calvinist, and Arian religions can freely be maintained everywhere."[4] Even then, restrictions remained directed against Jesuits and against Catholic patrons who tried to install priests in their churches. The Orthodox Church, meanwhile, only received limited privileges granted by princes.

The 1568 Turda resolution provides a distinctive Transylvanian variation on a common European theme during the early modern period. Many states responded to the challenges posed by religious diversity following the Protestant Reformation by offering some legal rights to religious minorities. This was not done out of any spirit of tolerance or mutual respect between those of different faiths, but rather out of social and political necessity. Laws aimed to try to prevent the outbreak of civil conflict over matters of religion or to try to bring such violence to an end. The Transylvanian diet's resolution reflected the particular circumstances of a fledgling state attempting to maintain internal political cohesion and to avoid being overwhelmed by the Ottoman and Habsburg Empires, its mighty Muslim and Catholic neighbors. Given the divisions in the diet between Lutheran, Reformed, and anti-Trinitarian supporters, there was no prospect of imposing a single faith within Transylvania. The diet therefore sanctioned some degree of religious diversity as the best means of securing social and political stability. Transylvania's laws on religion from this period remain distinctive not only because of the range of religions offered legal protection, but also because these laws provided a durable, stable, and peaceful resolution to the complex social legacy of the Protestant Reformation.

Notes

1 An early modern representative political assembly.
2 A superintendent was a high-level official in certain Protestant churches in early modern Europe.
3 Sándor Szilágyi (ed.), *Erdélyi Országgyűlési Emlékek. Monumenta Comitialia Regni Transsylvaniae*, 21 vols, Budapest: Magyar Tudományos Akadémia, 1875–1898, vol. 2, p. 343. Translated by Graeme Murdock.
4 Ibid., vol. 3, p. 472.

63 Who suffered? A row in the Dublin Privy Council, 1605

by Ute Lotz-Heumann

Ireland, a part of the multiple kingdoms of the English monarchs in the early modern period, was a country deeply divided by the religious strife of the sixteenth and seventeenth centuries. After the Protestant Reformation had been introduced in England, the English lord deputies (or viceroys) in Ireland tried to introduce Protestantism there as well. However, they did not succeed in their attempt at a state-sponsored Reformation. A majority of the Gaelic Irish and the Old English (descendants of medieval English settlers) defied all attempts by the state to convert them to Protestantism and staunchly adhered to the Catholic religion. This caused conflict in many areas, but especially in Dublin where the two religions clashed in a small urban space.

Protestant administrators sent over from England confronted an urban elite of mostly Catholic families who continued to find clandestine ways to practise their forbidden religion. In 1605, the Dublin administration tried yet another method to force the Dublin elite into converting to the Protestant Church of Ireland: They issued so-called 'mandates' to the most prominent Dublin office-holders, requiring them to attend Protestant church services. When the Dublin aldermen refused, they were imprisoned. In a letter to Robert Cecil, Earl of Salisbury and chief advisor to King James I, one of the Protestant councilors in Dublin castle, Sir John Davis, relates his expectations of the 'mandates.' He also mentions a revealing episode that provides us with a rare glimpse of an intense personal interaction in seventeenth-century Ireland:

"The principal business then in motion there was the reducing of the people of that town[1] to church. For Dublin being the principal city and seat of the State, all the eyes of the kingdom were turned upon it, expecting the event of the proceedings[2] there; and the Council presumed the people of other parts would be much led one way or the other by the example of that place. ... Touching this work of reformation (meaning the bringing of the people to church), the State was engaged in it; and it must be constantly pursued, or else they must ever thereafter despair to do anything in it. ... he was strongly persuaded that it would have a general good success, for the Irishry,[3] priests, people, and all, will come to church. ... The like is to be presumed of the multitude in general throughout the kingdom; for it so happened in King Edward the Sixth's days, when more than half the kingdom of England were Papists;[4] and again in the time of Queen Mary, when more than half the kingdom were Protestants; and again in Queen Elizabeth's time, when they were turned Papists again. The multitude was ever made conformable by edicts and proclamations; and though the corporations[5] in that realm[6] and certain of the principal gentlemen stood out, yet if this one corporation of Dublin were reformed, the rest would follow; ...

"P.S. – Had almost forgotten one circumstance, ... When Sir Patrick Barnewall[7] was committed from the Council table, 'Well,' said he, 'we must endure as we have endured many other things.' 'What mean you by that?' said the [Lord] Deputy; 'what have you endured?' 'We have endured,' said he, 'the miseries of the late war, and other calamities besides.' 'You endured the misery of the late war?' said the [Lord] Deputy. 'No, Sir, we have endured the misery of the war, we have lost our blood and our friends, and have indeed endured extreme miseries to suppress the late rebellion, whereof your priests, for whom you make petition, and your wicked religion, was the principal cause.'"[8]

Davies here formulates an expectation for Ireland that he derives from the 'lessons' of English history. In his view, the people of Ireland will conform to Protestantism if the administration succeeds in forcing the leading townspeople of Dublin to attend the services of the Protestant state church. He assumes that the common people will follow their superiors' example, and he feels confident in his assumption because he has witnessed similar developments in English history. In England, the official religion changed from Protestantism under Edward VI (ruled 1547–1553), to Catholicism under Mary I (ruled 1553–1558), and back to Protestantism under Elizabeth I (ruled 1558–1603), without much resistance from the population. Conformity to the religion prescribed by the monarch was the rule in the English kingdom. The Dublin administration, however, did not reckon with the Dublin aldermen. Their resistance was firm and their attachment to Catholicism did not waiver.

When Sir Patrick Barnewall, whom we can almost imagine mumbling his complaint about having to endure one more hardship under his breath, was accosted by Lord Deputy Arthur Chichester, he named the recent Nine Years' War, a rebellion by an Irish nobleman, as one of those hardships. This obviously raised the lord deputy's ire, who then told Barnewall in no uncertain terms that Catholicism was to blame for the rebellion in which only the Protestants in Ireland suffered, because they had staffed the army and had "lost our blood and our friends." This exchange draws attention to the very different meanings attached to the Nine Years' War in Ireland: While the Dublin merchants, whose trade had suffered because of the war and who did not have much sympathy for a nobleman's rebellion, saw themselves as its victims, the lord deputy regarded the war as a religious conflict and did not accept Barnewall's premise that the townspeople of Dublin had suffered. Rather, he turned the tables on Barnewall by accusing him, as a Catholic, of being responsible for the rebellion, and by defining Protestants as the only victims of the war. Overall, Sir John Davis's letter throws light on the personal, as well as the larger political, implications of early modern religious conflict.

Notes

1 Dublin.
2 The above-mentioned 'mandates.'
3 The Gaelic Irish.
4 Catholics.
5 Towns.
6 Ireland.
7 Sir Patrick Barnewall was an Old English Catholic who had been imprisoned for opposing the 'mandates.'
8 Letter from Sir John Davis to the Earl of Salisbury, 1605, in C. W. Russel and John P. Prendergast (eds), *Calendars of the State Papers Relating to Ireland, of the Reign of James I, 1603–1606*, London: Public Record Office, 1872, pp. 370–372.

64 Is the throne empty? James II's supposed desertion of 1688 discussed

by Peter Foley (†)

'The Glorious Revolution' is a positive name for events in British history set in motion in the fall of 1688 when the Protestant William, Prince of Orange and *stadtholder* in the Dutch Republic, landed in England with an army, causing the King of England, Scotland, and Ireland, the Catholic James II, to flee to France. Despite being a prince of royal and aristocratic bloodlines, William of Orange had achieved his political station at home through his successful military defense of the Netherlands against various European adversaries. Britain had at times ranked among his foes, but France had been by far the more consistent and immediately threatening neighbor. Ever a shrewd politician, William had sought to repair his relationships with the brothers of his mother, Charles II and James II, the successive British kings, and he had even married his cousin Mary, the eldest daughter of James II.

When Charles II died in 1685 and his brother, the openly Roman Catholic James II, who was unpopular in England, took over, William invaded the country with the support of a group of influential members of parliament. After the landing of William, members of the Houses of Lords and Commons[1] came together to debate and ultimately sanction William of Orange and his wife Mary Stuart taking over as monarchs for the reign we know as 'William and Mary.' In response to the first meetings of the Commons, the clergyman Jeremy Collier wrote a pamphlet entitled *The Desertion Discuss'd in a Letter to a Country Gentleman* that constituted a bold statement of James II's rights and at the same time questioned the legitimacy of deposing a ruling monarch. Framed as a putative letter to a friend, Collier laid out the illegitimacy of the claims of those defending the deposition of James II:

"I Don't wonder to find a Person of your Sense and Integrity so much surprised at the Report of the Throne's being declared Vacant, by the lower House of the Convention: *For how* (say you) *can the Seat of the Government be Empty, while the King, who all grant had an unquestionable Title, is still Living, and his Absence forced and involuntary? I thought our Laws, as well as our Religion had been against the Deposing Doctrine; therefore I desire you would Expound this State Riddle to me, and give me the Ground of this late extraordinary Revolution.* In answer to your Question, you may please to take notice, That those Gentlemen of the Convention, and the rest of their Sentiments, who declare a Vacancy in the Government, lay the main stress of their Opinion upon his Majesties withdrawing himself. ... give me leave to remind you, That a Parliament, and a Convention, are two very different Things: The latter, for want of the King's Writs and Concurrence, having no share in the Legislative Power. ... In order to the confuting of this Notion [of the throne being vacant], I shall prove ... That his Majesty, before his withdrawing, had sufficient Grounds to make him apprehensive of Danger, and therefore It cannot be called *an Abdication.* ... [and] That we have no Grounds, either from the Law of the Realm, or those of Nature, to pronounce the Throne void, upon such a Retreat of a King."[2]

Collier's pamphlet culminates in a striking parable:

"If a Man should forfeit his House to those who set it on Fire, only because he quitted it without giving some formal Directions to the Servants; and be obliged to lose his Estate, for endeavouring to preserve his Life. I believe it would be thought an incomprehensible sort of Justice. ... Now whether his Majesty has been well used in this Revolution, or not, I leave the World to judge now, but God will do it afterwards."[3]

What was going on was not the normal functioning of government and, for Collier, not part of a legitimate legal process. Parliament required the presence of the monarch in order to have legitimacy, and so the assembly that sanctioned the contention that the throne was vacant was called a "convention." In order to justify the proclamation of a new monarch (actually, there were eventually two, as William and Mary ruled jointly), some reason had to be given. This justification was found in declaring the position of monarch vacant due to James II leaving England.

Collier does his best to frame his arguments as not just those of one particular side but as universal in that they will appeal to anyone of "sense and integrity." He argues that James II had not abdicated but instead had been under threat, and that he left to save his life. Britain had seen the process of deposing a king before, when Charles I had been arrested and then executed in 1649, but supposedly the Restoration of Charles II in 1660 had signaled a final end to such heinous crimes in England. A monarch held his or her position by divine right, and it was a moral and religious crime to interfere with what God had ordained. The parallel between James II and his executed father Charles I is subtly rather than explicitly made: The laws and religion of England were meant to be against such "deposing doctrines."

As underlined by Collier, the weakness of the argument that James II's flight from England was tantamount to an abdication deeply complicated British politics almost to the end of the eighteenth century, and numerous Jacobite rebellions, named for the Latin version of the king's name, Jacobus, took place. Ultimately Collier's position failed, but it cast a long shadow.

Notes

1 The two houses of the English parliament.
2 [Jeremy Collier], *The Desertion Discuss'd in a Letter to a Country Gentleman*, [London]: s.n., 1689, pp. 1–2 (italics in original).
3 Ibid., pp. 7–8.

65 Dubrovnik: A Catholic state under the Ottoman sultan

by James D. Tracy

The Republic of Dubrovnik (Ragusa) became an Ottoman tributary in 1438. For more than two centuries thereafter, the ruling oligarchy – a patrician senate and small council – adhered to two fundamental principles. The first was that Dubrovnik's tributary status opened a vista of opportunity. Luxury cloth was much in demand among Ottoman elites, and Ragusans paid for goods imported into the sultan's lands a duty of only 2 percent, not the usual 5 percent. Thus, their merchant settlements in the Balkans replaced Italian colonies that largely disappeared after 1480. From Dubrovnik, horse-caravans wound up through the mountains and thence eastward to Istanbul. Dubrovnik had perhaps the largest merchant fleet in the Mediterranean by the middle of the sixteenth century, but everything depended on keeping its precious trading privileges. This sometimes meant making difficult choices. For example, since Spanish Naples was the hub for its merchant fleet, the republic had close ties to Spain, but in 1538 it lent no support to the conquest of nearby Herceg Novi (Castelnuovo) by a Spanish expeditionary force. Yet after the Ottomans reconquered the fortress in 1539, the Ragusans sent craftsmen and materials to help in rebuilding. As late as 1684, when victorious Catholic powers invited Dubrovnik to sever its Turkish connection, the republic chose instead to send a new tribute mission to Istanbul.

The second basic principle was that Dubrovnik was a Catholic state. Dubrovnik did not persecute its Orthodox subjects in the countryside, but from the fourteenth century it used a combination of inducements and pressure to draw them into the Latin Catholic fold. By law, if not always in fact, non-Catholics could not remain overnight within the walls of the capital. This included Ottoman officials, the Jewish merchants who organized the caravans, and the Orthodox, Vlach herdsmen who guided them. Because of its suspicious associations with Ottoman infidels and Orthodox schismatics, Dubrovnik depended on papal approval to warrant its Catholic character. There were long-standing papal prohibitions against trading with the infidel, but Dubrovnik was careful to obtain exceptions (e.g., 1548, 1566). Because of the paucity of secular clergy in this region (the Archbishop of Dubrovnik was pastor of the cathedral, but had no other parish churches under his authority), religious orders were of particular importance, and the magistrates used connections in Rome to have separate provinces created for Franciscans and Dominicans serving in the republic's territory. The Jesuits made several attempts to establish a base in Dubrovnik, but in the end they could not overcome the senate's reservations about an order known for its advocacy of holy war against the infidel.

The problem of reforming the Benedictine order was of particular concern. Discipline had become lax, and the houses were under ecclesiastical superiors based elsewhere. The magistrates had been working to bring all six Benedictine monasteries on Ragusan soil under a single congregation, based at St. Mary on the island of Mljet:

"You know how much trouble we have had bringing the Congregation of Mljet to the state in which it is now; desiring not merely to keep things as they are but to improve them, we bid you supplicate His Holiness[1] for a *breve*,[2] so that when there are up to five monks who wish to be part of a congregation, and who desire to enter the said Congregation of Mljet, they may be able to join it without any scruple of conscience. And to prepare whatever help may be needed to content His Holiness, and to bring him to the desired conclusion, you must use all the force of your eloquence, and also the good will of our friends, so that we may be granted this grace."[3]

Monastic reform was vital to keep the city "free from heretical depravity." Since the archbishop appointed the abbot of Mljet, there had to be a cooperative archbishop. Cardinal Giovanni Angelo de' Medici had been titular archbishop since 1545, and now that he had been offered a better prospect (at Cassano, in Campania) he intended to be succeeded in Dubrovnik by another absentee. The magistrates had other ideas. Once the ambassador in Rome had confirmed reports that the archbishop would be leaving, he was to arrange for a private audience:

"Having kissed the feet of His Holiness, tell him we have sent you on several matters ... We do not think our archbishop will leave us so soon, but we want His Holiness to know that we are by God's grace well populated, but situated among Turks and other heretical nations,[4] and we very much need a pastor who will be with us in person, to visit and instruct us, and who will teach what Holy Mother Church wills and commands, a man who is marked by fear of God, knowledge of Holy Scripture, and who is above all alien to the practices of this world."[5]

In fact, the persistence of the magistrates was repaid, and they eventually secured the man they wanted: Ludovico Beccadelli, a humanist from Bologna, proved a conscientious and reforming archbishop (1555–1560).

As the conflict between the Ottomans and various Catholic powers intensified, the Ragusans found themselves under attack for giving aid and comfort to the infidel, especially during the War of the Holy League (1570–1573), when Venice and the Habsburgs joined forces against the Turks. Dubrovnik indeed did give priority to its own interests, but so did Venice and the Habsburgs. Yet in a different sense the question of religious identity is not easy to separate from reasons of state. While popular belief in Dubrovnik has not been well

A Catholic state under the Ottoman sultan 245

studied, Beccadelli and other visitors were impressed by the avid participation of the people in the rites of the Catholic Church. On this frontier of Christendom, there was in practice no difference between being a citizen of Dubrovnik and being a Catholic.

Notes

1 Pope Paul IV.
2 A papal letter.
3 Dubrovnik State Archives, collection "Lettere de Levante," Small council to Dubrovnik's ambassador in Rome, 10 April 1545. Translated by James D. Tracy.
4 "Heretical nations" refers to Muslim countries. Islam was seen as a Christian heresy by many early modern Christians.
5 Dubrovnik State Archives, collection "Lettere de Levante," page from a letter to the ambassador in Rome inserted into a letter to Constantinople, 1 March 1553. Translated by James D. Tracy.

VI

Defining the religious other: Identities and conflicts

Introduction

by Ute Lotz-Heumann

This chapter explores the various ways in which elites and the populace in early modern Europe defined the religious 'other,' and how the formation of strong religious identities could lead not only to antagonism, but also to open conflict. The essay by Andrew Colin Gow shows how much the views of the Protestant reformers were influenced by medieval ideas and prejudices. In spite of their claim of 'Scripture alone,' reformers kept alive the concept of the 'red Jews,' alleged exotic but real Jews associated with the apocalypse.

The essays by Craig Koslofsky, Tom Scott, and Robert J. Bast exemplify aspects of how identities were defined and defended in the early Reformation in Germany. The former Franciscan monk Valentin Tham who had become an evangelical preacher entered into a mini-debate with the Bishop of Meissen and a Leipzig professor of theology during a visitation in 1522 (essay by Craig Koslofsky). An anonymous Freiburg citizen, accused of heresy – Protestant leanings – in 1524, defended himself by pointing out the connections between late medieval spirituality and Luther's teachings (essay by Tom Scott). And the weaver Augustin Bader took his new-found religious identity as an Anabaptist one step further by creating a community of believers which elevated him to kingly status (essay by Robert J. Bast).

The essays by Euan Cameron, Larissa Juliet Taylor, Irena Backus, Barbara Stollberg-Rilinger, and S. Amanda Eurich all show the various ways in which confessional identity was created and reinforced in early modern Europe. The Protestant theologian and pamphleteer Johannes Eberlin von Günzburg articulated what became a standard Protestant condemnation of consecration as a form of sorcery, thereby declaring important elements of Catholic ritual as superstitious (essay by Euan Cameron).

Catholics were no less active in denouncing Protestantism as heresy. In the lead-up to the French Wars of Religion François Le Picart, a popular Parisian preacher, used the antiquity and unity of the Catholic Church and the divisions within Protestantism as arguments to convince his audiences that Protestants were 'of the devil' (essay by Larissa Juliet Taylor).[1] Gabriel du Préau, in his

Catalogue of All Heretics of 1569, went even further by constructing a parallel between the Cynics, an ancient school of philosophy, and the Waldensians, a medieval Christian sect that quickly turned to Protestantism. His *Catalogue* was not a neutral description, but a piece of Catholic polemics trying to smear Protestants (essay by Irena Backus). Polemics did not only come as texts in the early modern period, but also as images which often carried even more powerful – and certainly more accessible – messages. An illustrated seventeenth-century broadsheet ridiculing the Luther family as the embodiment of carnal excess conveyed a strong anti-Protestant message (essay by Barbara Stollberg-Rilinger).

These aggressive propaganda and counter-propaganda campaigns characterized early modern Europe, and the 'preaching match' between a Calvinist pastor and a Catholic priest in the principality of Orange in 1678 attests not only to the acrimony associated with these interactions, but also to the shared beliefs in the supernatural (essay by S. Amanda Eurich).

Converting from one faith to another was a highly fraught decision in early modern Europe. As Scott M. Manetsch's and Monica Brennan's essays show, conversion was much more than an individual's decision to change his or her religious allegiance. Rather, a conversion could have wide-ranging consequences, both for the convert and for his or her family and community. Social and economic status, personal safety, and relationships were deeply affected by a decision to convert. Theodore Beza's thirteen-year struggle is an example of how difficult this decision could be. Beza was ultimately pushed to openly profess his Protestant faith after a severe illness. While Beza's case seems to clearly point toward inner conviction as the basis for his conversion, Catholic priests in eighteenth-century Ireland who decided to conform to the Protestant state church were often regarded with suspicion. Popular poems and songs attest to their difficult standing among their families and communities.

The last three essays show various ways in which individuals negotiated their identities within the religious landscape of the early modern European world. These three case studies, by David Cressy, Kevin Gosner, and Edward Muir, address very different persons and circumstances, thereby providing a glimpse of the broad range of early modern religious identities. John Milton, the famous English poet best known for his epic poem *Paradise Lost*, was also a keen observer of his time. As a so-called 'Puritan,' he thought that the Protestant Reformation in England had stalled, and that England was possibly even returning to Catholicism. Milton considered this a severe threat, and in his treatise *Of Reformation* he advocated for further reform (essay by David Cressy). Thomas Gage was a Dominican missionary who later converted to Protestantism and became a Puritan preacher. His account of his experiences as a friar in the Spanish American colonies provides rich details, but also hints at his changed attitude toward his former Catholic faith (essay by Kevin Gosner). Giovanni Francesco Loredan and Ferrante Pallavicino belonged to a group of "people who believe in nothing" in seventeenth-century Venice. As religious skeptics and critics of the papacy who questioned the foundations of Christianity, their beliefs were regarded as extremely dangerous in early modern Europe. In fact, Pallavicino lost his life for them (essay by Edward Muir).

Note

1 Several essays in this collection throw light on events leading up to and during the French Wars of Religion and the impact of these religious wars. Besides Taylor's essay see no. 18, Reid: Bourges: Public rituals of collective and personal identity in the middle of the sixteenth century; no. 19, Diefendorf: Castres, 1561: A town erupts into religious violence; no. 61, Mentzer: Assuring civil rights for religious minorities in sixteenth-century France.

66 The 'red Jews' and Protestant reformers

by Andrew Colin Gow

Around 1169/70, the famous *Historia Scholastica* was compiled by the Parisian scholastic Petrus Comestor. It was meant as a history of the entire world and it was one of the greatest bestsellers of the Middle Ages. In its pages, Bible stories jostled with the Alexander romance, fables, legends, and apocryphal writings attributed to imaginary sages of antiquity for space – and credibility. The Ten Lost Tribes of Israel (II Kings) – a group long understood in Christian exegesis to be identical with 'Gog from the land of Magog' (Ezekiel) or 'Gog and Magog' (Revelations), who would sweep down from the north at the end of time to destroy the world – were connected by Petrus Comestor with an element of the Alexander legend: God's imprisonment or enclosure, behind a great range of mountains and at Alexander's request, of a dangerous race of 'unclean peoples,' who would break out to devastate the world at the end of time. The *Historia Scholastica* made one story out of these disparate elements by a kind of imaginative medieval 'hyper-texting.'

Later, these imaginary apocalyptic destroyers came to be understood, in the German-speaking lands, as a race of exotic (but real) Jews – under the name 'red Jews,' a hostile designation given the connotations of the color red in medieval symbolism (falseness, wickedness, cunning). By the fourteenth century, the 'red Jews' were a staple of medieval religious texts in German: They would invade Christendom at the end of time, as servants of the Antichrist. Since the Antichrist was also imagined as a Jew in medieval popular theology, it made perfect sense to associate the apocalyptic 'red Jews' with the Antichrist.

Martin Luther and most of his fellow reformers believed they lived at the end of days. By casting the papacy in the role of the apocalyptic figure of Antichrist, Luther turned away from a centuries-old tradition that identified Antichrist as a Jew. But the strong connection between the end time and the Jews persisted, and the 'red Jews' (shorn of their association with the Antichrist) turned up in a large number of Reformation-era writings, including the works of Luther, Johannes Agricola, and Johannes Brenz, and most notably in a popular 1523 pamphlet entitled *Concerning a Great Multitude and Host of Jews*:

"A Jew has come from Latin parts,[1] supported by letters that were sent to my gracious Lord of Triest, which report that a good number of days ago, letters and genuine accounts sent from Jerusalem and Damascus and elsewhere reached cousins of his in his country. These letters relate that a great multitude and host of Jews, more precisely as many as five or six hundred thousand, have arrived in the land of Egypt and made camp thirty days' march from Jerusalem. They selected 12 Jews as ambassadors and sent them to the Turkish sultan to demand that he return the land inherited from their fathers, that is the Holy Land, to them or, should he refuse, they will conquer it themselves. And if the Turk[2] will not believe that they are real Jews, they will work wonders even Moses and the other prophets did not do. And this Jew reports that they are all black and red Jews, and have come out of the uttermost deserts or dunes of Africa, where until now they have been entirely hidden ..."[3]

Reports of war against the Ottomans in rebellious Mamluk Egypt may have been the origin of this pamphlet, but in the absence of any real information, the Augsburg author made his own sense out of the rumors, casting them in terms of medieval ideas, beliefs, and common-places about the coming events of the end times, as well as the (Jewish) actors in that great drama: Medieval Christians believed that the Antichrist would appear at the end of time and rebuild the Temple at Jerusalem, and that he would be served by (most) Jews, including the 'red Jews.' Published when Reformation preaching was only just reaching German cities beyond Luther's home, Wittenberg, this pamphlet reflects a 'vernacular' (not scholastic) pre-Reformation world view.

Only five years later, one of the great propagandists of the Protestant Reformation, Johannes Agricola, referred in his famous *Proverbs* to the 'red Jews' in a way that makes it clear they were well known – but as far as he was concerned, they were merely a fable:

"The scholastics have spent much time on the question whether the [individual] faith of each person will save that person. For they say that Alexander the Great fell on his knees and prayed earnestly, begging God to move the Caspian Mountains together and enclose the red Jews, and this is the origin of the fable concerning the red Jews, who are supposed to appear with Enoch and Elijah before the last judgment. Whatever we believe concerning this fable, it is certain that no belief saves except belief in Christ Jesus, as St. Paul teaches, and in God, who raised Christ from the dead. But he who confesses the faith is hated by the world. Hence arise disputes and differences, as has happened at all times of Gospel preaching, as Augustine writes."[4]

In casting the Alexander story as unimportant, Agricola seeks instead to insist on a central tenet of Luther's teaching and of evangelical faith ever since: the doctrine of salvation by faith alone (*sola fidei*). His treatment of the old legend and his preference for Scripture (St. Paul) over time-honored medieval texts (the Alexander story) is consonant with Luther's insistence on scriptural authority and his disdain for what he called the sophistries of scholasticism.

Yet Luther's views on the primacy of biblical texts and the unreliability of all 'man-made' exegesis did not stop him from writing extensive Bible commentaries himself. In his commentary on the Book of Ezekiel (1530), just a few years after Agricola's *Proverbs* appeared, Luther could not resist some hyper-texting of his own: "It has already been sufficiently proven that Gog the Turk is descended from the Tatars or red Jews, where the Great Khan is king ..."[5] For Luther, "the Turk" was an apocalyptic threat; and here he drew on medieval 'vernacular theology' and its ideas about Jews' role at the end of time to establish an apocalyptic genealogy for the Turks: They were descended from the 'Tatars' (by which he meant the Mongols, ruled by the Great Khan), who were the same as ... the red Jews! Despite his efforts to free himself from 'man-made' exegesis, Luther remained indebted to medieval ideas and ways of thinking, and exercised imaginative medieval hyper-texting based on established patterns.

Finally, in 1531, the less well-known but important reformer of the city of Schwäbisch Hall, Johannes Brenz, one of Luther's earliest companions, echoed Luther's apocalyptic identification of the Turks with the 'red Jews': "There are many reliable signs that the Turk will rise no higher, and that he will soon fall. If the [final] emergency is indeed at hand, let us manfully share in the struggle against these 'Red Jews.'"[6] Brenz, like Luther and like the author of the anonymous 1523 pamphlet, interpreted Ottoman expansion in his day as part of an imminent apocalyptic end-game.

All these interpretations, despite the reformers' dedication to Scripture as the only valid authority on religious topics, continued well into the Reformation era to appeal to and recycle ideas drawn not from learned or scholastic medieval writings, but from 'vernacular theology.' Medieval world views, Christian apocalypticism, anti-Jewish theology and legend, and Protestant theology all cross paths in these texts. Even Luther was still very much obligated to both traditional medieval ideas and to medieval ways of thinking and reasoning about the world, the past, and God's plan for humanity – ways that are usually imagined to have been abolished by the Reformation. Early modern Protestantism did not necessarily follow the neat pattern of 'progress' laid out for it by later interpreters. The Reformation was a deeply 'medieval' movement.

Notes

1 Italy.
2 The Ottoman sultan.
3 Anonymous, *Von ainer grosse meng unnd gewalt der Juden* ..., Augsburg: Steiner, 1523, fols Aii r–Aii v. Translated by Andrew Colin Gow.
4 Johannes Agricola, *Drey hundert Gemeyner Sprichworter der wir Deutschen uns gebrauchen und doch nicht wissen woher sie kommen*, Hagenau: Setzer, 1529, in Sander L. Gilman (ed.), *Die Sprichwörtersammlung*, 2 vols, Berlin and New York: de Gruyter, 1971, vol. 1, pp. 218–219. Translated by Andrew Colin Gow.

5 Martin Luther, "Commentary on 38 and 39 Ezekiel (1530)," in *D. Martin Luthers Werke: Kritische Gesamtausgabe*, 73 vols, Weimar 1883–2009, vol. 30/2, pp. 223–236, here p. 224. Translated by Andrew Colin Gow.
6 Johannes Brenz, *Wie sich Prediger und Leyen halten sollen so der Turck das deutsche land uberfallen wuerde*, Wittenberg: Rhau, 1531; quoted from John Bohnstedt, *The Infidel Scourge of God: The Turkish Menace as Seen by German Pamphleteers of the Reformation Era*, Philadelphia: Transactions of the American Philosophical Society, 1968, p. 50 and n. 3.

67 Debating the Reformation in Torgau, 1522

by Craig Koslofsky

During the early years of the Protestant Reformation, reform ideas from Wittenberg were preached and printed across Electoral Saxony and the Holy Roman Empire.[1] Martin Luther was the source of most of these sermons and pamphlets. Saxony was the center of the commotion, and in January 1522 the imperial council (*Reichsregiment*) in Nuremberg called on the temporal and spiritual rulers of Electoral Saxony to halt all changes to traditional Christianity. Bishop Johannes of Meissen took the imperial mandate as an opportunity for a visitation[2] of his diocese in the spring of 1522. The Elector of Saxony,[3] meanwhile, instructed his councilor to closely observe the bishop's visitation and ensure that reform-leaning clergymen would not be punished.

Bishop Johannes was not happy with what he found. Men like Valentin Tham, a former Franciscan monk, were challenging the sale of indulgences, the sacrament of penance, and the authority of the pope from the pulpits of churches in towns like Torgau. Tham engaged the bishop and a Leipzig professor of theology, Hieronymus Dungersheim, in a lively debate as they questioned him in the Saxon town of Torgau on 5 April 1522:

"Bishop of Meissen: Do you have anyone with you?"

"Preacher: Gracious Lord, I am in this by myself.

"Bishop: Listen you, people are saying about you, that you want to start a new faith in Torgau with your preaching.

"Preacher: Gracious Lord, I hope not. People are going around the city asking about what I preach. If anyone has something to accuse me of, I'll gladly answer for it.

"B. What have you been preaching about?

"P. Gracious Lord, I don't know how to preach anything but the Word of God and the Gospel.

"B. Right so. Then why have you let your tonsure grow out?

"P. Gracious Lord, I think the tonsure doesn't do anything for me; I want to be worthy of it.

"B. Am I to understand that you don't ever want to have it (the tonsure) again?

"P. I can take it or leave it, however it goes.

"B. How is someone supposed to see that you are a priest?

"P. From my words and deeds, and not from my clothes and tonsure.

"B. People will think you are the common hangman.

"P. Gracious Lord, I haven't learned that trade.

"B. That's vain Hussite[4] and Lutherite. Listen you – listen: what do you think of – or what is the holy Christian church?

"P. I believe any common gathering of Christians, whenever they come together, is the holy Christian church.

"B. Am I to understand that you think nothing of the pope?

"P. Yes, gracious Lord, I believe he is a pastor, so long as he teaches me Christian doctrine.

"B. Don't you know that the pope has been given authority from above, and that the pope gave it to me, I to the priest, and the priest to you?

"P. I know nothing but that I have it from God.

"B. Am I to understand that you think nothing of the church of Rome, [and] that it has the forgiveness of sins?

"P. Yes, gracious Lord. We have it [the forgiveness of sins] here in Torgau too, because we pray every day in faith in the forgiveness of sins.

"Then the bishop grew angry and said: Now listen – he's a fine one, because it's all Hussite and Lutherite. Doctor, sir, you talk with him; I can't get anywhere with him.

"Ochsenfahrt[5] walked up to him and said: Gracious Lord, in the name of God the Father I do want to speak with him. Then he said to the preacher: Listen you, were you born a Christian, baptized a Christian, and ordained a Christian?

"The preacher answered to each of these: I don't know otherwise.

"Doctor: Who ordained you? Was he also a Christian?

"P. That I don't know. I haven't looked into his heart.

"Bishop and Doctor together: What do you think of ordination?

"P. You two show me where it stands [written], so that it is proven to me; otherwise I don't believe in it.

"B. Don't you know that the holy twelve apostles were ordained?

"P. Lord, show me where it is written: otherwise I know nothing of it.

"B. Ey – listen you, would you like to be brought in for questioning?

"P. Gracious Lord, I'd like that fine and that's why I'm here.

"Doctor: Let me worry about him. Listen, were you not ordained in the Lord's Supper, in which the Lord gave the sacrament in both kinds?

"P. You yourselves don't have the least letter [of Scripture] for that.

"The Doctor took a letter out of his pocket and said: Look, I will prove to you that Doctor Martin wrote that the apostles were ordained at the Lord's Supper.

"P. I don't have anything to do with Doctor Martin. I stand here for myself alone and want to answer for myself. Martin will answer for himself as well, when he needs to.

"B. But you are willing to be questioned?

"P. Gracious Lord, I can suffer it well, that's why I'm here, so that I can be questioned right now.

"B. Everyone I need to question is not yet here. Would you also come if I summon you?

"P. Yes, I'd be glad to go to any place where I would be safe; I'd gladly appear.

"B. You will be quite safe, and I'll have you questioned, even if it costs me four or five hundred gulden.

"Then the bishop forbade him that he should ever preach again.

"P. If you won't allow it, then I must leave it alone.

"And he went away.

"Then Wolf von Schleynitz stood up and said: Gracious lord, you cannot get anything on that man. He met you halfway.

"B. He'd be a learned enough man if he didn't have so much Hussite stuff about him. Go ahead, tell him he can still preach, as long as he can answer for it."[6]

Such impassioned face-to-face religious debates echoed through the sixteenth century. The Leipzig Disputation of 1519 decisively shaped the ideas of Martin Luther and the Wittenberg reformers by forcing them to broaden their challenge to traditional sources of authority in the church. These 'great debates' stand alongside many other exchanges of words and ideas in the Reformation era by lay people and clergy, learned and simple, young and old.

Did the young 'evangelical' preacher really run rings around the bishop and the professor of theology in this impromptu debate? It is possible, but not probable. The report comes from officials sympathetic to church reform – these officials filtered what they heard, giving us an account of tongue-tied and exasperated stodgy supporters of traditional Christianity and a quick-witted, devout, yet humble model 'Protestant' reformer.

Notes

1 The Holy Roman Empire of the German Nation, usually called 'the Empire,' was a huge and complex political organization in central Europe in medieval and early modern times. It was a loose political union of mostly German and largely self-governing principalities and towns.
2 An inspection.
3 In early modern Germany, the electors were the princes who elected the emperor.
4 The Hussites were the followers of the Bohemian reformer Jan Hus (c.1369–1415), who was declared a heretic by the church and burnt at the stake.
5 'Ochsenfart' refers to the fact that Hieronymus Dungersheim, professor of theology at the University of Leipzig, was born in Ochsenfurt.
6 Ernestinisches Gesamtarchiv Weimar, Reg. N. No. 25 (Pag. 57, B. 10), No. 19, as printed in Karl Pallas, "Briefe und Akten zur Visitationsreise des Bischofs Johannes VII. von Meißen im Kurfürstentum Sachsen 1522," *Archiv für Reformationsgeschichte/Archive for Reformation History* 5, 1908, pp. 275–278. Translated by Craig Koslofsky.

68 A Freiburg citizen's response to Luther in 1524

by Tom Scott

Enthusiasm for reforming doctrines was widespread throughout all groups in German society. The Protestant reformers themselves believed that they were affirming a clear and decisive break with the practices and beliefs of the late medieval Catholic Church. The responses of layfolk, however enthusiastic, were much more ambiguous. Some saw in evangelical doctrines a weapon with which to bring the clergy, hitherto a privileged and separate caste, into the communal fold: 'Anticlericalism' was shorthand for creating a Christian community, the priesthood of all believers. Others, especially the rural population, saw the Gospel as a clarion of liberty from serfdom and an oppressive feudal regime which might justify recourse to violence.

Such strident voices were on occasion matched by quieter and more reflective views. In the town of Freiburg im Breisgau, a Catholic Habsburg stronghold on the Upper Rhine, which had a university from 1457, lay support for the new doctrines was muted. Within the university there were certainly sympathizers; Ulrich Zasius, the professor of law, who had earlier served as town clerk, was a cautious adherent of reform, though he drew in his horns after 1524. The town authorities, who saw their fortunes linked to continued Habsburg patronage, had no choice but to set their faces against the religious innovations, even taking action against members of the university, despite its immunity from civic jurisdiction. They were assiduous in surveying the population for the least sign of dissent. Into their net fell, probably in 1524, an anonymous citizen, who offered the following remarkable testimony or confession:

"Christ Jesus, our Saviour, teaches us in his Gospel, Matthew chapter 6, that we should not give heed to what we eat and drink or how we be clothed; rather, we should earnestly seek the kingdom of God and his righteousness. All other things the heavenly Father will give us himself. And I know not how better to seek that kingdom than in Holy Scripture. Therefore I bought several books, namely the entire Bible of Holy Scripture and the lives of the saints, many by the worthy Johann [Geiler von] Kaysersberg, Tauler, and Jean Gerson, and other teachers of Holy Scripture. On feast days and at other times I read [aloud] from these to myself, my wife, and servants for salvation' sake and to honour God. I have no other recreation with which, in my estimation, more profitably to spend my time. Over the last three years Luther's works have now been published, and I bought many of these. Where he writes against the papacy or its adversaries I have not much concerned myself: I seek not discord but instruction. As Paul writes, we should read everything, retaining the good and discarding the bad ...

"I know that our gracious overlord[1] has banned such books. Since I became aware thereof, I have not discussed Luther's teachings much with other people, and in future will refrain from doing so, for I well know that I am not sent to be a teacher to others, and in any case know not how to bring Luther's doctrines, albeit that they are grounded in Holy Scripture, to bear much fruit with those of little understanding, since they will not comprehend them."[2]

As with all such primary sources, we need to place it in its proper context. The citizen was being accused of heresy. Were his responses, therefore, deliberately exculpatory or evasive? For the Freiburg interrogators, his affirmation that he saw in Luther a committed searcher after religious truth who stood in the same tradition as the parade of late medieval Catholic theologians would not have saved his skin. If anything, it might have made his crime more heinous.

The citizen (about whom, alas, we know nothing) was by definition literate, though vernacular translations of his late medieval authorities do not require him to have known Latin. Some of his citations, such as Gerson, were in fact references to Thomas à Kempis's *Imitation of Christ*, the most widely read devotional tract of the fifteenth century, which was often mistakenly attributed to Gerson. Others, such as "the lives of the saints," refer to that medieval bestseller, Jacobus de Voragine's *Legenda Aurea*, available in an Alemannic German translation. The mention of Geiler von Kaysersberg, the preacher of Strasbourg cathedral, and of Johannes Tauler, the most practical of the late medieval German mystics, must refer to their printed collections of sermons. In other words, the anonymous citizen was not citing any texts with which an informed layman of pious disposition would have been unfamiliar.

What stands out is the direct lineage he traces from late medieval spirituality and lay piety to Luther. It is perfectly conceivable that in claiming not to be interested in Luther's denunciation of the papacy as Antichrist the citizen was speaking the truth: What mattered to him was the spiritual and theological message of Luther's teaching, not its ecclesiastical–polemical invective. This disavowal of polemic is perhaps the most striking feature of the testimony: "I seek not discord but instruction." It runs against the grain of everything that contemporaries caught up in confessional controversy, whether Catholic or Protestant, were supposed to have embraced. In that context, it is all the more remarkable that the anonymous Freiburg citizen fails to cite Erasmus, that apostle of Christian peace, whose popular tracts were readily available in the vernacular.

Notes

1 Archduke Ferdinand of Austria.
2 Stadtarchiv Freiburg im Breisgau, C 1 Kirchensachen 143, Confession of a Freiburg citizen, n.d. (*c*.1521 [*recte*: *c*.1524]). Translated by Tom Scott.

69 Augustin Bader of Augsburg (d. 1530): Weaver, prophet, messianic king

by Robert J. Bast

In the wake of the German Peasants' War (1524–1525), political authorities throughout Germany began to issue and enforce harsh new decrees against 'Anabaptists,' a subset of Protestant believers who practised adult baptism and rejected both the Catholic establishment and the emerging mainstream Protestant churches. The reputation of these sectarians for violence and revolutionary conspiracy was mostly unearned. Yet it is true that the most radical hopes for a Protestant Reformation that included social and ecclesiastical reform were to be found among these dissenters, who championed lay leadership over clerical hegemony, vernacular biblicism over theological degrees, and communal living over private property and the status quo. Persecution winnowed their ranks, eliminated the most educated and visible of their leaders, and intensified the already considerable apocalyptic expectation against which the Protestant Reformation played out.

This is the general context in which the short but remarkable career of Augustin Bader may be understood. Bader was an Augsburg weaver who rose to prominence as a lay elder among the city's Anabaptists in the mid-1520s. Fleeing just in advance of mass arrests launched by the regime in 1527, Bader spent several years wandering between other dissident communities throughout central Europe, sharpening the eschatological message he had first heard in Augsburg, while growing in the confidence of his own prophetic identity. By 1529 he and a small group of followers had established a communal existence in the hamlet of Lautern in the Duchy of Württemberg, then under the administrative control of the Habsburg regime.

It was there that the group's identity continued to evolve, bolstered by dreams, visions, and continuous reflection on the intellectual currents that ebbed and flowed through late medieval and early modern Germany. These defy easy categorization. Some were characteristic of the vivid demands for social justice that coursed through the populist preaching and pamphleteering of the early Protestant Reformation, especially in circles like Augsburg's, where lay people held prominent places. Others stemmed from what we think of as 'elite' religious culture, among them a fascination with Judaism probably mediated by Oswald Leber, a former priest among Bader's followers, who had drunk deeply from the sources of Christian Hebraism, and who played an important role in the evolution of Bader's status from end-times prophet to messianic king in the imminent millennial kingdom of Christ on earth. Others had their source in medieval prophecies of reform that long predated Protestantism, e.g., the anticipation of a universal world emperor who would unite all peoples under Christ. In this respect Bader's reformation stood as a rebuke to the ideological pretensions of the Habsburg monarchy.

These elements are especially important to remember when assessing the one aspect of Bader's communal life that most disturbed his contemporaries and that until very recently has prejudiced all subsequent historical interpretation of it: the elevation of Augustin Bader to kingly stature, graphically realized not only in rituals of deference by which the group signaled his status, but by the royal garb and imperial regalia – cheap copies, to be sure – that the group had manufactured on his behalf. The discovery of these objects by the Habsburg officials to whom the Bader sect was eventually betrayed touched off conflicting reactions. First came political paranoia, for the authorities felt their hold slipping on Württemberg and regularly jumped at the shadows of conspiracies involving the urban and rural poor, Jews, and the Protestant princes. The torture and interrogation of Bader and his associates failed to uncover such a conspiracy but elicited another predictable kind of testimony, the 'admission' that Bader had been motivated by nothing more than class envy and vainglory.

"The Interrogation of Augustin Bader: On the 27th day of January 1530, Augustin Bader of Augsburg confessed under torture that he is a prophet sent from God, and he and his youngest child, approximately six months old, are set as a sign of the coming Transformation which will begin during the coming Lent and endure about 2 ½ years before it ends. In it there will be great death, murder, tumult, plagues, and punishment.

"Thereafter a new understanding of Scripture will be revealed through Christ in the spirit, just as [Christ] in former times revealed things corporeally. Thus all external sacraments shall cease, so that there will be no baptism except suffering, no altar except Christ, no church except the community of believers, and all of this will come about and be fulfilled for those to whom the prophet reveals that which he has [received] inwardly from Scripture. And in this Transformation, Christ will teach them spiritually what one is to do or leave off doing.

"And for signifying, meaning and fulfilling these things, he [Augustin] caused to be made a crown, a scepter, a chain, a dagger, a sword, and clothing, and afterward at his house in Lautern also taught and announced these future things that will appear, and gave into the hands of another of his children, who is 5 years old, the scepter, and laid the crown and sword on the table, and wore the clothing, dagger, and chain in the presence of others of his companions, in order to indicate the authority that his youngest child, who is six months old, will have in the future. Also, Augustin permitted himself to be called a lord, and served with reverence as with kneeling, and in other ways, as a lord and king, though certainly not as if this should be understood of himself as a person, but rather he permitted it to honor Him who sent him, and [so] that their plans and intentions would finally be established ... And in the coming Lent he intended to send his companions to the four corners of the land and announce and cry out these beliefs about the coming things, as stated above, on the streets, and especially in the land of Nickolsburg, in Austria, and in other places where they believed the greatest number and most important of the Anabaptists would be found. And when they had assembled a great host of them, and when the Turk was again on the move, he [Augustin] would appear with his royal insignia and clothing as a sign of the future authority of his youngest son and reveal to them the things stated above and the meaning that all external [religious] things were nothing and should cease, and further that all things [property] were common and should be held in common, and whoever believed him and his proclamation of the things reported above but would not accept them, those they would shut out.[1] ...

"Further he indicated that he, Augustin, had contributed 100 gulden, his companion from Augsburg Gall Fischer 130 gulden, Gastel, his companion from Bavaria, more than 150 gulden. The entire sum they held in common and kept with them, to support themselves and to obtain the royal regalia. ... and although many other Anabaptists would eagerly have given them money, they certainly didn't want to take it.

"He also admitted that he was an Anabaptist, and had baptized others, and had become a leader of others as a prophet sent from God, as stated above. Therefore because of the signs which visibly and invisibly appeared and were revealed, seen and heard by himself and his companions and his wife, did he have made the crown and royal regalia, with which to signify the coming things that will take place."[2]

Publicity generated by the case, and perhaps a touch of guilt following its gruesome conclusion (public execution for the adult male sectarians, in Bader's case preceded by ritual humiliation and horrific mutilation), led some in its aftermath to opine that perhaps it had been madness rather than wickedness that drove the weaver–king. Until very recently, these two interpretations have held sway. Yet recent research suggests that, however irrational the behavior of this community might seem to modern eyes, in its own day it drew squarely on religious and intellectual traditions that were entirely mainstream.

Notes

1 Cast out, excommunicate.
2 For the critical edition of the trial transcripts, see Gustav Bossert (ed.), *Quellen zur Geschichte der Wiedertäufer*, vol. 1: *Herzogtum Württemberg*, Leipzig: M. Heinsius Nachfolger, 1930, pp. 924–925. Translated by Robert J. Bast.

70 Should you consecrate bells? Johannes Eberlin von Günzburg argues against an established religious practice in 1525

by Euan Cameron

Faced with the manifold insecurities and uncertainties of life, many premodern people resorted to ritual methods for protection against misfortune. The medieval church, hoping to dissuade people from the use of magical spells and tokens, offered a range of consecrated objects known as 'sacramentals': holy water, consecrated candles, herbs, salt, and certain religious amulets. It denounced popular magic as 'superstitious' and potentially demonic, but encouraged use of the approved sacramentals for protection.

The sixteenth-century Protestant reformers rejected any claim that ritual, no matter how orthodox, could constrain God's action or place the divine under an obligation. That argument, rooted in the doctrine of justification by grace, implied that sacramentals would be seen as both ineffective and ungodly. However, Luther and Zwingli did not at first focus particularly on consecrated objects. Less famous figures, such as the theologian and pamphleteer Johannes Eberlin von Günzburg (*c*.1470–1533), helped to frame what would become classic Protestant positions on the question. Before embracing the Reformation, Eberlin had been an Observant Franciscan friar and served as a teacher and preacher in Freiburg and Tübingen in southern Germany. In 1522, he went to Wittenberg and began to write a sequence of powerful polemical pamphlets, especially against the orders of friars, to which he had formerly belonged.

Eberlin wrote this pamphlet to join a dispute that had already broken out between Andreas Bodenstein, known as Karlstadt (*c*.1480–1541) and some Franciscans from Annaberg, Johannes Fritzhans and Franciscus Seyler. Karlstadt had argued that it was a gross error for priests to teach people that there was an actual spiritual benefit in the use of consecrated water or salt. Material objects used in worship were representations of spiritual things, not the spiritual things themselves. The Franciscans fought back against Karlstadt, and Eberlin took up the cudgels on his behalf. Eberlin wrote *Against the Profaners of God's Creatures through the Consecration or Blessing of Salt, Water, Palms, Herbs, Wax, etc.* probably in the spring or summer of 1523, although it was not published until 1525.[1] Unlike Karlstadt, Eberlin presented a coherent theological analysis of why the consecration of sacramentals was wrong.

Just before the extract translated below, Eberlin argued that all created things of God were good (therefore, by implication, not requiring purification or consecration). Even apparently harmful creatures such as lions or adders only seemed evil because fallen humanity had lost the authority over the creatures that it held in paradise. Looked at another way, things were good or bad depending on the disposition of the person using them. Here Eberlin provided an exegesis of Titus 1 [:15] "to the pure all things are pure." Priests, Eberlin argued, claimed that prayer should be made in the sacred space of a church to be heard, yet "the all-highest does not live in temples made with hands" (Acts 7:48); Christ directed believers to pray in secret places of their homes. Not only churches, but all their appurtenances and equipment were assigned for the convenience of common worship and needed no special consecration. Eberlin then denounced with biting sarcasm the common practice where bishops consecrated (colloquially, "baptized") the bells in the church steeples, assigning them names and attributing to their ringing the power to drive away evil spirits. He satirized the bishops as "village idiots" for baptizing bells but not children. He then cited the potential counterargument, that the ringing of bells called on people to pray for divine help against storms:

"If a violent storm appears in the skies, Christian people should fear God's wrath, and before God's face bow down in humble and devout prayer; this is useful and good for storms (they say), and that is why one rings the bells against the weather, so that the people should pray.

"I say to you, dear wine-bishop,[2] that task belongs to different bells than the ones that you consecrate: God must cast them (Titus 2); God must consecrate them (as in Romans 8); God must ring them or pull on them (Romans 10, Jeremiah 1). For these bells are really the true preachers of God's Word (Psalm 10). Through hearing such bells, one becomes faithful and prepared to pray, and to turn away all God's wrath. But not through your bells, which are so little use to turn away the weather, that sometimes even towers and bells have been destroyed by hail or lightning. Woe to you, you profaners of Scripture! You destroyers of souls! You enemies of God! There is no greater idol [devised] of Antichrist than bells, no greater idolatry than the use of bells. Should you consecrate bells? Woe to you. Do you wish to turn away God's wrath and chase away the devil with the use of bells? I can well believe that the devil sometimes arouses a terrible storm and then makes it cease, if people ring bells and sprinkle holy water, and burn consecrated palms and candles: in this way he promotes and strengthens idolatry among the people; for that purpose he uses you as instruments, by some secret ordinance of God. However, that is all the devil's work to cause greater harm."[3]

"God said through the prophets 'I will curse what you bless or consecrate.' For that reason a Christian person should use no created thing because it happens to be consecrated, when such consecration is a curse in the sight of God, and would give the devil more power to harm a person if he in his wrong faith uses a consecrated thing, than if he did not use it. That is the devil's cunning, that he makes for himself a means to harm us in God's name. ...

"See whether or not such consecration may be a secret mark of the devil, with which he marks out all those who are in God's curse, namely monks, nuns, priests, in short all those who belong to the false kingdom, where everything that is faithless belongs."[4]

"Nothing consecrates other than faith in Christ; nothing is consecrated besides a believing person; everything that such a person uses is consecrated by God. All other consecrations are masks, serving more for seduction than for salvation, more a sorcery than a blessing."[5]

Although Eberlin's pamphlet was not cited by later controversialists, his arguments against consecrations would be developed by other writers and become part of the definitive Protestant position. On one hand, Protestants applied to Catholic consecrations the following reasoning, already used in the later Middle Ages against popular magic. If a 'superstitious' rite worked, that was only because the devil had caused the problem (e.g., sickness or bad weather) in the first place, and removed it at the apparent prompting of the ritual, in order to encourage yet more superstitious activity. On the other hand, Protestants framed an entirely new argument, that material objects were assigned their properties and virtues at the creation, and no religious rite could transform them, enhance them, or assign them new powers. In that light Catholic consecrations represented nothing more than a form of sorcery.

Notes

1 Johannes Eberlin von Günzburg, *Wider die schender der Creaturen gottes, durch Weyhen, oder segnen, des Saltzs, Wasser, Palmen, kraut, wachss, fewr ayer, Fladen &c: nit zů verachtung der Creatur, allain meldung der gotslesterlichen betrüglichen falsch glaubigen yrrsalen*, Augsburg: Heinrich Steiner, 1525. Extracts translated by Euan Cameron.
2 On the previous page Eberlin referred to "unsere Weychbischoff," "our consecrated bishops" (also used in German to describe suffragan bishops): here he puns the term into "wine-bishop."
3 Eberlin von Günzburg, *Wider die schender*, p. Bi v.
4 Ibid., p. Ci r.
5 Ibid., p. Ciii v.

71 Catholic preaching on the eve of the French Wars of Religion: A eucharistic battleground

by Larissa Juliet Taylor

For several reasons, Roman Catholics did not respond quickly to the threats posed by Martin Luther and other Protestant reformers. From the twelfth century, the church had reacted to increasing threats posed by new 'heresies,' including those whose teachings on the Mass and Scripture would find echoes in the early sixteenth century. In the Middle Ages, church and state had effectively mounted responses to heresies by several methods: widespread teaching and preaching by the mendicant orders; inquisition and persecution; and, as a last resort, crusades. But the challenges of Martin Luther and other reformers differed from what the church had experienced before, largely because of the potential for the speedy dissemination of ideas provided by the printing press.

Unlike their Lutheran counterparts after 1520, Roman Catholics were deeply suspicious of using print propaganda. As a result, in the first four decades after Luther's challenge to the medieval church, the Catholic response was slow, leading to the spread of Reformed ideas in France and the beginning of the religious wars that tore the country apart between 1561 and 1594. Therefore, Catholic preachers – and thus spoken rather than printed words – remained at the forefront of the effort to combat Protestantism into the late sixteenth century.

As early as 1518, the works of Luther had circulated at the University of Paris, and the reforming tendencies of King Francis I and his sister, Marguerite de Navarre, allowed many suspected 'Lutherans' to gain a foothold at the court and throughout the country. 'Suspect' preachers attracted enormous crowds in Paris and elsewhere, outraging the Faculty of Theology of the University of Paris. The university attempted to mount a counterattack that was (in their view) undermined by the king and his sister. This situation changed in 1534 when anonymous placards smuggled from Switzerland denounced the "horrible, great, and intolerable abuses of the popish Mass; invented in direct opposition to the Holy Supper of our Lord and only mediator and savior." After being posted throughout Paris and even in the king's castle, Francis I was forced to take a strong stance that included the attempted suppression of all printing and the execution of suspected heretics. But by that time, the Reformed faith had already gathered strength in France.

After the Colloquy of Marburg in 1529 had shown insoluble divisions between Lutherans and Swiss reformers over the nature of the Lord's Supper, Catholics found a means to attack the reformers. The most popular preacher in Paris from 1530 until his death in 1556, François Le Picart, stood at the forefront of the counteroffensive. His 270 sermons are among the few printed Catholic sermons to survive during this critical period. A teacher and mentor to the earliest Jesuits in Paris, he condemned forcefully the new teachings on the Mass. Unlike most of his contemporaries, he understood the distinction between Luther and the later reformers, even though most Protestants at the time were simply referred to as 'Lutherans.' He asked in his sermons:

"Isn't it remarkable how they can't agree among themselves? Luther has one faith, one doctrine, Oecolampadius[1] has another, so who speaks the truth? ... There are those disciples of Martin Luther who say and do worse than he does ...

"Here we have that heretic Luther, and his disciple Melanchthon,[2] and Oecolampadius, and all of them have contrary opinions. Is this not a marvel and evident sign that they are deaf and mute, and that their edifice will not grow higher, but will fall into ruin? Luther says rightly that the body of Jesus Christ is in the holy sacrament of the altar, but he says that the bread is there too, which is false. Oecolampadius says that there is only bread, which is a complete error. God is not with those who are so divided ... There are five or six different opinions. One says it is only bread, the other that Jesus Christ is there but that the substance of the bread remains and is not transubstantiated. Another says that it is only the body and blood of Our Lord, but not a sacrifice. Yet another says that the sacrifice only profits the one who receives it, and not all the living and the dead. Another says that it is necessary to give the sacrament in both kinds to the laity. The division and variety of opinions that they hold is an argument and obvious sign that they do not have the Holy Spirit in them, but they speak in the spirit of Satan and the devil ... We must conclude that our congregation is the House of God, since there is unity, concord and common agreement in the faith."[3]

Echoing Johann Eck before him, who had asked Luther at Worms in 1517 how he dared go against all the teachings of 1500 years, Le Picart understood that the most effective response against the reformers was to emphasize their disagreements. The understanding of the meaning of the words of the Last Supper was central to the identity of all Christians, but the words themselves, as well as church tradition, made reconciliation impossible. It made some Christians burn others, while others willingly suffered the flames for their beliefs. Le Picart's preaching was especially important because his sermons were not delivered in the context of church meetings or esoteric theological discussions. They were public, highly attended sermons that exposed one of the key differences between Catholics and Protestants to all who came to hear. For Catholics in Paris and elsewhere, an attack on either the meaning of the Eucharist or the host was a call to arms. While Le Picart died five years before the religious wars, this was also the moment when Genevan preachers began to spread the Calvinist message in France and the first Reformed church appeared in Paris. And so began the French Wars of Religion.

Notes

1 Johannes Oecolampadius (1482–1531), the reformer of Basel.
2 Philip Melanchthon (1497–1560), Protestant reformer and Luther's colleague at the University of Wittenberg.
3 François Le Picart, *Les sermons et instructions chrestiennes, pour tous les Dimenches, & toutes les festes des saincts, depuis la Trinité iusques à l'Advent*, Paris: Nicolas Chesneau, 1566, pp. 41, 96–97. Translated by Larissa Juliet Taylor. See also François Le Picart, *Les sermons et instructions chrestiennes, pour tous les iours de caresme & Feries de Pasques*, Paris: Nicolas Chesneau, 1566, p. 87.

72 How to convince Catholics that Protestants have sex in the open air: Gabriel du Préau's *Catalogue of All Heretics*, 1569

by Irena Backus

During the Reformation period, the issue of religious and confessional identity became of capital significance. The definition of a religious identity inevitably entailed defining what one was *not*, and this meant attaching new importance to the definition of heresy. This in turn meant that Catholic theologians after the end of the Council of Trent in 1563, as confessional positions hardened, felt impelled to refute as heresies all systems of beliefs other than their own. Several of these theologians produced lists or catalogues of heresies, very often identifying 'heresies' of their own era or situating them on par with those of the early church on the principle attributed to Saint Jerome that "to point to the origin of a heresy is to refute it." The logic behind this was simple: Early heresies were systems of belief that had been refuted and condemned by the church. If they could be assimilated to more recent doctrinal movements that had sprung up before or during the Reformation era, these could be viewed as condemned from the outset.

This strategy is evidenced by the French Jesuit Gabriel du Préau or Prateolus (1511–1588) in his *Alphabetical Catalogue of Lives, Sects, and Doctrines of all Heretics*,[1] first published in Cologne in 1569. The *Catalogue* is especially interesting as du Préau in his preface draws a comparison between heresy and political rebellion on the one hand, and heresy and philosophical systems on the other hand. He can therefore establish in some cases parallels between "heretical sects" (as he calls the Protestant churches) and different schools of ancient Greek philosophy. His entry on Cynics and Waldensians is a very good example of this:

"The Cynics were a philosophical school and followers of Antisthenes[2] who was the first to introduce this type of philosophy. The name Cynics derives either from Cynosarges (or: Kunosarges), the gymnasium where Antisthenes taught or from their canine-like severity of speech with which they attacked people's lifestyles or else from the unhesitating way in which they had sexual relations in the open air like dogs. Diogenes Laertius talks about this in his *Lives of the Philosophers* referring to Crates and Hipparchia.[3]

"Waldensians and similar heretics some centuries back were not ashamed to imitate these carnal and bestial philosophers who asserted that anyone was allowed to couple with women shamelessly like dogs. In accordance with St. Peter's prophecy [1 Peter 4, 3–4], their licentiousness was copied by many others who also spurned the governing powers and blasphemed against authority."[4]

The Cynics were an ancient Greek school of philosophy who believed that the object of humans was to live a life of virtue in agreement with nature. This meant rejecting all conventional desires for wealth, power, health, and fame, and by living a simple life free from all possessions. As reasoning creatures, people could gain happiness by rigorous training and by living in a way which was natural for humans. The Cynics believed that the world belonged equally to everyone, and that suffering was caused by false judgments of what was valuable.

The Waldensians, so named after their founder Pierre de Valdes, were a Christian sect of twelfth-century origin combining various movements all condemned by medieval church councils. They practiced itinerant preaching and voluntary poverty, believed that the vernacular Bible should be made available to all Christians and opposed capital punishment. Most of them, however, continued to observe the Roman Catholic sacraments. Among the Waldensians, the 'perfect,' bound by vows of poverty, chastity, and obedience to their superiors, wandered about from place to place preaching. The 'perfect' were not allowed to perform manual labor, but were to depend for their subsistence on the members of the sect known as the 'friends' who continued to live in the world, married, owned property, and engaged in secular pursuits. The Waldensians quickly became interested in the Protestant Reformation and took advice from leading reformers as early as 1530. In the period between 1555 and 1565, the French and German Waldensians in particular formed themselves into Protestant communities.

Du Préau's purpose was not to put together a real catalogue in any sense of the word or to give an accurate account of either the Cynics or the Waldensians. His entry is based on unreliable and hostile sources and constitutes a classic piece of Counter-Reformation polemics. By the time he was writing, or rather compiling, his *Catalogue* from polemical works by his contemporaries and from a variety of works by earlier writers, almost all Waldensian communities had been absorbed into Protestant churches and so did not constitute a visible target. However, they did provide a hidden target, being an older religion than Protestantism and so an ancestor. As we saw, du Préau weaves together a horror story of the licentiousness of the Cynics, which is founded on the passing mentions of two of their philosophers (one of whom is, significantly, a woman) and their purported mating habits. It is difficult to see how he extrapolates from an anecdotal account of one married couple to the whole of the Cynic school of thought. It is even more difficult to see how he manages to draw a parallel between the alleged carnal lusts of the Cynics and the Waldensians and "similar heretics" whose carnal lusts, he implies, were copied by the Protestant Reformation. However, du Préau's purpose was not to inform but to persuade, and the power of his rhetoric is such that many readers of the successive editions of the *Catalogue* found his account convincing. He thus contributed to reinforcing the Counter-Reformation image of Protestantism as a carnal or bestial religion, based on the worst pagan customs.

As if that were not enough, he added that both the Cynics and the Waldensians (and hence the Protestant Reformation) were characterized by their lack of respect for civil authorities. This statement has more truth to it than the accusations of licentiousness. The Cynics did actually question the structures of civil society, while the Waldensians, at least in their early organization, lived on the margins of the society of their time and opposed capital punishment. All in all, du Préau manages to establish three parallels, one between the Reformation and pagan philosophy, another between the Reformation and licentious lifestyle, and the third between the Reformation and contempt for civil powers – all this using the already condemned heresy of the Waldensians as a link. His assault is typical of Counter-Reformation polemics and it leaves his Catholic readers in no doubt about what they should *not* be. We do not know whether it served to convert any Protestants to Catholicism.

Notes

1 Gabriel du Préau, *De vitis, sectis, et dogmatibus omnium haereticorum ... elenchus alphabeticus*, Cologne: Quentel, 1569.
2 Antisthenes (*c.*445–*c.*365 BC): Greek philosopher, disciple of Socrates and advocate of an ascetic and virtuous life. Later writers argued that he was the founder of the Cynics but this is not certain.
3 Diogenes Laertius (flourished 3rd century AD), *Lives and Opinions of the Philosophers*, although not reliable, was extremely popular in the sixteenth century as a source of information about ancient Greek schools of philosophy. Crates and his wife Hipparchia, one of the very few women to practise philosophy in ancient Athens, are mentioned by him in book VI, chapters 93–96. The couple are reputed to have lived out in the open air in the porticoes of Athens and to have practised sexual intercourse in the open air. According to the massive tenth-century Byzantine encyclopedia, the *Suda*, Crates described their union as *cynogamia* or 'coupling of dogs.'
4 Du Préau, *Elenchus*, p. 138. Translated by Irena Backus.

73 The Luther family's flight: A Counter-Reformation polemical broadsheet of the 1620s[1]

by Barbara Stollberg-Rilinger

Illustrated broadsheets were the first modern mass media: a central tool of political and religious propaganda that even people who were illiterate could understand. Broadsides and pamphlets were also a lucrative business in the early modern period: Printers published what people wanted to see and read. With a little caution, therefore, we can draw conclusions from what the 'common man' (and woman) in the street believed, wanted, and thought.

Not only did Protestants make use of these mediums, their Catholic antagonists also adopted them as propaganda tools. The primary source discussed here, a polemical broadsheet (see Figure 73.1), dates from the early 1620s, the beginning phase of the Thirty Years' War, when confessional polemic had reached its climax. After Emperor Ferdinand II had defeated the Bohemian revolt at the Battle of White Mountain in 1620, he pushed through a harsh policy of re-Catholicization in the Bohemian lands. The leaders of the revolts were executed; their followers had to flee and were dispossessed. Beginning in 1621, Protestant theologians, preachers, and schoolmasters were expelled from Bohemia with their families. This constituted an existential threat to the people affected. Soon after, all Protestant inhabitants were given the choice to convert or to leave the country. The broadsheet presented here refers to the expulsion of the ministers, and exists in several different versions. It must have been in high demand because it was reprinted several times. The artist and publisher are unknown.

The picture presents the Luther couple with child, dog, and belongings on their journey. A monstrously fat Martin Luther in a black minister's coat dominates the scene. In a wooden wheelbarrow, he carts not only his grotesquely large belly, but also books, and, scattered among these, the heads of Melanchthon, Zwingli, and Calvin. On his back, Luther carries a basket full of men dressed as burghers who are identified as "the servants of the [i.e., God's] Word" in the text below the image. With his left hand, Luther lifts a huge, magnificent drinking mug. In sharp contrast, Luther's wife, Katharina von Bora, is a picture of misery: thin and careworn, in a ragged short dress, burdened with a large wooden basket and a book on her back, a poodle on a rope, and a baby in her arms.

MARTHIN LVTHER.	CATHARINA.
Nuhn Muess es Ia gewandert sein,	O lieber Merth nimb deins Bauchs Wahr.
Hab gewandt ich bet mich erst gricht ein,	Leg ihn auff die Scheyb Truchen dar.
Weill ich dan hab Kham bleibente Orth,	Damit destbass Kanst Wandern forth,
Müesse ich Wider mein Willen fort.	Nach tragen Wil ich dir Gotts Wort.
Die Worths diemer mich Bschwdren sehr.	Gibst du mir auch Von deiner Storck,
Mein schwärer Leib aber noch mehr,	Thest du dran Warlich ein guets Werck,
Doch gibt mier Stärckh mein grosses glass.	Mein münd ist Spacr. die Fütess seind schwach.
Das ich forthin Khan gehen base.	Der Weg ist Vchr O gross Vngmach.

Figure 73.1 Broadsheet "Marthin Luther, Nuhn Muess es Ia gewandert sein ...," between 1620 and 1630, Herzog August Bibliothek Wolfenbüttel

The broadsheet combines three different motifs which were familiar to contemporary viewers into a caricature that equally derides the Luther family and the Protestant refugees in Bohemia. First, the broadsheet utilizes the well-known Luther portraits by Lucas Cranach the Elder as a motif, which is, however, exaggerated into a caricature. Luther's portrait, reproduced again and again in countless variations, was one of the most recognizable images of the early modern period. Second, the broadsheet employs the popular biblical motif of the holy family on the flight to Egypt. The juxtaposition of these two motifs gives rise to the derision of the viewer because the Luther family is depicted as anything but a holy family. The mother and child do not ride on a donkey but must drag a burden, and the father appears to be the very embodiment of carnal excess. The sacred motif of the holy family on the flight to Egypt is perverted into its opposite through the use of a third motif: the popular embodiment of crapulence in the figure of a grotesquely fat man with his stomach in a wheelbarrow. As early as 1520, this motif may be found in a woodcut by Hans Weiditz, and it is also present in the picture of gluttony (*gula*) that is part of the famous cycle of the seven deadly sins by Pieter Brueghel the Elder (1558).

The text, in two sets of four couplets and put into the mouths of Martin and Katharina, emphasizes this message. The first line is made up of words from a folksong, which would have been seen as an invitation to sing the verses satirically:

"MARTIN LUTHER.
Now I must roam,
It had seemed that I had found a home,
Since, then, I have no permanent place,
Against my will I must go apace.
The servants of the Word weigh me sore,
Yet my heavier belly burdens me still more.
Nevertheless my big glass gives me strength,
That I can henceforth go the length."

"CATHARINA.
O Dear Martin, for your stomach take care,
Rest it on the cart there,
So that you can better wander in exile,
Behind you, carrying God's Word, I file.
Give, also, of your 'strength'[2] to me,
In which you do a good work verily.
My mouth is dry, my feet are weak,
The journey is very long, O great affliction."[3]

This mockery of Luther as an unrestrained drunkard, glutton, and spendthrift was a popular anti-Protestant commonplace. For example, broadsheets from the years 1616–1618 featured a huge drinking mug and called it "Luther's Large Catechism." Besides the vice of corporal intemperance, Luther was attacked above all in his capacity as the head of his household. The caricature of Luther here, as the bad husband who did not take care of his wife and child, had a clear anti-Protestant slant. Because clerical marriage was a particular provocation for Catholics, the Roman church had reaffirmed celibacy rules for priests at the Council of Trent. Thus, the sheet presents a distorted image of a Protestant clergyman's household in general, and of Luther's marriage – which was considered by Protestants to be the model of the Christian state of marriage – in particular.

Notes

1 Translated by Benjamin A. Miller and Mary Kovel.

2 The mug of beer.
3 Caption, broadsheet "Marthin Luther, Nuhn Muess es Ia gewandert sein …," between 1620 and 1630, Herzog August Bibliothek Wolfenbüttel, shelf mark IH 23.

74 God intervenes: A eucharistic miracle in the principality of Orange, 1678

by S. Amanda Eurich

Situated between two great Catholic powers – the kingdom of France and the Comtat Venaissin (under papal control since the days of the Avignon papacy in the fourteenth century), the small principality of Orange experienced the full force of the religious wars that gripped early modern Europe. A feudal possession of the counts of Chalon in the fifteenth century, Orange became an enclave of Dutch power and authority when it passed into the hands of the House of Nassau in 1530. In the later decades of the sixteenth century, the princes of Nassau tried to impose a biconfessional regime on their Orangeois territories, but a powerful coalition of Calvinist clergymen, nobles, and notables drove many Catholics, including the Archbishop of Orange, into exile. In 1607, Prince Philip-William of Nassau finally succeeded in promulgating an edict of toleration which mandated the division of political authority between Catholics and Protestants. The famous edict of 1607 also ordered the restoration of Catholic worship and the public observation of Catholic holy days.

Until the French occupation of the principality in the 1660s, Catholics and Protestants grudgingly observed the decree, living cheek-by-jowl in relative peace. From the 1660s onward, however, religious tensions between the two communities increased. The week-long feast of Corpus Christi became a critical test case of religious coexistence. Authorized by a papal bull in 1264, Corpus Christi[1] celebrated the physical presence of the crucified body of Christ in the sacrament of the Eucharist or Mass. Protestant reformers from Martin Luther onward challenged the medieval belief that the ordinary elements of the Eucharist, the wafer of unleavened bread (or host) and wine, were transformed in substance (or 'transubstantiated') into the body and blood of Christ at the moment when the priest consecrated them by reiterating Christ's words at the Last Supper. Within Catholic Europe, however, secular and ecclesiastical officials promoted the feast of Corpus Christi, recognizing that processions of the host through urban streets functioned as a powerful metaphor of social cohesion and order. Members of religious orders renowned for their rhetorical skills preached a week-long cycle of sermons meant to excite the devotion of the faithful. By the seventeenth century, the Jesuits often performed this service and promoted the so-called Forty Hours' Devotion or adoration of the Eucharist, creating an air of revivalism that heightened religious passions and intensified confessional divisions.

In the late seventeenth century, Jacques Pineton de Chambrun, a Calvinist pastor from Orange, penned his autobiography, in which he described the events that transpired after a Jesuit preacher challenged him to refute the doctrine of transubstantiation during the Corpus Christi celebrations of 1678:

"One Sunday during the evening service, I attempted to refute all the sermons that he had made about this subject. I preached for more than four hours in the presence not only of my congregation but also before several strangers who had come in order to hear this refutation. I can say that I put him in a monstrous confusion by revealing his false reasoning and his false citations. I overwhelmed him with passages from the church fathers with which he had shown off up to that point, so that leaving the sermon he pulled his hair saying to a Catholic gentleman who is still living (named Villeneuve): 'Good God, how can I respond to so many quotations?' ... He contented himself by making several proclamations from the pulpit about what I had said that the veneration of the sacrament was an idolatrous cult. ... Then turning toward the altar where the host was exposed, he continued in these terms: 'Yes my savior I am addressing myself to you, to ask you to judge our cause by a miracle. If we are idolaters by venerating your holy sacrament make the fires of heaven descend upon us, as Elijah made them fall upon the priest of Baal. Strike our altars and we will be persuaded by this judgment that we are idolaters.' ...

"This was precisely the 19th of the month of June that this imprecation was pronounced. Ten days later, the 29th of the same month, on the feast of Saint Peter and Paul that is a Wednesday at nine in the morning, God revealed the miracle that the Jesuit had demanded. The air darkened with thick clouds, lightning bolts flashed everywhere, the thunder rumbled with an extraordinary racket. There was one that struck in a strange manner and fell right next to the great altar where the Canon Caulet was celebrating Mass. The thunderbolt made him fall backwards. It tore several stones from the vaulted ceiling and passing by the first chapel which is to the left of the choir, it burned the altar linens where Mass was also being celebrated. ... The thunder which had caused all of this disorder, exiting a window of the church, struck the bell tower where people worked until the evening to put out the fires it had ignited. There it is, an absolute fact known throughout Orange and environs that must give reasonable Roman Catholics something to think about."[2]

This passage is a powerful reminder of difficulties of religious coexistence in early modern Europe. In biconfessional regimes, the public recognition of religious holidays, church bell ringing, even routine processions of the host to the bedsides of the sick and dying could all be occasions for verbal denunciations and physical violence. In the pulpit and in the streets of Orange, both Catholics and Protestants used Corpus Christi to score points against the opposition. Chambrun clearly takes great pleasure in using the writings of the early church fathers – traditional texts defended by the Catholics rather than the biblical texts so favored by Protestant reformers – to debunk the claims of his rival. By linking the narrative to the Old Testament story of the prophet Elijah, who called upon God to destroy the altars of Baal by fire, Chambrun underscores the Calvinist conviction that the followers of the Reformed religion, like the Hebrews, were indeed God's 'chosen' ones – a 'fact' confirmed, in his view, by divine intervention.

Notes

1 'Body of Christ,' Latin.
2 Jacques Pineton de Chambrun, *Les Larmes de Jacques Pineton de Chambrun* (1688), Paris: Charpentier, 1854, pp. 15–18. Translated by S. Amanda Eurich.

75 Different confessions, difficult choices: Theodore Beza converts after thirteen years of inner struggles

by Scott M. Manetsch

The Protestant Reformation in sixteenth-century Europe divided territories, cities, and families. Many townspeople and peasants remained loyal to the traditional church and its teachings, suspicious of doctrinal innovation and horrified by the popular violence that racked the Holy Roman Empire[1] and France beginning in the 1520s. Hundreds of thousands of other people – particularly from Europe's towns and cities – defied the Roman church and embraced the religious message championed by reformers such as Martin Luther and (later) John Calvin. These Protestant leaders attacked the systemic abuses of medieval Catholicism and espoused an understanding of Christianity that emphasized God's gracious acceptance of sinners through faith in Jesus Christ alone.

No doubt numerous converts to Protestantism were influenced by political pressure or personal expediency. But for many others, the decision to leave the traditional church issued from deep religious convictions, arrived at after inner struggles, and resulted in the rupture of relationships, the loss of property, and personal danger. In the letter preface to his popular *Confession of the Christian Faith* (1560), the Geneva minister Theodore Beza (1519–1605) relates the intense struggle and personal cost that was involved in leaving the religion of his childhood and becoming an openly Protestant believer:

"In the meantime, I was still stuck in the mire. My friends urged me to undertake some kind of livelihood. My uncle placed all of his wealth at my disposal. On the one side my conscience pressed hard on me, and my wife Claudine Denosse called on me to fulfill my promise [to make public our marriage]. On the other side, Satan, hiding behind a most peaceful countenance, tempted me with his blandishments. My income was made greater by the death of my brother. And so I was rendered helpless, incapable of making a decision due to all of these worries.

"But here I will most happily narrate the amazing way the Lord had compassion on me. For it happened that the Lord afflicted me with a very serious illness, so that I almost despaired of life itself. What could I do, wretched man that I am, when I saw nothing before me except the terrible judgment of God? What more can be said? After endless tortures of both mind and body, the Lord showed pity toward his runaway slave and consoled me so that I harbored no doubts about the gift of his pardon to me. Therefore, I renounced myself with tears, I asked for forgiveness, I renewed my vow to embrace his true worship publicly – in short, I devoted myself completely to God. And so it happened that the image of death, which stood before me, awakened in me a desire for true life that had previously been dormant and buried, and that illness was for me the beginning of true health. How wonderful is the Lord that, in one and the same stroke, he both knocks down and lifts up, wounds and makes whole again.

"Therefore, as soon as I was able to leave my bed, I broke all the chains that bound me and collected my belongings. I left behind my native land, my relatives, my friends in order to follow Christ. And, accompanied by my wife, I went to Geneva in voluntary exile. Accordingly, on 24 October 1548, having fled Egypt,[2] I arrived at that city and discovered what I previously could not even have believed, although I had heard that commonwealth greatly praised by a number of pious men."[3]

Theodore Beza's decision to embrace Protestantism and flee Catholic France in the fall of 1548 occurred after years of personal turmoil. Born into France's lower nobility, Beza grew up in privilege and wealth. In 1528, when Beza was 9 years old, he was sent to Orléans to study with the famous pedagogue (and secret Lutheran) Melchior Wolmar, who instructed him in the liberal arts and imparted to him a love of classical literature. Beza learned to write elegant French and Latin, and began to study the Greek New Testament. He discovered a gift for writing poetry. He also came to share the conviction of Catholic humanists that a recovery of the Christian Scriptures in their original languages would hasten the reform of the church. In 1535, shortly before he left the household of Wolmar, Beza was introduced to the writings of the Zurich reformer Heinrich Bullinger, which (he will report later) "caused me to look toward the light of truth."[4] Beza made a personal vow to repudiate one day the Catholic religion and find a safe haven for his conscience in Germany.

Beza's 'spiritual awakening' was stillborn, or at least delayed for the next thirteen years. When Wolmar left for Germany, Beza remained back in France, earning a degree in civil law, writing provocative love poetry, and associating with a talented coterie of young French humanists. His livelihood was supported by two generous benefices from the Catholic Church. Hence (as Beza described it), the three-fold snare of Satan – the allurements of pleasure, the ambition for literary glory, and the expectation of public honors – dulled his conscience and bound him to the Catholic religion. Marriage to a chambermaid named Claudine Denosse in the mid-1540s made matters still more complicated, since the marriage had to be contracted in secret to avoid forfeiting his benefices. He promised Claudine that one day their marriage would be confirmed in public. Beza finally achieved literary fame when he published a collection of poetry entitled *Poemata* in the summer of 1548 – but the triumph was short-lived. Within weeks he was stricken with a life-threatening illness. During his convalescence, Beza resolved to fulfill his promises to God and Claudine if he recovered. Thus, in the fall of 1548, Beza and Claudine fled the spiritual 'Egypt' of Catholic France for the 'promised land' of Reformed Geneva, where the couple confirmed their marriage in a public ceremony presided over by John Calvin. With his conversion, Beza forfeited his financial security, renounced his literary ambitions, alienated family members, and began a new life in exile. The dictates of conscience and the true worship of God justified these substantial sacrifices, he believed.

Notes

1 The Holy Roman Empire of the German Nation, usually called 'the Empire,' was a huge and complex political organization in central Europe in medieval and early modern times. It was a loose political union of mostly German and largely self-governing principalities and towns.
2 'Egypt' here denotes France. Beza uses the biblical story of the Israelites' exodus from Egypt to describe his own experience moving from France to Geneva, which is implied to be his 'Holy Land.'
3 Beza to Melchior Wolmar, 12 March 1560. Letter-preface to the *Confessio christianae fidei*, Geneva, 1560, in *Correspondance de Théodore de Bèze*, vol. III (1559–1561), compiled by Hippolyte Aubert, published by Henri Meylan and Alain Dufour, Geneva: Librairie Droz, 1963, pp. 42–52. Translated by Scott Manetsch. A slightly different English translation of this letter is in Henry Martyn Baird, *Theodore Beza. The Counsellor of the French Reformation, 1519–1605*, New York: G. P. Putnam's Sons, 1899, pp. 355–367, here pp. 364–365.
4 Beza to Bullinger, 18 August 1568, in H. Meylan, A. Dufour, C. Chimelli, and B. Nicollier (eds), *Correspondance de Théodore de Bèze: 1568*, vol. IX, Geneva: Librarie Droz, p. 121. Translated by Scott Manetsch.

76 "A priest you were on Sunday / Monday morning a minister": Clerical conformity in eighteenth-century Ireland

by Monica Brennan

Between 1695 and 1760, the Irish Parliament passed a series of anti-Catholic laws, referred to as 'penal' or 'popery' laws, to ensure that Protestant supremacy in Ireland would never again be threatened as it had been by the Catholic rebellion of 1641 and the Jacobite War (1688–1691).[1] This legislation, it is important to note, did not outline a system of religious persecution, nor did it prohibit the practice of the Catholic religion. It sought to safeguard and strengthen the Protestant interest in Ireland by eliminating Catholic access to political and social power. The most important provisions concerned land ownership. By 1780, Protestants were in possession of 95 percent of the island's land (compared to 41 percent in 1641).

While efforts to convert Ireland's Catholics to the Protestant Church of Ireland, the so-called 'Established Church,' were limited largely to the country's remaining Catholic landowners (and in this they were successful), laws were passed banishing bishops and regular clergy. As a result, by the beginning of the eighteenth century the Irish Catholic Church's diocesan structure and its parochial system were in a state of virtual collapse. Most sees were vacant and their bishops in exile. The secular clergy, though required to register and provide sureties of fifty pounds for good behavior, were generally left alone and free to minister to their people. It was the government's expectation, though, that banishing bishops, combined with laws against educating Catholics abroad, would result in the gradual extinction of the Catholic clergy in Ireland. This did not happen, but the absence of Catholic seminaries and universities in Ireland resulted in the ordination of many men who lacked proper theological training or a true religious vocation. Disciplining these individuals was extremely difficult. Some were suspended from performing their priestly duties; others were excommunicated.

Faced with financial difficulties stemming from a loss of employment or to revenge themselves on their bishops, some 'degraded' priests conformed to the Established Church. Their conformity was encouraged by the "Act for Registering the Popish Clergy," which promised that "Every popish priest who shall convert and conform to the Church of Ireland as by law established shall have 20 pounds yearly for their maintenance and till they are otherwise provided for, said money to be levied on the inhabitants of such county or city or town when such converted priest did last officiate. And such converts shall publickly read the liturgy of the Church of Ireland in the English or Irish tongue, in such places as the archbishop or bishop of that diocese shall appoint."[2]

While the Irish press in the eighteenth century was generally more concerned with foreign, rather than domestic, news, the public was interested in the scandalous and the sensational, particularly, it seems, when Catholics – especially Catholic priests – were involved. Both lay and clerical recantations made the news, as did the obituaries of 'former' Catholic priests, like Rev. Richard Archbold, who supposedly conformed "from a sincere and rational conviction, renounced Popery and embraced the Protestant faith."[3]

The exact number of Catholic priests who conformed to the Established Church in this period cannot be determined, but the 'Convert Rolls,' the government register of converts to the Church of Ireland, and eighteenth-century newspaper accounts record approximately 100 clerical recantations.[4] Anecdotal material – including poems and songs – bears witness to others.

When a priest changed his religion, he risked earning the contempt of the layfolk he once served and rejection by his family. His actions were all the more galling since the annual maintenance with which he was provided was levied off the people among whom he lived. Protestant bishops regarded most conforming priests with suspicion, and few appear to have been granted good livings. Most lived obscurely; some as teachers, others as couple-beggars, making a living by assisting at clandestine weddings. This was usually neither honorable nor decent, and therefore such men often led a degraded and drunken existence and frequently fell afoul of the law. Some of the bitterest poems in the Irish language lampoon the men who abandoned the Catholic faith of their fathers. "Fill, Fill a Rún Ó" (*c*.1739) is the lament of a Donegal mother whose son, Dominic O Domhnaill, abandoned the church of "Peter and Paul" and became a minister in the Church of Ireland:

> "Torment on you, Dominic O Domhnaill
> Aren't you a pathetic sight
> A priest you were on Sunday
> Monday morning a minister.
>
> "Come back darling and don't leave me:
> Come back from that other world,
> You won't achieve glory till you return.
>
> "You foresook Peter and Paul
> On account of gold and silver.
> You forsook the Queen of Glory[5]
> And you turned to the coat of a minister.
>
> "When you're in hell for a while
> And tears streaming from your eyes,
> That's the place where you'll discover
> Which is better to be – priest or minister."[6]

While these lines suggest the mother's concern for her son's soul, in one version of the song she curses him for making her a figure of ridicule:

> "When I attend Mass on Sunday
> I hide my shame in my mantle,
> I hear the young girls say;
> There goes the minister's mother."[7]

Eighteenth-century press reports highlight the sincerity of those Catholic priests who abjured 'popery' and embraced the Protestant faith. Popular literature in Irish, on the other hand, excoriates these men as ignorant and avaricious – disgraces to both faith and family.

Notes

1. The 'Jacobite War,' also called the 'Williamite War,' refers to the conflict over the kingship of England, Scotland, and Ireland between James II and William of Orange after the so-called 'Glorious Revolution' of 1688, when James II had been deposed as king of England and William and Mary installed in his place.
2. "Act for Registering the Popish Clergy," 2 Ann, c. 7 (1703). 8 Ann, c. 3 (1709) raised the annual maintenance to thirty pounds.
3. *Cork Evening Post, 2 July 1767*, quoted in Anne R. Chamney, "Catholic Converts Recorded in Some 18th Century Irish Newspapers," *The Irish Genealogist* 11:1, 2002, 31.
4. In 1742 there were reportedly 1,400 priests in Ireland. About half are believed to have been secular priests while members of religious orders comprised the rest.
5. The Virgin Mary.
6. Quoted in Maureen Wall, *Catholic Ireland in the Eighteenth Century: Collected Essays*, ed. Gerard O'Brien, Dublin: Geography Publications, 1989, pp. 32–33. Translated by Annette Byrne.
7. "Fill, fill a run O." Online. Available at https://mudcat.org/thread.cfm?threadid=14833 (accessed 5 May 2018).

77 A great poet describes his own times: John Milton's *Of Reformation*, 1641

by David Cressy

The poet John Milton (1608–1674) believed that the political corruption of the Roman Catholic Church dated back to the reign of Constantine in the fourth century, and that its spiritual corruption sprang from the papacy that contaminated religion in the west for over a thousand years. The Protestant Reformations of the sixteenth century, in Milton's view, served only to begin the process of cleansing, and in England, he charged, that process had been thwarted by prelates and other regressive interests. In his own day, especially under Charles I in the 1630s, God's church in England suffered from haughty and aggressive bishops who had usurped the power of the evangelical ministry. The Protestant Reformation had not just stalled, but was going backward. By 1641, however, when Milton wrote *Of Reformation*,[1] the Established Church[2] was under attack, episcopacy was discredited, and a revolutionary parliament seemed to be considering the thorough reform of religion. Milton's pamphlet not only advertised his ideas and his learning, in his distinctive Latinate style, but promoted a view of Reformation history that looked at the past to advocate for further reform in the future:

"HENRY the 8. was the first that rent this *Kingdome* from the *Popes* subjection totally; but his Quarrell being more about *Supremacie*, then other faultinesse in *Religion* … it is no marvell if hee stuck where he did. The next default was in the *Bishops*, who though they had renounc't the *Pope*, they still hugg'd the *Popedome*, and shar'd the Authority among themselves, … In *Edward* the 6. Dayes, why a compleate *Reform* was not effected, to any considerate man may appeare. … we all know by Examples that exact *Reformation* is not perfited at the first push, …"[3]

"From hence then I passe to Qu. ELIZABETH, the next *Protestant* Prince, in whose days why *Religion* attained not a perfect reducement … I suppose the hindering Causes will be found to bee … the weak Estate which Qu. MARY left the Realme in, the great Places and Offices executed by *Papists*, the *Judges*, the *Lawyers*, and the *Justices* of Peace for the most part *Popish*, the *Bishops* firm to *Rome*, from whence was to be expected the furious flashing of Excommunications, and absolving the *People* from their Obedience. Next, her private *Councellours* … perswaded her … that the altering of *Ecclesiasticall Policie* would move sedition. … From this period I count to begin our Times …"[4]

"... now the gravest, and worthiest Minister ... shall be revil'd and ruffl'd by an insulting, and only-Canon-wise Prelate ... stones & Pillars, and Crucifixes have now the honour, and the almes due to *Christs* living members; the Table of Communion now become a Table of separation stands like an exalted platforme upon the brow of the quire, fortifi'd with bulwark ... And thus the people vilifi'd and rejected by them, give over ... the search of divine knowledge as mystery ... only for Churchmen to meddle with, which is what the Prelates desire, that when they have brought us back to Popish blindnesse we might commit to their dispose the whole managing of our salvation, ..."[5]

"... what numbers of faithfull, and freeborn Englishmen, and good Christians, have bin constrain'd to forsake their dearest home, their friends, and kindred, whom nothing but the wide Ocean and the savage deserts of America could hide and shelter from the fury of the Bishops ... Thus as they have unpeopl'd the Kingdome by expulsion of so many thousands, ... so have they hamstrung the valor of the Subject by seeing to effeminate us all at home. ... upon that day which Gods Law ... hath consecrated, that we might have one day at least of seven set apart wherein to examin and encrease our knowledge of God, ... and by *Bishops* the pretended *Fathers of the Church* instigated by publique Edict, and with earnest indeavor push't forward to gaming, jigging, wassailing, and mixt dancing is a horror to think. ... Now I appeal to all wise men, what an excessive wast of Treasury hath beene within these few yeares in this Land ... in the Idolatrous erection of Temples beautified exquisitely to out-vie the Papists, the costly and deare-bought Scandals, and snares of Images, Pictures, rich Coaps, gorgeous Altar-cloths: ... If the Splendor of *Gold* and *Silver* begin to Lord it once againe in the Church of *England*, wee shall see *Antichrist* shortly wallow heere, though his cheife Kennel be at *Rome*."[6]

"Thou therefore that sits's in light & glory unapprochable ... thee I implore ... looke upon this thy poore and almost spent, and expiring *Church*, leave her not thus a prey to these importunate *Wolves*, ... O let them not bring about their damned *designes* ... to re-involve us in that pitchy *Cloud* of infernall darknes, where we shall never more see the *Sunne* of thy *Truth* againe."[7]

According to Milton, the Tudor Reformations of Henry VIII, Edward VI, and Elizabeth I were lost opportunities, false and faint efforts, compromised above all by the worldliness and ambition of the bishops. James I's church was barely half-reformed, its doctrine compatible with the best Reformed churches, but its discipline and worship 'popishly' affected. This was a position that Milton shared with many Puritans, though he moved away from predestinarian Calvinism. The ceremonial revival of the reign of Charles I, associated with the theology of Arminianism and the ascendancy of Archbishop William Laud, promoted altar-like communion tables, ecclesiastical vestments, and the beauty of holiness. According to Milton, the church's worship was polluted by lavish ceremony and ornament that presaged a return to Rome. Puritans (and Milton) were further alienated by the king's approval of sports and games on the sacred Sabbath.

Milton did not join the thousands who moved to New England for godly as well as social reasons, but he blamed the episcopal Church of England for their exodus. England's religious future was uncertain as Milton penned his pamphlet, but true Reformation seemed possible. Within a year, however, conditions worsened as the country spiraled into religious civil war.

Notes

1. John Milton, *Of Reformation Touching Church-Discipline in England and the Causes that hitherto have hindred it. Two bookes, written to a freind [sic]*, [London]: Thomas Underhill, 1641.
2. The Protestant state church in England.
3. Milton, *Of Reformation*, pp. 8–9, 13.
4. Ibid., pp. 15–16.
5. Ibid., pp. 21–22.
6. Ibid., pp. 56–57, 60–62.
7. Ibid., pp. 86–87.

78 Thomas Gage in Guatemala: A Puritan's memoir of preaching among the Maya, 1648

by Kevin Gosner

In 1648 the Puritan preacher Thomas Gage (*c*.1597–1656) published *The English-American, His Travail by Sea and Land, or A New Survey of the West India's [Indies]*,[1] an account of his twelve-year sojourn in Spanish America, where as a young Dominican friar he served in Indian parishes in southern Mexico and Guatemala. Gage's personal history would seem to disqualify him as a reliable source for understanding the history of local religion in New Spain, and yet he produced an engaging and convincing description of 'living among the Indians' that is – in spite of being deeply imbued with Christian values – empathetic, richly detailed, and insightful. The son of a prominent English Catholic family, Gage trained for the priesthood at Jesuit colleges in Flanders and Valladolid, Spain, but abandoned the Society to join a Dominican mission to the Philippines in 1625. On route to Manila, he fled his entourage in Mexico City and made his way first to Chiapas and then to Guatemala.

After three years of study at the Dominican convent in Santiago, Guatemala, he was assigned a parish in the K'iche' Maya towns of Mixco and Pinula, with a congregation that included Spaniards and African slaves. He served there for nearly five years, until 1635, when he moved to nearby parishes at Amatitlán and then Petapa. In 1637, he abandoned Guatemala and eventually returned to England, where he renounced Roman Catholicism, briefly joined the Church of England,[2] and finally, by 1642, cast his fate with that of Oliver Cromwell.

A New Survey of the West India's was written, in part, to raise support for Cromwell's ambition to challenge Spanish control of the Caribbean. Gage himself sailed as chaplain with the English fleet that attacked Hispaniola in 1655. The Spanish successfully defended the island, but the English did take Jamaica and there Gage lived until his death in 1656.

In this excerpt, Gage tells the story of discovering a case of idolatry outside his parish in Mixco. The clandestine cult was betrayed by a local Mayan man to a Spanish parishioner, and Gage organized a small band to find the hidden shrine:

"At the entrance the cave was broad, and went a little forward, but when we were in, we found it turn on the left hand towards the mountain, and not far, for within two rods[3] we found the idol standing upon a low stool covered with a linen cloth. The substance of it was wood, black shining like jet, as if it had been painted or smoked; the form was of a man's head unto the shoulders, without either beard or mustachios. His look was grim with a wrinkled forehead and broad startling eyes. We feared not his frowning look, but presently seized upon him; and as we lifted him up we found under him some single reals,[4] which his favorites had offered unto him, and that made us search the cave more diligently.

"Our effort was not amiss, for we found upon the ground more single reals, some plantains and other fruits, half-burned wax candles, pots of maize, one little one of honey, and little dishes wherein frankincense had been burned. I perceived the idolaters and Christians agreed in their offerings, and had I not been informed that they called this idol their god, I would have blamed them no more than the rest of the towns who worship, kneel before, and offer such offerings unto the saints made of wood, and some no handsomer than this idol. I thought it might have been some beast's shape; but being the shape and form of a man, they might have named him by the name of some saint, and so some way excused themselves. But they could not or would not do this because they persisted in this error that he was their god, and had spoken and preached unto them. Afterwards, on being asked by me whether it were the picture of any saint, such as were in Mixco, and other churches, they answered, no, but that he was above all the saints in the country. ...

"On the Sabbath day in the morning, when the pulpit was made ready by him who had care of the church and altars, I had Miguel Dalva carry the idol under his cloak and leave it in the pulpit upon the ground that it might not be seen, till such time as I should think fit in my sermon to produce it. ... The Fuentes and all the rest that were suspected to be that idol's favorites came also that day to church, little thinking that their god was brought from his cave, and now lay hid in the pulpit to shame them. ...

"Mass being ended, I went up to preach, and when I rehearsed the words of my text, I perceived both Spaniards and Indians to look upon one another, for they were not used to sermons out of the Old Testament. I went on to expound this command of God to have no other gods before him, so that the doctrine might seem to convince all that were present. I showed that no creature could have the power of God the Creator of all things, neither could do good or harm without the living God's commission. This was especially true of inanimate creatures such as stocks and stones, which by the hands and workmanship of man might have eyes, and yet are dead idols and see not, might have ears and not hear; might have mouths and not speak; might have hands and not work, nor help or defend with them such as worship them, and bow unto them.

"Having half finished my sermon, I bowed myself down in the pulpit, and lifted up the black, grim, and staring devil, and placed that Dagon on one side of the pulpit. I fixed my eyes on some of the Fuentes and others, who I perceived changed color, blushed, and were sore troubled looking upon one another. I desired the congregation to behold what a god was worshipped by some of them, and all to take notice of him, if any knew what part of the earth was the dominion of this god, or from whence he came. I told them that some had boasted that this piece of wood had spoken and preached against what I had taught of Christ, and that therefore he was worshipped by them for God, and they had offered him money, honey, and the fruits of the earth unto him, and burnt frankincense before him in a secret and hidden cave under the earth, showing thereby that they were ashamed to own him publicly, and that he by lurking in the darkness of the earth showed certainly that he belonged to the Prince of Darkness.[5] ...

"I assured them that if they would renounce and abjure from that time all heathenish idolatry of their forefathers, I would intercede for them, and secure them from what punishment might be inflicted upon them by the President and the Bishop, and if they would come to me, I would spend my best endeavors for the helping and furthering of them in the way of Christianity.

"Concluding without having named any person, I went down out of the pulpit, and caused the idol to be brought after me. Sending for an axe and for two or three great pans of coals, I commanded it to be hewn in very small pieces, and to be cast in the fire and burned before all the people in the midst of the Church."[6]

Writing years after his service in Guatemala, Gage, as a Puritan, compares Mayan paganism to Catholic rituals to honor the saints. The case offers an opportunity to explore two important themes in early modern history: the local social contexts for the transformation of ritual and the history of emotions among rival religious communities. Gage's larger work also reminds us that the forces that shaped the history of religion in this period – in Europe and the Americas – were transatlantic and global in scale.

Notes

1 Thomas Gage, *The English-American, His Travail by Sea and Land, or, A new Survey of the West-India's Containing a Journall of Three Thousand and Three Hundred Miles within the Main Land of America*, London: R. Cotes, 1648; here quoted from J. Eric S. Thompson (ed.), *Thomas Gage's Travels in the New World*, Norman: University of Oklahoma Press, 1958.
2 The Protestant state church in England.
3 A unit of length. One rod is 16½ feet, about five meters.
4 Spanish coins.
5 The Devil.
6 Thompson (ed.), *Thomas Gage's Travels*, pp. 281–285.

79 The morality of doubt: The religious skeptics of seventeenth-century Venice

by Edward Muir

Gabriel Naudé, one of the forefathers of the French Enlightenment, famously claimed that seventeenth-century Italy at the height of the Counter-Reformation was "full of libertines, atheists, and people who believe in nothing."[1] The "people who believe in nothing" were primarily members of the Venetian Academy of the Unknowns, many of whom the Frenchman had met while studying at the University of Padua, which was a hotbed of free thinkers. The liberty of the Unknowns depended on their founder and patron, Giovanni Francesco Loredan (1607–1661), a member of one of Venice's most prominent patrician families. Loredan himself was usually circumspect about his personal religious beliefs, but his private secretary, Ferrante Pallavicino (1615–1644) was not. A popular novelist and historian, Pallavicino was the most extreme papal critic and religious skeptic in seventeenth-century Catholic Europe. The nephews of Pope Urban VIII took Pallavicino's writings so seriously that they hired a secret agent to lure him away from the safety of Venice to papal Avignon, where he was executed at age twenty-eight.

Soon after his death someone, probably Loredan himself, penned *The Soul of Ferrante Pallavicino*, the most virulent attack on the church to come from the circle of the Unknowns.[2] The conceit of the book is that the soul of the deceased Ferrante Pallavicino returns to earth one evening to carry on a conversation with an old friend named Henrico who may have been a stand-in for Loredan. In their dialogue, Ferrante and Henrico feed off one another's skepticism as might happen in a real conversation between two like-minded friends:

"We find reasons to conclude why the infidels and the heretics have had occasion to laugh at our religion, while the abuses and scandals make it totter … The upright judgment they have made can be shown in the capitals of Christianity, which are full of all kinds of debauchees, gamblers, whores, transvestites, thugs, and of every enormous vice. How can they believe the faith of Christ to be the truth and unique when they see all the Catholics lead the life of atheists? How can they believe that the sacrament of the Host is the true, immaculate body of the second person of the Most Holy Trinity when they see that our temples are not full of the devout but of lovers; when they see no respect, less even than in the square for street performers."[3]

The two friends cite one simple fact that seemed to prove their point. The Council of Trent established penalties for many sins, including fornication. However, "it is laughable that the church has prohibited fornication, but then the pontiffs have tolerated many thousands of prostitutes, indeed taxed them ... to take the earnings from the trade."[4] These criticisms of papal corruption were standard fare in Protestant countries, but Loredan and Pallavicino were not Protestants. Their thoughts were far more subversive, and had they lived in a Protestant country, they would certainly not have been tolerated. In *The Soul of Ferrante Pallavicino* they questioned the immortality of the soul and the sovereignty of God, the very foundations of Christianity.

Henrico asks Ferrante how it is that souls, which are without bodies, can be subjected to physical penalties after death, the torments of purgatory and hell so often described in sermons and depicted in paintings. To render souls capable of feeling physical pain, they must have organs, but if after death souls can feel pain without a body, then there was no need for God to have given them bodies in the first place. Henrico posits that the only solution to the problem is to reject the belief in suffering souls after death and to accept that the only real punishment after death is the deprivation of divine grace. Henrico's position, of course, is an assault on the doctrine of purgatory and the entire apparatus of penance administered by the Catholic Church. Pallavicino's wandering soul, however, disagrees. Many theologians have argued as has Henrico, but Pallavicino reports that bodily death is much worse than the deprivation of salvation. Without life one does not have the capacity to comprehend the state of glory from which one has been deprived by the loss of grace. In other words, the recently executed Pallavicino claims that the living only imagine salvation because they do not want to lose life.

Pallavicino and Henrico move on to discuss the Last Judgment: "And it is very true and constant that men do not sin with the intention of offending God but to satisfy their appetites; they are not made less guilty by punishment, which is incompatible with the infinite mercy of God." Infinite mercy is infinite. Despite this evident truth, the Christian religion has become a thing of fear, "indeed even the fear of a madman." The only way to eradicate the madness of Christianity, therefore, is to recognize that "men have the ability to establish laws over God."[5] That is a radical claim. If humans can impose laws on God, then what is God? Does he have any influence, let alone power, over human events? Pallavicino's soul, speaking from the beyond in the conceit of the book, has taken the Christian promise of divine salvation and turned it on its head. The whole scheme, not just of penalties imposed by the church but of divine judgment itself, contradicts the Christian claims of God's infinite mercy. Morality does not require God. Human laws can guarantee morality better than belief in God. This, in the end, is the strongest claim of the "people who believe in nothing."

Notes

1 Quoted in Giorgio Spini, *Ricerca dei libertini: La teoria dell'impostura delle religioni nel Seicento italiano*, revised edn., Florence: La Nuova Italia, 1983, p. 6. Translated by Edward Muir.
2 Anonymous [Giovanni Francesco Loredan?], *L'Anima di Ferrante Pallavicino*, Villafranca [false place of publication, the real location may have been Amsterdam or Geneva]: s.n., 1643. Translated by Edward Muir.
3 Ibid., pp. 52–53.
4 Ibid., p. 65.
5 Ibid., p. 80.

Map

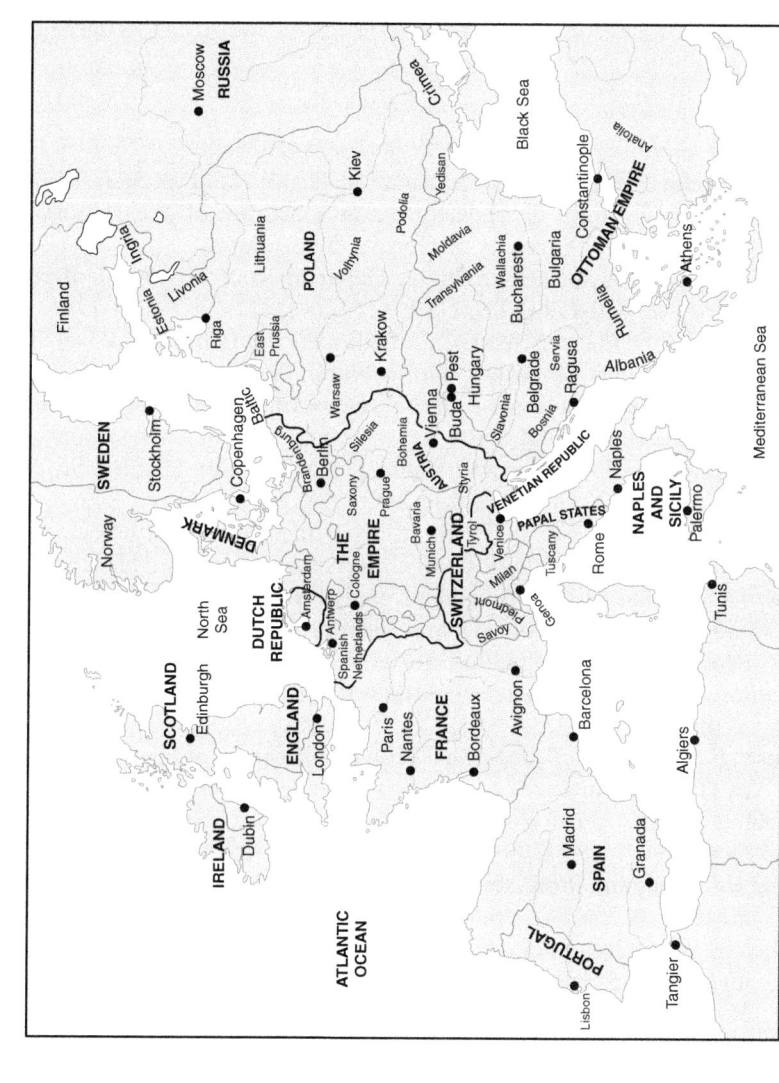

Europe after 1648

List of contributors

Irena Backus: Professor of Reformation History and Ecclesiastical Latin, Institut d'histoire de la Réformation (Institute of the History of the Reformation), University of Geneva, Switzerland

Robert J. Bast: Associate Professor, Department of History, University of Tennessee, Knoxville, TN, USA

Jill Bepler, PhD: Former Head of the Fellowship and Conference Department, Herzog August Bibliothek, Wolfenbüttel, Germany

Alan E. Bernstein: Professor Emeritus, Department of History, University of Arizona, Tucson, AZ, USA

James Blakeley: Professor and Chair, Department of History, St. Joseph's College New York, Patchogue, NY, USA

Curt Bostick: Professor of History, Department of History, Sociology, and Anthropology, Southern Utah University, Cedar City, UT, USA

Lynn A. Botelho: Distinguished University Professor, Department of History, and Director of Women's and Gender Studies, Indiana University of Pennsylvania, Indiana, PA, USA

Katherine G. Brady: Master of Arts in Religion, Columbia University, lives in Berkeley, CA, USA

Thomas A. Brady, Jr.: Peder Sather Professor Emeritus of History, Department of History, University of California, Berkeley, Berkeley, CA, USA

Helmut Bräuer: Professor Emeritus of History, University of Leipzig, Germany

Monica Brennan: Professor Emerita and Chair Emerita, Department of History, St. Joseph's College New York, Patchogue, NY, USA

Michael W. Bruening: Associate Professor of History, Department of History and Political Science, Missouri University of Science and Technology, Rolla, MO, USA

Amy Nelson Burnett: Paula and D. B. Varner University Professor of History, Department of History, University of Nebraska-Lincoln, Lincoln, NE, USA

Euan Cameron: Henry Luce III Professor of Reformation Church History, Union Theological Seminary, New York, and Professor, Department of Religion, Columbia University in the City of New York, NY, USA

Robert Christman: Associate Professor, Department of History, Luther College, Decorah, IA, USA

Victoria Christman: Associate Professor, Department of History, Luther College, Decorah, IA, USA

Michael Crawford: Associate Professor, Department of History, McNeese State University, Lake Charles, LA, USA

David Cressy: George III Professor of British History and Humanities Distinguished Professor Emeritus, Department of History, Ohio State University, Columbus, OH, and Research Professor of History, School of Arts and Humanities, Claremont Graduate University, Claremont, CA, USA

Pia F. Cuneo: Professor of Art History, School of Art, University of Arizona, Tucson, AZ, USA

Barbara B. Diefendorf: Professor Emerita, Department of History, Boston University, Boston, MA, USA

Irene Dingel: Professor of Church History and the History of Dogma, Faculty of Protestant Theology, Johannes Gutenberg University, and Director, Department 'Abendländische Religionsgeschichte,' Leibniz Institute of European History, Mainz, Germany

Kathryn A. Edwards: Professor, Department of History, University of South Carolina, Columbia, SC, USA

James M. Estes: Professor Emeritus, Department of History, University of Toronto, Toronto, ON, Canada

S. Amanda Eurich: Professor, Department of History, Western Washington University, Bellingham, WA, USA

Andrew Fix (†): Charles A. Dana Professor of History, Department of History, Lafayette College, Easton, PA, USA

Peter Foley (†): Associate Professor, Department of Religious Studies and Classics, and Director of the Institute for the Study of Religion and Culture, University of Arizona, Tucson, AZ, USA

Richard L. Gawthrop: Honorable Roger D. Branigin Professor of History, Department of History, Franklin College, Franklin, IN, USA

Bruce Gordon: Titus Street Professor of Ecclesiastical History, Yale Divinity School, Yale University, New Haven, CT, USA

Kevin Gosner: Associate Professor of History and former Chair, Department of History, University of Arizona, Tucson, AZ, USA

Andrew Colin Gow: Professor of History, Department of History and Classics, University of Alberta, Edmonton, AB, Canada

David Graizbord: Associate Professor, Arizona Center for Judaic Studies, University of Arizona, Tucson, AZ, USA

Kaspar von Greyerz: Professor Emeritus of Early Modern History, University of Basel, Switzerland

Berndt Hamm: Professor Emeritus of Modern Church History, University of Erlangen-Nuremberg, Germany

Craig Harline: De Lamar Jensen Professor of Early Modern History, Department of History, Brigham Young University, Provo, UT, USA

Sigrun Haude: Associate Professor, Department of History, University of Cincinnati, Cincinnati, OH, USA

Randolph C. Head: Professor, Department of History, University of California, Riverside, Riverside, CA, USA

Scott H. Hendrix: Professor Emeritus of Reformation History and Theology, Princeton Theological Seminary, Princeton, NJ, USA

Siegfried Hoyer: Professor Emeritus of Early Modern History, Department of History, University of Leipzig, Germany

Milton Kooistra: PhD in History, University of Toronto, lives in Williamsburg, ON, Canada

Craig Koslofsky: Professor, Department of History, University of Illinois, Urbana-Champaign, Urbana, IL, USA

Nicole Kuropka, Dr. habil.: Pastor in Wuppertal and Lecturer at the Kirchliche Hochschule in Wuppertal/Bethel, Germany

Marjory E. Lange: Professor of English and Humanities, Department of English, Western Oregon University, Monmouth, OR, USA

Ute Lotz-Heumann: Heiko A. Oberman Professor of Late Medieval and Reformation Studies, Division for Late Medieval and Reformation Studies and Department of History, and Director of the Division for Late Medieval and Reformation Studies, University of Arizona, Tucson, AZ, USA

Karin Maag: Professor, Department of History, and Director of the H. Henry Meeter Center for Calvin Studies, Calvin College, Grand Rapids, MI, USA

Scott M. Manetsch: Professor of Church History and the History of Christian Thought, Trinity Evangelical Divinity School, Trinity International University, Deerfield, IL, USA

Thomas B. de Mayo: Associate Professor of History, J. Sargeant Reynolds Community College, Richmond, VA, USA

Raymond A. Mentzer: Daniel J. Krumm Family Chair in Reformation Studies, Department of Religious Studies, University of Iowa, Iowa City, IA, USA

Paul Milliman: Associate Professor, Department of History, University of Arizona, Tucson, AZ, USA

Cornelia Niekus Moore: Dean Emerita, College of Languages, Linguistics, and Literature, University of Hawaiʻi at Mānoa, Honolulu, HI, USA

Edward Muir: Clarence L. Ver Steeg Professor in the Arts and Sciences and Charles Deering McCormick Professor of Teaching Excellence, Department of History, Northwestern University, Evanston, IL, USA

Graeme Murdock: Associate Professor in European History, Department of History, Trinity College Dublin, Dublin, Ireland

Christopher Ocker: Professor of Church History, San Francisco Theological Seminary, San Anselmo, CA, and Chair of the Department of the Cultural and Historical Studies of Religion, Graduate Theological Union, Berkeley, CA, USA

Marjorie Elizabeth Plummer: Susan C. Karant-Nunn Professor of Reformation and Early Modern European History, Division for Late Medieval and Reformation Studies and Department of History, University of Arizona, Tucson, AZ, USA

Allyson M. Poska: Professor of History, Department of History and American Studies, University of Mary Washington, Fredericksburg, VA, USA

Helmut Puff: Elizabeth L. Eisenstein Collegiate Professor of History and German, and Director of the Eisenberg Institute for Historical Studies, University of Michigan, Ann Arbor, MI, USA

Jonathan A. Reid: Associate Professor, Department of History, East Carolina University, Greenville, NC, USA

Catherine Richardson: Professor of Early Modern Studies, School of English, University of Kent, Canterbury, England

Bernard Roussel: Directeur d'études (Director of Studies), Sciences religieuses (Religious Studies), École Pratique des Hautes Études, Paris, France

Ulinka Rublack: Professor of Early Modern European History, and Fellow of St John's College, University of Cambridge, Cambridge, England

Heinz Schilling: Professor Emeritus of Early Modern European History, Department of History, Humboldt University, Berlin, Germany

Anne Jacobson Schutte (†): Professor Emerita, Department of History, University of Virginia, Charlottesville, VA, USA

Tom Scott: Honorary Professor, School of History, University of St Andrews, St Andrews, Scotland

Michael S. Springer: Professor of History, Department of History and Geography, and Director, Office of High-Impact Practices, University of Central Oklahoma, Edmond, OK, USA

Barbara Stollberg-Rilinger: Rektorin, Wissenschaftskolleg zu Berlin (Institute for Advanced Study, Berlin), and Professor of Early Modern History, Department of History, University of Münster, Germany

Ulrike Strasser: Professor, Department of History, University of California, San Diego, La Jolla, CA, USA

Larissa Juliet Taylor: Professor, Department of History, Colby College, Waterville, ME, USA

Nicholas Terpstra: Professor, Department of History, University of Toronto, Toronto, ON, Canada

B. Ann Tlusty: Professor and Chair, Department of History, Bucknell University, Lewisburg, PA, USA

James D. Tracy: Professor Emeritus, Department of History, University of Minnesota, Minneapolis, MN, USA

J. Jeffery Tyler: Professor and Chair, Religion Department, Hope College, Holland, MI, USA

Joel Van Amberg: Professor of History and Chair, Department of History and Museum Studies, Tusculum University, Greeneville, TN, USA

Günter Vogler: Professor Emeritus of German History, Department of History, Humboldt University, Berlin, Germany

Merry E. Wiesner-Hanks: Distinguished Professor, Department of History, University of Wisconsin-Milwaukee, Milwaukee, WI, USA

Gerhild Scholz Williams: Vice Provost, Barbara Schaps Thomas and David M. Thomas Professor in the Humanities, and Professor of Germanic Languages and Literatures and Comparative Literature, Washington University in St. Louis, St. Louis, MO, USA

Heide Wunder: Professor Emerita of Social and Constitutional History of the Early Modern Period, University of Kassel, Germany

Charles Zika: Professorial Fellow, School of Historical and Philosophical Studies, University of Melbourne, Melbourne, Parkville, VIC, Australia

Index

Note: The names of authors in this volume are in italics.

Agricola, Johannes 251–253
à Kempis, Thomas *see* Kempis, Thomas à
a Lasco, John *see* Lasco, John a
Albert, Archbishop of Mainz 153–155
Alsace 41, 115
Antwerp 62, 74–76
Aragon 3, 15
Aristotle 187
Augsburg 25, 49, 61–62, 71–73, 77–79, 106, 121–122, 136, 190, 192, 194, 209, 252, 261–263
Austria 15–16, 263
Austrian Habsburg lands *see* Austria

Backus, Irena 247–248, 270–272
Bader, Augustin 247, 261–263
Barnewall, Sir Patrick 238
Basel 21–22, 38, 40–41, 68, 86–88
Bast, Robert J. 247, 261–263
Beccadelli, Ludovico, Archbishop of Dubrovnik 244–245
Becon, Thomas 118–120
Bekker, Balthasar 190, 194
Bepler, Jill 106, 142–144
Bern 87–88, 116, 200, 218–219, 221–222
Bernstein, Alan E. 61–62, 89–91
Beza, Theodore 248, 280–282
Blakeley, James J. 200, 218–220
Bodenstein of Karlstadt, Andreas 203, 264
Bohemia 10, 13, 29, 101, 150, 156, 158, 175–176, 224, 273–274
Boleyn, Anne 212–213
Bologna 62, 92–93, 244
Bolz, Valentin 86–87

Bora, Katharina von 273–275
Borna 203
Bostick, Curt 105, 118–120
Botelho, Lynn A. 106, 145–147
Bottati, Francesco (father of Francesco Antonio Bottati) 139–141
Bottati, Francesco Antonio (son of Francesco Bottati) 106, 139–141
Bourges 62, 80–82
Brady, Katherine G. 62, 95–97
Brady, Thomas A., Jr. 61–62, 68–70, 95–97
Brandenburg-Prussia 16–17, 57
Brandmüller, Johannes 22, 40–42, 107
Bräuer, Helmut 22, 55–56
Brennan, Monica 248, 283–285
Brenz, Johannes 227, 229, 251, 253
British Isles 11, 13, 15, 17; *see also* England; Ireland; Scotland; Wales
Bruening, Michael W. 200, 221–223
Brussels 74–75
Bryson, Alexander 105–106, 124–125
Bucer, Martin 136, 162
Bugenhagen, Johann(es) 172, 209
Bullinger, Heinrich 160, 281
Burnett, Amy Nelson 21–22, 40–42

Calvin, Jean *see* Calvin, John
Calvin, John 11, 124, 149, 160, 162–164, 166, 200, 221, 273, 280, 282
Cameron, Euan 247, 264–266
Canterbury 22, 46
Capito, Wolfgang 136–137
Caroens, Maria 150, 181–183
Caroline Islands *see* Palaos archipelago
Castile 3, 15, 32, 185
Castres 62, 83–85, 232

Index

Charles I, King of England 16–17, 241, 286–287
Charles II, King of England 17, 240–241
Charles V, Emperor 10, 15, 74, 199, 204, 209
Chichester, Arthur, Lord Deputy of Ireland 238
Christman, Robert 200, 215–217
Christman, Victoria 61–62, 74–76
Cisneros, Francisco Ximénes de, Archbishop of Toledo 10
Collier, Jeremy 240–241
Columbus, Christopher 2
Comestor, Petrus 251
Constantine, Emperor 207, 286
Constantinople 2, 243
Contreras Figueroa, García de 21, 32–34
Cranach, Lucas, the Elder 3, 274
Crawford, Michael 21, 32–34
Cressy, David 248, 286–288
Croce, Giulio Cesare 92–93
Cromwell, Oliver 17, 289
Cuneo, Pia F. 21, 25–28, 61, 65–67

Davis, Sir John 237–239
de Contreras Figueroa, García *see* Contreras Figueroa, García de
de Mayo, Thomas B. *see* Mayo, Thomas B. de
Denmark 13, 15
Denosse, Claudine 280–282
de Sierra, María *see* Sierra, María de
Deutsch, Niklaus Manuel *see* Manuel Deutsch, Niklaus
de Werve, Hermann *see* Werve, Hermann de
Diefendorf, Barbara B. 61–62, 83–85
Dingel, Irene 199, 209–211
Dresden 65, 187
Dublin 237–238
Dubrovnik 201, 243–245
Dungersheim, Hieronymus 255–257
du Préau, Gabriel *see* Préau, Gabriel du
Dürer, Albrecht 3, 149, 168–170
Dürer, Barbara 168–170
Dutch Republic 17, 181, 240; *see also* Netherlands

Eberlin von Günzburg, Johannes 247, 264–266
Edward IV, King of England 30
Edward VI, King of England 118, 237–238, 286–287
Edwards, Kathryn A. 149–150, 175–177

Elisabeth of Braunschweig–Lüneburg, Duchess 106, 142–144
Elisabeth of Calenberg *see* Elisabeth of Braunschweig–Lüneburg, Duchess
Elizabeth I, Queen of England 13, 118, 238, 286–287
England 4, 8, 10, 13, 15–18, 30, 46, 101, 105, 118, 165, 199, 201, 212, 237–238, 240–241, 248, 286–289
Erasmus of Rotterdam, Desiderius 3, 10, 38, 159, 162, 212, 259
Erich of Braunschweig–Lüneburg, Duke (son of Elisabeth of Braunschweig–Lüneburg) 106, 142–144
Eschwege 127
Estes, James M. 199, 206–208
Estienne, Catherine 124–125
Eurich, S. Amanda 247–248, 277–279

Faurin, Jean 62, 83–85
Fernández, Antonio 43–44
Fix, Andrew 150, 187–189
Flacius Illyricus, Matthias 209–210
Flanders 32, 289
Foley, Peter 200, 240–242
France 10–13, 16, 31, 62, 80–81, 83–84, 91, 101, 124, 213–214, 225, 231–233, 240, 267–269, 277, 280–282
Francis I, King of France 29, 80, 267
Francis II, Emperor 4
Francke, August Hermann 22, 57–59
François de Valois (son of Henri de Valois) 80–81
Frederick I, Count Palatine 30
Frederick III, Elector of Brandenburg–Prussia 57
Frederick the Great, King of Prussia 17
Frederick the Wise, Elector of Saxony 10, 153, 199, 203–205
Freiberg (Saxony) 55–56
Freiburg (Breisgau) 247, 258–259, 264
Freke, Elizabeth 106, 145–147
Froben, Johann 38
Fröhlich, Georg 200, 227–229
Fugger, Marx 25–27

Gage, Thomas 248, 289–291
Gallmeyer, Hans 105, 121–123
Gast, Johannes 87
Gawthrop, Richard L. 22, 57–59
Geiler von Kaysersberg, Johann 258–259
Geneva 11, 83, 106, 124–125, 149, 162, 166, 269, 280–282

Index 303

Gent 181–183
Germany 3, 10–12, 29, 52, 57, 59, 62, 101, 127, 129, 133, 142, 144, 150, 172, 178, 187, 190, 247, 261, 264, 281; *see also* Holy Roman Empire (of the German Nation)
Gerson, Jean 168, 258–259
Glaumeau, Jean 62, 80–82
Glotz 121–122
Goldschmidt, Peter 190, 194
Gordon, Bruce 21–22, 38–39
Gosner, Kevin 248, 289–291
Gottskálk the Cruel, Bishop *see* Nikulásson, Gottskálk, Bishop of Hólar
Gow, Andrew Colin 247, 251–254
Graizbord, David 150, 184–186
Graubünden 62, 98
Greyerz, Kaspar von 61–62, 86–88
Guatemala 289, 291
Gutenberg, Johannes 2

Hahn, Johann Philip 187–189
Haimblichen, Wenceslaus 150, 175–177
Halle 57–59, 190, 192
Hamm, Berndt 200, 227–230
Harline, Craig 150, 181–183
Haude, Sigrun 200, 224–226
Head, Randolph C. 62, 98–100
Hendrix, Scott H. 149, 153–155
Henri IV, King of France 13, 200, 231
Henri de Valois (*dauphin*, son of Francis I, King of France) 80–81
Henry VIII, King of England 4, 13, 29, 199–200, 212–214, 286–287
Hólar 195–196
Holderbuel, Henrich 105–106, 127–129
Holy Roman Empire (of the German Nation) 2, 4, 6, 15–16, 203, 209, 215, 224, 226, 255, 280; *see also* Germany
Horky, Martin 224–225
Hornhausen (village in northern Germany) 150, 178–179
Hoyer, Siegfried 22, 52–54
Hungary 55, 124, 234
Hus, Jan 10, 156
Hütterodt, Johannes 127–129

Iceland 195, 197
Ignatius of Loyola 12
Ireland 13, 15–16, 200, 237–238, 240, 248, 283–284
Istanbul *see* Constantinople
Italy 2, 32, 35–36, 252, 292

James I, King of England 13, 237, 287
James II, King of England 17, 201, 240–241
Jerusalem 30, 252
Johannes, Bishop of Meissen 203, 247, 255–257
John, Count of Werdenberg and Bishop of Augsburg 71–73

Kangiesser, Orthie 105–106, 127–129
Karlstadt *see* Bodenstein of Karlstadt, Andreas
Kempis, Thomas à 258
Klein, Paul 101–103
Kooistra, Milton 106, 136–138
Koslofsky, Craig 247, 255–257
Krantz, Kaspar 95–97
Kratzer, Ernst 49–51
Kuropka, Nicole 149, 159–161
Küsel, Melchior 192–193

Lange, Marjory E. 199–200, 212–214
Lasco, John a 149, 165–166
Lausanne 200, 221–222
Lautern (village in the Duchy of Württemberg, Germany) 261–262
Leipzig 57, 156, 172–174, 192–193, 247, 255, 257
Leo of Rožmitál *see* Lev of Rožmitál
Le Picart, François 247, 268
Lev of Rožmitál 29–30
Lewys, Magdalen 46–47
Leyser, Polykarp, Jr. 173–174
Loftur 195–197
Löhneysen, Georg Engelhard 65–66
London 16, 59, 165–166
Loredan, Giovanni Francesco 248, 292–293
Lotz-Heumann, Ute 1–19, 21–22, 61–63, 105–107, 109–114, 149–151, 178–180, 199–201, 237–239, 247–249
Louis XIV, King of France 13, 16, 233
Loyola, Ignatius of *see* Ignatius of Loyola
Lucerne 86
Luther, Martin 3, 7, 9–12, 59, 74–75, 83, 136, 149, 153–156, 159–160, 166, 170, 172, 199, 203–206, 215, 227, 247–248, 251–253, 255, 257–259, 267–268, 273–275, 277, 280

Maag, Karin 105–106, 124–126
Magdeburg 178, 209–210

Manetsch, Scott M. 248, *280–282*
Mansfeld, territory of 200, 215–217
Manuel Deutsch, Niklaus 87
Margaret of Austria 74–76
Mary I, Queen of England 238, 286
Mary II, Queen of England 17, 240–241
Maurice, Elector of Saxony 209–210
Mayo, Thomas B. de 150, 195–197
Melanchthon, Philip 3, 149, 153, 159–160, 172, 199, 206–211, 268, 273
Mentzer, Raymond A. 200, *231–233*
Mexico City 32–33, 289
Milliman, Paul 21, 29–31
Milton, John 248, 286–288
Mixco 289–290
Moore, Cornelia Niekus 149–150, 172–174
More, Thomas 199, 212–214
Morhardt, Caspar 49–51
Mühlich, Hector 71–73
Muir, Edward 248–249, 292–294
Müntzer, Thomas 11, 149, 156–158
Murdock, Graeme 200, 234–236

Netherlands 10–13, 15, 17, 74, 240
New England 288
New Spain 32, 289
Nikulásson, Gottskálk, Bishop of Hólar 195–197
Nuremberg 3, 29, 35–36, 68, 95, 97, 106, 109, 130–132, 168, 170, 200, 203, 227–229, 255

Ocker, Christopher 105, 115–117
O Domhnaill, Dominic 284
Oecolampadius, Johannes 268
Orange, principality of 248, 277–279
Ore Mountains 55
Ottoman Empire 2, 10, 29, 201, 235, 243–244, 252–253

Palaos archipelago 62, 101–103
Pallavicino, Ferrante 248–249, 292–293
Paris 31, 62, 89–91, 212–214, 232, 247, 251, 267–269
Pastrana (village in La Mancha, Spain) 184–185
Paumgartner, Balthasar (father) 35–36
Paumgartner, Balthasar (son) 35–36
Paumgartner, Magdalena 21, 35–36
Pays de Vaud 200, 218–219
Pellikan, Conrad 21, 38–39
Philippines 101, 289

Piedmont 139
Pilsen 175–177
Pineton de Chambrun, Jacques 278–279
Platter, Felix 86–87
Plummer, Marjorie Elizabeth 105, 121–123
Poland 15, 55, 234
Polish–Lithuanian commonwealth *see* Poland
Poska, Allyson M. 21–22, 43–45
Praepositus, Jacobus 74
Praetorius, Johannes 133–134, 193–194
Prague 29, 156
Prateolus, Gabriel *see* Préau, Gabriel du
Préau, Gabriel du 247, 270–272
Prussia *see* Brandenburg–Prussia
Puff, Helmut 149–150, 168–171
Puller of Hohenburg, Richard 105, 115–117

Rabelais, François 62, 89–91
Ragusa *see* Dubrovnik
Raven, Margaret 46–48
Reid, Jonathan A. 61–62, 80–82
Rémy, Nicholas 190
Rhegius, Urbanus 78
Richardson, Catherine 22, 46–48
Richardson, Margaret 46–48
Röhrscheidt, Christian 150, 172–174
Roman Empire (ancient) 2, 181
Rome 3, 154–155, 165, 244
Roussel, Bernard 149, 162–164
Rublack, Ulinka 21, 35–37

Santiago de Compostela 29–30, 43
Šašek, Václav 29–31
Saxony 22, 52, 55, 156, 173–174, 203, 215, 255
Schilling, Hans 77–79
Schilling, Heinz 199, 203–205
Schutte, Anne Jacobson 106, 139–141
Scotland 13, 16, 124, 132, 240
Scott, Tom 247, 258–260
Shakespeare, William 4, 212
Sierra, María de 150, 184–186
Sobrino, Gregorio 43–44
Spain 13, 15, 17, 29, 43–44, 101, 150, 243, 289
Spengler, Lazarus 227–229
Spitzel, Gottlieb 190–191, 194
Springer, Michael S. 149, 165–167
Stollberg-Rilinger, Barbara 247–248, 273–276

Index   305

Strasbourg 39, 61, 68–70, 115–117, 136–137, 259
Strasser, Ulrike 62, 101–103
Sweden 13, 15–16, 225
Swiss confederation *see* Switzerland
Switzerland 7, 11, 62, 68, 87, 98, 115–116, 219, 221, 267

Tauler, Johannes 258–259
Taylor, Larissa Juliet 247, 267–269
Terpstra, Nicholas 61–62, 92–94
Tetzel, Gabriel 29–31
Tham, Valentin 247, 255–257
Thomasius, Christian 190, 194
Tlusty, B. Ann 22, 49–51
Torda *see* Turda
Torgau 255–257
Tracy, James D. 201, 243–245
Transylvania 200, 234–236
Turda 234–235
Tyler, J. Jeffery 61–62, 71–73

Ulm 68, 121–122

Van Amberg, Joel 61–62, 77–79
van Zutphen, Hendrick *see* Zutphen, Hendrick van
Venice 36, 244, 248, 292
Vienna 2, 122
Viret, Pierre 200, 221–222
Vogler, Günter 149, 156–158

von Bora, Katharina *see* Bora, Katharina von
von Greyerz, Kaspar see Greyerz, Kaspar von

Wales 15
Wartburg castle 203
Wendelstein (village in Franconia, Germany) 62, 95–97
Werve, Hermann de 225–226
Wiesner-Hanks, Merry E. 106, 130–132
William of Orange, *stadtholder* of the Netherlands and King of England 17, 201, 240–241
Williams, Gerhild Scholz 106, 133–135
Wittenberg 3, 74, 149, 153, 155, 159, 166, 172, 203–206, 209, 252, 255, 257, 264
Wolfhart, Boniface 106, 136–138
Wolmar, Melchior 281
Wunder, Heide 105–106, 127–129
Wycliffe, John 9

Zika, Charles 150, 190–194
Zizers (village in Graubünden, Switzerland) 62, 98–100
Zurich 11–12, 21, 38–39, 115–117, 281
Zutphen, Hendrick van 74–75
Zwickau 22, 52–54, 156
Zwingli, Huldrych *see* Zwingli, Ulrich
Zwingli, Ulrich 11, 12, 38–39, 200, 222, 227, 264, 273